Studies in Neurolinguistics

VOLUME 1

PERSPECTIVES IN
NEUROLINGUISTICS AND PSYCHOLINGUISTICS

Harry A. Whitaker, Series Editor
DEPARTMENT OF PSYCHOLOGY
THE UNIVERSITY OF ROCHESTER
ROCHESTER, NEW YORK

HAIGANOOSH WHITAKER and HARRY A. WHITAKER (Eds.).
 Studies in Neurolinguistics, Volumes 1 and 2

In preparation

NORMAN J. LASS (Ed). Contemporary Issues in Experimental
 Phonetics

Studies in Neurolinguistics

Volume 1

Edited by

HAIGANOOSH WHITAKER

HARRY A. WHITAKER

Department of Psychology
The University of Rochester
Rochester, New York

ACADEMIC PRESS   New York San Francisco London 1976

A Subsidiary of Harcourt Brace Jovanovich, Publishers

ACADEMIC PRESS, INC.
111 Fifth Avenue, New York, New York 10003

United Kingdom Edition published by
ACADEMIC PRESS, INC. (LONDON) LTD.
24/28 Oval Road, London NW1

Library of Congress Cataloging in Publication Data

Main entry under title:

Studies in neurolinguistics.

   (Perspectives in neurolinguistics & psycho
linguistics)
      Includes bibliographies and index.
      1.   Speech, Disorders of.   2.   Languages—
Physiological aspects.   3.   Neuropsychology.
I.   Whitaker, Haiganoosh.   II.   Whitaker, Harry A.
[DNLM: 1.   Lanugage.   2.   Neurophysiology.   WL102
S933]
RC423.S74   616.8'552   75-13100
ISBN 0-12-746301-1 (Pt. A)
PRINTED IN THE UNITED STATES OF AMERICA

Contents

4 The Role of Phonology in Linguistic Communication: Some Neurolinguistic Considerations   139

Marc L. Schnitzer

5 Neurogenic Disorders of Output Processing: Apraxia of Speech   161

Donnell F. Johns and Leonard L. LaPointe

6 Broca's Area and Broca's Aphasia   201

J. P. Mohr

List of Contributors

Numbers in parentheses indicate the pages on which the authors' contributions begin.

Alfonso Caramazza (261), Department of Psychology, The Johns Hopkins University, Baltimore, Maryland

Harold Goodglass* (237), Boston Veterans Administration Hospital and Department of Neurology, Boston University School of Medicine, Boston, Massachusetts

Donnell F. Johns (161), Department of Surgery, University of Texas Health Science Center at Dallas, Southwestern Medical School, Dallas, Texas

Leonard L. LaPointe (161), Veterans Administration Hospital, Gainesville, Florida

Yvan Lebrun (1), Neurosurgical Clinic and Neurolinguistics Laboratory, University of Brussels, Belgium

Esther Milner (31), Brooklyn College of The City University of New York, New York

J. P. Mohr (201), Behavior Laboratory, Stroke Service, Massachusetts General Hospital, Boston, Massachusetts

George A. Ojemann (103), Department of Neurological Surgery, University of Washington School of Medicine, Seattle, Washington

Marc L. Schnitzer (139), The Pennsylvania State University, University Park, Pennsylvania

Alan B. Rubens (293), Aphasia Unit, Hennepin County Medical Center, Minneapolis, Minnesota

Edgar B. Zurif (261), Aphasia Research Center, Department of Neurology, Boston University School of Medicine and Boston Veterans Administration Hospital, Boston, Massachusetts

*Present address: Psychology Service, Veterans Administration Hospital, 150 S. Huntington Avenue, Boston, Massachusetts 02130.

Preface

In the fall of 1972, we were asked to edit a volume of papers that surveyed the current research in neurolinguistics and explicated the historical roots of each of the major topics. At that time, the journal *Brain & Language* was only a proposal, there was only one recent anthology and that was of reprinted papers, and the best-known books in the field were both dated and lacking in broad scope. At the same time, many people sensed the surge of interest developing in neurolinguistics and we readily agreed to undertake the task. The surge of interest has exceeded our expectations, to the point that it is possible to assert without qualifications that neurolinguistics has become a field of scientific research. Four years ago, it might have been feasible to publish a single volume of studies in neurolinguistics and believe that the major topics of research had been covered. It is clearly not possible to do so today. What originally was to have been a single volume has grown to at least four and possibly five or more. Because of the fivefold increase in size, and the well-known difficulties of obtaining all papers from all authors at the same time, we have elected to begin publishing the volumes now with the papers that have been completed. This, of course, makes it harder to subdivide each volume into more specialized interest areas. On the other hand, it is questionable whether such a subdivision would be genuinely useful; even though the field of neurolinguistics is frankly inter-disciplinary, there is a common theme of the relationships between language and brain. Ultimately, we have been guided by the intrinsic interest in certain topics in this field rather than by a desire to represent each and every aspect of it. Some of the papers espouse viewpoints that will not meet with uniform agreement in the readership; some of the papers will present material that in piecemeal is widely known but in synthesis is original as summary and as prediction; some of the papers will present new research published for the first time here, research that we feel represents some of the best examples of the interdisciplinary effort that is neurolinguistics; some of the papers are straight-forward reviews of topics or problems in this field which have never before been reviewed. To impose a uniformity of style, format, length, or approach would, in our opinion, be as misleading as to impose a uniformity of theoretical viewpoint. Neurolinguistics is a young discipline which still reflects its interdisciplinary heritage in all respects. Both the clinician and the research scientist will find material of interest in these volumes. For the clinical neurologist or speech pathologist, neurolinguistics can represent the addition of powerful and interesting theories and methods from the behavioral sciences. For the linguist, neurolinguistics can represent the addition of a new realm of empirical evidence against which to test theories of language, as well as the addition of the successful methodologies of research in clinical and behavioral sciences. For the psychologist, neurolinguistics can represent a means for neuropsychology and physiological psychology to focus on problems of language, much in the manner that experimental psychology had earlier made use of, and developed into, psycholinguistics. For all of us, neurolinguistics can represent a synthesis of the brain sciences, the behavioral sciences, and the clinical sciences, regardless of whether one's primary interest is in language, in the brain, or in the rehabilitation of the brain-damaged individual. These volumes are the first in this field to present a multiauthored, multitopic study of neurolinguistics. These chapters will give the reader a sense of the breadth, and some insights into many of the interesting problems, of neurolinguistics.

Lebrun's frankly historical approach to *Neurolinguistic Models of Language and Speech* (Chapter 1) primarily considers models of output or language production. In the course of his analysis, he presents three cases that exemplify his views of articulatory deficits. Lebrun traces the use of the term "neurolinguistic," an appropriate beginning to the five volumes.

Milner's discussion of *CNS Maturation and Language Acquisition* (Chapter 2), which includes a number of tables by way of summary, is a novel approach to synthesizing much of the early and mid-twentieth century neurological literature. Some readers may find the newly coined terms a bit difficult to remember; all readers will recognize that recent studies of language acquisition, cognitive development, neural substrates of maturation, and electrophysiological correlates of behavior have raised questions with the older literature and thus require some reinterpretations of Milner's ideas. Nevertheless, as Ralph Gerard said of Milner's 1967 treatise on this subject, it would be a mistake to not look beyond these "superficial blemishes" to the wide-ranging synthesis Milner attempts. We often fail to attempt such synthesis ourselves because of commitments to specialized research problems.

Ojemann's presentation of *Subcortical Language Mechanisms* (Chapter 3) focuses on the role of various thalamic nuclei in language, with particular attention given to object naming. He provides further documentation to the view that, like the cerebral cortex, there is a dominant and a nondominant thalamus.

Schnitzer addresses the question of *The Role of Phonology in Linguistic Communication* (Chapter 4), specifically inquiring whether or not the phonological system that is a component of oral–aural communication is also a component of other forms of communication such as the visual–graphic. The evidence that bears on this question is derived from aphasic patients of several language backgrounds as well as deaf and blind patients.

Johns and LaPointe begin their chapter on *Neurogenic Disorders of Output Processing* (Chapter 5) with a detailed review of the literature on motor speech disorders since Auburtin and Broca, 1861. Following the review, they delineate the differences between dysarthria, oral apraxia, apraxia of speech, and aphasia.

Mohr addresses one of the more controversial issues in neurolinguistics, the problems of *Broca's Area and Broca's Aphasia* (Chapter 6), giving a detailed review of case histories which support as well as question various viewpoints on this topic. His analyses and conclusions provide challenges for future research.

Goodglass presents both the historical and current research on *Agrammatism* (Chapter 7), showing its relationship to child language and providing experimental evidence that the linguistic impairment includes the morphological, syntactic, and prosodic aspects of language. The documentation he cites clearly shows how agrammatism is related to normal language use.

Zurif and Caramazza employ hierarchical cluster analysis on data taken from a relatedness judgment task given to agrammatic Broca's aphasics, in their paper on *Psycholinguistic Structures in Aphasia* (Chapter 8). The data indicate that the knowledge of syntactic forms is as deficient as the productive use of these forms in these patients.

Rubens' paper is a clinical, anatomic, and behavioral analysis of *Transcortical Motor Aphasia* (Chapter 9), which provides a number of insights into this deficit of spontaneous initiation of speech. He blends the classic historical cases with the current, more thoroughly analyzed cases, leading to a comprehensive overview of this syndrome.

Contents of Volume 2

1 Neurolinguistic Models of Language and Speech

Yvan Lebrun

UNIVERSITY OF BRUSSELS

INTRODUCTION

One of the earliest occurrences of the word *neurolinguistic* seems to be in the title of a dissertation submitted by M. Kendig for a master's degree at Columbia University in 1935. The dissertation was entitled "A proposed research investigation valuable in the improvement of teaching on the junior college level: Application of a method for scientific control of the neuro-linguistic and neuro-semantic mechanisms in the learning process" (Korzybski 1936–1937b). In December of the same year, Kendig, who was later to become director of the Institute of General Semantics in Lakeville (Conn.), read a paper on "Language re-orientation of high school curriculum and scientific control of neuro-linguistic mechanisms for better health and scholastic achievement" before the Educational Section of the American Association for the Advancement of Science, in St. Louis. At the same meeting Alfred Korzybski (1936–1937a) presented a paper called "Neuro-semantic and neuro-linguistic mechanisms of extensionalization." In this talk, the author did not define the word *neurolinguistic* but used it once or twice in connection with verbal behavior. The same year and in the same journal, Douglas Gordon Campbell, in an article entitled "General semantics" and devoted to Korzybski's theory, also used the word a few times, e.g., in the curious statement that "mathematics appears to be a neurolinguistic device capable of representing the structural correspondence between the invariant relations of electro-magnetic phenomena occurring outside our skins and the invariants of 'colloidal aggregation change' at the basis of neuro-physiological and neuro-semantic reactions inside our skins."

1

While the word *neurolinguistic(s)* appeared a few more times before 1962, e.g., in a short paper by Edith Trager (1961) entitled "The field of neurolinguistics," it is only after this date that it began to be used in connection with speech pathology.

In 1963 a "Groupe de Recherches Neuropsychologiques et Neurolinguistiques" came into existence at the St. Anne Hospital in Paris. In the subsequent years, the team repeatedly used the word *neurolinguistique* in their publications (e.g., Cohen & Hécaen, 1964; Dubois, 1967; Dubois, Hécaen, Angelergues, Maufras du Chatelier, & Marcie, 1964; Dubois, Marcie, Irigaray, Hécaen, & Angelergues, 1965; Hécaen, 1969; Hécaen & Dubois, 1971; Hécaen, Dubois, Angelergues, Vedrennes, & Marcie, 1964; Hécaen, Dubois, & Marcie, 1967). The Parisian group construed the discipline rather narrowly, however. In their view, the neurolinguist's task is to investigate acquired and developmental language disorders. Speech impairments such as <u>dysarthria</u> and stuttering fall outside the scope of neurolinguistics. Hécaen and Dubois (1971) write:

lower order

> La neurolinguistique peut être définie comme l'application des méthodes et des modèles de la linguistique à l'étude des perturbations des réalisations du langage entraînées par des lésions corticales. Si son domaine est donc essentiellement celui des aphasies, elle n'exclut pas les troubles du langage au cours des démences dites organiques (artérioscléreuses, dégénératives . . .). Elle s'efforce de distinguer dans ces troubles la part due aux troubles 'aphasiques', si souvent présents, de celle qui reflète l'effondrement global des facultés cognitives. Le champ de la neurolinguistique inclut également les troubles de développement du langage, que leur origine soit lésionnelle ou qu'ils répondent à des déficits de maturation; mais cette neurolinguistique génétique implique des connaissances particulières, aussi constitue-t-elle à nos yeux un champ spécifique de recherches, nécessitant une nouvelle spécialisation. En revanche, la neurolinguistique exclura de son domaine les troubles de la parole dus à la malformation des organes périphériques (alalie, blésité . . .), ou aux dysfonctionnements des organes d'exécution d'origine centrale (asynergie, ataxie cérébelleuse, paralysie pseudobulbaire, etc. . .). A un autre pôle, elle ne retiendra pas non plus les troubles de l'énoncé résultant d'un état psychotique ou neurotique.[1]

[1] Neurolinguistics may be defined as the application of the methods and models of linguistics to the study of disturbances of the realization of speech caused by cortical lesions. Although its scope is primarily that of aphasia, it does not leave out speech problems that occur in the so-called *organic dementias* (arteriosclerotic, degenerative, etc.). It tries to separate among these problems those which are caused by aphasia, so frequently present, from those which reflect a total loss of cognitive capacities. The scope of neurolinguistics also includes problems of speech development, whether they are caused by a lesion or whether they represent a developmental problem. But this genetic neurolinguistics implies a special knowledge; it is for us a specific research field that requires a new specialization. On the other hand, neurolinguistics leaves out of its scope the speech problems that are caused by a malformation of the peripheral organs (alalia, lisping, etc.) or by a malfunction of the execution organs of central origin (asynergia, cerebellar ataxia, pseudobulbar palsy, etc.). It also excludes the speech problems that are associated with a psychotic or neurotic condition.

This view was restated in Hécaen's (1972) recent book *Introduction à la Neuropsychologie*: "La neurolinguistique représente un sous-ensemble de la neuropsychologie en tant qu'étude des troubles des réalisations verbales survenant après lésions corticales. Elle se sépare selon qu'elle prend comme objet la pathologie du langage de l'adulte ou celle de l'enfant" (p. XI).[2]

In contradistinction to the Parisian group the Dutch neurologist Grewel (1966), in a paper entitled "Neurolinguïstiek," defined *neurolinguistics* as the study of language and speech disorders due to neurological impairment, and he rejected the identification of neurolinguistics with aphasiology: "De neurolinguïstiek tot de afasie(leer) te beperken is onjuist, want er zijn vele neurologisch veroorzaakte stoornissen van het taalgebruik die buiten de afasie vallen."[3] Grewel furthermore expressed the view that the neurolinguistic investigation, if properly conducted, in a number of cases permits a better diagnosis of neurological impairments.

Luria (1967) published in French a paper entitled "Problèmes et faits de la neurolinguistique," in which he stated: "Les dernières décennies ont vu se constituer une nouvelle branche des sciences de l'homme, qui se situe à la frontière des sciences sociales et des sciences exactes et qu'on pourrait appeler 'neurolinguistique'."[4] He further wrote: "Précédée de travaux qui se sont étendus sur plus de cent ans, elle n'a pris sa forme définitive qu'à une époque récente."[5] After briefly reviewing the development of aphasiology since 1861, Luria concluded:

> Toutes ces recherches ont permis d'accumuler une abondante documentation sur les multiples formes de troubles du langage dont s'accompagnent les lésions localisées du cerveau. . . . Cependant, tous ces faits de neurologie clinique ne représentent que la phase préliminaire de la création de cette nouvelle discipline scientifique à laquelle nous avons donné le nom de 'neurolinguistique.'[6]

According to Luria, the task of the neurolinguist is to use the available clinical data to uncover the physiological and neuropsychological mechanisms under-

---

[2] Neurolinguistics is a subspeciality of neuropsychology, insofar as it is the study of problems of realization of speech that result from cortical lesions. It is separated into two fields, depending on whether the object of the investigation is the speech pathology of children or of adults.

[3] To limit neurolinguistics to aphasiology is inaccurate, for there are many neurologically caused disturbances of language usage that fall outside aphasia.

[4] During the last decades, a new human science was born, which is at the frontier between social sciences and exact sciences, and which we could call neurolinguistics.

[5] Preceded by research that has lasted more than 100 years, it has adopted its definitive form only recently.

[6] All this research has made it possible to collect much information on the various forms of speech difficulties that are associated with lesions of the brain. Nevertheless, all the facts pertaining to clinical neurology represent only the preliminary phase of the creation of this new scientific field that we have called neurolinguistics.

lying language disorders and to arrive at an integrated view of speech pathology of central origin.

Harry Whitaker (1970), one of the editors of the present volume, wrote a paper entitled "A model for neurolinguistics." In his view, "neurolinguistics differs from linguistics per se by implying a broadened empirical domain that considers, as evidence for linguistic hypotheses, various observables not usually entertained by the linguist—in particular, aphasic speech." Whitaker maintained that neurolinguistic findings should serve as the touchstones of linguistic theories, for "it is not acceptable to remove linguistic hypotheses to an abstract level outside of neurological correlation and refutation."

In 1965, a "unité de recherches neurolinguistiques" was created in the Neurosurgical Clinic of the University of Brussels by J. Brihaye. Four years later, a neurolinguistics laboratory was brought into existence by Y. Lebrun. And in 1972, a postgraduate seminar in neurolinguistics was initiated. Neurolinguistics as it is pursued at the University of Brussels is the study of language and speech disorders caused by a dysfunction, disturbance, or lesion of the central nervous system. These disorders may be either developmental or acquired. Their organic substratum may be obvious, as in bulbar dysarthria, or unknown, as in some cases of stuttering.

Recently, publication of an international series called *Neurolinguistics* was begun. The series consists of monographs on speech physiology and speech pathology, with special emphasis on the neurological foundation of language and language impairment. It is edited by R. Hoops of Ball State University (Indiana) and by the author of the present chapter.

In his paper, Luria (1967) stated that neurolinguistics should transcend the mere clinical description of language disorders. Working from the findings of aphasiology and psycholinguistics, as well as from the tenets of current linguistic theory, neurolinguistics should set up models that help uncover the neuropsychological basis of language impairment: "[Il faut] que derrière les descriptions cliniques des troubles du langage apparaissent les mécanismes physiologiques et neuropsychologiques qui les provoquent."[7] On the other hand, Whitaker (1970) has warned that "the neurolinguistic model should not account for abilities other than language even though it should be able to integrate such abilities in the more comprehensive theory of mind."

Keeping these principles in mind, a number of neurolinguistic models have been evolved. They are presented in the following together with a discussion of some of their implications.

---

[7] [It is important] that behind the clinical descriptions of speech problems, the physiological and neuropsychological mechanisms become evident.

SOME NEUROLINGUISTIC MODELS

Articulatory Defects in Aphasia

Paul Broca (1861) described a pathological condition in which articulation is severely impaired or even impossible, while comprehension of spoken language, reading, and writing are unabated. The loss of expressive speech is not due to paralysis or to buccofacial apraxia:

Cheeks

> Les malades comprennent parfaitement le langage articulé et le langage écrit. . . .
> Ceux qui sont lettrés, et qui ont le libre usage de leurs mains, mettent nettement
> leurs idées sur papier. . . . L'appareil auditif est intact [et] tous les muscles, sans en
> excepter ceux de la voix et ceux de l'articulation, obéissent à la volonté. . . . Ces
> malades peuvent exécuter librement avec leur langue et leurs lèvres tous les mouve-
> ments autres que ceux de l'articulation; ils peuvent porter immédiatement, lorsqu'on
> les en prie, la pointe de leur langue, en bas, à droite ou à gauche. . . . Ce qui a péri
> chez eux, ce n'est donc pas la faculté du langage, ce n'est pas la mémoire des mots,
> ce n'est pas non plus l'action des nerfs et des muscles de la phonation et de
> l'articulation, c'est autre chose, c'est une faculté particulière considérée par M.
> Bouillaud comme la faculté de coordonner les mouvements propres au langage
> articulé, ou plus simplement comme la faculté du langage articulé, puisque sans elle
> il n'y a pas d'articulation possible.[8]

At the dawn of aphasiology, Broca thus posited the existence of a specific impairment of oral expression that is not concomitant with paralysis, or apraxia, of the buccofacial musculature. He called this condition *aphemia* and in 1865 upheld the view that it results from a lesion of the third frontal convolution of the dominant hemisphere (Broca, 1865). This part of the brain was to become known as Broca's area.

In his *Clinique médicale de l'Hôtel-Dieu*, Armand Trousseau (1885) reported a case that corresponds to Broca's description of aphemia. The patient, an auctioneer at Les Halles in Paris, lost his power of speech, although he had no paralysis and no apraxia of the tongue. "Il n'avait aucun symptome de paralysie, mais il ne pouvait articuler un seul mot. La langue se mouvait parfaitement, la

---

[8] The patients understand spoken and written language perfectly. Well-read persons who have the free use of their hands formulate their ideas very clearly on the paper. The auditory system is intact and all the muscles, including the voice and articulatory muscles, obey the patients' will. These patients can carry out all movements, except for the articulatory ones, with their tongue and lips. When they are asked to do it, they can immediately carry the tip of their tongue to the left or right. What is lost is thus not the language power; not the memory of words; nor the action of the nerves and muscles of phonation and articulation. It is something else. It is a special aptitude, which M. Bouillaud considers to be the ability to coordinate the movements pertaining to articulated speech, or more simply, the articulated-speech ability, since no articulation is possible without it.

déglutition était facile"[9] (p. 712). There was no disorder of comprehension and
the patient could write correctly. As a matter of fact, he kept looking after his
business, giving his orders in writing.

Fernand Bernheim (1900), proposed to distinguish between aphemia, which he
called *subcortical motor aphasia*, and what he termed *cortical motor aphasia*.
According to Bernheim, a patient with cortical motor aphasia is always agraphic
and he is unable to indicate how many syllables comprise the words that he
cannot speak. His inner speech is disturbed, while in patients with subcortical
motor aphasia, inner speech is intact. Bernheim thus contrasted aphemia with
what is now called *Broca's aphasia* and he regarded both as pathological entities.
Moreover, he upheld the view that aphemia is due to a subcortical lesion, while
Broca's aphasia results from a lesion of the third frontal convolution of the
dominant hemisphere.

In 1906, Pierre Marie started to use the word *anarthric* to denote a patient
"qui ne peut plus parler tout en ayant conservé intactes l'intelligence, la notion
du mot, la lecture et l'écriture,—sans qu'il soit aucunement question de phénomènes pseudo-bulbaires ou paralytiques."[10] He insisted that anarthria, which in
fact is identical with aphemia, is by no means a motor problem: "C'est la
fonction elle-même de la phonation qui est entravée."[11] Anarthrics, therefore,
may be compared with abasics, who can no longer walk although their legs are
not paralyzed. According to Marie, anarthria can be brought about by a lesion in
the dominant as well as by a lesion in the nondominant hemisphere. In either
case the lesion lies in the vicinity of the lenticular nucleus. Moreover, Marie
contrasted anarthria with aphasia. In his view, "l'aphasie est une."[12] This
single-entity aphasia is Wernicke's aphasia. Broca's aphasia, i.e. what Bernheim
called cortical motor aphasia, is not a single pathological entity but the combination of Wernicke's aphasia and anarthria. Consequently, the articulatory defects
in Broca's aphasia and those in anarthria are identical (Marie, 1926, pp. 3–64).

In the 1914 revised edition of his treatise *Sémiologie des affections du système
nerveux*, Dejerine (1914) upheld the view that there are two kinds of motor
aphasia: Broca's aphasia, in which inner speech is disturbed, and *pure motor
aphasia*, which is identical with aphemia and anarthria. Dejerine shared Marie's
opinion that articulatory disorders are exactly the same in both kinds of motor
aphasia. Quite incidentally, however, he noted that most patients with pure
motor aphasia can no longer sing (they can only hum—Dejerine, 1914, p. 82)

[9] He had no symptoms of paralysis, but he could not articulate a single word. His tongue
moved perfectly well. He could swallow easily.

[10] . . . who cannot speak, although he still fully possesses concepts of words, understanding, reading and writing abilities, without the condition being a matter of pseudobulbar or
paralytic phenomenon.

[11] It is the function of phonation per se which is hindered.

[12] Aphasia is a single entity.

while a number of patients with Broca's aphasia can still sing pretty well (Dejerine, 1914, p. 149). Furthermore he pointed out that Broca's aphasia may evolve into pure motor aphasia:

> L'aphasie motrice pure [peut survenir] comme stade d'amélioration au cours d'une aphasie qui, d'abord totale, s'est transformée en aphasie de Broca puis se termine par une aphasie pure, le langage intérieur revenant complètement à l'état normal bien que l'aphasie motrice subsiste [Dejerine, 1914, p. 83].[13]

Marie's and Dejerine's views that articulatory disorders are the same in Broca's aphasia and in anarthria (pure motor aphasia) was adhered to by Alajouanine, Ombredane, and Durand (1939) in their monograph on "Le syndrome de désintégration phonétique dans l'aphasie" and by Alajouanine, Sabouraud, and Scherer (1957) in their oscillographic study of anarthria. Alajouanine and his associates claimed that articulatory defects in anarthria and in Broca's aphasia are due to paresis, apraxia or dystonia of the speech musculature, or to a combination of the three factors. In the Alajouanine *et al.* (1939) essay, one reads that articulatory errors "présentent une homogénéité et une constance remarquables; elles se laissent facilement ramener à un petit nombre de principes" (p. 116).[14] These rules resemble those of a child's articulation: "La phonétique du malade présente de grandes analogies avec celle de l'enfant" (p. 122).[15] The Alajouanine *et al.* (1957) study, however, insists on the great variability and inconsistency of anarthric errors. It also stresses the effortful speech of anarthrics and their repeated attempts at correct pronunciation:

> Les anarthriques arrivent épisodiquement ou régulièrement à des émissions assez proches du normal, mais au prix d'un effort considérable, et, dans bien des cas, après plusieurs essais. Leur trouble est de gravité inégale, leur performance est de type variable, d'un moment à l'autre.[16]

In the 1939 monograph one may also read that the articulatory defects are often concomitant with oral apraxia (Alajouanine *et al.*, 1939, p. 116).

Marie's view survives in Hécaen's conception of *phonematic aphasia* (Hécaen, 1972, pp. 12–20). This is "un désordre de la programmation phoné-

---

[13] A pure motor aphasia may occur as an amelioration phase during an aphasia which is at first total, then becomes Broca's aphasia, and eventually becomes a pure aphasia; the internal language recovers to a fully normal condition although the motor aphasia still persists.

[14] . . . show remarkable homogeneity and consistency; they are easily summarized by a few principles.

[15] The patient's phonology has much in common with that of a child.

[16] Occasionally, or regulary, anarthrics manage to produce speech that comes close to being normal, but at the cost of considerable effort, and in many cases after several attempts. The seriousness of their deficit and their performance varies from one moment to the next.

matique,"[17] which occurs isolatedly in only very few cases. Most of the time, it
is accompanied by agraphia but the graphic disturbance does not parallel the
articulatory disorder. There may also be some degree of alexia. Very often there
is a concomitant right hemiplegia, and bucco-linguo-facial apraxia is not rare.
Hécaen points out that the existence of phonematic aphasia implies that the
phonological level may be selectively disturbed, with relative preservation of the
morphological and syntactical levels. It also implies a dissociation between
speech production and speech perception. Phonematic aphasia should not be
confused with articulatory disorders resulting from a lesion of the inferior part
of the motor cortex. According to Hécaen, such disorders are paretic and
therefore show a great consistency. In phonematic aphasia, on the contrary,
articulatory erros are unsystematic: "Il est difficile de déterminer des règles, ou
même s'il y a des règles valables pour tous les sujets examinés" (Cohen, Dubois,
Gauthier, Hécaen, & Angelergues, 1963).[18]

Bay also follows in Marie's footsteps. However, in contradistinction to Hécaen,
he regards articulatory defects in Broca's aphasia as motor disorders that are
"independent of language" (De Reuck & O'Connor, 1964, p. 329). Nonetheless,
such disorders can be brought about only by a lesion in the dominant hemisphere, "because articulation corresponds with writing, drawing, sewing and
other skilled movements which are confined to the right hand" (p. 128). They
but rarely occur in isolation. Generally, they combine with true aphasia to form
Broca's aphasia. Bay holds that this articulatory disorder, which he calls *cortical
dysarthria*, is "typified by apraxia of the face." However, when Critchley at the
Ciba Foundation Symposium on Disorders of Language asked him whether he
regarded cortical dysarthria as a variety of apraxia, Bay answered: "I would call
it a slight spastic paresis of the articulatory muscles" (p. 329).

Sollberg (1966) contends that cortical dysarthria is a spastic disorder:

> Pathophysiologische Grundlage dieser Artikulationsstörung ist eine spastische Be-
> wegungsstörung der unter der Artikulationsmuskulatur zusammengefassten Ge-
> sichts-, Mund-, Hals- und Kehlkopfmuskulatur. Sie betrifft ausser der Artikulation
> auch alle nichtsprachlichen Leistungen dieser Muskulatur und äussert sich hier in
> einer Vergröberung des Bewegungsablaufes, in einem Verlust der Fähigkeit zu
> feinmotorischen Bewegungen.[19]

According to Sollberg, glossograms and electromyograms of patients with cortical dysarthria fully confirm the spasticity of the articulatory organs. Broca's
aphasia is a combination of cortical dysarthria and genuine aphasia.

[17] A disturbance of the phonematic programming.
[18] It is hard to set rules; it is even harder to decide if there are any rules that apply to all
of the subjects examined.
[19] The pathophysiology of this articulatory disturbance is a spastic movement disorder of
the muscles of articulation, viz., the facial, oral, neck, and laryngeal muscles. In addition to
articulation, it also affects all movements unrelated to verbalization, manifesting itself in a
coarseness of the movement, in a loss of the capacity for fine motor control.

Luria (1970), on the contrary, posits two different kinds of articulatory disorders: one that is part of a syndrome called *afferent motor aphasia*, and another that is part of a clinical entity named *efferent motor aphasia*. In the latter, the sequential organization of articulation is disturbed. Isolated sounds can still be uttered, but the production of words and phrases is impaired. The patient finds it difficult to switch quickly from one articulation to the other, and he tends to perseverate. In afferent motor aphasia, on the contrary, the dynamics of speech production are not reduced, but the patient finds it hard to correctly articulate each individual sound. This articulatory disorder results from an oral apraxia, which itself is due to an impairment of kinesthesia.

In Denny-Brown's opinion (1963) the articulatory defects in anarthria (which he calls *subcortical dysarthria*) and in Broca's aphasia are not identical. In subcortical dysarthria, "the defect is constant, and is simply the result of incomplete, dystonic movement of the tongue, palate and lips." The condition stems from lenticular and external capsular lesions. In Broca's aphasia, on the contrary, articulatory disorders are apraxic in nature. They are often associated with oral apraxia. "The essential lesion in Broca's aphasia must lie in the audito-motor connections of the cortical areas controlling movements of the lips and tongue."

The neurolinguist who wants to set up a model of articulatory defects in aphasia is thus faced with a double problem: Are these defects unitary, as Marie, Dejerine, Bay, and Sollberg maintain, or do they constitute several clinical entities, as Luria and Denny-Brown contend? And if they are unitary, are they spastic (Sollberg), apraxic (Bay), paretic-apraxic-dystonic (Alajouanine, Ombredane, and Durand), or linguistic (Hécaen) in nature? In other words:

> Jusqu'où va, dans l'aphasie, le trouble apraxique des organes de la parole, et même ne peut-on pas trouver dans les difficultés d'élocution des aphasiques des désordres de niveau plus élémentaire que l'apraxie? Jusqu'à quel point aussi des symptômes de cet ordre peuvent-ils être considérés comme partie intégrante de l'aphasie ou doivent-ils être éliminés du cadre de l'aphasie comme constituant un syndrome extrinsèque? [Ombredane, 1951, p. 321].[20]

In an attempt to find an answer to these questions, three cases of articulatory defects concomitant with predominantly expressive aphasic symptoms have been analyzed.

1. Mathilde V. was born in 1909. She is well-educated. She speaks French. She writes with her right hand but is ambidextrous for other manual activities. In 1963 she started to suffer from Jacksonian convulsions characterized by clonic movements of the right eyelid, chewing, pharyngeal stricture, slight respiratory

---

[20] At what point do the apraxic speech difficulties merge into aphasia? Can we find some disorder more elementary than apraxia among the speech difficulties of aphasics? To what extent may this syndrome be considered as a part of aphasia; or must it be rejected as being a syndrome extrinsic to the domain of aphasia?

difficulty, and inability to speak and to swallow. Eventually, brain scan and arteriography revealed a tumor in the left hemisphere and the patient underwent surgery. A meningioma that compressed the inferior part of the precentral gyrus was excised (Surgeon, J. Brihaye). After surgery the patient had a right facial paralysis accompanied by hypoesthesia. The tongue, when protruded, deviated to the right. Its mobility was considerably reduced. The palatal and pharyngeal reflexes were present. Nonetheless, swallowing was difficult. Respiration was very shallow. The right hand was paretic. The patient could not speak at all. She could express herself in writing but frequently misspelled words. There was some degree of dyscalculia. After a few weeks the dysgraphia and the dyscalculia cleared up and speech returned. But the patient's delivery was slow and her articulation defective. Her articulatory errors were fairly constant. Sibilants and velar plosives were the most distorted sounds. The phonemes /R/ and /w/ were very often omitted. On the whole, articulation tended to be dedifferentiated. Moveover, pulmonic air was short so that the ends of most sentences were barely audible. The same articulatory mistakes obtained regardless of the kind of speech (conversation, reading aloud, reciting) the patient used. There was no oral apraxia. The patient was dysphonic. Two years after surgery, the articulatory deficit and the dysphonia were still present. Chewing firm food (such as crisp apples) remained arduous. The right hand was still slightly paretic. The patient complained about numbness in the right cheek, the right half of the lips, and the right thumb.

2. Joseph V. was born in 1913. He is foreman in a factory. He speaks French. On September 11, 1965, late in the evening, he was assailed by bandits who severely beat him. Joseph succeeded in reaching a hotel, the owner of which telephoned for a doctor. The physician arrived and found a stupefied patient with several scalp wounds. He had Joseph taken to a hospital. The next morning, it was discovered that Joseph, though quite in his senses, could not speak a word. No other neurological symptom could be discovered, however. The patient was referred to another clinic for further investigation. Joseph wrote his daughter that he was lying in the hospital because he had had a fall, and he told her not to worry. Some words in the note exhibited omissions or substitutions of letters (e.g., he wrote *grawe* instead of *grave, vou* instead of *vous,* and *reen* instead of *rien*). A week after the assault, the patient's condition suddenly deteriorated. Joseph was in a fever and complained, in writing, about violent headaches. A roentgenographic investigation of the head revealed a left temporo-parietal fracture with skull depression. On September 23, Joseph was trepanned; his wound was cleansed and the bone fragments tied together (Surgeon, P. Martin). Four days after surgery the patient was still completely speechless: All his attempts at speaking resulted in unintelligible grunts. However, there was no paralysis of the speech musculature and no oral apraxia. Joseph could chew and swallow without difficulty. Comprehension of spoken and written language was

normal. The patient communicated by means of grimaces and gestures, which were very expressive indeed. He could also express himself in writing, but made occasional mistakes (e.g., he wrote *lesant* instead of *lisant* and *complèlement* instead of *complètement*). There was also a slight dyscalculia. The patient was shown in succession three sets of objects. Each time, he was asked whether he knew the names of the five objects in front of him. As he nodded, he was requested to point to the two objects among the five whose names began with the same sound (e.g. *pencil* and *pipe* in a set comprising these two objects as well as a screw, an eraser, and a knife). In each case, he gave the correct answer. After a few days, speech slowly returned. The patient was soon able to make himself understood but his articulation was grossly disturbed. His wound having healed and there being no neurological deficit other than the speech disorder, the patient was discharged. He was re-examined one year later. It was found that he was talkative, but did not always complete the sentences he had begun. Sometimes he would stop midway as if finding it difficult to proceed with the syntactic structure he had chosen; and he would begin another sentence to convey his idea. No other aphasic symptom could be discovered. On the other hand, the patient's delivery was still very impaired. His speech showed syllabic prominence and syllabic isochronism, slow articulation rate, and abnormal vowel formation. As a result, the patient seemed to be using scanning speech (Lebrun, Buyssens, & Henneaux, 1973). Moreover, he often mispronounced words. His articulatory errors were either phonetic or phonemic. A phonetic error is a sound that cannot be identified as any of the phonemes of the language used. A phonemic error is an omitted phoneme or a phoneme used inappropriately. Analysis of the phonemic errors showed that no phoneme was systematically dropped or added. No vowel was ever substituted for, or replaced by, a consonant. Nor was a back vowel ever substituted for, or replaced by, a front vowel. Apart from these limitations, substitutions were completely unsystematic and did not form any patterning of phonemic disintegration. Phonetic errors were equally inconsistent and unpredictable. On the other hand, many substitutions appeared to be anticipations. Most of them occurred across word boundaries (e.g., *bien faire* /bjẽfɛʀ/ was pronounced /bɛʀfɛʀ/); a few of them occurred across syllable boundaries (e.g., *cinéma* /sinema/ was pronounced /simnema/). A number of substitutions were perseverations (e.g., *équateur* /ekwatəʀ/ was pronounced /ekwatwəʀ/). The patient's articulation was often faulty, but never indistinct. Pronunciation was frequently incorrect but it was not weak nor dedifferentiated. A balanced repetition test indicated that the number of articulatory errors increased with word length. While in monosyllabic words, one syllable in less than seven contained an error, in trisyllabic words one syllable in less than four was incorrect. There was no word the patient could not pronounce at all. To be sure, repeated attempts were sometimes necessary before a given word could be uttered in its entirety (e.g., *philo-philos-philosoph-ph-s-*

philosophiquement). Or the word might contain one or more articulatory errors. But one way or another, the patient always succeeded in saying whatever word he wanted. Moreover, delivery was abnormal and articulation was impaired regardless of the kind of spoken language resorted to by Joseph. The severity of his speech disorder was constant, whether he held a conversation, recited series he knew by rote, or repeated words pronounced by the examiner: So-called automatic speech was as badly articulated as propositional speech. On the other hand, the very same word might be articulated correctly or nearly so at one time and be considerably distorted a few seconds later although nothing had changed either in the speech situation or in the kind of speech used.

3. Yvette W. was born in 1914. She works as an accountant and speaks French. In 1967, she suffered a vascular accident in the left temporal region that caused a right-sided hemiplegia and a severe aphasia. The hemiplegia cleared up after a few days but a significant language disorder remained. In May 1968, the patient could understand simple questions and uncomplicated orders but experienced difficulty in dealing with complex ones. She had no facial paralysis, no oral apraxia, and no dysphagia. She was agraphic, but could easily copy script or typewritten texts. She could understand written language but read much more slowly than she did before the stroke. Her speech was made up of islands of fair fluency alternating with periods of effortful delivery or of groping toward word production. The words that slowed her down were often mispronounced (e.g., *octobre* /ɔktɔbR/ was pronounced /ɔkstɔbR/ and *Bruxelles 1* /bRysɛlɑ̃/ was pronounced /bRyθɛljɑ̃/). Her phonemic errors were unsystematic and unpredictable. Her omissions, insertions, and substitutions formed no definite pattern (Lebrun, Lenaerts, Goiris, & Demol, 1969). Phonemic anticipations and perseverations were few. Moreover, they did not occur across word boundaries. On the other hand, more than once the patient found it impossible to utter the word she needed. When she experienced a breakdown in speech production, she would often resort to such standing phrases as *How shall I say?, I know it, you know, but . . .*, or *I'm so sorry*, which were always pronounced correctly and fluently. When she stumbled over a word, prompting would often help her. Indeed, showing the patient the first articulatory movement frequently sufficed to enable her to say the whole word. Her speech contained many filled pauses (*er*), numerous expletives, and frequent iterations (e.g., *On p- on p- on peut f s on peut euh r on pf- on peut comment dirais-je? on peut essayer*). There were also occasional word perseverations and some semantic pharaphasias. Remarkably enough, repetition of simple words and short sentences was correct and always fluent. Routinized series (days of the week, months of the year, figures from 1 to 20, etc.) once they had been thrown into gear, did not present any difficulty either.

Each of the three patients described above thus showed disturbed articulation associated with aphasic symptoms that were predominantly or exclusively expressive in nature. These symptoms were transitory in the first case, slight in the *rapid motor recovery is typical*

second, and rather severe in the third. Although they all occurred in conjunction with some form of motor aphasia, the articulatory defects that were observed in these three patients obviously are not identical.

The first case, Mathilde V., very much resembles the case reported by Alajoua-nine, Boudin, Pertuiset, and Pépin (1959a). Their patient was a 57-year-old male who was admitted to the hospital for a speech disorder. Neurological examination revealed that the right corneal reflex was diminished. The right masseter contracted far less than the left. There was a paralysis of the musculature innervated by the seventh cranial nerve on the right. The right half of the velum and of the pharynx was paretic. The palatal and gag reflexes were abolished. The tongue, when protruded, deviated to the right. The right sternocleidomastoid contracted less than the left. The patient had a severe articulatory disorder, with slow delivery and hyperrhinolalia. His articulatory errors were rather constant. There was also a slight aphasia. The right hand was paretic. EEG and arteriog-raphy disclosed a tumor in the left hemisphere. The patient was craniotomized and a glioblastoma was removed from the inferior part of the precentral gyrus. 16 months after surgery, the articulatory disorder was still present, although it was slightly less pronounced than before the operation.

A rather similar case was reported by Sollberg (1966). His patient was a 36-year-old worker who had fallen from a scaffold. When he was admitted to the hospital he had a right-sided hemiplegia and aphasia. The motor impairment soon cleared up, although the speech disorder improved slowly. There were word-finding difficulties and some impairment of comprehension. Six weeks after the accident the patient was still very silent. When he did speak, he used very short sentences. His choice of words was correct, but his delivery was slow and his articulation defective. He always made the same articulatory errors. These mispronunciations occurred regardless of the kind of speech the patient was using. Articulatory movements tended to be dedifferentiated:

> Die verwendeten Wörter sind ausnahmslos richtig, kommen jedoch zum grossen Teil entstellt heraus, wobei immer wieder die gleichen oder ähnliche Fehlleistungen zu beobachten sind, welche vom Patienten nicht korrigiert werden können. Sie ziehen sich durch alle sprachlichen Teilleistungenn... Es besteht also eine Artikulations-störung, die durch eine mangelnde Unterscheidungsfähigkeit zwischen verwandten Lautbildungen gekenntzeichnet ist [Sollberg, 1966].[21]

There was no comprehension difficulty and no further anomia. Three months posttrauma, the articulatory disorder was still present. No other neurological deficit could be found. According to Sollberg, the articulatory defects were due

[21] The words used were invariably correct, but did on the whole come out distorted, in the course of which the same or similar errors, which could not be corrected by the patient, could be observed again and again. These mistakes occurred regardless of the kind of speech used. There exists thus an articulatory disturbance that is characterized by an inability to differentiate between sound sequences that resemble one another.

solely to the spasticity of the patient's speech musculature. Because of this spasticity, the patient was also unable to smack and to cluck. There was no facial paralysis, however.

It can hardly be doubted that, in the case of Mathilde V. and in the similar case reported by Alajouanine and his associates, the articulation impairment resulted from the paresis of the speech musculature. Most probably this explanation applies also to Sollberg's patient. In the first two cases, the paresis was due to a lesion of the inferior part of the precentral gyrus. There can thus be an articulation disorder that is paralytic in nature and is concomitant with predominantly expressive aphasic symptoms. Interestingly enough, this dysarthria may be a lasting deficit despite the fact that the lesion which causes it is unilateral. Moreover, it may be so severe as to render the patient speechless. To be sure, one might argue that immediately after surgery Mathilde V. was not only dysarthric but also severely aphasic and that is the reason why she could not speak at all. It should be pointed out, however, that patients occasionally are rendered completely speechless by a unilateral lesion that does not at the same time make them aphasic. In other words, oral speech may be totally suppressed as a result of a motor deficit caused by a unilateral hemispheric lesion. A case in point was reported by Alajouanine, Lhermitte, Cambier, Rondot, and Lefebvre (1959b). Their patient was a 27-year-old, right-handed male who woke up one morning to find himself unable to speak and to move the right side of his body. He was admitted to the hospital and neurological examination revealed a severe hemiplegia affecting the face, the arm, and the leg on the right side. The patient could only produce a few guttural sounds. His pharynx, velum, and tongue remained completely immobile when he tried to speak. There was no aphasia, however. The patient understood language perfectly. He could still read, and what he managed to write with his left hand was correct. He could not move his tongue voluntarily nor purse his lips. He could not blow out a match or drink through a straw. He was unable to make faces or to frown on command. The palatal reflex was abolished, while the gag reflex was preserved. Curiously enough, spontaneous facial gesticulation and laughing were normal (though weaker on the right side). Chewing was unimpaired and swallowing, once the bolus had reached the pharynx, presented no difficulty. The left limbs exhibited no deficit whatsoever. On the basis of bilateral arteriography, Alajouanine and his co-workers concluded that this symptomatology resulted from a vascular lesion affecting the lenticular nucleus, the internal capsule, and the caudate nucleus in the left hemisphere.

It thus appears that a condition resembling pseudobulbar dysarthria may obtain as the result of a unilateral hemispheric lesion. It is not clear, however, whether a *permanent* speechlessness may result from such an injury. Mathilde V. recovered her speech after a few weeks and so, it would seem, did Alajouanine's case (see Alajouanine & Lhermitte, 1960). On the contrary, it is an established

sequencing needed for speech

fact that a bilateral hemispheric lesion may entail an irreversible loss of speech. It also remains to be shown whether a lesion in the *nondominant* hemisphere may bring about a lasting articulation disorder.

For want of a better term, the articulation disturbance exhibited by Mathilde V. might be called *cortical paralytic dysarthria*.

On the other hand, the articulation disorder that was observed in Joseph V. corresponds to the condition referred to as *apraxia of speech* by Johns and Darley (1970) and Deal and Darley (1972). Deal and Darley conceive apraxia of speech "as a motor speech disorder—a disorder of the programming of the complex sequencing of neuromuscular events required for speech." In patients having this impairment "the speech musculature does not show significant weakness, slowness, or incoordination when used for reflex and automatic acts." Since oral apraxia is generally defined as "the inability to perform voluntary movements with the muscles of the larynx, pharynx, tongue, lips and cheeks, although automatic movements of the same muscles are preserved" (De Renzi, Pieczuro, & Vignolo, 1966), whether or not apraxia of speech is part of oral apraxia may be questioned. It would seem that this query has to be answered in the negative. In the case cited above (Joseph V.), apraxia of speech was not concomitant with oral apraxia, even when apraxia of speech was so severe as to render the patient completely speechless. In a group of 13 patients with apraxia of speech, La Pointe and Wertz (1974) could identify only 9 with oral apraxia. Moreover, when both disorders obtain in one patient, their courses are not always parallel, as was shown by Tissot, Rodriguez, and Tissot (1970). Indeed, in one of the cases reported by these authors, the buccofacial apraxia, which was very severe at the beginning of the affection, cleared up after six months while the articulatory impairment remained. Conversely, oral apraxia may be occasionally observed in patients without articulatory disorders. One such case has been reported by De Renzi *et al.* (1966). It would appear, therefore, that articulatory eupraxia is subserved by cerebral areas that do not completely coincide with those commanding voluntary nonverbal movements of the oral structures. This observation, after all, is not surprising, for a similar dissociation has been shown to exist in relation to finger movements. At the Ciba Foundation Symposium on Disorders of Language, Broadbent reported that

well *articulation vs voluntary movement of articulators*

typists can, as one might expect, type more efficiently sequences which are more probable. A very interesting case arises however in teleprinter operators, since numbers on a teleprinter keyboard occur on the same keys as do letters. It is therefore possible to construct sequences of numbers which require the pressing of the same sequence of keys as do probable sequences of letters, although there is of course no reason to suppose that these are particularly common sequences of numbers. If therefore the teleprinter operator had practised a particular sequence of finger movements, it should be possible to type out these sequences of numbers more rapidly than sequences which correspond to improbable sequences of letters. In fact this is not so. Exactly the same pattern of finger movements is easy when it corresponds to the sequence of letters, but shows no particular advantage when it corresponds to a sequence of numbers [De Reuck & O'Connor, 1964, pp. 85–86].

This phenomenon suggests that the typing of a routinized string of letters cannot be equated with a sequence of individual motor actions. On the contrary, there seem to exist verbomotor engrams that facilitate the typing of such strings and can only be used to perform verbal tasks. Similarly, there seem to exist articulatory engrams that insure fluent and orderly delivery and cannot be viewed as sequences of pure motor commands. Disturbance of these engrams would result in the slow, jerky, and dishevelled pronunciation typical of apraxia of speech.

Alajouanine, Pichot, and Durand (1949) had occasion to examine a patient who had sustained a stroke two months before. The initial writing disorder, dyscalculia, and right-sided hemiplegia had cleared up almost entirely. There was no intellectual impairment, but the patient had a significant apraxia of speech (which the authors called *pure anarthria*). This man was bilingual, having a French father and an English mother. Living in France, he used to speak English at home and French at school. Before he started to go to school at the age of four he had spoken only English. The patient's relatives drew Alajouanine's attention to the fact that the speech impairment was less severe in English than in French. A phonetic analysis of a sample of the patient's speech production showed the family's judgment to be correct. This result testifies to the verbal nature of the disorder called apraxia of speech. If this speech disturbance resulted from oral apraxia, no difference would have been observed between French and English. In reality, the articulatory engrams that had been formed first were less affected by the stroke.

Pilch and Hemmer (1970) reported a case that they called "phonematische Aphasie, ein Sonderfall motorischer Aphasie." Their patient in fact very much resembles Joseph (case number 2 in this chapter). Surgery was performed on the Pilch and Hemmer patient because he had a precentrotemporal tumor in the left hemisphere.

Nach der Operation vertauschte der Patient bestimmte deutsche Phoneme gegen andere deutsche Phoneme oder brachte sie überhaupt nicht heraus. Er sprach stets klar und deutlich. Es bestand nie ein Zweifel, welches deutsche Phonem im Einzelfall ausgesprochen wurde. Der Patient war sich über seine Fehlleistungen zum grossen Teil im klaren und beschrieb sie *expressis verbis*. . . . Die stereotype Rede des Patienten unterschied sich nicht von seiner spontanen Rede. . . . Der Patient verstand mühelos alle spontane Rede, die er hörte. . . . Häufig setzte der Patient, wenn ihm eine Aussprache nicht gelang, mehrfach an. . . . Der Patient kapitulierte häufig vor mehr als zweisilbigen Wörtern. . . . Bei der spontanen Rede verbesserte der Patient sich selbst sehr häufig. . . . Er wusste selbst meistens wo es fehlte. . . . Er hatte zwar auch beim Schreiben gewisse Schwierigkeiten, jedoch schrieb er besser, als er sprach. . . . Er las, wie er berichtete, Bücher langsam and musste jeden Satz zweimal lesen. . . . Scheinbare Schwierigkeiten des Patienten bei der Wortfindung liessen sich in fast allen Fällen ohne weiteres als blosse Schwierigkeiten bei der Aussprache des gesuchten Wortes verstehen.[22]

Pilch and Hemmer concluded that the disorder lay essentially "im Bereich der Umsetzung der Sprechabsicht in eine artikulierte Aeusserung."[23]

It would appear, however, that in apraxia of speech articulatory engrams, in addition to being disordered, tend to interact when they are being made ready for activation. This causes anticipations, perseverations, and transpositions across word boundaries. Such a disturbance is somewhat akin to the crush of sentence constituents that is observed in agrammatism (Lebrun, Brihaye, & Lebrun, 1971). It may therefore not be purely coincidental that some patients with apraxia of speech also show some degree of agrammatism (Lebrun *et al.*, 1973).

[margin annotation: crush of sentence constituents]

It should further be noted that in apraxia of speech articulatory difficulty increases with word length. This suggests that the articulation of a word is not programmed piecemeal as a series of discrete movements, but on the contrary as an integrated complex motion.

Apraxia of speech thus appears to be a disorder of the articulatory gesture and of the temporal organization of this gesture. As such, apraxia of speech seems to correspond to Broca's aphemia and to Marie's anarthria.

Obviously, the third patient described above, Yvonne W., had a motor aphasia of the Broca type. Was this syndrome a combination of genuine aphasia and anarthria? Although her articulatory errors are as inconsistent and as unpredictable as Joseph's, it would appear that the two articulation impairments are essentially different. There are many words—and not necessarily long ones—that Yvonne cannot pronounce at all in ordinary conversation, while Joseph can say any word he likes, even though he may misarticulate it. Conversely, Joseph speaks haltingly whatever kind of language he may be using, and so did the anarthric patient of Alajouanine, Pichot and Durand (1949), whereas Yvonne speaks fluently when she repeats words or short sentences, when she recites automatized series, and when she resorts to expletives or standing phrases. When

---

[22] Postoperatively, the patient substituted certain German phonemes for other German phonemes, or failed completely to produce them. He always spoke clearly and distinctly. There was never any doubt about which German phoneme was being articulated. The patient was on the whole aware of his errors and described them *expressis verbis*. . . . The stereotyped speech of the patient was not different from his spontaneous speech. . . . The patient understood without any problems all spontaneous speech which he heard. . . . Often, the patient would start over again if he failed to articulate something. . . . The patient frequently gave up on words with more than two syllables. . . . In spontaneous speech, the patient often improved himself. He knew in most cases what was wrong. . . . He also had some difficulties with his writing, although it was better than his speech. . . . When he read books, he proceeded slowly and he had to read each sentence two times. . . . Apparent word-finding difficulties could in almost all cases be understood as problems with the pronunciation of the word he was seeking.

[23] . . . in the domain of converting the speech intention into an articulated expression.

Yvonne experiences a breakdown in speech production she can often be helped by prompting. In Joseph's case, prompting is ineffective. As a matter of fact, he does not need it. Finally, many of Joseph's phonemic errors are anticipations that occur across word boundaries, and so were most of the errors made by the patient of Alajouanine *et al.* (1949). Such anticipations do not obtain in Yvonne's speech. These differences seem to justify the conclusion that the mechanisms underlying Yvonne's articulatory defects, although they cannot be easily specified, do not identify with the mechanisms underlying Joseph's disorder of articulation. It would appear, therefore, that Bernheim (1900) was correct in contrasting aphemia (i.e., apraxia of speech) with Broca's aphasia and in regarding both as distinct clinical entities.

The articulatory errors of Joseph V. differ also from those of Mathilde V. However, immediately after surgery, the two patients exhibited approximately the same neurolinguistic deficit: speechlessness, dysgraphia, dyscalculia. If Joseph had had a facial paralysis, the two patients would have looked very much alike and a differential diagnosis would have been very difficult. Indeed, it might be presumed that a number of neurologists, had they seen Mathilde immediately after surgery, would have regarded her as an anarthric patient, since, according to Alajouanine and Lhermitte (1960), "une paralysie faciale centrale accompagne toujours l'anarthrie."[24] Retrospectively, it would seem that the fierce controversy between Pitres, Marie, and Moutier on the one hand, and Dejerine and Bernheim on the other, at the beginning of the twentieth century, sprang in part from the failure to distinguish between apraxia of speech and cortical paralytic dysarthria.

Afferent Dysgraphia

Patients having a lesion in the minor hemisphere not infrequently exhibit a writing disorder, whose main feature is an inappropriate number of letters and of strokes. Figure 1 shows how a Dutch-speaking patient (Verd.) with a right temporal hematoma wrote the following sentences under dictation:

Wij gaan voor eerst naar school.
"We are going for the first time to school."
Wij zijn voor eerst in de school.
"We are for the first time in school."
Ze liep naar hem toe zodra ze hem zag.
"She ran to him as soon as she saw him."

Figure 2 shows how a French-speaking clerk (Dur.) having a right parietotemporal hematoma wrote the following sentences under dictation:

[24] Anarthria is always associated with a central facial paralysis.

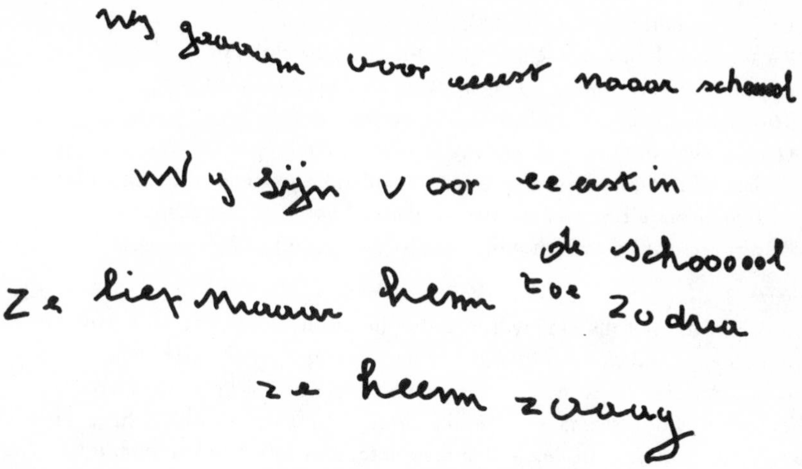

Figure 1 Sentences written under dictation by a Dutch-speaking patient having a right temporal hematoma.

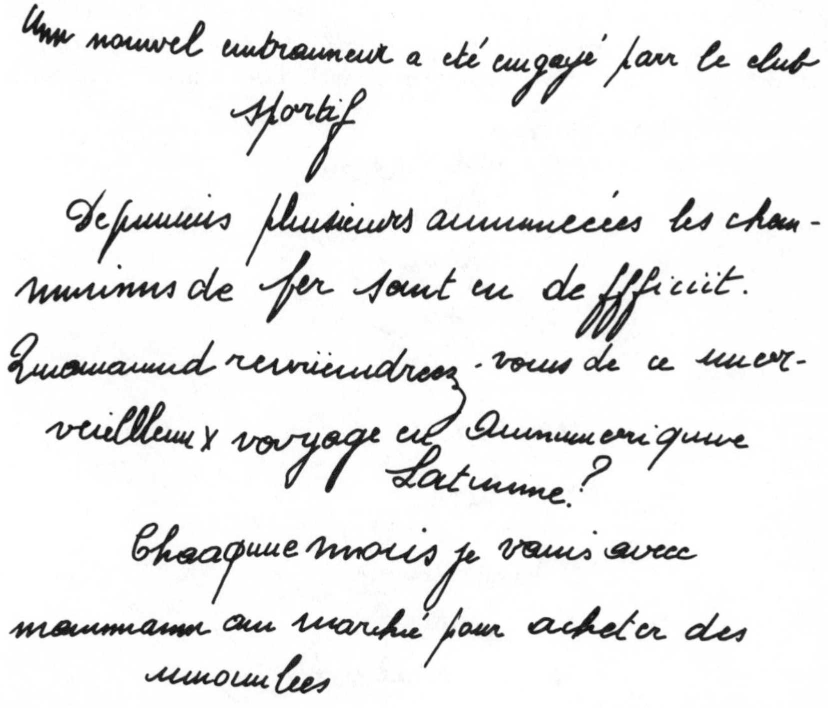

Figure 2 Sentences written under dictation by a French-speaking patient having a right parietotemporal hematoma.

Un nouvel entraîneur a été engagé par le club sportif.
"A new coach has been engaged by the sporting club."
Depuis plusieurs années les chemins de fer sont en déficit.
"For several years the railways have shown a deficit."
Quand reviendrez-vous de ce long voyage en Amérique Latine?
"When will you be returning from this splendid journey in South America?"
Chaque mois je vais avec maman au marché pour acheter des moules.
"Every month I go with my mother to the market to buy mussels."

Figure 3 shows how a French-speaking patient (Delh.) having a right parietal tumor wrote the following words under dictation: *minimum, mur, mine, femme, munir, neuve, inutile, inimitable, écume, mienne, miel, lune, mince, madame, mousse.* As may be seen, the *m* in the second word has four downstrokes, while the fourth word seems to contain three *m*'s, two of which have only two downstrokes. The *u* in *neuve* is incomplete, and so is the *b* in *inimitable.* The *m* at the beginning of *mine* and of *mienne* has only two downstrokes. Similar mistakes were made by a French-speaking accountant (Andr.), who had sustained a vascular accident in the right hemisphere, e.g., *oeuffs* instead of *oeufs, bellle* instead of *belle, ongrie* instead of *Hongrie, cuche* instead of *couché, qatre* instead of *quatre, joerrr* instead of *jouer.* Remarkably enough, this patient, who was very well educated, never erred when she spelled words aloud from memory.

Figure 3 Words written under dictation by a French-speaking patient having a right parietal tumor.

Indeed, when she spelled aloud the words she was writing down, she would always spell correctly although she <u>reduplicated</u> or <u>omitted</u> quite a number of letters. This indicates that her knowledge of orthography was intact, but when she had to manifest this knowledge in writing, she used an inappropriate number of signs. In other words, the disorder exhibited by the patient was not an impairment of written language but a disturbance of the act of writing.

The view that the duplications and omissions under consideration do not result from acquired dysorthography is corroborated by Marcie, Hécaen, Dubois, and Angelergues (1965): In a group of 28 right-brain-damaged patients, they found 7 who made reduplications of strokes and 2 who made reduplications of letters and of strokes. They also found 9 patients with a slight dysorthography and 2 with a moderate dysorthography. Of these 20 patients, only 3 exhibited both disorders. These 3 patients had a slight dysorthography and showed a tendency to reduplicate strokes.

Also, Verd., Dur., Delh., and Andr. made as many reduplications and omissions when they copied a text as when they wrote under dictation, which would not have been so if the errors in question were spelling mistakes.

Marcie *et al.* (1965) observed that the nine patients in their study who made reduplications of strokes and/or of letters also tended to perserverate in grammatical tests.

> L'exécution de ces tests met en évidence, par la forme même qu'ils présentent, [des] perturbations qui résultent d'un phénomène général que l'on a nommé d'une manière purement descriptive *pe* (persévération). On entend par là la difficulté pour un malade de passer d'un schéma de transformation à un autre schéma dans une succession de tests grammaticaux; l'inertie du schéma perturbe la réalisation du schéma suivant ou même des schémas ultérieurs.[25]

It might therefore be wondered whether the reduplications under discussion are not perseverations. Perhaps the patient cannot inhibit in due time the gesture which is tracing, say, the downstrokes of *m*; there results, as in the examples quoted above, a letter with far too many strokes. As a matter of fact, this point of view has been adopted by Assal and Zander (1969), who note that the script of right-brain-damaged patients often exhibits "des phénomènes de persévération: itération de syllabes ou de groupes de lettres, de lettres, de jambages. Ces persévération se retrouvent dans l'écriture des nombres."[26] However, this

---

[25] Through their procedural methods, the performance on these tests emphasizes some disturbances resulting from a general phenomenon which is called, in a purely descriptive way, *pe* (perseveration). One means by that the difficulty experienced by a patient in switching from a transformation scheme to another scheme in a succession of grammatical tests; the inertia of the scheme disturbs the realization of the following scheme, and even of the subsequent ones.

[26] perseverative phenomena: repetition of syllables or groups of letters, letters, and downstrokes of letters. This perseveration is also found in the writing of numbers.

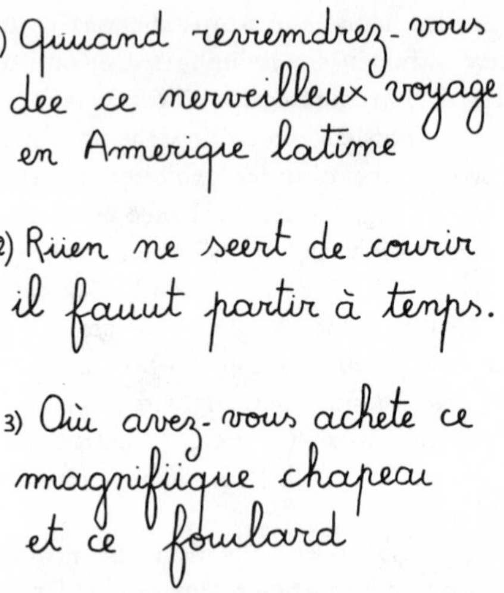

Figure 4 Text used to test whether or not right-brain-damaged patients can spot duplications and deletions made by others. (English translations: (1) "When will you be returning from this splendid journey in South America?" (2) "It is no good hurrying, you must start punctually." (3) "When did you buy this beautiful hat and this scarf?")

explanation fails to account for the omissions of strokes and of letters that also occur in the writings of these patients. And it fails to reveal why the patients most of the time overlook their reduplications and omissions when they read over what they have written. Indeed, they tend to disregard duplications and deletions also in the writings of others. Delh. was once shown the text reproduced in Figure 4. When requested to read the text aloud, he did so correctly and without making any comment. When asked whether or not there were spelling mistakes in the text, he read it over again and said that there should have been an interrogation mark after the third sentence. This was the only mistake he could discover. He was then requested to look for reduplications and omissions. He re-read each sentence slowly and crossed out the third downstroke of the *n* in *reviemdrez* and in *latime*, the second *i* in *Riien*, the second *e* in *seert*, and the third upstroke of the *u* in the very last word. Pointing to the word *tenps* at the end of the second sentence, he remarked that the *m* should have had a third downstroke, and he proceeded to correct the mistake by writing above the incomplete *m* another *m*, which had two downstrokes! The first word of the third sentence caused him to pause. Then he said he must have seen double, for he had thought at first that the *u* had too many upstrokes!

The patient's behavior suggests that the cause of the reduplications and omissions made by some right-brain-injured people may be perceptual. In order to get a better insight into this matter, 10 right-handed French-speaking subjects, having no sign of dysorthography or of neurological disease, were requested to write down the sentence, *ma maman mange une bonne pomme avec un monsieur* ("My mother is eating a nice apple with a gentleman"), with their eyes closed. In the experiment, the following mistakes were made:

ma: One subject added a fourth downstroke to the *m*, and another redoubled the circle of the *a*.

maman: Two subjects added a fourth downstroke to the first *m*, and two others added a fourth downstroke to the second *m*; one subject omitted the second downstroke of the final *n*.

mange: Three subjects added a fourth downstroke to the *m*.

bonne: One subject added a third downstroke to the first *n* and another subject added a third downstroke to the second *n*; yet another subject deleted the second downstroke of the second *n*.

pomme: One subject added a fourth downstroke to the first *m*; three subjects added a fourth downstroke to the second *m*; one subject omitted the third downstroke of the first *m*.

avec: One subject deleted the second upstroke of the *v*.

un: One subject added a third downstroke to the *n*.

monsieur: One subject added a fourth downstroke to the *m*; another subject added a third upstroke to the *u*; yet another dropped the *s*.

The same experiment was repeated with 16 Dutch-speaking university students, all of whom were healthy and right handed. The test sentence was *moeder mijmert naast de nieuwe mahoniemeubels van mijnheer Bellemans, de vitterige nettenmaker.*[27] The following errors were made:

moeder: One subject added a fourth downstroke to the *m*.

mijmert: One subject doubled the *r* and two others duplicated the *i*; one subject added a fourth downstroke to the initial *m*.

naast: One subject added a third downstroke to the *n*.

nieuwe: One subject redoubled the *i*; three subjects added a third upstroke to the *u*; three others deleted the last upstroke of the *w*; yet another added a fourth upstroke to the *w*.

meubels: Two subjects added a fourth downstroke to the *m*; another dropped the third downstroke of the *m*; one subject added a third upstroke to the *u* while another deleted the second upstroke of this letter; one subject doubled the *l*.

van: One subject added a third downstroke to the *n*.

mijnheer: One subject doubled the *i* and another doubled the *r*; one subject added a third downstroke to the *n*.

---

[27] Mother muses next to the new mahogany furniture of Mr. Bellemans, the faultfinding netmaker.

right hemisphere damage is connected with perception (handwritten annotation)

Bellemans: Two subjects dropped the third downstroke of the *m*; one subject deleted the second downstroke of the *n*.

vitterige: One subject doubled the second *i* and another duplicated the *r*; one subject dropped the *v* and another added a third upstroke to it.

nettenmaker: Two subjects doubled the first *e* and one subject reduplicated the second *n*; one subject omitted one of the *t*'s; another dropped the third downstroke of the *m* and yet another deleted the second downstroke of the initial *n*.

The mistakes that were made in these experiments very much resemble those made by the aforementioned right-brain-damaged patients. Yet, reduplications of strokes or of letters by these patients are often far more dramatic than those made by normal individuals writing with their eyes closed. Duplications by normals generally consist in the addition of only one supernumerary stroke or letter, while reduplications by patients may consist in the addition of several superfluous strokes or in the triplication of a letter.

There is another similarity between normals who write with their eyes closed and the patients under discussion: Subjects who write with suppressed visual feedback not infrequently split their words into two or more parts. An analogous tendency to word tearing can often be observed in the writings of right-brain-injured patients. For instance, in Delh.'s written production one finds *mes mei llleurs amiitiiés* (instead of *mes meilleures amitiés*), *rem versé* (instead of *renversé*), *mi ches* (instead of *miches*).

The patients under consideration may not only be compared with normals writing with their eyes closed, but also with normals writing under conditions of delayed visual feedback. K. Smith (1962, p. 83) has reported the results of an analysis of 64 errors in writing words with delayed visual feedback. The greatest number (40.8%) were letter duplications. The second most numerous kind of error (26.6%) was the insertion of letters or parts of letters. There were a few errors of omission (7.8%) and a variety of miscellaneous errors in writing (23.4%). These results parallel the findings of van Bergeijk and David (1959) and of Kalmus, Fry, and Denes (1960). However, while normals under conditions of delayed visual feedback tend to make the same kinds of errors as some right-brain-damaged patients, they do not multiply strokes or triplicate letters. Despite this quantitative difference the resemblance between the two groups is striking. Moreover, it is not limited to errors in number of letters and of strokes. As a rule, right-brain-injured patients who make duplications and deletions do not write horizontally. Their lines are oblique or wavy. When they are oblique they generally have an upward slant. An illustration of this can be found in Hécaen (1972, Figure 21 on page 79) and in Brain (1965, Figure 24 facing page 135). The same trend can be observed in the words reproduced by W. Smith, McCrary, and Smith (1960) in their paper. These words were written by normals with delayed visual feedback.

visual feedback

K. Smith (1962, p. 83) also points out that when visual feedback is delayed, most subjects can still write legibly. In a few cases, however, handwriting is so degraded as to become illegible. Similarly, most patients who make reduplications and omissions still have a readable hand. "[Les] altérations ne dissimulent pas la véritable structure du mot qui reste lisible" (Hécaen, 1972, p. 78).[28] In a few cases, however, script degenerates into a scribble, notably because letters are drawn above one another.

When they are made to write on a ruled sheet of paper, right-brain-injured patients who make reduplications and omissions, usually find it difficult to heed the lines: Very often their downward strokes overrun. Delh. was once earnestly requested not to let his strokes go farther down than the line. Despite his obvious desire to please the examiner, he frequently made his downstrokes too long. A few times he noticed it and excused himself on the ground that he had seen the line too late. Interestingly enough, Kalmus *et al.* (1960) reports that, with delayed visual feedback, normal subjects find it difficult to drop a perpendicular onto a line without letting the perpendicular overshoot the line.

Also, the kind of patients under consideration, when they draw, tend to go over their pencil strokes time and again. A similar oscillatory type of movement was observed by K. Smith (1962, p. 83) in normals who had to draw with delayed visual feedback.

These numerous resemblances support the view that the duplications and omissions made by right-brain-injured patients are due to a disorder of visual feedback. However, since these patients tend to overlook such errors also when they read, this impairment of visual feedback may be conceived as part of a more general visuospatial disorder that consists essentially in a difficulty in analyzing one's visual percepts, notably when these percepts relate to series of similar elements (such as the downstrokes of an *m*). This difficulty is akin, it would seem, to the "troubles du dénombrement (impossibilité d'énumérer une série d'objets identiques)"[29] which, according to Hécaen (1972, p. 219) have been mentioned by C. Best, and to the difficulty in visual counting of objects that was observed by Paterson and Zangwill (1944) in two patients having right cerebral lesions. The disturbance also resembles the visual deficit described by Luria (1959). If he was presented with a pattern of dots forming a triangle, Luria's patient could easily recognize the geometric figure. However, if he was requested to tell how many dots there were, he was at a loss. In this case, the lesion was bilateral but the damage suffered by the right hemisphere was greater since there was a left-sided hemiparesis, partial left visual neglect, and EEG anomalies that were more pronounced on the right side.

The handwriting of Luria's patient showed disturbed alignment. Moreover, the spatial organization of the strokes was not always correct. Performance im-

[28] The changes do not dissimulate the real structure of the word, which can still be read.
[29] difficulties with enumeration: inability to count a series of identical objects.

both visual and Kinesthetic feedback

proved, however, when the patient wrote with his eyes closed. A similar observation has been reported by van Dongen and Drooglever Fortuyn (1968). Their patient, who had a right parieto-occipital lesion, could not draw a cube with his eyes open but could do so with his eyes closed. Thus, in both cases, suppression of the visual feedback improved the graphic ability. It might be wondered therefore whether or not patients who, like Dur. and Verd., make many reduplications would not write more correctly if they closed their eyes. In fact, an investigation carried out by Leprince, Hasquin, and Bamps in the Neurosurgical Clinic of the University of Brussels has shown that right-brain-damaged patients who make duplications with their eyes open make just as many errors with their eyes closed. This observation should be contrasted with the finding that some of the normal subjects, who were used in the closed-eye experiments described above, made no mistake while writing with suppressed visual feedback. These subjects stated that during the experiment they had slowed down their writing speed and consciously relied on proprioceptive feedback to control the action. It would appear, therefore, that in the right-brain-injured patients who multiply strokes and triplicate letters, there is an impairment not only of visual but also of kinesthetic feedback. If their kinesthetic feedback were not disturbed, these patients should, when they write with their eyes closed, make approximately the same errors as normals. In fact, they make duplications that are much longer (i.e., the duplicated sign is repeated a greater number of times) than those made by normals. Again, if their kinesthetic feedback were not impaired, patients should, when they write with their eyes open, make approximately the same mistakes as normals who write with their eyes closed or under conditions of delayed visual feedback, i.e., proprioception should prevent the errors from becoming enormous.

It is now generally accepted (see Warrington, 1969) that visuo–spatial functions depend primarily on the right hemisphere in right-handed people. Accordingly, a right hemispheric lesion may conceivably result in a failure to incorporate visuospatial information into the constructive act. The view that the reduplications and omissions discussed above originate from an impairment of visual feedback is therefore consistent with the current theory on asymmetry of hemispheric functions.

But what about the disorder of kinesthetic feedback that has been inferred above? Is there also some degree of cerebral asymmetry as regards somesthesis? Teuber (1962) has observed that patients having a right hemispheric lesion are more impaired than left-brain-damaged patients in a task that requires the subject to fit variously shaped blocks (under exclusion of vision) into the appropriate holes in a board. Weinstein (1962) has found that right-brain-injured patients are considerably more impaired than patients having a left hemispheric lesion on a haptic task involving the discrimination of three-dimensional size. Corkin (1965) has demonstrated the inferiority of patients with right-sided cortical excisions on a <u>tactual-maze task.</u> Pizzamiglio and Carli (1974) have indicated that on a tactile-embedded-figures test, right-brain-damaged patients perform significantly worse than left-brain-damaged patients not having aphasia and worse (though not significantly) than left-brain-damaged patients having aphasia. Carmon and Benton (1969) have shown that right-hemisphere disease leads to a severe impairment in tactile performance involving a spatial component. Replicating Carmon and Benton's experiment but using a simpler experimental technique, Fontenot and Benton (1971) were able to confirm the view that "the right hemisphere plays a distinctively important role in mediating spatial perception in the tactile as well as in the visual ... modalities." This conclusion is further supported by Benton, Levin, and Varney's findings (1973). Carmon (1970) has reported impaired utilization of kinesthetic feedback in right hemispheric lesions. Hermelin and O'Connor (1971) have shown that the reading of braille by blind subjects (including the recently blinded) is faster and/or more accurate with fingers of the left than of the right hand. Rudel, Denckla, and Spalten (1974) have found that normal right-handed children learn braille letters better with their left than with their right hands. It thus appears that the right hemisphere plays a leading part in processing somesthetic data involving spatial components. The view propounded above that lesions of the minor hemisphere may entail an impairment of kinesthetic feedback which reflects negatively on writing, fits in with this conclusion. Consequently, the writing disorder discussed above may well be considered an *afferent dysgraphia.*

CONCLUSION

At the end of the seventeenth century, a controversy, known as the *Querelle des Anciens et des Modernes,* arose in France. The dispute was about the excellencies of the ancients as compared with contemporary writers. Some held the classics to be superior to the moderns; others maintained that, thanks to the expansion of knowledge that had taken place since Antiquity, the moderns surpassed the ancients. Someone submitted that moderns were like dwarfs perched on the shoulders of giants. The giants were the classics. The dwarfs could see farther and better than the giants. But obviously this was so because the giants carried the dwarfs on their shoulders. This metaphor also applies to neurolinguistics. Neurolinguists are in a position to better understand language pathology because they can benefit from the numerous observations made during the first hundred years of aphasiology. For more than a century, clinical data have been gathered and tentative explanations put forward. The challenge for neurolinguistics is to scrutinize this material and to critically review these hypotheses in order to open up new vistas on disorders of language. In other words, a threefold task awaits performance:

classement et description plus précis des désordres impliquant des hypothèses sur les facteurs qui perturbent spécifiquement les performances; recherches de corrélations entre les types ainsi isolés et les topographies lésionnelles; enfin, à partir de ces analyses et en tenant compte des données anatomophysiologiques, tentatives d'interprétation du rôle des mécanismes nerveux dans les réalisations du langage et essai de vérification de ces hypothèses [Hécaen & Dubois, 1971].[30]

It is hoped that the neurolinguistic models offered here may contribute to this end.

REFERENCES

Alajouanine, T., Boudin, G., Pertuiset, B., & Pépin, B. 1959a. Le syndrome unilatéral de l'opercule rolandique avec atteinte contralatérale des territoires des V, VII, IX, X, XI et XIIe nerfs crâniens. *Revue Neurologique, 101*, 168–171.
Alajouanine, T., & Lhermitte, F. 1960. Les troubles des activités expressives du langage dans l'aphasie. Leurs relations avec les apraxies. *Revue Neurologique, 102*, 604–633.
Alaljouanine, T., Lhermitte, F., Cambier, J., Rondot, P., & Lefebvre, J. P. 1959b. Perturbations dissociées de la motricité facio-bucco-pharyngée avec aphémie dans un ramollissement sylvien profond partiel. *Revue Neurologique, 100*, 493–498.
Alajouanine, T., Ombredane, A., & Durand, M. 1939. *Le syndrome de désintégration phonétique dans l'aphasie.* Paris: Masson.
Alajouanine, T., Pichot, P., & Durand, M. 1949. Dissociation des altérations phonétiques avec conservation relative de la langue ancienne dans un cas d'anarthrie pure chez un sujet français bilingue. *Encéphale, 28*, 245–265.
Alajouanine, T., Sabouraud, O., & Scherer, J. 1957. Contribution à l'analyse oscillographique des troubles de la parole. *Larynx et phonation.* Paris: Presses Universitaires de France. Pp. 145–158.
Assal, G., & Zander, E. 1969. Rappel de la symptomatologie neuropsychologique des lésions hémisphériques droites. *Archives Suisses de Neurologie, Neurochirurgie et de Psychiatrie, 105*, 217–239.
Benton, A., Levin, H., & Varney, N. 1973. Tactile perception of direction in normal subjects. *Neurology, 23*, 1248–1250.
Bernheim, F. 1900. *De l'aphasie motrice.* Paris: Carré.
Brain, R. 1965. *Speech disorders.* London: Butterworth.
Broca, P. 1861. Remarques sur le siège de la faculté du langage articulé, suivies d'une observation d'aphémie (perte de la parole). *Bulletin de la Société d'Anatomie, 6*, 330–357.
Broca, P. 1865. Sur le siège de la faculté du langage articulé. *Bulletin de la Société d'Anthropologie, 6*, 377–393.
Campbell, D. G. 1936–1937. General semantics. *American Journal of Psychiatry, 93*, 789–807.

[30] A more precise classification and description of the disorders that imply hypotheses about the factors specifically disturbing the performance; a search for correlations between the different types of deficits identified in this way and the topography of the lesion; finally, starting from these analyses and considering the anatomophysiological data, attempts at interpreting the role of the nervous system in the realization of speech and verification of the aforementioned hypotheses.

Carmon, A. 1970. Impaired utilization of kinesthetic feedback in right hemispheric lesions. *Neurology, 20,* 1033–1038.

Carmon, A., & Benton, A. 1969. Tactile perception of direction and number in patients with unilateral cerebral disease. *Neurology, 19,* 525–532.

Cohen, D., Dubois, J., Gauthier, M., Hécaen, H., & Angelergues, R. 1963. Aspects du fonctionnement du code linguistique chez les aphasiques moteurs. *Neuropsychologia, 1,* 165–177.

Cohen, D., & Hécaen, H. 1964. Remarques neurolinguistiques sur un cas d'agrammatisme. *Journal de Psychologie Normale et Pathologique, 62,* 273–296.

Corkin, S. 1965. Tactually guided maze learning in man: Effects of unilateral cortical excisions and bilateral hippocampal lesions. *Neuropsychologia, 3,* 339–351.

Deal, J., & Darley, F. 1972. The influence of linguistic and situational variables on phonemic accuracy in apraxia of speech. *Journal of Speech and Hearing Research, 15,* 639–653.

Dejerine, J. 1914. *Sémiologie des affections du système nerveux.* Paris: Masson.

Denny-Brown, D. 1963. The physiological basis of perception and speech. In L. Halpern (Ed.), *Problems of dynamic neurology.* Jerusalem: Department of Nervous Diseases, Rothschild Hadassah University Hospital. Pp. 30–62.

De Renzi, E., Pieczuro, A., & Vignolo, L. 1966. Oral apraxia and aphasia. *Cortex, 2,* 50–73.

De Reuck, A., & O'Connor, M. 1964. *Disorders of language.* London: Churchill.

Dubois, J. 1967. La neurolinguistique. *Langages, 5,* 6–17.

Dubois, J., Hécaen, H., Angelergues, R., Maufras du Chatelier, A., & Marcie, P. 1964. Etude neurolinguistique de l'aphasie de conduction. *Neuropsychologia, 2,* 9–44.

Dubois, J., Marcie, P., Irigaray, L., Hécaen, H., & Angelergues, R. 1965. Analyse distributionnelle en neurolinguistique: le comportement verbal des aphasiques dans les épreuves de langage répété. *Langage et Comportement, 1,* 111–134.

Fontenot, D., & Benton, A. 1971. Tactile perception of direction in relation to hemispheric locus of lesion. *Neuropsychologia, 9,* 83–88.

Grewel, F. 1966. Neurolinguïstiek. *Tijdschrift voor Logopedie en Foniatrie, 38,* 159–162.

Hécaen, H. 1969. Clinico-anatomical and neurolinguistic aspects of aphasia. In G. Talland & M. Waugh (Eds.), *Memory disorders.* Boston: Atlantic Press. Pp. 10–28.

Hécaen, H. 1972. *Introduction à la neuropsychologie.* Paris: Larousse.

Hécaen, H., & Dubois, J. 1971. La neurolinguistique. In G. Perren & J. Trim (Eds.), *Application of linguistics.* London: Cambridge University Press. Pp. 85–99.

Hécaen, H., Dubois, J., Angelergues, R., Vedrennes, C., & Marcie, P. 1964. Comparaison neurolinguistique et neuropsychologique de deux cas anatomo-cliniques d'aphasie. *Revue Neurologique, 111,* 401–411.

Hécaen, H., Dubois, J., & Marcie, P. 1967. Critères neurolinguistiques d'une classification des aphasies. *Acta Neurologica et Psychiatrica Belgica, 67,* 959–987.

Hermelin, B., & O'Connor, N. 1971. Functional asymmetry in the reading of braille. *Neuropsychologia, 9,* 431–435.

Johns, D., & Darley, F. 1970. Phonemic variability in apraxia of speech. *Journal of Speech and Hearing Research, 13,* 556–583.

Kalmus, H., Fry, D. B., & Denes, P. 1960. Effects of delayed visual control on writing, drawing, and tracing. *Language and Speech, 3,* 96–108.

Korzybski, A. 1936–1937a. Neuro-semantic and neuro-linguistic mechanisms of extensionalization. *American Journal of Psychiatry, 93,* 29–38.

Korzybski, A. 1936–1937b. The science of man. *American Journal of Psychiatry, 93,* 1343–1351.

La Pointe, L., & Wertz, R. 1974. Oral-movement abilities and articulatory characteristics of brain-injured adults. *Perceptual and Motor Skills, 39*, 39–46.

Lebrun, Y., Brihaye, J., & Lebrun, N. 1971. On expressive agrammatism. *Journal of Communication Disorders, 4*, 126–133.

Lebrun, Y., Buyssens, E., & Henneaux, J. 1973. Phonetic aspects of anarthria. *Cortex, 9*, 126–135.

Lebrun, Y., Lenaerts, M., Goiris, K., & Demol, O. 1969. Aphasia and the concept of the phoneme. *Tijdschrift voor Logopedie en Foniatrie, 41*, 127–135.

Luria, A. 1959. Disorders of "simultaneous perception" in a case of bilateral occipito-parietal brain injury. *Brain, 82*, 437–449.

Luria, A. 1967. Problmes et faits de la neurolinguistique. *Revue Internationale des Sciences Sociales, 19*, 39–55.

Luria, A. 1970. *Traumatic aphasia.* The Hague: Mouton.

Marcie, P., Hécaen, H., Dubois, J., & Angelergues, R. 1965. Les réalisations du langage chez les malades atteints de lésions de l'hémisphère droit. *Neuropsychologia, 3*, 217–245.

Marie, P. 1926. *Travaux et mémoires.* Part 1. Paris: Masson.

Ombredane, A. 1951. *L'aphasie et l'élaboration de la pensée explicite.* Paris: Presses Universitaires de France.

Paterson, A., & Zangwill, O. 1944. Disorders of visual space perception associated with lesions of the right cerebral hemisphere. *Brain, 67*, 331–358.

Pilch, H., & Hemmer, R. 1970. Phonematische Aphasie. *Phonetica, 22*, 231–239.

Pizzamiglio, L., & Carli, R. 1974. Visual, tactile and acoustic embedded figures tests in patients with unilateral brain damage. *Cortex, 10*, 238–246.

Rudel, R. Denckla, M., & Spalten, E. 1974. The functional asymmetry of braille letter learning in normal, sighted children. *Neurology, 24*, 733–738.

Smith, K. 1962. *Delayed sensory feedback and behavior.* Philadelphia: Saunders.

Smith, W., McCrary, J., & Smith, K. 1960. Delayed visual feedback and behavior. *Science, 132*, 1013–1014.

Sollberg, G. 1966. Neuere Untersuchungen zum Aphasieproblem. *Folia Phoniatrica, 18*, 45–58.

Teuber, H.-L. 1962. Effects of brain wounds implicating right or left hemisphere in man: Hemisphere differences and hemisphere interaction in vision, audition, and somesthesis. In V. Mountcastle (Ed.), *Interhemispheric relations and cerebral dominance.* Baltimore: Johns Hopkins Press. Pp. 131–157.

Tissot, A., Rodriguez, J., & Tissot, R. 1970. Die Prognose der Anarthrie im Sinne von Pierre Marie. In A. Leischner (Ed.), *Die Rehabilitation der Aphasie in den romanischen Ländern.* Stuttgart: Thieme.

Trager, E. 1961. The field of neurolinguistics. *Studies in Linguistics, 15*(3/4), 70–71.

Trousseau, A. 1885. *Clinique médicale de l'Hôtel-Dieu de Paris.* (7th ed.) Paris: Baillière.

van Bergeijk, A., & David, E. 1959. Delayed handwriting. *Perceptual and Motor Skills, 9*, 347–357.

van Dongen, H. R., & Drooglever Fortuyn, J. 1968. Drawing with closed eyes. *Psychiatria, Neurologia, Neurochirurgia, 71*, 275–280.

Warrington, E. 1969. Constructional apraxia. In P. J. Vinken & G. W. Bruyn (Eds.), *Handbook of clinical neurology.* Vol. IV. Amsterdam: North-Holland Publ. Pp. 67–83.

Weinstein, S. 1962. Differences in effects of brain wounds implicating right or left hemispheres: Differential effects on certain intellectual and complex perceptual functions. In V. Mountcastle (Ed.), *Interhemispheric relations and cerebral dominance.* Baltimore: Johns Hopkins Press. Pp. 159–176.

Whitaker, H. 1970. A model for neurolinguistics. *Occasional Papers, 10.* (Language Center, University of Essex, Colchester.)

2

CNS Maturation and Language Acquisition[1]

Esther Milner

BROOKLYN COLLEGE OF THE CITY
UNIVERSITY OF NEW YORK

INTRODUCTION

In the continuing evolution of matter, new levels of complexity are superimposed on the individual units by the organization and integration of these units into a single system. *What were wholes on one level become parts of a higher one.* Each level of organization possesses unique properties of structure and behavior which, though dependent on the properties of the constituent elements, appear only when these elements are combined in a new system. Knowledge of the laws of the lower level is necessary for a full understanding of the higher level; yet *the unique properties of the phenomena at the higher level can not be predicted, a priori, from the laws of the lower level. The laws describing the unique properties of each level are qualitatively distinct, and their discovery requires methods of research and analysis appropriate to the particular level.* These laws express the new organizing relationship, i.e., the reciprocal relationships of elementary units to each other and to the unit-system as a whole [Novikoff, 1945, p. 209] (Italics EM's).

Evolution signifies the local rise of new systems with new properties. Such [novel] properties must not be considered to be "stuck on" externally and miraculously, but to be functions of the [new] organization [Sellars, 1938, p. 462].

From a phylogenetic standpoint, it is possible to group all behavior expressed by human beings into three generalized categories:

1. Unlearned behaviors which man shares with other, lower, mammals. The inborn processes of growth and maturation ordinarily see to it that such basic physiological and psychological functions as: breathing, sucking, chewing, swallowing, digesting, coughing, feeling hungry and thirsty, urinating and defecating, basic-temperament

[1] ©Esther Milner, 1976, and Academic Press, Inc., 1976.

tendencies, sexual tension, anger, feeling primary fear; ability to smell, taste, hear, touch, vocalize, distinguish gradations of light, orient self in space; primary curiosity, will all appear before, at, or not long after birth, so long as food and responsive physical care are provided.

2. Learned behaviors which we share with other higher mammals; for example: the manner in which we see the physical world around us and the basic-recognition meanings of what we see, hear, smell, touch, taste and so on.

3. Learned behaviors which we share with no other form of life; for example: language spoken and written, self-awareness and self-judgment, abstract thought, values and ethics.

Physiology and ethology and psychology have shared the study of the first category, comparative-experimental psychology has also concentrated on the second—and the surface of the third category has scarcely been scratched by any scientific discipline. Nor has the comparative-experimental tradition shown sufficient appreciation in the past that "learning and many other higher processes are secondary modification of innate mechanisms," and that therefore *a study of man's higher processes must be preceded by a study of the innate foundations of behavior in man* (adapted from Tinbergen, 1951, p. 6) [E. Milner, 1967, pp. 10–11] (Italics EM's).

The three foregoing excerpts have provided the bare-bones point of departure for this chapter. Because language and cognition are very much "other higher processes," the last sentence of the last excerpt serves as the chapter's basic rationale. It has also influenced organization of the topics under discussion. In line with Tinbergen's prescription, a comprehensive, albeit selectively formulated, overview of current knowledge of the developmental patterns and functional organization of the human nervous system precedes a discussion of the more delimited issue that is the subject of this chapter.

The initial selective overview is drawn chiefly from E. Milner (1967) and was formulated by a social-psychologically oriented developmental and personality psychologist who wished to arrive at a picture of human postnatal neural development both broad and specific enough to answer the question: What role does level of nervous system development and functional organization play in the developmental timing of the various personality structurings?

When the writer's pursuit of data bearing on this question revealed that the related literature did not—and apparently still does not—contain enough specific postnatal data to permit deductions from such data alone, she was obliged to turn to other, related, sources. If ontogeny really does recapitulate phylogeny to a reasonable degree, material on neural phylogeny should yield some useful clues. And, because ontogeny had theretofore apparently meant only embryology to neurophysiologists, to take advantage of the "law of anticipatory development" seemed a good idea: perhaps the extensive *pre*natal data available would yield additional useful clues. Also, because some notion of the nature and magnitude of the gap between the status of the nervous system at birth and its status at neurological maturity would lend more meaning to the scanty data on the developmental events between, knowledge of the matured nervous system was also germane. All these data sources entered into the conceptual background basic to the central aspect of the author's monograph, the systematic relating of neural and behavioral developmental data. Indeed, it would have been impossible to make coherent sense of the bits and pieces information available in the literature, or to arrive at the answers eventually arrived at, without this preparatory background.

PREPARATORY BACKGROUND

Our Species' Neural and Behavioral Inheritance

In light of the writer's negative reaction to theoretical psychology's traditional overreliance on data derived from the study of lower animals, it would seem to constitute a self-contradiction to assert that psychological attempts to study the structure and behavior of lower forms have been minimal and that especially developmental psychology has much to gain from such a study. But when it is added that we need to know a great deal more about the structural and functional legacy of previous evolutionary stages as *this legacy is expressed in the form and the functioning and the development of the human nervous system*, the contradiction should become only apparent.

The list of 20 "phylogenetic principles," following, represents an attempt to formulate the manner in which the structural and functional legacy of previous evolutionary stages is expressed in the form, the functioning, and the developmental patterns of the human nervous system. These principles, some merely restated and some originally formulated, are based on two types of material:

1. Data on neural phylogenesis, located in a variety of standard sources and originally organized into a three-part table (E. Milner, 1967, pp. 52–57); only the third section, "Structural Phylogenesis of the Mammalian Neocortex" is being reproduced in this chapter (as Table 1).
2. Additional conceptual-order resources, including especially Judson Herrick's (1956) and Hughlings Jackson's (1882, 1884) contributions.

Principles 1 through 4 embody *phylogenetic carryovers.*

Phylogenetic Principle 1. Man shares with prevertebrates the basic structural pattern of his spinal cord and medulla, the two most primitive parts of his central nervous system (CNS), as well as the nature and intimate unity of their functional interrelationship: The medulla has the functionally dominant role of coordinating spinally mediated reflexes. Although in man, spinal cord and medulla both transmit and are subject to the controlling influences of higher neuraxial centers, *together they form a discrete subsystem within the human neuraxis*—a subsystem closely similar in structure, in functional relationships, and in ontogenetic growth patterns to the entire prevertebrate fourth- (and final-) stage nervous system.

Phylogenetic Principle 2. Bishop's (1956) material on the electrical properties of the nerve impulse appears to indicate that all the basic conduction character- istics of the neuron have manifested themselves in the prevertebrate evolutionary stages. Various patterns of subsequent phyletic change in neural functioning are dependent on changing organizations of nerve cells, rather than on any funda- mental changes in the conduction characteristics of the individual cell; the various types of neurons present in man as well as their conduction characteris- tics constitute one or another of the types first found in prevertebrate and lower-vertebrate forms.

Phylogenetic Principle 3. The phylogenetic retention of both the nerve net and the specialized neuron prompts the question: Are these structural differences correlated with unique functions? Herrick's (1956) answer is *yes*, and he dis- cusses at length the functional significance of the two conduction modes expressed by the nerve net (slow rate of conduction and a diffuse, graded, fields-of-force type electrical functioning), and the specialized nerve fiber (fast rate of conduction and a specific, all-or-none type electrical functioning) (Her- rick, 1956, Chapter VIII). The specialized, rapidly conducting nerve cells exist within fixed, localized (i.e., partial-pattern) pathways and centers that subserve the organism's interactions with its environment—sensory, correlational, and motor functions which Herrick terms "analytic." The diffuse, slow-conducting nerve net is not as firmly bound to definitely localized pathways and centers, parallels and/or surrounds the specialized cells, and is more labile and whole- pattern in its functioning. This conduction apparatus is concerned with main- taining the identity of the body and with coordinating the various subparts of the analytic system—functions that Herrick terms "synthetic" or, better, "inte- grative." These two neural apparatuses are structurally intertwined and their functions, integrative and analytic, are obviously complementary; in Herrick's (1956) words: "Both kinds of vital processes are primordial and essential components of the action systems of all animals, from the lowest to the highest" (p. 101).

Phylogenetic Principle 4. Another order of duality, the visceral–somatic dual- ity of chordate neural structure to which Romer (1958) points (and Herrick too—he treats them as subdivisions of the analytic conduction system) also appears to have been retained in man's nervous system. It seems to constitute one of the basic functional organization patterns of the human nervous system and will be subsequently referred to in that context.

Principles 5 through 16 express *phylogenetic trends.*

Phylogenetic Principle 5. The overall direction of nervous-system phylogenesis has been towards increasing structural differentiation of parts and specialization of function, together with increasing interdependence of the parts on the whole and on each other—that is, toward increasing degrees of organization. An example of this trend directly pertinent to linguistics is, according to Lenneberg (1967), the emergence of hemispheric dominance in man.

Phylogenetic Principle 6. The principle of encephalization has obtained, both in structure and in function: New phyletic structures have been added on progressively at the head end; as each new structure is added on, there is a tendency for functions originally performed by lower, more primitive parts of the CNS to be transferred cephalically to the new structure. But on the basis of neurophysiological knowledge not included in Table 1, it is necessary immediately to supplement the classic neural principle of encephalization with two additional principles, following directly.

Phylogenetic Principle 7. The first supplementary principle may be termed the "principle of successive lowest-center duplication." As each new head part is added on phyletically, the oldest neuraxial part's basic segmental or topological organization pattern is reduplicated on each newly evolved sensory or motor center. That is, the basic segmental organization pattern of the lowest motor center, the spinal cord, is successively duplicated on each new motor center when it differentiates phylogenetically. Similarly, the segmental or topological organization pattern of the first receiving center for the particular sensory modality is successively duplicated on each new sensory center as *it* differentiates phylogenetically.

Phylogenetic Principle 8. The "principle of hierarchical dominance" is also a necessary supplementation of Principle 6. As new structures are added on at the head end, they tend to assume functional dominance over the older sections that have the same type function, sensory or motor.

Phylogenetic Principle 9. But in spite of their functional dominance, phylogenetically newer parts tend to be both highly vulnerable to external influences and unstable in their functioning as compared with the older, lower centers; see especially Himwich (1951) for documentation of this point. Principle 8 is complicated still further by other concurrent functional organization patterns of the nervous system, described subsequently.

As the vertebrate scale is ascended, as shown in Table 1, the size and the complexity of the brain part of the primitive neuraxis increase; the part of the brain that increases most in size and in complexity is the cerebral cortex. As the mammalian scale is ascended, the part of the cerebral cortex that increases most in size and in complexity is the cerebral neocortex. Table 1 provides concrete evidence that the mammalian cortex has made what Eiseley (1955) and other anthropologists call "a quantum jump" in its development from the lower primates to man. Structural evidence of such a quantum jump of the neocortex includes the following:

1. Its prefrontal section increases markedly in proportional size from chimpanzee to man.

TABLE 1 Structural Phylogenesis of the Mammalian Neocortex[a]

Index of phylogenesis	General trends	Lower mammals	Middle mammals	Lower primates and man
Size of the four lobes	The higher the animal, the greater the proportion of neocortex in the brain. In frontal lobe, prefrontal section (association functions) increases most in size.	Proportion of cortical area taken up by prefrontal area: 3.4% in the rabbit.	Proportion of cortical area taken up by prefrontal area: 7% in the dog.	Proportion of total cortical area taken up by prefrontal association area: 11% in the macacque, 17% in the chimpanzee (about half the frontal lobe), and 29% in man (¾ of the frontal lobe).
Number of cellularly distinct areas	Increases steadily up the mammalian scale.	13 neocortical areas in the albino rat[b]	36 neocortical areas in the adult cat[b]	At least 52 neocortical areas in man[b]
Localization and specialization of sensory and motor functions; multiplicity of connections with lower centers.	Increase steadily up the mammalian scale[c]	Of the subhuman forms studied, the degree of overlap of the two basic somatosensory areas of the parietal lobe is greatest in the rabbit[d]		Of subhuman forms studied, degree of overlap of two basic somatosensory areas of parietal lobe is least in monkey.[d] Much greater impairment of function in man than in rodents when specific cortical areas are destroyed.
Proportion of neocortex associational in function	Increases steadily up the mammalian scale[e,f]	In rodents, 90% is sensorimotor in function, 10% associational[e]	In cats, 70% is sensorimotor and 30% associational[e]	In monkeys, 40% is sensorimotor and 60% associational. In man, 15% sensorimotor and 85% associational.[e]

Thickness and number of neocortical layers	Neocortex thickens, number of layers increases, and their cellular composition becomes more complex as mammalian scale is ascended.	A supragranular layer is added to submammalian granular and subgranular layers (that continue to be typical of the archicortex). The meso/paleocortex also adds supragranular layer.	Supragranular layer increases steadily in thickness up the rest of the mammalian scale. Granular layer's thickness increases variably; subgranular's remains about the same.	In man, the supragranular layer differentiates into the upper three layers of the six-layered neocortex; these "outer three layers are much better developed than in lower forms."[f] In man, the middle granular layer thickens and the subgranular layer divideds into the two bottom layers.
Fissuration pattern	The higher the mammal, the larger the number of cortical fissures	All mammals have at least three fissures		Fusiform gyrus emerges on underside of occipital lobe. Secondary and tertiary sulci (only in human brain), markedly increase size of associational area of neocortex.
Number of unmyelinated areas at birth.	Increases as the mammalian scale is ascended			In man, no cortical areas are myelinated at birth.

[a] Abstracted from Ariïens-Kappers et al. (1936) except where otherwise indicated.
[b] Tilney (1934).
[c] Viz., Lashley's reversal of his earlier postulation of lack of cortical differentiation.
[d] Gellhorn (1953).
[e] Zubek and Solberg (1954).
[f] Hamilton, Boyd, and Mossman (1952, p. 300).

2. Its supragranular layer, which emerges only in mammals, increases markedly in further stratification and in cellular complexity in man.
3. Its proportion of total area which is associational in function increases markedly from chimp to man, as shown in the following small extract from Table 1:

Mammal	Sensorimotor neocortex	Associational neocortex
Rodent	90%	10%
Cat	70	30
Monkey	40	60
Man	15	85

Note the almost complete reversal in proportions in man from the rat, comparative psychology's favorite experimental animal!

Phylogenetic Principle 10. Several functional shifts accompanied the continuous cephalic development referred to in Principle 6:

1. The visceral and olfactory senses predate the other senses in functional importance phylogenetically (for vertebrates in general and mammals in particular); the skin and proprioceptive senses follow; and then the distance-receptor senses and kinesthesis, which are of major functional importance only in mammals.
2. The capacity for refined movement develops in direct proportion to provision for exactness of sensory reception and sensory localization.
3. Emancipation from chemically (i.e., hormonally) and external-stimulus dominated behavior is in direct proportion to the size and complexity of the cerebral neocortex.
4. Structurally innate factors in the determination of behavior decrease relatively up the mammalian scale, while the role of individual experience and learning increases.

Phylogenetic Principle 11. The infant's period of immaturity and dependence on older members of the same species increases steadily up the phyletic scale, and makes a marked jump from lower primates to man. This circumstance, together with Principle 18, following, suggests an evolved, physical basis for our species' strongly social nature.

Phylogenetic Principle 12. Ability to adapt to a constantly widening range of external situations increases up the phyletic scale, and is accompanied by a repertoire of adaptive responses that increases steadily in range, complexity, and flexibility—that is, in degree of individual control. (This principle as well as the succeeding four—12 through 16—are adapted from Nissen's (1951) enumeration of phylogenetic changes in behavior.)

Phylogenetic Principle 13. Cognitive capacities and types of behavior increase steadily up the phyletic scale, and most of all in man. This increase is at least partially related to the circumstance that the length of delay of response to an external stimulus is potentially by far the greatest in man, and as a result: abilities to abstract, generalize, transfer, transpose, all increase steadily; sensory discrimination increases variably; an organism's "influencing environment" expands both temporally and spatially; the period of perceptual-growth improvement becomes longer; the gap between initial and ultimate perceptual ability increases; ability to perceive a relationship between objects appears earlier, phylogenetically, than does the ability to perceive the intrinsic properties of an object.

Phylogenetic Principle 14. The complexity of what can be learned, the potential for training, and the capacity to form complex habits, all increase up the phyletic scale.

Phylogenetic Principle 15. The number, range, and complexity of an organism's needs and motives increase up the phyletic scale; the proportion of these needs that are psychogenic—including curiosity or desire to perceive, exploration, play, anticipation, goal orientation, need to make sense of what is perceived, prudent foresight or capacity to direct one's behavior towards delayed goals, and ethical–altruistic–esthetic motives—increase most (the latter two appear to be peculiar only to man).

Phylogenetic Principle 16. The incidence of conflict, frustration, and guilt is much increased in man, as well as vulnerability to derangement of his "higher" behaviors.

Finally, the four characteristics that follow are unique to man and, as such, they represent *departures from man's phylogenetic heritage.*

Phylogenetic Principle 17. Data on mammalian neural phylogenesis imply a most fundamental development, but one so obvious it is easily overlooked: The genetic endowment of our species includes uniquely human neural structures, apparently superimposed upon the more basic mammalian structures. Just how this dual genetic endowment expresses itself in human ontogenesis becomes in light of this departure an important focus of inquiry.

Phylogenetic Principle 18. In man, it is only after birth that those neural centers which mediate all uniquely human behaviors begin to function, as subsequent embryological data will further document. Additional structural and functional development of these centers occurs after birth. That is, *the "human principle" in our species' genetic endowment is present only as potential at birth.* This characteristic implies not merely that such behaviors do not develop within a stable, physiologically regulated environment; it further implies that they are subject throughout the course of their postnatal development to an increasingly variable and complex social milieu. It is this species characteristic that makes man, to a far greater degree than any other biological form, dependent on his opportunities for experience subsequent to birth. He is so dependent not only for the degree to which his implanted potentialities for behavior will be developed, but beyond sheerly somatic and vegetative development, even for the *form* many of his behaviors will take.

Phylogenetic Principle 19. Ability to become an object within one's own perceptual field—self-awareness with its associated accumulation of self-referrent feelings and experiences—is peculiar only to man. One can interpret the biblical story of Adam and Eve symbolically, as the point in phyletic time when this awareness emerged: "And the eyes of them both were opened, and they knew that they were naked."

Phylogenetic Principle 20. "The great basic innovation among all varieties of mankind was the production of the sociocultural world itself," and once having created this "second, invisible environment," man's behavior was thereafter fundamentally and irrevocably influenced by it (Eiseley, 1955). The qualitative aspect of the difference between man and all other animals may well stem from just this "great basic innovation." Although the structural differences between man and other forms may indeed be conceived of as ones only of degree, once certain of these structural developments permitted the linkage of sustained self-awareness and symbolization, man developed cumulatively a highly complex emotional, moral, and symbolic learning environment—and subjected each new generation to it. This postulation implies that if this complex learning environment were not made directly available to any one human generation of a particular society as a result of a complete interruption in interpersonal communication (in the subtlest sense) between it and members of the parent generation, the new generation, *if* it survived physically (which is highly doubtful) would, at physical maturity have at best a behavioral repertoire akin to that of other primates. At worst, it would be so emotionally disturbed as not to be able to produce another generation, as the work of Harlow (1962) and others strongly suggests. Indeed, it is possible to conceptualize most emotional disorders, including those of personality and perhaps also some of speech and language, as products of some sort of interruption, in especially the early mother-figure ←→ child communication process.

The phylogenetic overview given in the foregoing list of principles attests that the gap in neural evolution between man and his mammalian relatives is great, not small, as Eiseley (1955) has pointed out. It further suggests that psychology needs to emulate modern anthropology in recognizing the width of that gap— and the implications of it for the study of man's behavior.

Patterns of Prenatal Neural Development

Schneirla's (1957) cautionary reminder concerning the phyletic roots of behavioral development applies in this context: "Behavioral development on any

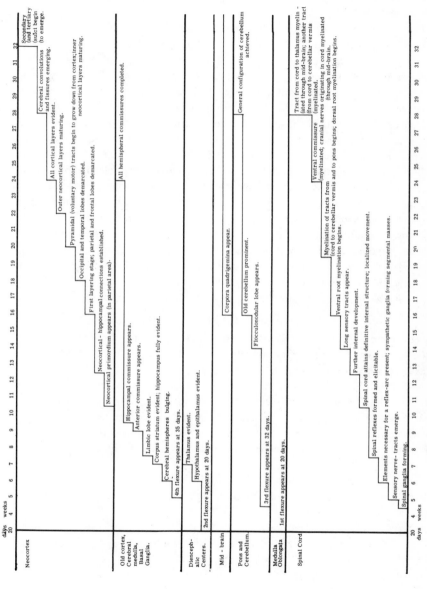

Figure 1 Embryological neurogenesis: CNS developmental sequence.

41

phyletic level is not so much a retracing through the stages and levels of successive ancestral forms as a new composite leading to a new pattern distinctive of that level" (p. 102).

The first relevant and detailed source of data about the human "new composite" is the prenatal phase of neural ontogeny which, unlike the postnatal phase, has been thoroughly researched. The postnatal phase of neural development also needs to be consulted to answer the question, "Do phylogenetic trends provide clues as to how previous evolutionary stages express themselves in the form and functioning of the human nervous system?"

Figure 1, a composite analysis of the developmental timing of the several neuraxial centers, was derived from data in human prenatal ontogeny in authoritative secondary sources (Arey, 1954; Carmichael, 1951; Zubek & Solberg, 1954) which were organized and presented in a three-part table: from 2½ to 7 fetal weeks, from 7½ to 15 fetal weeks, including also elicited responses and spontaneous function, and from 16 weeks to birth, including also elicited responses and spontaneous behavior (E. Milner, 1967, pp. 64–69). Figure 1 is organized to show both a horizontal perspective—i.e., the over-time pattern of the development of each neuraxial center (see especially spinal cord and neocortical development); and a vertical perspective—i.e., the developmental status at particular prenatal stages of the various CNS centers.

A quick inspection of Figure 1 along its vertical dimension shows:

At 32 days, (5½ weeks), the spinal ganglia are forming, at the same time that the third or pontine flexure appears (which sets off the section of the neural tube in which the pons and cerebellum develop, from the section where the medulla is already differentiating).

At 5 weeks, the first spinal nerve tracts emerge, at the same time that the fourth or telencephalic flexure appears in the upper section of the neural tube.

At 6 weeks, the elements necessary for a reflex arc emerge in the developing spinal cord, at the same time that the hypothalamus and epithalamus of the diencephalon first become evident and the cerebral hemispheres are beginning to bulge.

At 7 to 7½ weeks, spinal reflexes are fully formed and elicitable, just a few days after the thalamus, the hippocampus, and the basal ganglia (corpus striatum) first emerge.

At 10½ weeks, the spinal cord attains its definitive internal structure, with localized fetal movements appearing as a direct consequence, at the same time that the primordium of the cerebral neocortex differentiates.

At 14 weeks, intersegmental sensory tracts appear in the cord, at the same time that the flocculonodular lobe of the cerebellum first appears.

At 16 weeks, ventral-root (motor function) myelination (an index of functioning) begins in the cord, at the same time that the old cerebellum is prominent, the corpora quadrigemina (auditory and visual tracts) appear in the midbrain, the first neocortical layering stage begins, and the parietal and frontal lobes of the neocortex are demarcated by the central fissure.

At 20 weeks, dorsal-root (sensory function) myelination begins in the cord, a few days before the pyramidal tracts, which eventually play a key role in voluntary behavior, begin to grow down from the motor neocortex.

At 24 weeks, the cranial nerves, which originate in the spinal cord, are myelinated up through the midbrain, at the same time that all hemispheral commissures are completed and all neocortical layers become evident.

At 28 weeks, a second tract from the cord to the cerebellar vermis is myelinated, and the tract from the cord to the thalamus is myelinated through the midbrain, at the same time that the full configuration of the cerebellum is achieved and neocortical convolutions and fissures are beginning to appear. Neural mechanisms permitting vocalization have developed by this age since crying occurs during the seventh through ninth prenatal months. (Authorities consider the birth cry to be a respiratory-related reflex.)

Eight developmental patterns may be derived from these and other prenatal data. The first four suggest that basic aspects of prenatal neural ontogeny constitute an almost unqualified continuation of established phylogenetic trends:

1. The time pattern of the embryological emergence of the respective structural derivatives of the neural tube parallels the phylogenetic emergence of the respective neuraxial centers closely enough—i.e., the lowest centers phylogenetically differentiate first and the highest centers last—to indicate that neural structural ontogeny would indeed seem to recapitulate neural phylogeny.

2. The overall gradient of development of the neuraxis is from tail (spinal cord) to head (neocortex).

3. This structural growth gradient foreshadows the pattern of spontaneous functioning of the CNS both prenatally and (as subsequent data will document) postnatally.

4. However, (a) the spinal cord within itself, as a discrete subunit of the CNS, develops and becomes functional in a head-to-tail direction; and (b) the pattern of development of voluntary motor behavior, which is dependent on the onset of functioning of the motor neocortex, repeats the spinal-cord pattern: i.e., the onset of voluntary motor behavior also reflects a head-to-tail gradient. The myelination patterns of myelinated nerve tracts—a recognized index of onset of function—also reflect dual growth gradients. As has just been described, above the spinal cord, myelinated sensory tracts become myelinated (and functional) ahead of myelinated motor tracts. But within the cord itself, motor neurons and tracts myelinate (and become functional) ahead of the sensory ones. Not at all

incidentally, this overall neuraxial versus spinal cord growth pattern duality, together with its behavioral concomitants, provides the basis for a final resolution of the now-dormant Coghill–Windle controversy (viz., E. Milner, 1967, pp. 89–92).

The next three of the eight embryologically derived patterns reflect the influence of a phylogenetically based organizational principle:

5. The organizational structure of the CNS is hierarchical, with the sequence of the emergence of the respective neural-tube derivatives correspondingly timed—that is, the lowest levels in the hierarchy develop first and the highest levels last.

6. This structural hierarchy is directly related to the functional organization of the matured human nervous system. Just how it is so related will be discussed subsequently; at this point, Hughlings Jackson's principle of the "continuous reduction of succession to coexistences" provides the central clue.

7. The coherent functioning of the fully matured nervous system represents the end-product incorporation of a progressive series of organized functional patterns that develop in a vertical-hierarchical ontogenetic sequence—another proposition to be examined subsequently.

The last of the eight embryologically derived developmental patterns is based on this combination of sources: the behavioral and neural status of the human neonate at birth and at one month (viz., E. Milner, 1967, Tables IVA and IVB), considered as an extension of the data on prenatal neural ontogeny and matched against information on the functioning of the matured nervous system. All these data imply that at birth, human behavior is mediated primarily by hindbrain and midbrain centers, with probably some forebrain (chiefly diencephalic) participation; and that toward the end of the first postnatal month, forebrain involvement increases, including some participation of the primary-sensorimotor and primary-visual areas of the neocortex. Anticipating the data and discussion of the section directly following, it can be further concluded that the coordinated forebrain–lower-brain feedback circuits have not yet established themselves, especially the integrating, reinforcing, inhibiting, controlling, stabilizing, refining roles of the higher, intraforebrain centers of thalamus, hypothalamus, old cortex, basal ganglia, and neocortex. That is, the related data imply the eighth developmental pattern.

8. At birth, the mammalian legacy in human development, referred to previously in phylogenetic principle 17, is dominant, and the human endowment, although clearly indicated structurally, is present *only as potential*. This pattern introduces an extraphylogenetic factor; and understanding of just how this new, human-species principle both expresses itself and influences other neurogenic patterns must await examination of pertinent postnatal data.

The Matured Nervous System: Functional Organization Patterns

At this stage of our understanding of the functioning of the single most complex physical system known, to refer to *the* overall functional organization pattern of the human nervous system would betray an overly specialized orientation. At least three such patterns seem so basic to this enterprise that their analysis in some depth in this preparatory section is necessary; they include:

1. the hierarchical–reduplicative phylogenetic-legacy pattern;
2. the neuropsychological functional-subsystems pattern; and
3. the triple-system phylogenetic-legacy pattern (of the writer's formulation).

A survey of the functional contributions of the subcortical, supracord forebrain centers is given in Table 2. The cerebral cortex will be dealt with separately and explicity in context.

```
THE HIERARCHICAL–REDUPLICATIVE
PHYLOGENETIC-LEGACY PATTERN
```

The principle that the CNS is organized in a complex lowest-center reduplicative fashion, with the highest centers functionally dominant over the lower centers, has been a basic assumption of biologists such as Weiss and Tinbergen

TABLE 2 Functional Contributions of Subcortical, Supracord Human Neuraxial Centers[a]

Lower-Brain Centers

Medulla oblongata

Acts as a relay station for both the motor and the sensory division of the auditory nerve. Provides for the continuation of major nerve tracts, which maintain efficient relations between body receptors and effectors. Mediates phonation and articulation. Has fundamental autonomic functions, mediating the more coordinated (than spinal cord) vegetative functions and reflexes: its respiratory center generates periodic bursts of impulses; it regulates cardiac action, chewing-tasting-swallowing, coughing-sneezing-salivation, vomiting, and sucking in the newborn.

Pons

Chiefly composed of major nerve tracts connecting the cerebellum and the cortex in both directions. Also mediates some protective and orientation reflexes.

Cerebellum

Sensory:

Receives tactile, visual, and auditory impulses, which apparently contribute to execution of its motor functions. Like the somesthetic cortex, has a double tactile representation of the body surface on its two lobes.

Continued

TABLE 2 (Continued)

Lower-Brain Centers

Motor:

Through the medium of a reverberatory circuit between it and the higher motor centers, plays a major role in (a) the maintenance of muscular tonus and posture and equilibrium, and in (b) the regulation of voluntary movements. Is somatotopically organized. The motor cortex controls the purpose and initiates the execution of voluntary movements, while the cerebellum regulates the overall pattern of these acts through inhibitory and facilitatory activity.

The two parts of the cerebellum develop at different phylogenetic and ontogenetic stages: the neocerebellum develops along with the motor neocortex, later than the archicerebellum.

Midbrain Centers

Reticular formation

Sensory:

Is the lowest component of the ARAS (ascending reticular activating system). Ascending sensory tract conveying visceral, somatic, auditory, visual impulses give off branches to the RF. Contains a wakefulness/alertness center: affects neocortex via hypothalamus and thalamus.

Motor:

Facilitates spinally mediated reflexes. Exerts a modifying influence upon, and transmits higher-centers feedback to, the primary receptors.

Superior colliculi

Help to mediate the least complex visual reflexes: those related to light and visual accommodation, and to control of eyeball movements (also the inferior colliculi, which have auditory functions).

Red or ruber nucleus and substantia nigra

Are important parts of the extrapyramidal (unmyelinated-motor) tract; are sometimes grouped with the basal ganglia.

In general, the midbrain centers provide for the continuity of ascending and descending nerve tracts. A pain center is located in the RF, a pleasure center in the septal nuclei (upper section)[b]

Diencephalic Centers

The thalamus and hypothalamus work in close collaboration with one another and with the cortex.

Thalamus

Sensory:

1. All sensory tracts except the olfactory synapse in its lateral portion (which is phylogenetically newer than its anterior portion). Representation of bodily sensation is localized by dermatomal segments within the thalamic nuclei; richness of sensory endings in the skin determines the size of the thalamic area allocated, not the size of the body-part (also true of the somesthetic cortex, to which the thalamus projects).
2. The anterior portion acts as a relay station, allowing for cortical integration of visceral

TABLE 2 (Continued)

Diencephalic Centers

functions. It also provides for the affective aspect of sensation (as opposed to the discriminative aspect, which is cortically mediated).

3. Passes on wakefulness impulses from the reticular formation and hypothalamus to the cortex, through the medium of a reverberatory circuit.
4. Allows for such crude awareness as the recognition of contact, temperature, pain.

Motor:

1. Its many connections with the basal ganglia, cerebellum, motor neocortex, indicate it plays an important role in motor functions.
2. Its connections with the vagus nerve and with the hypothalamus indicate participation in visceral and autonomic functioning.[c]

Hypothalamus

Sensory:

Sends on impulses from the reticular formation which keep the cortex awake, via the thalamus; has a direct effect on the brain-wave activity of the neocortex.

Motor:

1. The reflex dilatation of the pupil is dependent on it.
2. Is the principal integrative center for the entire autonomic nervous system. In man, it performs this function in concert with the "old cortex." Has the richest blood-supply of the entire brain and its blood-vessels are reciprocally connected with the pituitary, the "master gland." Plays a major role in homeostasis: coordinated interaction between its forepart (parasympathetic) and back-part (sympathetic) results in such complex physiological functions as *regulation* of: body temperature, water metabolism and excretion, and food-intake. It is essential for the overall sexual behavior pattern; a "pleasure" center has been located in the same sex-related nuclei. Also regulates certain of the pituitary's hormone secretions.
3. Is the major subcortical component of the ' limbic system," a functional subsystem. Magoun attributes the mediation of "emotional vocalization" to this system, apparently among all mammals[d]

Cerebral Medulla

Basal ganglia:

1. Help to coordinate and smooth complex voluntary movements and posture, acting in concert with the neocortex and cerebellum.
2. The amygdaloid nucleus helps regulate visceral activity and emotional behavior; functionally, it is also part of the limbic system.

Nerve tracts:

They allow for coordinated functioning of the neocortex with subcortical centers, the two neocortices, the areas within each half of the cortex.

---

[a]Abstracted from Fulton (1955) and Ruch and Fulton (1960) except where otherwise indicated.

[b]Olds and Milner (1954).

[c]Jasper (1952).

[d]Magoun (1967).

and neurophysiologists such as Fulton and Himwich for some time. The phylogenetically (and ontogenetically) oldest parts of the CNS are lowest in this
functional hierarchy, its phylogenetically (and ontogenetically) youngest parts
are highest, and there is a successive re-representation, at each ascending level, of
each level below. The functional corollary of this anatomical arrangement is the
emergence, with each reduplication, of a greater degree and scope of functional
coordination, along with a greater degree of refinement of functioning. This
pattern must, however, be considered in conjunction with the two functional
organization patterns to be subsequently discussed, and be qualified by them.

The hierarchical–reduplicative pattern is especially relevant for psychology
because it provides the framework for the over-time–phylogenetic and ontogenetic–investigative perspective, which has hitherto been slighted by behavioral
theory. Without this perspective, the complex behaviors of the matured organism during a particular moment in time, the typical psychological and neurophysiological experimental design, cannot be adequately conceptualized.

Reference to the hierarchical–reduplicative pattern necessitates interjection of
the thinking of Hughlings Jackson, the later-nineteenth-century English neuro-
surgeon–psychiatrist. Although many of Jackson's neurological specifics have
since proven inaccurate because of the relatively primitive status of neuro-
anatomy during the second half of the nineteenth century, his prolific theoriz-
ing, based on keen observation of his patients, has proved to be so heuristic that
he has been periodically rediscovered by neurophysiologists. He is now considered to be one of the three "patron saints" of modern neurophysiology, along
with Ramon y Cájal, formulator of the neuron theory, and Sir Charles Sherring-
ton, the great experimentalist. The newest, methodologically impeccable
research continuously rediscovers that Jackson was "already there." The following passages, exerpted from his (reprinted) writings, embody much of his
thinking; three modern restatements of his ideas will be cited thereafter.

> The higher the centre, the more numerous, different, complex and special move-
> ments it represents, and the wider the region it represents, equals *evolution*. The
> highest centers represent innumerable, most complex and most special movements
> of the whole organism, and . . . each unit of them represents the whole organism
> differently. In consequence, the higher the centre, the more numerous, different,
> complex and special movements of a wider region are lost from a negative lesion of
> equal volume, equals *dissolution*.
>
> The higher nervous arrangements inhibit (or control) the lower, and thus, when
> the higher are suddenly rendered functionless, the lower rise in activity [Jackson,
> 1882, p. 34].
>
> There is no localisation in the sense that each unit of the [highest motor] centre
> represents only a part of the muscular region; each unit represents, or coordinates,
> the whole region. And there is no localisation in the sense that every unit of the
> centre represents the whole region similarly; each represents, or coordinates, the
> whole region differently [Jackson, 1882, p. 38].

[A lowest motor centre is] one which represents some limited part of the body most nearly directly; . . . is one of simplest yet compound coordination. . . . The sum of these representations in detail is the first, most direct representation of the whole body. A middle (motor) centre represents over again in still more complex coordinations what many or all of the lowest have represented in comparatively simple combinations, and thus represent a less limited part of the body. The middle centres are re-representative; they are centres of doubly compound coordination. . . . The sum of these representations is . . . a doubly indirect representation of the whole organism. . . . The highest (motor) centres are . . . re-re-representative; they represent parts of the body triply indirectly. They are centres of triply compound coordination. The sum of their representations is the third and triply indirect representation of the whole of the body. [In each higher centre, there is] increase in complexity of representation of parts of the greater range represented, and increase in the speciality of representation [Jackson, 1882, p. 41–42].

Evolution is a passage from: 1. the most to the least organised, from centres comparatively well organised at birth to those, the highest centres, which are continually organising throughout life. 2. the most simple to the most complex. 3. the most automatic to the most voluntary. [Thus, the highest centres] are the least organised, the most complex and the most voluntary. *Dissolution* is the reverse of the process of evolution. It is a "taking to pieces" in the order from the least organised, most complex and most voluntary towards the most organised, most simple and most automatic. The symptomatology of nervous disease is a double condition; there is a negative and there is a positive element in every case. Evolution not being entirely reversed, some level of evolution is left. "To undergo dissolution" has the same meaning as "to be reduced to a lower level of evolution." I submit that disease only produces negative emotional symptoms answering to the dissolution and that all positive mental symptoms (illusions, hallucinations, delusions and extravagant conduct) are the outcome of activity of nervous elements untouched by any pathological process; that they arise during activity on the lower level of activity remaining. [As a concrete example, take Aphasia; it consists of loss of intellectual or more voluntary language, but persistence of emotional, the more automatic, language, including gesticulation.] [Jackson, 1884, p. 46]

The data in Table 2 in themselves embody a modern restatement of Jackson's thesis (more clearly if spinal cord functions are included). Here are two more: Patten (1953, p. 318), the embryologist, echoes Tinbergen's (1951) postulation of a hierarchical system of Innate Releasing Mechanisms (IRMs) in a table representing the levels of the somatic–motor system in the human being:

Level	Highest mediating center (read up)	Function or behavior (read up)
Arc 6	Neocortex	Voluntary and regulatory control
Arc 5	Basal ganglia (striatum)	Automatic associated control
Arc 4	Cerebellum plus midbrain	Synergic control (automatic control of muscle movements)
Arc 3	Cerebellum plus medulla plus cord	Equilibratory control
Arc 2	Several spinal segments acting in coordination	Intersegmental reflex
Arc 1	Only one spinal segment	Intrasegmental reflex

And Arieti (1955) utilizes Jacksonian concepts to account for the symptomatology of schizophrenia:

> In schizophrenia, there is an altered functionality of the [old cortex].... If we follow again Hughlings Jackson's principles, a *hypo*functionality of neopallic areas should be accompanied by a release and *hyper*functionality of the archipallium. Such a syndrome presents negative symptoms, caused by hypofunctionality of highest levels, and positive symptoms, caused by the prominence of released lower centers.... Dysencephalization, the reverse of encephalization, seems to occur in schizophrenia [pp. 422–423].

Jackson's hierarchical thesis is so taken for granted by neurophysiologists that the adjective "Jacksonian" is routinely used to refer to this principle in the literature. In the context of this paper, his thesis raises the question: What are the implications for speech production and language acquisition of the postnatal functional emergence of each higher CNS center and its assumption of functional dominance over lower neural centers? The answer to this question should help to explain why chimpanzees such as Washoe are able to master some of the competencies necessary for advanced levels of spoken and written language and not others.

Another of Jackson's postulations of direct relevance for speech and language, that the two hemispheres function in complementary rather than in dominant–secondary (or indispensable–dispensable) fashion, has also been corroborated by modern neurophysiological research. At the end of a survey of the known language-related functions of the parietal lobe, Hécaen (1967) explicitly agrees with Jackson's conclusion that the two hemispheres do not have different functions but, rather, "different aspects of the same function" (p. 158). And Falconer (1967) states that data on ictal dysphasia and ictal speech atomatisms support Jackson's dictum that the right hemisphere is "the one for the most automatic use of words," while the left is "the one in which the automatic use of words merge into their voluntary use—into speech" (p. 185).

A major factor contributing to the hierarchical–reduplicative schema is a consistent patterning of nerve-tract connections in the neuraxis. Each of the major nerve centers, with only minor exceptions:

1, 2. Sends impulses *to* centers above (if any) via ascending (sensory) nerve tracts and *to* centers below (if any) via descending (motor) tracts.

3, 4. Receives projections *from* centers above (if any) via descending tracts and *from* centers below (if any) via ascending tracts.

5, 6. Within each major nerve center, a specific nucleus sends impulses *to* other nuclei of the same complex nerve center, and receives impulses *from* other nuclei of the same center, via interconnecting tracts. [In the neocortex itself, such intracenter connections apparently obtain only within certain broad functional areas (viz., Myers, 1967).]

Each of the nine major CNS nerve centers—spinal cord, medulla, pons and cerebellum, midbrain, hypothalamus, thalamus, basal ganglia, old cortex, neo-cortex—may thus have anywhere from three to six of these categories of connecting tracts, not allowing for the two kinds of sensory and motor tracts, diffuse and specific. The circumstance that the neocortex apparently does not contain any of its own autogenous (i.e., initiators of electrical activity) neurons/ centers demonstrates the most crucial functional role of subcortical–cortical–subcortical nerve tracts: nerve tract interruption between neocortex and subneo-cortex rapidly results in the elimination of characteristic electrical activity in all neocortical centers. The neocortex may serve as the driver, but the lower centers provide the engine!

This intra-CNS formulation should not be interpreted as either overlooking or excluding those nerve tracts which connect various central loci with the periph-ery. The recent discovery of modifying-in-effect efferents from the midbrain to the various receptor cells provides a specific example of how much more complex than previously conceived are central–peripheral interconnections. These connections are further discussed under Pattern 2.

Nor does this formulation mean to ignore the existence of both myelinated and unmyelinated connecting tracts, within the CNS as well as between the CNS and the PerNS (peripheral nervous system). The discovery of diffuse afferent and efferent unmyelinated connecting systems, existing side by side and/or over-lapping with the myelinated, more specific in distribution myelinated motor and sensory pathways, indicates what is in actuality another type of phylogenetically derived duplication, one that Herrick anticipated in his functional division of the nervous system into integrative and analytic systems. The older, diffuse nerve-net type of structure and of electrical transmission has been retained in the human nervous system along with the more recently evolved, more focused, more specialized, and directly associated with highest-center connections. It is logical to assume that this dual style of conduction plays a role in speech production and in language acquisition: <u>What role does it play?</u>

This dual diffuse- and specific-pathways arrangement, and the key role played in its activity and coordination by the brain stem reticular formation (BSRF; to be discussed under Pattern 2), have together led the neurophysiologist Living-ston (1959), to group the interconnecting neural pathways into a different sort of schema than that heretofore presented. He identifies the following six conduction systems in the CNS:

1. the classical, lemniscal, myelinated ascending sensory pathways to the primary sensory receiving areas of the neocortex;
2. the parallel, extralemniscal, unmyelinated ascending sensory pathways via the BSRF to more widespread regions of the cerebral cortex;
3. centrifugal, "sensory control" motor mechanisms that seem to involve

fibers going in reverse directions to 1 and 2 and that may implicate, through the BSRF, projections from cerebral and cerebellar loci;

4. the BSRF as such, which exerts modifying influences upward on both cerebral and cerebellar hemispheres and downward on both sensory and motor synaptic relays;

5. the classical, pyramidal (corticospinal), myelinated descending motor pathways, projecting directly from neocortex to lower motoneuron aggregates;

6. the parallel, extrapyramidal, unmyelinated motor pathways, descending to the motor nuclei indirectly—by way of basal ganglia and the BSRF.

In Herrick's terminology, systems 1, 3, and 5 subserve analytic functions, while systems 2, 4, and 6 subserve integrative functions. All six conducting systems are interdependent and are knitted together at subcortical levels in the BSRF.

It is this exceedingly complex maze of interconnecting nerve tracts, here merely outlined, that contributes to one of the two necessary qualifications of the hierarchical—reduplicative functional organization pattern—and possibly to both. Such qualifications comprise (1) functional organization Patterns 2 and 3, to be described subsequently, and (2) Jackson's ontogenetic dictum of the "continuous reduction of succession to co-existences"—which must be applied when the hierarchical—reduplicative pattern is related to neural functioning at any one moment in time.

At the top of Jackson's functional hierarchy is the cerebral neocortex. So much more is known about this most recently evolved part of the human neuraxis now than at Jackson's time, an updated description of key aspects of its structural and functional characteristics must be interjected at this point.

Brain mapping of cortical functions is no longer the simple topological matter it was considered not long ago to be because of:

1. the high degree of functional interdependence of every level of the neuraxis with every other level and with the PerNS; and of the nervous system with the organism's chemical order of functioning (these findings are serving to re-emphasize how unsatisfactory a word "psychosomatic" continues to be, with its reification rather than elimination of the old mind—body dichotomy);

2. a much greater degree of cortical-area overlap of sensory, motor, and association functions and of visceral and somatic sensory projections than was earlier appreciated; mapping of sensory areas is now approached in terms of termination points of nerve-tract projections from specific subcortical centers, especially from the thalamus (Bailey & Von Bonin, 1951).

A cautionary reminder by Hebb (1958) is especially germane at this point:

> [When] reference is made to "cortical processes," [it is] usually a brief way of saying "higher processes in which the cortex is essentially involved." The cortex, in other words, is not a functional system in itself; and when we speak of cortical

processes, what we mean is corticothalamic processes (or cortico-subcortical), since there are probably other subcortical structures also involved. . . . No psychological function can exist within a segment of the cortex by itself. We commonly say that vision is located in the visual area, a part of the occipital lobe; but this does not mean that the whole process of seeing (or even of visual imagery) can occur in the occipital lobe. What it means is that *an essential part of the process occurs there, and only there.* Speech is "localized" in the cerebral cortex on the left side (for most persons). This again does not mean that the mediating processes of speech can occur in that tissue alone; it does mean that their organization depends on it [p. 83].

Then which functional principle obtains in the cortex, localization or equipotentiality? As might be anticipated from the circumstance that—continuing to use Herrick's terminology—the analytic and the integrative systems are closely intertwined in the neocortex, the former with its delimited and specialized functional style and the latter with its general and diffuse modus operandi, the long-standing argument as to whether there is localization or equipotentiality of function is being resolved in the classical manner pointed to by Tinbergen (1951); both principles, localization and equipotentiality, obtain! It is now correct to speak of a few foci of functional specialization, supplemented by concepts of statistical probability of neuronal excitation within homogeneous regions (Hebb, 1949; Sholl, 1956).

Recourse to the developmental perspective also helps to resolve the old contradiction. Initially, the intact presence of the various function-specific areas of cortical tissue is essential for its particular sensory or motor or association functions to emerge as neocortical maturation proceeds. But after that specialized bit of tissue has begun to function and, as a result, has established a complex network of interconnections with all cortical layers, with other areas of the cortex, and with subcortical centers, both these interconnections *and* the overlap principle provide for the spread of the area's function well beyond its own originally delimited locus. Maps of cortical-area function would accordingly seem to have their greatest applicability to the young child's cortex. Certainly, speculation as to behavioral implications is provoked by such interesting topological findings as the following (Ariëns-Kappers, Huber, & Crosby, pp. 1620–1657):

1. the neocortical areas mediating the sensibility of the corner of the mouth and of the thumb are directly adjacent to each other;
2. the areas that mediate touch overlap with visual areas, and
3. the areas that mediate handedness and the motor aspects of speech are directly adjacent to each other.

As for the functional arrangement of the two cerebral hemispheres, a similar argument has gone on, this one related to specialization versus duplication: does each half of the cortex have a unique function or do the two halves duplicate each other, functionally? The evidence is that, again, both principles obtain: Certain functions are specific to only one side, while other functions are located on both sides.

The gross sensory, motor, and association functional divisions of the neocortex are delineated in the two parts of Figure 2. The most frontal section of the frontal lobe in both illustrations is the prefrontal (PF) association area. In the bottom diagram, except for the frontal striped area, all shaded areas, both striped and stippled, comprise the T-O-P (Temporal-Occipital-Parietal) association area.

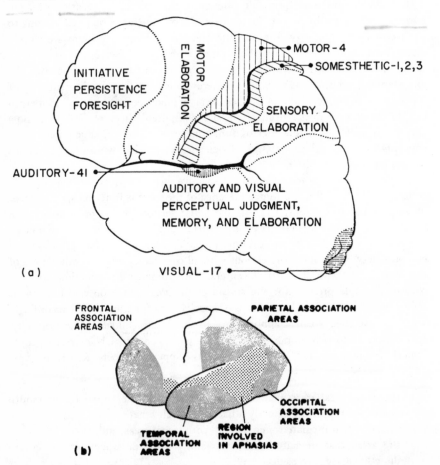

Figure 2 Major functional divisions of the human neocortex. Two diagrams of the lateral surface of the left cerebral neocortex highlighting the association (or "elaboration") areas. In (*b*), with the exception of the frontal striped area, all shaded areas both striped and stippled comprise the T-O-P association area. ((*a*) is from Herrick (1956, p. 417) and is reproduced by courtesy of the University of Texas Press. (*b*) is from Gardner (1963) and is reproduced by courtesy of W. B. Saunders and the author, Ernest Gardner.)

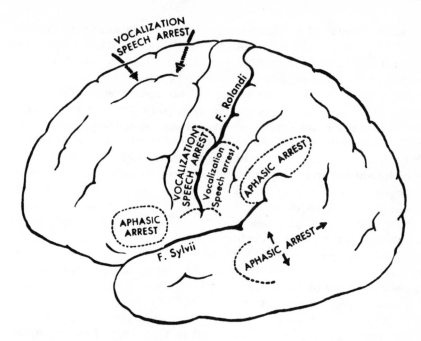

Figure 3 "Dominant" hemisphere areas involved in vocalization and speech. (From Penfield & Rasmussen, 1952, p. 107.)

Penfield and Rasmussen's (1952) diagrammatic summary of the dominant (?)-hemisphere areas in which stimulation may interfere with speech and/or produce vocalization (Figure 3) is also presented for comparison purposes.

The basic anatomical divisions of the neocortex are the frontal, parietal, occipital, and temporal lobes. The central fissure, which runs across the top of the two hemispheres almost from ear to ear, is the usual point of departure for discussing cerebral functions, not only because it provides the demarcation of the frontal lobe from the parietal lobe, but because its front and back walls and the long, striplike areas immediately to the front and the back of it are the first cortical areas that begin to function after birth.

Parietal lobe. Its overall function is to provide a picture of what is going on in and on the body. It is primarily somatosensory, viscerosensory, and sensory associative in function. It receives projections from the thalamus; and the primary somatoviscerosensory area, like the thalamus, has a dermatomal representation of the entire body.

Occipital lobe. It is necessary for seeing the external world and for recognizing what is seen. It is primarily visuosensory in function; the reaction of the pupil to light appears to be the only visual function not mediated by the visual cortex.

Temporal lobe. It is necessary for hearing, for understanding what is heard, for maintenance of body balance in space, for speech comprehension (left lobe), and for visual appreciation and discrimination and manipulation of form and spatial relationships (right lobe) (B. Milner, 1954). Penfield (1952b) has located stream-of-consciousness affective memory centers in it; it also has other complex intellectual and emotional functions not yet fully identified.

Frontal lobe, posterior sections. The first two areas directly forward of the central fissure mediate all voluntary motor behavior. The body is represented, part by part, in the motor cortex; the size of cortical area devoted to each part is proportional to the discreteness and exactness of the movement involved rather than to the actual size of the part's musclemass. Another area makes speech possible. Another area mediates movements of the eyeballs and acts as a visual association area, integrating stimuli from the eye muscles and from the retina (projected to it from the visual cortex), and appears to play a role in the focusing and maintenance of attention. Two further body-projection areas have been located in this section of the frontal lobe.

Frontal lobe, pre- (or orbito-) frontal sections. One prefrontal area is the primary respiratory center of the cortex, along with other autonomic-regulation functions; it is one of the two neocortical areas entering into the limbic system, a functional subcircuit related to emotional behavior. The gyrus cinguli is usually grouped with the frontal lobe, although it is meso–paleocortex, not neocortex; it is also part of the limbic system, and is reciprocally connected with the anterior thalamic nuclei. The PF association area performs life-essential autonomic regulations, mediates affective reactions to pain, and is the seat of recent memory. Its ablation or injury results in impaired learning ability as well as in a number of personality changes that vary from person to person. Foresight and the pursuit of long-term goals seem also to depend on the PF area.

Since the determination of the functions of the neocortex, especially of the association areas, is an active research frontier, the foregoing summary cannot be taken as definitive.

Herrick's (1956) description of the entire amphibian brain vis à vis the intimate structural and functional relationships between the integrative and the analytic networks applies with only minor modifications to these same relationships within the human neocortex; this description provides a pertinent introduction to a discussion of the cortex's internal pattern of organization [especially significant passages are italicized by the present author] :

> The nervous elements concerned with the analytic functions are generally recognizable, and among these nerve-cells and fibers there are others that are integrative in function. The latter form a very closely woven fabric of interlaced thin naked fibers, the neuropil. *The bodies of all nerve-cells and their widely spread dendritic branches are embedded within this fibrous mat and closely enveloped by it.* . . . This web of neuropil permeates the entire [neocortex] and acts as a nonspecific conducting system which puts every part of the [neocortex] into physiological connection with every other part. It is the primary integrating mechanism, but it is much more than

this. *It is germinative tissue with potentialities for further differentiation in an endless variety of ways* [Herrick, 1956, p. 249].

Second only to the dual conduction arrangement to which Herrick points, the most obvious intrastructural characteristic of the neocortex is its horizontal, multilayered organization, each layer distinguishable on the basis of distinctive cellular characteristics. Although six is the consensus, there is some disagreement in the literature as to the exact number of layers—perhaps because they vary in thickness and in relative degree of development in different sections of the cortex (Ruch & Fulton, 1960, p. 248). These layers have both a phylogenetic and an embryological history. By convention, the numbering of each layer proceeds from the surgeon's or dissector's perspective and so goes from the outside in—i.e., the layer closest to the skull is designated one and the deepest layer, directly contiguous with the cerebral medulla, is numbered six. However, the gradient of layer development is in the diametrically reverse direction.

Experimental evidence "suggests strongly that the upper three cortical layers form a unit in themselves" (Ariëns-Kappers *et al.*, 1936, p. 1571). These are the layers that differentiate from the supragranular layer during embryology; this layer is by far the thickest in man, as pointed out in Table 1. Layer 3 is a thick layer in most parts of the cortex and is made up of large pyramidal cells (plus enveloping neuropil). It is frequently subdivided; for example, Conel (1939– 1967), whose material is extensively drawn on in the developmental section following, refers to Layers 3a, 3b, 3c, with 3a directly contiguous with Layer 2, and 3c, the deepest layer, directly contiguous with Layer 4. Very many vertical and horizontal fibers originating both outside and inside the cortex are found in the various layers. Horizontal fibers, which are believed to be concerned with higher, association functions, have been estimated as continuing to increase up to at least 38 years of age (Ariëns-Kappers *et al.*, 1936, p. 1576). There are a great many cells having short axons in the human neocortex. Cájàl's assumption that such cells provide for the delicacy of function of man's brain is now taken as fact (Ruch & Fulton, 1960, p. 252).

The distinctive functional contributions of the multiple layering pattern have not yet been fully determined. This writer's speculations are in line with Jackson's principle of repeated re-representation up the neuraxis together with a "continual adding-on of new organizations" with each reduplication. That is, the six-layered neocortex adds not one but six more functional levels to the human neuraxis: Layer 6 re-represents all subcortical levels, Layer 5 re-represents Layer 6, Layer 4 re-represents Layer 5, and so on up to Layer 1, which re-represents all representations below it. This schema would account for a number of heretofore puzzling cortical characteristics. It helps explain the brain's remarkable ability to recover functionally after damage. If the re-representation is not isomorphic, that is, topographically precisely duplicated from the bottom to the top layer—

which this writer believes it is not—then the overlapping of functional areas that has been consistently observed would also be explained.

Gooddy's (1956) criticism of the point-by-point stimulation technique as a means of ascertaining localization of function becomes especially germane in this context; he points out that this technique reveals only bits of a particular unit of behavior, never the whole, integrated behavior pattern that actually occurs *in situ*. For example, despite the circumstance that ongoing speech can be arrested by carefully placed electrical stimulation, Gooddy specifically points out that so far as the evocation of speech is concerned, the point-stimulation technique has brought forth only sounds, never speech.

Phylogenetically, the supragranular layer is an exclusively mammalian acquisition, while its further subdivision into Layers 3, 2, 1(?) is an exclusively human characteristic. Is alert consciousness in man mediated by Layers 3 and 2? This functional role would not exclude subcortical contributions to alert consciousness, specifically the ARAS (ascending reticular activating system), to be described under Pattern 2 following, on p. 60. This conception of the functional role of the layering pattern would also provide for the successively higher levels of adaptive behavior that emerge as postnatal development proceeds—from the first sensorimotor coordinations of the first month of life, to ideation and ideational integration at neural maturity.

It is tempting to speculate that Piaget's (1952) postulated stages in the development of "intelligence" are directly correlated with the postnatal onset of functioning in the various ascending layers of the neocortex. It may be that sensorimotor coordinations are mediated by the lower layers of the T-O-P association area, while the upper layers of the same area make possible increasingly refined perceptual discriminations. It is tempting also to speculate that while mere vocalization is mediated by subcortical centers, man's preverbal babbling stage entails the functioning of the three lower layers (6, 5, 4) of the cortical speech areas, and verbalization—i.e., speech—entails the functioning of the upper layers. This question will be kept in mind for future reference: Does speech emerge postnatally as Layer 3 becomes functional? The anatomical and developmental characteristics of the chimpanzee cortex should provide an independent data source bearing on such speculation: Do chimps have a cortical area corresponding to the human speech area and, if so, how many layers does it manifest at neurological maturity?

Conel (1939–1967, Vol. 5 [1955]) points out that the layering or horizontal organization of neurons in the neocortex is supplemented by striation, a discontinuous vertical cellular arrangement at direct right angles to the horizontal pattern and with no direct contact between the horizontally and vertically arranged cells anywhere in the cortex. Although this dual pattern is clearly evident by six fetal months (the layering pattern emerges a month earlier), Conel does not refer to the striation arrangement as being a dominant neocortical characteristic until 15 months after birth. Is it possible that the vertical cellular arrangement provides for a kind of sedimentation process whereby recent experience, which is originally mediated by higher layers and registered, in Hebb's (1949) terminology, as a phase sequence, gravitates to the bottom layers, spreading in locus as it does so? Such a process would mean that Layers 6 and 5 serve as a memory "reservoir" for current functioning. Interestingly enough, the deepest layers are the only ones that continue to function during lighter, typically dream-filled, sleep.

Conel (1939–1967, Vol. 8 [1967]), apparently influenced by Herrick, has a complex (albeit not contradictory of the foregoing) hypothesis concerning the functional correlates of the cortex's dual vertical–horizontal neuronal organization:

> Careful search has not revealed any contacts between exogenous fibers and dendrites of neurons or between fibers. The arrangement of apical dendrites and vertical exogenous fibers in the vertical plane and the tangential, horizontal and subcortical-association fibers in the horizontal plane throughout the entire extent of the cortex is a structural manifestation of some function. The unswerving right-angle relationship between the vertical and horizontal elements throughout the cortex suggests an electromagnetic field. The exogenous fibers are undoubtedly axons and are transmitting impulses. The absence of collateral or terminal branches on them and the absence of contacts between one fiber and another or between fibers and dendrites suggests that there may be electric and/or electronic transmission of impulses in the cerebral cortex *in addition to* axo-dendritic and axo-somatic synapses [p. 278].

The remarkably complex cellular organization described means that functionally, every part of the cortex can both relay and receive impulses, and is in potential contact with every other part of the cortex as well as with all subcortical centers. A particular cortical afferent can relate to a cortical efferent in a variety of ways: It can go directly via one fiber to one cortical efferent; it can effect multisynaptic connections with an efferent; it can form, through recurrent collaterals from both afferents and efferents, circular chains capable of re-excitation or reverberation, i.e., "feedback circuits" (Lashley, 1951). More extended analysis of the behavioral correlates of this last functional mode is being reserved for the next functional organization pattern. But from the description already given, it is evident just why the physiological and the behavioral universes of discourse, kept rigidly separate until recently, have begun not merely to come closer together but to overlap.

THE FUNCTIONAL SUBCIRCUITS PATTERN

Recent research of both neurophysiologists and physiological psychologists, independently and in collaboration, provides the basis for the second functional organization pattern. The mammalian nervous system is now seen as being made up of countless overlapping unilevel and multilevel functional subsystem or "circuits," many of them closed-loop or reverberatory in character. Each of these circuits functions both as an organized whole and with the rest of the nervous system in an instantaneous and coherent manner. Although these subsystems are primarily central in locus and regulatory in function, the essential contributory role of peripheral neural structure is expressly acknowledged.

Here are only a few examples of a feedback or reverberatory circuit: A nerve impulse darts from a specific nucleus in the thalamus to a particular section of the parietal neocortex, thence to a particular section of the frontal lobe, thence to the hippocampal formation, back to another thalamic nucleus, whence it goes to the original one—and the cycle of activity is repeated many times before it ceases (Ruch, 1951). The sensory nerve cell in a muscle spindle of the PerNS sends its signal to the reticular formation of the brainstem and the reticular formation promptly sends a modifying impulse back to the muscle spindle, in a constant, never-ceasing circuit that is subject to higher-center influences (Brodal, 1957). In a similar manner, receptor cells in the retina send impulses to the BSRF which promptly sends a modifying impulse back to the retina (Granit, 1955). The motor neocortex sends a chain of impulses to the neocerebellum via the corticopontine tracts, the pontine nuclei, and the middle peduncle of the cerebellum; the neocerebellum sends a chain of impulses right back to the motor neocortex via the superior cerebellar peduncle and the ventrolateral nucleus of the thalamus—and this circle is repeated several times before activity ceases (Ruch, 1951).

There appear to be two general types of functional subcircuits:

1. those of a relatively limited scope, involving either only one CNS center or more than one subcortical level; and
2. those of a more complex character, involving either several neuraxial centers, one of which is neocortical, or interaction between the CNS and the PerNS; the autonomic nervous system is an example of the second type of complex functional subcircuit.

There seems to be no end to the number of both types of subcircuits that have been and are still being identified. Three of the more complex ones are:

1. The ascending reticular activating system (ARAS), which comprises the following circuit: BSRF (brainstem reticular formation) → thalamus → hypothalamus → BSRF. It provides for the BSRF's alerting function, so basic to the behavioral phenomena of wakefulness—consciousness and attention. It also provides for neocortical influence on the functioning of the BSRF—that is, for cortical feedback.
2. The centrencephalic integrating system (CIS), derived entirely from observation of human functioning: an upper-brainstem circuit made up of dien-

cephalic and midbrain centers, and feed-ins from old and new cortex. Penfield (1952a) separates the CIS into two related mechanisms, one of which can function independently of the other. The *B-mechanism* is the CIS proper, and is used in the integration of the sensory and motor systems, the acquired skills of speech and manual dexterity, and in recollection of past experience. The *A-mechanism* is seen as an adjunct to the CIS and is made up of two subcircuits: the frontal-lobe subdivision, involving prefrontal areas, and the temporal-pole subdivision, involving prefrontal areas, and the temporal-pole subdivision; both are used to record one's current perceptions.

3. The *limbic system* or *visceral brain*, an old-cortex-centered circuit. It is reverberatory; structurally, it comprises an inner ring—part of the hippocampal formation, the archicortex, and the olfactory structures—which projects to the septal region, the hypothalamus, and the midbrain via the fornix; and an outer ring—cingulate gyrus, orbito-insulo-temporal cortex, and presubiculum—which projects to subcortical centers via the striatum and is closely associated with the septal nuclei and the basolateral amygdalar nuclei. According to Cobb (1950), "It seems to set the emotional background on which man functions intellectually." Magoun (1967) maintains that it mediates "emotional vocalization" among all mammals.

Speech and language undoubtedly involve feedback circuits of both the first and the second types enumerated earlier. For expressive language, the multilevel (Type 2) circuit would undoubtedly involve at least these neuraxial centers: subcortically mediated vocalization centers plus neocortical motor speech centers, left temporal lobe, and T-O-P assocation area. That such a complex circuit has not already been unequivocally identified is probably due to the circumstance that suitable neuroelectric investigative techniques have not yet been developed.

Pattern 2, the functional subsystems pattern, is clearly apparent when one observes the functioning of the nervous system *in situ* for any limited period of time. But a hierarchic patterning, i.e., each higher level having functional dominance over lower levels, would definitely not be apparent. Does not Pattern 2 contradict Pattern 1? How can both apply simultaneously? The necessity of explicitly raising these questions constitutes a reflection on the theoretical limitations of the moment-in-time observational perspective, to which experimental neuropsychology and physiology have hitherto been almost exclusively devoted in the design of their investigations.

The hierarchical organizational principle is clearest when the over-time or developmental observational perspective is resorted to. All lower motor centers and activities eventually subject to neocortical influences cannot come under such influence until related primary motor and association areas have begun to function. Effective sensorimotor relations—that is, refined sensory control over (voluntary) motor activities—can only be established after primary sensory neocortical areas and related association areas have begun to function. And all the complex cognitive and intellectual functions of the human brain, centered in the neocortex, can emerge only as the neocortex becomes functional. Yet at birth, the human infant's neocortex (as well as such lower centers as the neocerebellum) is simply not transmitting impulses! This state of affairs means that all functional subcircuits that include neocortical centers, or are subject to the influence of such centers, emerge subsequent to birth, in accordance—it is here hypothesized—with a hierarchical organization principle that, in line with Jackson's dictum of the "continuous reduction of succession to coexistences," expresses itself at neurological maturity in vertically organized, functionally coherent and instantaneous subcircuits.

When the over-time perspective is included in this manner, functional organization Patterns 1 and 2 become complementary rather than contradictory organizational principles. Future study of the nervous system must, therefore, include not only sheerly structural changes subsequent to birth. It must also include as a major area of inquiry how, when, and under what conditions each one of the more complex functional subcircuits emerges, both structurally and functionally.

Herrick (1956) has applied the newer physical concepts of electrodynamic fields to cortical organization and functioning, and the implications of this application for the perceptual process:

> To explain the observed facts, the new theory of quantum mechanics was developed. . . . The "quantum field" [is one] in which objects are not . . . regarded as separate entities in fixed positions that react with the field. While still called elementary particles, their properties are identical with those of quanta of energy and *the particles are loci or patterns of energy.* The field can be defined only by its dynamic properties. The particle and the field are inseparably one . . . [This way of looking at the electromagnetic field directs attention] to the system as a whole, exhibited in the form of the *relations of the motions of the parts.* Different individual particles may be engaged from time to time *but the pattern persists* [p. 264] (Italics EM's).

> So also if mentation is a vital process carried on in a field of metabolic activity, then the mind must not be regarded as an entity separable from its field of operation, a being which somehow pulls the strings that move a mechanical robot. *The mind and the field are inseparably one.* . . . The field in question is not a structure; *it is a pattern of process.* But such a pattern may occur only in some particular region of the brain with the requisite structural organization, and this region, which has more or less definite boundaries, may be called the field of this particular type of process; that is, a field defined in terms of its relations in space to other parts of the brain [p. 266] (Italics EM's).

> The distinction which we draw between awareness on the one hand and on the other hand the projection outward of some components of experience as things known about, including objects set in the frame of space and time, all observable behavior of ourselves and others, and all symbols of mental processes—this distinc-

tion . . . is a methodological artifact which results from the structural limitations of the human apparatus of perception. *The knowings and the known are intrinsic components of a field of experience within which they are inseparable* [p. 279]. (Italics EM'S)

An inseparable feature of perceptual integration is the polarization of the perceiving subject against the thing perceived, of the self against the not-self [p. 349]. [That is], I experience myself in action as immediately as I experience things acted upon [p. 207]. This clear-cut conscious polarization of subject and object, [which] arises late in human psychogenesis, is basic for perception and all mental processes derived from it [p. 323].

As for behavioral psychology's tenacious adherence to one or another version of the S → R model of behavior, Lashley, Hebb, and recently also Pribram (among others) have been trying to convince fellow psychologists that the classical intra- and intersegmental spinal reflex arc does not provide an adequate mechanistic foundation for most of human behavior. If they and such neurophysiologists as Gerard and Livingston have their way, and there are encouraging signs that they are, the latest behavioral schema must at the very least be conceptualized, as Gerard (1960) has put it, in the form of "input and output to the CNS"; that is, as s → C → r, in which C represents the explicitly acknowledged—and increasingly well documented—highly complex role of the central nervous system, and s and r represent the functional roles of the peripheral nervous system which, as we shall shortly see, not only influences but is influenced by the CNS.

More specific documentation of the validity of the proposed s–C–r model requires that new understandings of the extent to which the CNS influences the functioning of the PerNS be added to the CNS-centered information already presented.

First, the sensory or, rather, stimulus aspect. All receptor cells have a common, truly remarkable function: Each type of receptor organ acts as a highly specialized, high-speed "transformer," instantaneously converting a particular kind of physical energy (pressure, sound waves, light waves, chemical substances) into electrical energy. We now know that they also play a screening, and therefore a perceptual, role as a result of central efferent influences on them. Not even the subjective concomitants of higher-level functioning—consciousness, self-awareness, thought—exceed the almost metaphysical complexity of receptor-organ functioning.

The BSRF (brainstem reticular formation) acts as a second-level checkpoint or modifier of incoming sensory impulses: It receives collaterals from nearly all the sensory modalities and, under the influence of higher centers, selects which stimuli will go on to higher levels and which shall not; hence it also plays a major role in the perceptual process. Also, at the same time that higher-order functions are being subserved by thalamic projections to specific sensory areas of the neocortex, the BSRF is responsible for a more fundamental biological function: It determines, through the ascending reticular activating system, the neocortex's degree of receptivity to the specific sensory impulses being sent to it from the thalamus. The thalamus, working in feedback intimacy with the old cortex and hypothalamus, contributes an important preconscious perceptual attribute to those sensations which have survived their previous "inspection points:" their feeling-tone associations. Perceptual selectivity and discrimination reach their greatest degree of refinement at the neocortical level: The neocortex has a recognition–discriminative role in which memory processes are involved; these in turn involve the limbic system, which appears to have a strong self-referrent aspect.

The necessary involvement of motor activities in the sense organs' role of "presenting a detailed report" is stressed by Lord Adrian (1959):

> All the actions which focus the sense-organs on the stimulus will evoke afferent signals of their own to be related to the signals from the sense-organ itself. Thus the full report which comes to the CNS will be far more complex and informative than anything which could be furnished by a sense-organ isolated from the body and controlled by the electrophysiologist [p. 366].

This cautionary reminder provides an apt introduction to the response aspect of the nervous system. Here we must start where we left off in the quick overview of its sensory aspects: the highest centers. Not only the highest levels of perception and meaning and thought and volition are exercised on the body musculature by the neocortex, but also the body's emotional reactions to the incoming sensory messages may be transmitted from cortical centers to both skeletal and visceral musculature. In the execution of coordinated voluntary movement, the reverberatory circuit comprising cerebral–striatal–cerebellar–striatal–cerebral centers comes into play. Both autonomic and emotional reactions depend heavily on hypothalamus-centered circuits; and *the hypothalamus, through its close association with the pituitary gland, both affects and is affected by the body's chemical order of functioning.*

Denny-Brown reciprocates Lord Adrian's emphasis on central motor factors in sensory functioning by stressing the importance of central sensory factors in motor functioning (Denny-Brown, 1960). He posits two basic principles of motor integration (p. 793): (1) Every motor reaction has an adequate stimulus, immediate or remote. (2) "The nervous system as a whole contributes to each motor act." He amplifies the second principle by stating: "It is not possible to indicate separate mechanisms for posture and for movement: postural reactions are fundamental in neural organization, and movement in its most elementary form is seen as modifications of postural responses" (p. 793).

Livingston (1959) has pointed out that unknowingly inadequate investigative methods are partially accountable for the delay in confirming the existence of a sensory-modifying motor system, the lower parts of which were first noticed many years ago by Cájàl and others, a system of connections that permits central influences to "modify sensory-input patterns anywhere from peripheral sense organs to at least the sensory neocortex" (p. 741). The use of anesthesia and cortical extirpation in investigating motor connections and functions, both of which eliminated cortical influences, had much to do with this oversight. These central processes are tonically active and usually inhibitory in effect, acting to reduce or eliminate potential sensory experiences in *initial* stages of sensory integration. Since such central influence allows both past experience and the direction of attention to play a part, says physiologist Livingston, "central interference with sensory transmission appears to be regulatory and to *constitute a goal-seeking physiological mechanism*" (p. 742; italics EM's).

THE TRIPLE-SYSTEM PHYLOGENETIC-LEGACY PATTERN

Phylogenesis has apparently bequeathed not one but three relatively discrete neural-structure legacies to the human species: a visceral, internally oriented subsystem; a sensorimotor subsystem interactive with the external environment; and a third system that coordinates the first two systems into a coherently functioning whole. Each one is functionally organized along the vertical (i.e., hierarchical) dimension. Close consideration of Herrick's (1956) functional division of the neural networks of the vertebrate nervous system into "analytic" and "integrative" *and* of Romer's (1958) dual-structure phylogenetic-legacy postulation, which coincides with Herrick's subdivision of the "analytic" conduction system, underlies this formulation—for which the writer must take full responsibility. This pattern also takes into account the two functional organization patterns just presented.

It is accordingly postulated that the human nervous system is made up of three separate, but interrelated, components: the intraorganismic subsystem, the transactional subsystem, and the integrative system. A description of the essential characteristics of each follows.

The Intraorganismic Subsystem

The first of the two subsystems, termed the *intraorganismic vegetative and feeling-tone subsystem*, is conceived as subserving the organism's internal milieu, that is, its basic life processes, as well as the organism's orientation to—its feelings about, attitudes towards—self and external world. Such behavioral concepts as organismically centered drives or instincts (including Freud's id) and emotions can be related to it. There is a strong possibility that it also subserves at its higher levels a still more complex, subjective function for the human individual: awareness of its own reactivity. Its sensory pathway reaches the thalamus via the hypothalamus, and from the thalamus it goes to the cingulate gyrus of the frontal mesopallium (and thence to the PF association area). Its motor pathway goes from the cingulate cortex (with feed-ins from the PF area) to the hippocampal formation, thence to the hypothalamus and the rest of the ANS (Autonomic Nervous System).

The intraorganismic subsystem functions through two discrete, yet overlapping, sensorimotor circuits; one short and one long. The short circuit subserves the vegetative-homeostatic processes of the body; its highest correlating center is the hypothalamus. Neurophysiology's updated picture of the ANS—that is, as having both CNS and PerNS components—provides the motor aspect of the short circuit. Significantly, in light of Romer's (1958) formulations, the body's chemical order of functioning is closely interrelated with its neural order through the hypothalamus' close functional relationships with the pituitary, the "master gland." Fulton's (1955) levels of ANS formulation, documents the hierarchical—reduplicative organization of the short circuit. The long circuit entails the connections to the (right?) cingulate gyrus and (right?) prefrontal association area referred to earlier, thence to the hypothalamus (and the ANS) via the hippocampal formation—that is, it is the limbic system plus the PF area. The long circuit provides for the "orientation" aspect of the intraorganismic subsystem's hypothesized role: It transforms inner, physiologically derived sensations into (psychological) experience, a function analogous to receptor cells' transformation of physical energy into neuroelectric energy. It affects physiological functioning in turn through the hypothalamus and influences the motor component of the transactional subsystem through relevant integrative system circuits.

The Transactional Subsystem

The other of the two subsystems is being termed the "transactional-perceptual" system. It is seen as directly subserving both the organism's interactive transactions with the physical world external to it, and its awareness—perception of itself as a physical entity in relation to the outside world. The posterior, T-O-P association area is believed to be the core locus of this perceptual process.

The sensory aspect of this subsystem is comprised of the specific sensory pathways direct to the thalamus, and also the sensory aspect of the cerebellar—striatal—thalamic subcircuit; thence its pathways lead to the (left?) sensory cortex and the T-O-P association area. The motor aspect of the transactional subsystem has two distinct components: the rapid pyramidal "short circuit" to the skeletal muscle via the cerebellum, which ordinarily functions almost automatically; and those pathways that modify sensory input, motor pathways that Livingston has described as paralleling every ascending neural pathway on a one-to-one basis and as providing for central regulation of sensory transmission. The cortical processes and centers from which these modifying pathways derive, the pathways themselves, and the incoming sensory tracts on which they exert highest-center influences, together comprise the transactional "long circuit;" its functional role is to transform externally derived sensation into (psychological) experience and, via relevant integrative-system circuits, to initiate the purposeful bodily activity that may result.

The Integrative System

At this point, we have two vertically organized, apparently functionally discrete subsystems, except for their convergence in the thalamus. In actuality, *in situ* there is much interaction between them—and here is where the slower conducting, diffusely organized integrative system comes in. The extralemniscal pathways, the BSRF, the UTCIS (unspecific thalamocortical integrating system), and the extrapyramidal motor pathways are key components of this system, which will hereafter also be termed, collectively, the "central integrating circuits," or CI circuits.

The CI circuits comprise six forebrain branches or categories, all included in the corpus callosum. They are listed here in their hypothesized *developmental order*; this schema is derived from integrative networks that are already known:

1. Those networks paralleling the mode-specific sensory pathways to and from the posterior cortex (these feed into and out of the posterior thalamic nuclei).
2. Those networks paralleling the motor pathways from and to the precentral and midfrontal cortex (these feed into and out of the basal ganglia).
3. Those pathways paralleling the ANS networks of the forebrain—i.e., paralleling the limbic system; these feed into and out of the anterior, midline, and centromedial thalamic nuclei. (Or is the limbic system in itself a CI circuit?)
4. The heavy reciprocal connections between the T-O-P association area and the posterior thalamic nuclei.
5. The heavy reciprocal connections between the temporal pole and the posterior thalamic nuclei.
6. The reciprocal connections between the PF association area and the intralaminar and medial thalamic nuclei.

In the matured, conscious brain, all branches function together as a coherent unit.

Branches 1, 2, and 4 collect data from and feed data to the transactional subsystem from other forebrain centers and from subforebrain centers. Branch 3 collects data from and feeds data to the intraorganismic subsystem. Branch 5 serves both the intraorganismic and transactional subsystems. Branch 6, which develops well after birth, as we shall see, is related somewhat differently to the integrative system than are the other branches. This CI circuit projects to the PF association area (via the thalamus) data deriving from the ongoing functioning of the transactional and intraorganismic subsystems, and in turn feeds back data via the thalamus to cortical centers involved in the functioning of the intra-organismic and transactional subsystems; thus, Branch 6 is the most heavily dependent of all the CI circuits on the accumulated experiences of the individual. It appears not to develop at all in the autistic and early-schizophrenic child, to be defectively developed in psychopaths, and to be minimally developed in persons having limited mental ability, whether the limitation is due to organic factors, or to environmental deprivations, or to a combination of both. *Branch 6 appears to have emerged phylogenetically only with the human species.*

The third functional organization pattern, which has been presented here in tentative, outline form, is at once the most comprehensive and the most conjectural of the three postulated. In essence, it implies that the organization of the human nervous system at neurological maturity represents the outcome of a continuous, largely (and perhaps entirely) postnatal developmental process involving the knitting together of the two disparate structural and behavioral legacies here termed the intraorganismic and transactional subsystems; the thalamus is a core factor in the "knitting" process. The details of this neurogenic, chiefly forebrain, process have yet to be documented by whole-system-oriented research. It is further hypothesized that (1) each of the three systems has its own developmental timetable, and (2) the integrative process referred to in the second-last sentence (i.e., the postnatal knitting together of the intraorganismic and transactional subsystems) is heavily influenced by the growing individual's life experiences.

With the postulation of the triple-system functional organization pattern, we are now in a position to determine from the postnatal data whether the seventh developmental pattern earlier formulated—that the coherent, unified functioning of the physiologically mature nervous system represents the end-product incorporation of a progressive series of organized functional patterns that develop in a vertical-hierarchic ontogenetic sequence—is borne out. We may also be in the position to answer the following question, at least speculatively: What role does the triple-system functional organization pattern play in the acquisition of speech and language?

Ontogenetic Patterns

As has already been postulated, at birth the infant's behavior is mediated primarily by hindbrain and midbrain centers, with probably some forebrain (diencephalic, striatal, and old cortex) participation; by the end of the first month of postnatal life, there is also some participation of primary-sensorimotor and visual areas of the neocortex. We are not born with the ability for complex motor and eye–hand coordination and skills; for the use of language in a complex and sophisticated manner; for sustained mental manipulation of symbols; with the ability to formulate a long-range plan and carry it out; with awareness of and strong feelings about self; or with attitudes, values, ethics, and religious beliefs.

If we accept the fundamental assumption of this discussion, that all the behaviors just enumerated are directly dependent on a nervous system which obviously continues to develop after birth, and which makes possible all individual experience, performance, and learning, we are confronted with a very wide gap indeed between the status of the nervous system at birth and its status at neural maturity. This gap prompts the question: *What* neural maturative changes occur between birth and neural maturity, and *when* do they occur? A detailed answer to this question necessitates a prior description both of the nature of the neurogenic data utilized and of the writer's rationale for their use.

The neurogenic data related to the first few years of life are comprised of gross structural, histological (including myelination), and EEG analyses. For subjects beyond six years of age, only gross structural and EEG studies could be located. It is especially unfortunate, in light of the important role of unmyelinated nerve tracts in the functional organization of the matured nervous system, that data on the pre- and postnatal development of these tracts appear to be nonexistent. Also, since the postnatal neural data to be cited are chiefly neocortical, important lacunae are left from a developmentalist's point of view: What of postnatal patterns of development of other forebrain centers (especially the thalamus), and of the cerebellum (especially the neocerebellum)?

Before proceeding to a more extended introduction to the neural data, it is important to acknowledge explicitly at the outset that behavioral changes that occur with age cannot be ascribed solely to neural maturation. Growth changes in accessory structures—in the receptor organs, in the bones and skeleton and muscles, in the organ systems, in the glands and in related biochemical factors—also occur after birth and obviously contribute to behavioral change. Even more complicative is the circumstance that learning enters into the shaping of behavior at every stage of human development; less so in the early months, more and more so as time goes on. How then can behavioral changes that are manifestly due to a multiplicity of factors be justifiably attributed to only one of these factors? More important, how can one with confidence ascribe a particular change in behavior to particular maturative changes in the nervous system rather than to the individual child's experience subsequent to birth?

Such an enterprise is indeed untenable and is not the writer's goal. Her goal within this context is more realistic. It is, rather, to be guided by this question:

Can one reasonably conclude from the data that a particular evidence of neural change has contributed to or played a role in a particular behavioral development?

"But why can't the relationship be in the opposite direction: Could not the child's experience have brought about the neural change?" a not-so-imaginary challenger might further question. The best answer this writer can give to this difficult query is her present idea of how neural development factors are related to learning, summarized in these propositions:

1. Learning is dependent on the individual organism's having an experience, either conscious or unconscious. An experience may or may not have an overt motor component.

2. An organism's "having an experience" is dependent, as a minimum, on conduction in central supramidbrain neural tissue (perhaps only in cortical tissue), conduction that is in turn dependent on two equally essential contributing conditions: first, relevant stimulation, and second, maturational readiness to conduct of neural sensory tissue that is enabling of that particular category of experience. Previously nonconducting neural tissue, which is stimulated to conduct by conduction in adjoining tissue, will do so only if it is sufficiently advanced in cellular (and so forth) maturation to be able to function.

The foregoing formulation provides for this further proposition:

3. Where the neural evidence indicates continued functional immaturity of neural tissue known or believed to be enabling of a particular category of behavior that has not yet emerged at the age observed, then it is tenable to assume that continuing maturation of such tissue is prerequisite to the eventual emergence of that behavior.

The third postulation is important to this discussion because it provides for heuristic speculation beyond the as yet scanty neurogenic data—speculation believed to be warrantable in the context of a theoretical paper.

Biochemical aspects and accompaniments of postnatal neurogenesis are not being systematically included in this survey. Nevertheless, this question needs to be interjected: Why is it that cortical cells begin to function immediately after viable birth and not before, while cells directly subjacent to the cortex are apparently functioning before birth? The answer appears to be: because of the "oxygen barrier," which prevents the presence of function-essential oxygen in the blood supply of the cortex until birth (Barcroft, 1938). Only with the inspiration of the birth cry and subsequent onset of aerobic respiration can subcortical electrical conduction at last trigger cortical-cell conduction. Thereafter three, rather than the earlier postulated two, factors seem to be operative in the spread of cortical functioning:

1. shift from anaerobic to aerobic respiration in a particular cortical area and layer;
2. a sufficient degree (??) of cellular maturation in the same area or layer; and
3. presence of stimulative conduction in adjacent or subjacent neural tissue.

Impulse conduction appears to serve not merely an "enabling" function, but also a growth-promoting function, causing an increase in blood oxygen in adjacent cortical tissue and consequent acceleration of cellular maturation. It is this intervening physiological process that seems to underlie the maturation-promoting influence of individual experience which has frequently been pointed to.

As background basic to the subsequent age-organized analysis, three generalized overviews of the overall neurogenic trends deducible from each of the categories of neurogenic data that were utilized follow:

1. TURNER'S (1948, 1950) STUDIES OF GROSS STRUCTURAL CHARACTERISTICS

Turner's studies show that the cortex as a whole continues to grow after birth in both surface area and in fissuration. This growth is especially rapid (fourfold) between birth and six years, with minor or localized changes thereafter. As for lobe subpatterns of growth, Table 3 shows relative rates of growth of each of the four neocortical lobes, as derived from Turner's discussion. The rapid rate of growth for the two-to-six-year period in the frontal and temporal lobes is especially noteworthy: Certain frontal-lobe areas are necessary for speech production and certain temporal-pole areas are necessary for speech comprehension.

2. CONEL'S STUDIES (1939–1967 [1939, 1941, 1947, 1951, 1955, 1959, 1963, 1967])

Conel has utilized nine maturative criteria in his meticulous histological studies of the postnatal cerebral cortex from birth to six years. On the basis of these criteria, Conel finds these maturative trends to be histologically consistent throughout the developmental periods so far studied by him:

1. The width, or thickness, of the entire neocortex and of each cortical layer increases with age.
2. The number of nerve cells per study unit decreases with age because
3. the size of nerve cells increases.
4. There is a progressive change in the condition of the chromophil substance of the nerve cells, from small granules (immature state) to clumping of granules to Nissl bodies (mature state).
5. Nerve fibrils emerge within neurons (from random granules to rows of granules to solid strands to nerve fibrils), and increase in number with age.

TABLE 3 Relative Growth Rates of Neocortical Lobes[a]

Age period	Parietal lobe		Occipital lobe		Temporal lobe		Frontal lobe	
	Surface area	Fissuration	Surface area	Fissuration	Surface area	Fissuration	Surface area	Fissuration
0–2 yrs.	Most rapid	Rapid	Same as overall pattern (see text)	Same as parietal lobe	Moderate	Rapid in auditory portion	Rapid	Moderate
2–6 yrs.	Same as overall pattern (see text)	Moderate	None →	→	Very rapid	Rapid in temporal pole	Moderate, even until near-max. at 10 (total at 20)	Rapid
6 and after	Practically none; total at 24.	Moderate to submax. at 10	None	→	None	None		Moderate to submax. at 10

[a]Based on Turner (1948, 1950).

6. The caliber, length, and compactness of nerve processes (axons and dendrites) increase with age.
7. Pedunculated bulbs on the dendrites increase in each cell and show up on more cells with increasing age.
8. Both the quantity and size of exogenous fibers increase with age.
9. Myelination of nerve cells and nerve processes spreads with age.

Wide individual differences obtained on all these criteria at all ages studied; possible sex differences were not taken into account.

On the basis of the various criteria just listed, Conel's data show that the cells of the human cerebral cortex manifest these simultaneous or overlapping growth gradients:

(A) *Topologically or horizontally*
1. Beginning first and proceeding fastest: the primary motor and primary sensory areas; the central-fissure area develops earliest and fastest of all.
2. Beginning second and proceeding at a slower pace than the first gradient: areas directly adjacent to the primary areas that have a primary-area-modifying function (termed secondary areas); and a few old-cortex areas.
3. Beginning third and proceeding at a slower pace than the first two gradients: secondary areas in the frontal lobe and old cortex; and the posterior, T-O-P, association area. (The outer edges of it, i.e., the areas closest to the sensory-receptive areas, become functional first and the innermost area last.)
4. Beginning last, the prefrontal association area, which lags well behind the posterior association area in onset and in pace of maturation.

(B) *Vertically*
5. Growth proceeds from the inner or bottom neocortical layers up to the outer or upper layers; Layer 1, the top layer, is the possible single exception to this trend.

Conel's data on the postnatal development of the old cortex are puzzling in light of embryological and phylogenetic growth patterns: they show that the cells of the hippocampus and the limbic lobe lag behind those of the primary sensorimotor, central-fissure area. Nor is it possible to know from Conel's data alone (with the possible exception of Trend 9) the exact maturation point at which conduction in a particular cell or area or layer actually begins. Conel himself had recourse in his first few volumes to data of developmental psychologists such as Carmichael, McGraw, and Gesell to deduce functional status. Nor is anything known of the experiences, or of the behavior status at time of death, of any of the children whose brains were studied. Also, the possibility that consistent sex differences exist in development, which the behavioral and EEG data clearly indicate, was not checked until Volume 8, at which point Conel (1939–1967 [1967]) maintains none exists. Lansdell (1964) reanalyzed Conel's basic data on the four-year cortex (Conel, 1939–1967, Vol. 7 [1963]) and found that in the hand subarea of the primary motor area, there was more myelin in the left hemisphere than in the right in the female cortices (four out of five), with the reverse situation obtaining in the male cortices (two out of three). He also found that the number of exogenous fibers in Layer 1 of both the primary motor and primary sensory areas was greater in the right hemisphere in all the female brains (four) for which Conel provided data, but was greater in the left one for two of the three male brains reported on. Lansdell also refers to Matsubara's finding of a sex difference in cerebral venous drainage: The right "vein of Troland" is larger than the left one among girls but not among boys.

3. EEG STUDIES OF CHANGES IN NEOCORTICAL ELECTRICAL ACTIVITY WITH AGE

EEG studies reveal that at least nine parameters of the EEG record show developmental changes; both these parameters and the overall developmental trend of each one is summarized in Table 4. Girls' EEG records are more mature than boys' at every age studied. Also, wide ranges of individual variation in rate and pattern on every EEG index are typical. Clinical use of the EEG shows that whether a particular EEG pattern is to be considered normal or abnormal is frequently a function of the patient's age. That is, persistence of patterns typical of—and normal for—the young child into adolescence and adulthood is almost invariably associated with at least some categories of behavior disorder, especially of "acting out" and psychopathic categories. In light of such findings, a question deserving investigation is: Which parameters of the EEG record are entirely (or almost entirely) maturational and which are materially affected by the individual's life experiences?

4. ADDITIONAL SOURCES OF INFORMATION

As a further preamble to an analysis of the more delimited issue of the postnatal neurogenic bases of speech and language, two additional informational resources are being included. The first consists of the sequential reproduction of five tables that summarize various neural-developmental indices from one month to neural maturity, age-organized as follows: one to three months, three to twelve months, one to two years, two to six years, seven years to the thirties.

The second additional resource is one of the outcomes of the writer's extensive neural-behavioral inquiry: a table summarizing the postulated successive neural organizations underlying particular stages of human development.

TABLE 4 Postnatal Developmental Trends in the EEG

EEG parameter	Overall trend
Continuity and stability—regularity	1. The young infant's EEG is labile and diffuse in patterning, with periods of total lack of activity. Continuity of activity and stability—regularity of activity and of overall patterning steadily increase up to neurological maturity. Also, a child's EEG is more affected by overbreathing than an adult's.
Frequency; proportion of each type of frequency; voltage or amplitude	2. Frequency tends to increase with age, while 3. Amplitude tends to decrease. Delta activity (up to 1½–3 Hz) is the most typical wave band up to one year; theta (4–7 Hz) is the dominant activity from two to five years, theta and alpha (8–13 Hz) are about equally frequent at five to six years, and alpha is increasingly the most common frequency after six years. Beta waves (14 Hz and higher) increase variably with age; fast records become increasingly common between 15 and 60 years.
State of consciousness differentiation; patterns characteristic of the various stages of sleep	4. Initially, the EEG record shows no difference between waking and sleeping; by maturity, it shows consistent differences not only between sleeping and waking but between seven stages of sleep: drowsiness, very light sleep, light sleep, moderately deep sleep, deep sleep, early-morning sleep, arousal. Most of the activity in the waking record comes from lower-than-vertex and posterior areas; during sleep, most activity is at the vertex and from the frontal areas.[a] 5. The electrical activity associated with the various stages of sleep shows characteristic developmental-level patterns.
Transition from a deep-sleep re-record upon arousal.	6. In children, there is an intermediate phase, electrically, between the sleeping and the aroused-waking record. Beyond the midteens, arousal is usually abrupt, without this intermediate phase.
Asynchrony vs. synchrony	7. Asynchrony of the wave forms from analogous areas is typical of the infant's record. Synchrony increases steadily during the first several years.
Asymmetry vs. symmetry.	8. Asymmetry—activity in only one hemisphere—is frequent during infancy and early childhood. With increasing age, matched activity from corresponding areas in both hemispheres becomes typical.
Area differentiation or degree of organization.	9. Electrical activity is originally diffusely and unpredictably distributed over the neocortex. With age, activity becomes increasingly organized and delimited according to cortical areas, and there is also a developmental progression in intra-area activity and in acquisition of mature patterning: The parietal area shows regular activity first, the primary-motor and occipital lobe (visual) areas are next, with the occipital areas shortly overtaking the parietal lobe in proportion and regularity of activity. The activity of the prefrontal region differentiates last and takes the longest to attain a fully adult pattern. In general, electrical activity becomes more monomorphic, localized, systematized and structured, with definite irreversibility: Once a more mature pattern is acquired, it will not regress to the previous stage, unless disease occurs.[b]

[a]Pond (1963).
[b]Monnier (1957).

TABLE 5 Neural Developmental Indices: One to Three Months

A. Myelination of Neuraxis at Two Months[a]

   1. Pyramidal-tract fibers are myelinated down through the medulla oblongata and lightly down through the upper and middle cord; there is practically no myelin in the caudal portions of the spinal cord.

   2. The myelination pattern of the rubrospinal tract is much the same as above.

   3. Spinocerebellar fibers are heavily myelinated.

   4. Myelination of the cerebellar hemispheres has advanced markedly.

   5. The tract from the cerebellar peduncles to the ruber nucleus (in midbrain) is heavily myelinated; the upper continuation of this tract is myelinated to the ventral nucleus of the thalamus.

   6. The olivocerebellar tract shows myelin for the first time.

   7. The tract from the globus pallidus (a basal ganglion) to the ruber nucleus is myelinated.

   8. The thalamo-olivary (pons) tract shows myelin for the first time.

   9. Tectobulbar and tectospinal fibers from the subthalamic region are beginning to show myelin.

  10. Optic nerves, chiasma, and tracts (Cranial II) are almost completely myelinated (now more advanced than the acoustic nerve, even though the latter began to show myelin in the sixth fetal month).

  11. There is no myelin in the fornix and only a little around the mammillary bodies of the hypothalamus and on the mammillothalamic tract.

  12. These thalamic nuclei show myelin: ventral centrum medianum, semilunaris, the geniculates. The anterior, medial-lateral, and pulvinar nuclei still do not.

  13. Fibers from the geniculate nuclei of the thalamus show myelin up into the internal capsule of the cerebral medulla, as do projection fibers from the ventral nucleus. There is much myelin on the sensory section of the posterior limb of the internal capsule (auditory, optic, and somesthetic fibers); there is less myelin on the motor section.

  14. Olfactory (?) tracts show first signs of myelin. The hippocampus has scattered and lightly myelinated fibers, as do the olfactory tracts in the septum pellicidum and surface of the corpus callosum. The stria medullaris and stria semicircularis are fairly well myelinated.

  15. Temporo-pontine fibers are lightly myelinated, fronto-pontine fibers not at all.

  16. Few fibers of any type to the frontal lobe anterior to the primary motor areas are myelinated.

B. Neocortical Cellular Changes Between One and Three Months[b]

   1. Layer pattern

     a. In order of degree of growth since one month: Layers 1, 6, 3, 2, 5, 4.

     b. Functioning cells are almost all in Layers 6 and 5; there are also a few in Layer 4 and in the lower section of Layer 3. At 3 months, the cells in the upper sections of Layer 3 and in Layers 2 and 1 are too poorly developed to be functioning.

     c. The axon-mesh is dense in Layer 4 in most sections of the old cortex.

TABLE 5 (Continued)

2. Area pattern
   a. In order of the extent of growth since one month: primary motor area (upper trunk and arm subareas have advanced most), primary somesthetic area (trunk, arm, and hand subareas have advanced most), primary visual, primary auditory.
   b. Myelin has increased rapidly in the nonauditory parts of the temporal lobe and in the part of the frontal lobe directly anterior to the primary motor area, with wide individual differences in the degree of increase. Myelin has increased since one month in the old cortex.
3. Fiber pattern
   a. The greatest increase in horizontal exogenous fibers and in subcortical association fibers is in Layer 6.
   b. There are more vertical exogenous fibers in the limbic lobe than in the hippocampus.

C. Electrical Activity From One to Three Months
   1. Low-voltage arrhythmic activity is characteristic of this period, with slightly higher amplitude and slower dominant frequency in the posterior regions. Prior to 3 months in the occipital region there are only slow and irregular potential changes; rhythmic activity is present here only in the 3–4 Hz range. As the infant goes to sleep, there is a dampening of activity, along with overall slowing and increase in amplitude. At 3 months, for the first time, photic stimulation produces a clear arousal. At 3 months, waves of 4–5 Hz (theta) are present in all areas[d].
   2. After one month, steady high-voltage slow waves (2–4 Hz) appear during drowsiness (up to 6 months). After the second month, bursts of 14-Hz activity in central areas in both hemispheres are typical during light sleep. Also, after 2 months, in half of the records examined, high-voltage slow waves appear continuously during arousal. At 3 months, waves of 4–5 cps (theta) are present in all areas [d].
   3. From 1 to 3 months, the sleep delta from the posterior areas becomes continuous. A diffuse pattern of activity appears on top of the earlier waking pattern. There is also a slowing of frequency and an increase in regularity of rhythm and in amplitude. At 3 months, a "second important stage in the maturation of the waking EEG" emerges: a definite topographic organization appears for the first time, along with occipital predominance. Preciseness of activity is shown by blockage of the occipital rhythms by all sensory and psychic stimulation. Diffuse waking activity increases proportionately. Synchronous and asynchronous spindles of 12–13 Hz emerge in the primary sensorimotor region. The earlier brief lack of activity periods drops out permanently.[e]

---

[a] Langworthy (1933).
[b] Conel (1939–1967 [1947]).
[c] Pond (1963).
[d] Gibbs and Gibbs (1950).
[e] Dreyfus-Brisac et al., 1958.

TABLE 6 Neural Developmental Indices: Three to Twelve Months

A. Gross Structural[a]
   1. Increase in surface area of the neocortex between birth and 2 years; the parietal lobe increases most.
   2. Rapid increase in the fissuration of the parietal and occipital lobes until 2 years, also of the auditory sections of the temporal lobe. Frontal lobe fissuration increases moderately.
   3. The corticospinal (pyramidal) motor tract is rapidly myelinated during the latter part of the first year and the early part of the second year.[b]

B. Neocortical Changes between Three and Six Months[c]
   1. Layer pattern
      a. Bottom part of Layer 3 has advanced throughout the cortex, especially in the growth of neurofibrils and of large pyramidal cells. The chromophil substance in Layer 3 in the frontal lobe is more advanced than in any other layer in that lobe.
      b. Nerve processes continue to be densest in Layer 4.
      c. Layers 6 and 5 have increased most in width in the hippocampal areas.
   2. Area pattern
      a. In the primary motor area, the subarea of the hand is now as developed as the trunk and arm subareas.
      b. Limbic areas are about as developed as secondary frontal lobe areas.
      c. Myelination had advanced in all hippocampal areas.
      d. Secondary areas in all lobes have continued to advance.
   3. Fiber pattern
      a. Subcortical association fibers are most numerous in areas where development has been most active: primary motor, primary somesthetic, primary visual, primary auditory.
      b. There are practically no myelinated fibers above the bottom section of Layer 3 at 6 months.

C. Electrical Activity from Three to Twelve Months
   1. Delta is the dominant rhythm up to one year; is usually diffuse and asymmetrical.[d]
   2. At 3 months, occipital wave frequency ranges from 3.3 to 7 Hz, with a mean amplitude of 37 microvolts.[e] These waves are highly variable until 5 months.[f] By 6 months, activity in the occipital area is the most developed of all other cortical areas.[g]
   3. Slow, high-voltage waves of drowsiness are between 2 and 4 Hz from 3 to 6 months.[g]
   4. At 5 months, occipital electrical activity acquires a rhythmic, sinusoidal character much like the adult alpha rhythm in its purity and stability, although its frequency is 4–6 Hz (theta) at this stage.[h]
   5. There is a rapid rise in occipital frequency, from 3 to 4 Hz at the end of 3 months to 7 Hz at 15 months. There is much overlap in wave frequency from the sensorimotor and occipital areas.[f] At 6 months, the occipital rhythm ranges from

TABLE 6 (Continued)

4.0 to 4.8 Hz, with a mean amplitude of 42 mV (millivolts); at 12 months, it ranges from 5.5 to 7.0 Hz.[e]

6. At 6 months, the diffuse waking activity noted at 3 months continues to increase in proportion, and a hypersynchrony emerges and gradually increases up to at least 3 years. At 7 to 8 months, going-to-sleep becomes characterized by a slow, diffuse hypersynchrony of 3–4 Hz, usually a bit slower in the occipital regions, attaining an amplitude of 100–150 mV. Between 8 months and 2 years, this activity has an occasional paroxysmal character. At 9 months, the continuous sleep delta drops out and diphasic spikes emerge in the primary motor area.[h]

7. Between 6 and 12 months, biparietal "humps" appear during very light sleep—high-voltage, spike-like waves, usually diphasic, and with a duration of 1/3 to 1/8 of a second; they are of highest voltage in the parietal areas. They are also associated with lower-voltage disturbances in the frontal and occipital areas and with waves that appear independently in the left and the right temporal areas. About 20 percent of children between 6 months and 6 years have bursts of low-amplitude fast activity (20–30 Hz) interspersed between these biparietal humps.[g]

8. Asynchrony and asymmetry are normal until 6 months during wakeful periods; by one year, these become abnormal characteristics. Drowsiness is accompanied by general slowing, plus increase in voltage, most marked in the parietal leads. The difference between drowsiness and light sleep is not clear until after 6 months. Sleep spindles show up toward the latter part of the age period: 13–15 Hz, clearest in the parietal leads, least clear in the frontal areas. The basic pattern is: irregular 3–6 Hz waves with superimposed low-voltage fast activity. Some children show 18–22 Hz activity while awake and at all times except during deep sleep. Deep sleep is accompanied by further slowing and irregular high waves without humps and spindles. An arousal pattern becomes differentiated between 4 and 12 months: paraxysmal, synchronous slowing, with high-voltage, sinusoidal 2–4 Hz waves appearing in all leads. Some persisting occipital slowing is frequent after arousal.[i]

9. There is a steady increase from birth to 2 years in the voltages in the theta band; they decline thereafter.[g]

10. The A-wave of the electroretinogram shows up at 12 months, for the first time; this represents achievement of the adult ERG pattern.[j]

D. Neocortical Changes between Six and Fifteen Months[k]
   1. Layer pattern
      a. Layers *2, 6, 1, 3, 4, 5* have all grown, in order of the number of areas that have increased in width since 6 months.
      b. Myelination of exogenous fibers is very scant above the bottom section of Layer 3.
      c. The cells of Layers 4 and 2 have increased in size in all neocortical areas. In the hippocampus, only pyramidal cells in Layers 6 and 3 have incrased in size. In all frontal lobe areas, the greatest development has been in the pyramidal cells in Layer 3. In most of the cortex, cell development in the upper parts of Layer 3 has almost caught up with that of the lower part.

Continued

TABLE 6 (Continued)

   2. Area pattern
- a. The large cells in Layers 3 and 5 are especially large in the motor eye field and in Broca's area for coordinated speech (both in the frontal lobe). The anterior portions of the frontal lobe are still minimally developed.
- b. The order of degree of development of subareas in both the primary motor and primary somesthetic areas is: hand, upper extremity, head, lower extremity. The primary auditory area continues to be less advanced than the primary visual area.
- c. Limbic areas are more advanced in growth; are now in about the same state as secondary areas in the frontal lobe forward of the basic motor areas. Hippocampal areas have also advanced.
- d. Growth in the primary, "leading" areas in each lobe seems to slow down between 6 and 15 months, while development in the secondary areas increases in rate, so that although the primary areas are still ahead of the other areas, the gap between the primary and the secondary areas is not as great at 15 months as it was at 6 months.

   3. Fiber pattern
- a. Exogenous fibers make no direct contact with the dendrites and axons of cortical neurons; there are no branches on any of these fibers.
- b. Many nerve processes originating in Layers 6 and 5 extend tangentially into Layer 1; the tangential fibers in Layer 1 are as developed as the horizontal fibers in Layer 5a.
- c. The mesh formed by axons on Golgi type-II cells is present in all layers in all areas of the cortex; it is thickest in the primary afferent areas and thinnest in the primary motor areas.
- d. Dendrites and axons of all neurons in all parts of the cortex have increased in size, length and compactness.
- e. Horizontal exogenous fibers are still little developed in Layer 2. Subcortical association fibers are more numerous than horizontal fibers in Layer 6 in all areas.
- f. Very few vertical exogenous fibers go higher than Layer 4 (which occurs only in the primary visual area) at 15 months; they are more numerous than subcortical association fibers in all neocortical areas.
- g. Fiber myelination lags behind cortical fiber formation.

E. The cerebellum, the major subcortical motor center, attains 80% of its adult weight by 2 years.[l]

---

[a]Turner (1948, 1950).
[b]Patten (1953).
[c]Conel (1939–1967 [1951]).
[d]Pond (1963).
[e]Lindsley (1939).
[f]Smith (1938).

[g]Gibbs and Gibbs (1950).
[h]Dreyfus-Brisac et al. (1958).
[i]Fois (1961).
[j]Zubek and Solberg (1954).
[k]Conel (1939–1967 [1954]).
[l]Himwich and Himwich (1957).

TABLE 7 Neural Developmental Indices: One to Two Years

A. Cortical Changes between Fifteen and Twenty-four Months[a]

   1. The frontal lobe grows more between 15 and 24 months than any other section of the cortex, especially in its middle and anterior sections. But the PF association area is still little developed. The difference in degree of development between the primary motor area and the rest of the frontal lobe is not as great at 24 as at 15 months. The area directly in front of the primary motor area now seems to be exerting control over it. Myelinated vertical exogenous fibers have increased in only two frontal areas: the subarea of the head in the primary motor area and Broca's speech center. What little development has gone on in the prefontal section has occurred mostly in Layer 3.

   2. Layer pattern

     a. Order of increase in layer width since 15 months is 6, 4, 5, 1 and 3, 2.

     b. The axon mesh is densest in Layers 4 and 3c; it has more elaborate branching than at 15 months. (At 24 months, this mesh is thickest in the primary afferent areas and thinnest in the frontal lobe.)

     c. Layer 1's tangential fibers are more developed in its outer than in its inner half.

     d. There are still very few horizontal exogenous fibers in Layers 3 and 2. Layer 6 has more, and more developed, subcortical association fibers than horizontal exogenous fibers.

   3. Area pattern

     a. The primary somesthetic and primary motor areas are equally developed on most growth criteria.

     b. Secondary areas in the parietal, occipital, and temporal lobes have all developed since 15 months; the primary auditory area is still not as developed as the primary visual.

     c. Limbic areas have advanced in all growth criteria; their status is like midfrontal secondary areas. Hippocampal areas have also advanced in growth; the large pyramidal cells in their deepest layer are as advanced as in Layer 6 of the neocortex. There is some evidence of handedness at 24 months: The hemisphere of the preferred hand is slightly more developed than the other.

   4. Fiber pattern

     a. The vertical exogenous fibers (v-e-fs) are the earliest cortical fibers to develop, then the subcortical association fibers (s-a-fs), then the tangential fibers in Layer 1, then the horizontal exogenous fibers (h-e-fs). The ascending v-e-fs lie at right angles to the s-a-fs and h-e-fs in all areas of the cortex. In the earliest stages of development, these v-e-fs end in Layers 6 and 5, and in later stages in Layers 4 and 3c. (Conel speculates that the v-e-fs are afferent and efferent fibers connecting the cortex with subcortical neurons, while the other three types of fibers are all intracortical.)

     b. In the subareas for the head and the lower extremity of the primary motor area, the tangential, horizontal, and s-a fibers are equally numerous, but v-e-fs are less numerous in the lower-extremity subarea. More v-e-fs end, and go higher up, in

Continued

TABLE 7 (Continued)

the primary somesthetic area than in any other cortical area. Myelinated v-e-fs go higher in the temporal lobe than at 15 months, but none goes higher than Layer 3b. The v-e, h-e, and s-a fibers are all larger in the primary somesthetic area than in the primary motor area at 24 months. Myelinated tangential fibers in Layer 1 are more numerous in the primary somesthetic area than in any other parietal lobe area.

c. There are more, and more heavily myelinated, fibers of all types in the old cortex than at 15 months. V-e-fs end higher and have more myelin in the gyrus cinguli than they did at 15 months.

B. Electrical Activity from One to Two Years

1. At 12 months, occipital frequencies range from 5.5 to 7.0 Hz, with mean amplitude of 52 mV; such high-voltage slow waves are common at one year.[d]

2. At 15 months, occipital frequency goes up to 7 Hz. The rate of increase slows down beginning about 15 months.[b]

3. The steady high-voltage slow waves during drowsiness, which showed up after one month, still appear in the majority of one year old subjects, and are 4–6 Hz (theta) at one year. They have a very high voltage and occupy long stretches of drowsy-state records. During the second year they break up into short runs or paroxysmal discharges, looking much like the high-voltage waves of petit-mal epilepsy.[c]

4. Sleep spindles of 12–15 Hz are synchronous and are more marked in the parietal leads, but are also seen in occipital and frontal areas.[c]

5. There is a steady increase from birth to two years in the voltages in the 4–6 Hz (theta) band; they decline thereafter. At 2 years, a hump develops in the 9-Hz range.[c]

6. At 2 years, the occipital frequency ranges from 5.0 to 9.6 Hz, with a mean amplitude of 49 mV.[d]

7. At 2 years, the hypersynchrony, diphasic-spike pattern, sensorimotor area spindles, and diffuse electrical activity cited at the previous age period all reach the highest proportions of the period studied (fifth fetal month through 2 years). From 5 to 18 months, there is very little change in the EEG.[e]

8. Up to 2 to 3 years, theta frequencies are augmented by emotional episodes (crying, laughing, hunger) and by closing the eyes. The occipital alpha is rarely responsive to visual stimuli before 3 years (but is frequently so after 3 years).[f]

9. The electrical discharge of the infant's and young child's brain is ten times as great as that of the adult brain.[d]

---

[a]Conel (1939–1967 [1959]).
[b]Smith (1938).
[c]Gibbs and Gibbs (1950).
[d]Lindsley (1939).
[e]Dreyfus-Brisac et al. (1958).
[f]Pond (1963).

TABLE 8 Neural Developmental Indices: Two to Six Years

A. Gross Structural Changes
 1. The increase in the surface area of the parietal and occipital lobes continues at a rapid pace up to 6 years, while their fissuration continues at a moderate pace between 2 and 6 years. The rate of increase in the surface area of the temporal lobe is at its most rapid between 2 and 6 years. The temporal pole fissurates rapidly between 2 and 5 years and then stops. The increase in the surface area of the frontal lobe continues at a moderate and even rate from 2 to 10 years. Its rate of fissuration is most rapid between 2 and 6 years.[a]
 2. The brain is 80% of its adult weight at 4 years and 90% at 6 years.[b]
 3. Myelination of the pyramidal tract (voluntary motor) is well advanced during this period.[c]
B. Cortical Changes between Two and Four Years[d]
 1. Layer pattern
    a. Layer 3 has increased most in width in the frontal and limbic lobes. Layer 6 has increased most in width in the temporal lobe (while Layers 3 and 2 have increased least).
    b. The cells in Layer 3c have increased most in size in all parts of the new and old cortex; those in Layers 3b and 3a have also increased a good deal in most sections.
    c. The nerve cells and fibers in Layers 6 and 5 in the primary motor area are equally developed in the head and lower-extremity subareas, but those in Layers 4, 3, and 2 are more advanced in development in the head subarea than in the lower-extremity subarea. All layers are equally advanced in the other subareas of hand and upper extremity, which are more advanced than are the head and lower extremity.
 2. Area pattern
    a. In the frontal lobe, the primary motor area continues to be most advanced in development on all criteria, and the gradient of development decreases from the back to the front of the lobe on all criteria; the PF area is still little developed.
    b. The primary sensory areas in the parietal, occipital, and temporal lobes continue to be the most developed areas in each lobe, with the secondary areas in each lobe decreasing in development in proportion to their distance from the primary reception area.
    c. Cell processes have increased appreciably in all areas except the insula and the gyrus cinguli.
 3. Fiber pattern
    a. No vertical exogenous fibers end higher than Layer 3b except in the primary motor and primary somesthetic area, where a few end in Layer 3a and a very few end in Layers 2 and 1. They are larger in all sections of the frontal lobe except in the subarea for the lower extremity in the primary motor area.
    b. The horizontal exogenous fibers have increased most in Layers 4, 3c, and 3b in the frontal lobe and are most numerous in the subarea for the lower extremity in the primary motor area. They have also increased in primary and secondary areas in the other lobes.
    c. All types of fibers have advanced in development in most of the old-cortex areas.
    d. All myelinated fibers have more myelin at 4 years than they did at 24 months.

Continued

83

TABLE 8 (Continued)

Except for the PF section of the frontal lobe, there are more myelinated fibers in every layer in every area of the cortex; in the frontal pole and anterior part of the three frontal gyri, there are no myelinated fibers in Layers 3a and 2. (There were wide individual differences in the amount of myelin in each area and on the other criteria of development, in all brains studied.)

    e. From birth onward, the order of development of nerve cells and fibers in the cortex is (1) v-e-fs in the cores of the gyri; (2) the s-a-fs; (3) the neurons and h-e and v-e fibers in Layers 6 and 5, and tangential fibers in Layer 1 (which originate in Layer 5); (4) neurons and exogenous fibers in Layers 4, 3c, 3b, and 3a, respectively; (5) neurons in Layers 2 and 1, and exogenous fibers in Layer 2 (after 4 years). The tangential fibers appear to originate in the cingulum, which extends the entire length of the corpus callosum.

  4. No area and no layer has reached full maturity on the nine growth criteria at 4 years.

C. Cortical Changes between Four and Six Years[e]

  1. Layer pattern

    a. Substantial increase in width has occurred only in Layers 6, 4, 3, and 2 in the frontal lobe, and only in seven of its 16 areas; however, the layer width at age 6 in all areas is as yet less than in the adult brain.

    b. Gradient of layer development throughout the cortex since 4 years is, from most to least: 6, 5, 4, 3c, 3b, 3a, 2. There are only a few neurons in Layer 1 and these are in about the same state of development as those in Layer 2.

    c. In the frontal lobe, layer development decreases in an anterior gradient; all other lobes continue the same gradients as earlier established; there has been some increase in development in each area since 4 years.

  2. Area pattern

    a. The primary motor and sensory areas in each lobe continue to be, to paraphrase Conel (1939–1967, Vol. 8 [1967]), more advanced in development than any other areas in their respective lobes, and there is a gradual decrease in the degree of development in all areas as the cortex proceeds away from each of these areas.

    b. In the frontal lobe, the middle frontal gyrus is more advanced than the inferior gyrus, and the latter is more advanced than the superior gyrus.

    c. In the primary motor area, the lower extremity subarea is more advanced than the head subarea, while in the primary sensory area, the order of development is: upper extremity including hand, head, lower extremity.

    d. No significant differences in the two hemispheres in Broca's speech area were detected at 6 years.

    e. The anterior and posterior transverse temporal gyri (area TC) are larger and longer at 6 than at 4 years.

    f. The size of the neurons in the parietal lobe has grown much more in Layer 3c than in 3b and 3a since 4 years.

    g. Layer 3 is less developed in the gyrus cinguli than in all four cortical lobes (with the single exception of the prefrontal section).

  3. Fiber pattern

    a. From birth onward, tangential exogenous fibers (that apparently originate in the old olfactory area) are in the same state of development in Layer 1 as they are in Layers 6 and 5; still the case at 6 years.

    b. H-e and s-a fibers show a growth gradient from Layer 6 to Layer 2; they have grown since 4 years.

TABLE 8 (Continued)

    c. At 6 years most v-e-fs end in Layer 4 in the most advanced areas; a few end in 3c and a very few in 3b; Layer 3 seems to be their terminal layer. More myelinated vertical fibers end in Layers 4 and 3 than at 4 years.

    d. Myelinated fibers of all three types are more numerous, larger, and darkly stained than at 4 years. But not all eventually myelinated fibers are myelinated at 6 years.

D. Electrical Activity from Two to Six Years

    1. After 2 years, the frequency continues to rise, while the amplitude begins to decrease. From 5 months to 3 years, the amplitude decreases from 75–110 mV to about 50 mV; it continues to decrease thereafter to adulthood. Most of the decrease occurs between 2 and 3 years; see Lindsley's data, in Item 4 below.[f]

    2. From 15 months, there is a tapering off in the rate of increase in the occipital frequency, to a preadolescent maximum of 9 Hz at 8 years.[g]

    3. The delta rhythm declines steadily between 1 and 6 years; after 6 years it appears normally only in sleep records. Theta is the dominant rhythm from 2 to 5 years; theta and alpha are about equal at 5 to 6 years. Theta waves are more pronounced in the dominant hemisphere; are diffusely distributed up to about 5 years, and are more delimited to the temporal lobe among older children; are polyrhythmic in younger children and monorhythmic (4–6 Hz) in later childhood.[h]

    4. Frequency and amplitude pattern of occipital rhythms from 2 to 6 years is summarized in the following table.[i]

Age, years	Frequency range, Hz	Mean amplitude, mV
2	5.0– 9.6	49
3	4.3– 8.5	51
4	6.0– 9.2	27
5	7.3– 9.4	31
6	7.3–10.3	27

    5. a. Two years: 14-Hz spindles disappear during moderately deep sleep; deep sleep is now marked by irregular slow waves of 1½–3 Hz, with intermittent 4–8 Hz waves mixed in.

       b. Three years: biparietal humps, which showed up during light sleep between 6 and 12 months are still very evident from 3 to 9 years. 10–40% of all Ss over 3 years have 10 Hz spindles diffusely distributed during moderately deep sleep.

       c. Four years: a steady 7–8 Hz occipital frequency is typical by the fourth year. After 4, 12-Hz spindles occur during light sleep, usually in only one hemisphere, and have their highest voltages in the frontal areas.

       d. Five years: 25% of 5-year-olds record like normal 10-year-olds. From 5 to 6 years, high-voltage 4–8 Hz waves appear continuously in the parietal areas during arousal.[j]

[a]Turner (1948, 1950).
[b]Himwich and Himwich (1957).
[c]Langworthy (1933).
[d]Conel (1939–1967 [1963]).
[e]Conel (1939–1967 [1967]).

[f]Dreyfus-Brisac *et al.* (1958).
[g]Smith (1938).
[h]Pond (1963).
[i]Lindsley (1939).
[j]Gibbs and Gibbs (1950).

TABLE 9 Neural Developmental Indices: Six Years to the Thirties

A. Gross Structural Changes

1. Although the increase in the surface area of the parietal and occipital lobes stops at 6 years, fissuration continues at a moderate pace to a submaximum at 10 years. The increase in the surface area of the frontal lobe continues at a moderate pace to its near-maximum at 10 years; the fissuration pattern is similar.[a]
2. The cerebellum achieves its full adult weight at 13 years, but the entire brain does not achieve its full weight and volume until "during the third decade".[b]
3. Between 6 years and mid-adolescence, the dark pigment of the substantia nigra (in the upper midbrain), which is associated with finely controlled movement, develops rapidly.[c]

B. Electrical Activity

1. From 6 to 10 years, theta rhythm declines in proportion; The EEG record vacillates between theta and alpha rhthms. The adult pattern of alpha dominance emerges clearly at about 10 years, although it begins to emerge after 6 years, and is stabilized at about 12 years. Alpha rhythms are more prominent on the right side from 6 to 8 years and from 10 years on; at 9 years, they are nearly symmetrical in distribution.[d]
2. After the sixth year, the low-amplitude fast activity found in 20% of the 6 to 12 months records disappears; it is not present in normal adults. [e]
3. Occipital-alpha range and amplitude from 6 to 16 years:[f]

Age, years	Range, Hz	Mean amplitude, mV
6	7.3–10.3	27
8	7.3–10.3	21
10	8.0–11.6	19
12	8.0–12.0	20
14	8.7–12.2	18
16	9.0–11.0	13

4. Individual and sex differences from 5 to 17 years:[g]
   a. There is considerable individual variability in the age when the occipital alpha becomes stabilized at the adult level.
   b. Individuality of pattern is consistent: a child with initially fast alpha tends to remain on the fast side as he (she) grows older; similarly for a child with an initially slow alpha.
   c. Girls showed faster mean alpha frequencies than boys throughout the period studied; also a low voltage, fast type record is more common among girls; both are characteristics of maturity.
   d. Girls have significantly faster delta activity from the occipital area at 8 years, faster delta activity from the central areas at 10 years, more delta activity from the motor area at 10 years.
5. Development patterns between 8 and 15 years for three brothers:[h]
   a. The alpha rhythm becomes more monorhythmic and monomorphic; it becomes more localized in the occipital region and better organized into harmonious spindles.
   b. In the temporal area, percent-time delta decreases, and the theta frequency band becomes narrower and decreases in voltage. From 12 to 15 years, theta disappears altogether during the resting state, emerging thereafter only during emotional states. Thus, "the activity of the temporal region also becomes less polyrhythmic and polymorphic."
   c. In general, electrical activity become more monomorphic, localized, systematized, and structured—i.e., shows growing equilibrium, with definite irreversibility: Once a more mature pattern is acquired, it will not regress to the previous stage, unless disease occurs.
6. Area patterns:[e]
   a. During the ninth year, the record from the occipital area is very much like that

TABLE 9 (Continued)

of an adult, but there is more slow and 7–9 Hz activity in the parietal and frontal areas than is common among adults.

    b. In the tenth year, 9- and 10-Hz activity reaches its maximum.

    c. From 10 to 19 years, 12-Hz spindles during light sleep are most evident.

    d. Years 12 to 17 are characterized by the commonness of short runs of 5–7 Hz waves during drowsiness in the frontal and parietal areas.

7. From 14 to 30 years:[e]

    a. All types of adult records are obtained, but many exhibit childish characteristics.

    b. The low-voltage fast activity in the occipital areas found in 20% of adult records hardly ever occurs before age 14; slow activity in the form of a shifting baseline diminishes after 14 years.

    c. The adult arousal response consists of a quick return of the normal waking pattern without transition through a stage of high-voltage fast activity, typical of children.

    d. Paroxysmal slow waves, first seen during the second year, are rare after 15 years.

    e. 5–7 Hz (theta) waves in the frontal area are a normal EEG feature from 15 to 20 years; the frequency is faster thereafter.

    f. The highest voltage of the 14-Hz light-sleep spindles is reached between 15 and 20 years; they are entirely absent in 20% of adults over 60 years.

    g. Except for the prefrontal section, most persons have normal adult records after 19 years.

    h. The voltage of frequencies from 1–3 Hz (delta) declines up to at least 29 years; frequencies between 11 and 19 Hz increase gradually until at least 29.

    i. Biparietal humps during light sleep are typical of 20 to 50 year records.

    j. Between 15 and 60 years, fast records are increasingly common, while slow records become increasingly atypical; after 60 years, more slow records emerge.

8. From the thirties on:[e]

    a. The adult drowsiness pattern (flattening and some slowing) is found in almost all subjects during their thirties and forties; this pattern does not become common until the tenth year. Positive spike-like patterns are also common during light sleep during the thirties and forties.

    b. Isolated 6–8 Hz waves appear in the temporal lobes after 40 years, and in other areas such slowing appears after 60 years. [Are the temporal areas more vulnerable to aging?—EM]

    c. During the fifties and sixties, large slow delta (1½–3 Hz) waves in both frontal areas during drowsiness become common.

9. A fully adult pattern from all parts of the brain including the PF area emerges between 25 and 35 years.[i]

10. EEG patterns associated with various psychological disorders from 5 to 55 years:[j]

    a. Aggressive, paroxysmal rage pattern or a low frustration threshold is related to focal theta activity in the temporal region; psychomotor seizures show the same relationship. The percentage of abnormal records among the behavior-problem sample was at its highest point between 5 and 12 years.

    b. Schizophrenics showed a high percentage of fast activity in the frontal poles. The percentage of abnormal records among the schizophrenic sample was at its highest point between 5 and 11 years.

    c. The psychopaths exhibited a significant relationship between high alpha index and theta activity.

[a]Turner (1948, 1950).
[b]Himwich and Himwich (1957).
[c]Patten (1953).
[d]Pond (1963).
[e]Gibbs and Gibbs (1950).
[f]Lindsley (1939).
[g]Henry (1944).
[h]Monnier (1957).
[i]Walter (1953).
[j]Levy and Kennard (1953).

TABLE 10 Postulated Neural Organizations Underlying Successive Stages of Human Development

Dominant species principle	Age span	Underlying neural organization	Associated cortical layers	Associated EEG pattern
Domination by the "mammalian principle"	First several weeks after birth	Stable establishment of Intraorganismic short circuit	6 and 5	Delta dominance
	1 to 9 months	Establishment of: Phase 1 of Transactional Subsystem Sensory: thalamus ⟷ primary and modifying primary sensorimotor cortex Motor: motor cortex → cerebellum → motor cortex CI branches 1 and 2 Phase 2 of Intraorganismic Subsystem: thalamus and lower layers of gyrus cinguli added to short circuit	6, 5, 4, 3c	Emerging theta dominance
	8 to 24 months	Establishment, in succession, of: Phase 2 of the Transactional Subsystem: outer sections of the T–O–P association area begin to function, plus thalamic ⟷ T–O–P area connections CI branches 3 and 4, and coordinated functioning of branches 1, 2, 3, 4. Phase 3 of the Transactional Subsystem: first sensory-modifying cortical-in-origin motor tracts	6, 5, 4, 3c, 3b	Theta dominance

1½ to 4 years	Establishment of: Intraorganismic long circuit, emergence of "limbic system" (Continuation of the Transactional long circuit) CI branches **4** (additional tracts) and **5**.	6, 5, **4**, all of 3	Theta dominance
Transition period, 3 to 6 years	Establishment of the CI "short circuit": branches 1 to 5 join in an unstable functional unity.	6, 5, 4, 3, 2 in primary areas	Shift towards alpha dominance begins
Domination by the "human principle", 5 to 12 years	More central parts of the T–O–P area and further sections of the frontal lobe become functional. Stably coordinated functioning of CI branches 1 to 5 is established.	6, 5, 4, 3, 2 except in PF area	Emergence of alpha dominance; development of adult alpha frequency
11 to 14 years	Changes in the T–O–P area; shake-up of the Intraorganismic short and long circuits and in CI circuits functioning. Onset of functioning in lower layers of the PF area.	6, 5, 4, 3, 2, 1	Greater EEG stability and organization; sudden transition from sleep to waking
13 to 17 years (F): 15 to 20 years (M):	Restabilization of Transactional, Intraorganismic, and CI circuits functioning. Continuing T–O–P and PF association areas development. Initiation of as yet unstable CI "long circuit."	Through 3 in the PF area?	Theta in frontal areas
16 to 35 years	Continuing functional development of the PF area; stabilization of the CI long circuit and of the entire CNS.	All layers in all parts of the cortex	Systematized, mature EEG

THE TITLE ISSUE

This concluding section, specifically focused on speech and language, is of necessity the most conjectural of an already speculative paper. Of necessity, because definitive data on the neurogenic bases of the emergence of speech and language are, due to the peculiar experimental difficulties involved, almost entirely of the earlier-criticized bits and pieces variety [helpfully summarized in Whitaker's recent discussion (1975)].

But there is another, more idiosyncratic reason for the conjectural character of this section. The writer was a developmental psychologist with a strong interdisciplinary orientation, not a specialist in either neurophysiology or linguistics, at the time she undertook the theoretical inquiry which culminated in the monograph that has been heavily drawn on in writing this chapter. Her explorations into neurophysiology territory have had the effect of strengthening rather than weakening that orientation. It is this background and its associated biases that have led to her explicit recognitions that:

1. Greater knowledge of the nature and the development of speech and language must be closely related to growing knowledge of the development and the functional organization of the human nervous system; premature specialization—i.e., isolating the field of linguistics from its supporting-knowledge underpinnings—can be, has been, and will continue to be a serious mistake.

2. There is a close and reciprocal relationship between speech and language development and emotional, social, perceptual, and self development.

3. The time-graded interaction of environmental, especially social (that is, individual-experiential) influences with biological potentialities is the fundamentally significant dimension in our species' development of its higher abilities, including speech and language.

These interrelated recognitions clearly imply the writer's rejection of a narrowly mechanistic approach to the title issue—a rejection intended as an essential preamble to any attempt on her part to apply a broadly interdisciplinary orientation to the delimited investigative specialty of speech and language. Nor does she wish to enter into the controversy concerning the nature of the relationship between language and cognition/mentation. The data on behavioral development—as well as analyses such as that of Werner and Kaplan (1963)—show that some categories of cognition developmentally predate verbalization, some categories parallel language acquisition, and some (perhaps very few, judging from cognitive development among the profoundly deaf) are explicitly dependent upon language (per se language rather than symbolization) acquisition.

On these explicit bases, it is here hypothesized that there are three separate-but-overlapping CNS systems that mediate speech and language, each with its own developmental timetable:

Speech–Language System E, for expressive of inner-states speech. It is intraorganismically mediated, projects indirectly from the thalamus to the right hemisphere, and is least dependent of the three postulated S–L systems on the individual's life experience. It is quite possible that we share with other mammals all except the explicitly verbal components of this system.

Speech–Language System C, for intentionally communicative speech and language. It is transactionally mediated, projects directly from the thalamus to the left hemisphere, and is strongly dependent on the individual's life experience.

Speech–Language System S, for symbolizing language and language-mediated mentation. It is chiefly dependent on the progressive integration of Systems E and C and therefore, as part of the earlier-postulated integrative system, is heavily dependent on the individual's life experience.

Common or basic to all three S–L systems are the peripheral neural mechanisms and the subcortical speech-related centers in the medulla and midbrain, and the thalamus. Each of these speech–language systems is further detailed in tabular form according to ascending age range (see Tables 11–13).

1. SPEECH–LANGUAGE SYSTEM E

The full S–L System E entails the linking up of the limbic-system circuit and the frontal neocortex's motor-speech centers with the basic (or common) centers. This system, detailed in Table 11, continues as the foundation of all human verbalization throughout life.

2. SPEECH–LANGUAGE SYSTEM C

The full S–L System C entails the linking-up of the basic common-speech centers to: (*1*) additional subcortical speech-related centers in the neocerebellum and the striatum, (*2*) the temporal-pole neocortical areas for speech comprehension, (*3*) the T-O-P association area, and (*4*) the frontal motor-speech areas. This system is delineated in Table 12; the first two stages in the Werner–Kaplan organismic-developmental theory of symbol formation (Werner & Kaplan, 1963) are explicitly included in the behavioral column.

3. SPEECH–LANGUAGE SYSTEM S

The full S–L System S entails the four-stage emergence of a CI circuit that links Systems E and C at both the intrathalamic and (more questionably) the intracortical levels:

TABLE 11 Speech–Language Neural System E (for Inner-States Expressive Speech)

Age range	Behavioral events	Postulated associated CNS mechanisms
At birth	Only vocalization, with predominance of (front) vowels	Medulla, plus medulla—old-cerebellum connections
Birth to 1 month	Dominance of vowels; vocalization reflects inner physiological states	Layers 6 and 5 of primary motor-speech (Broca's) area of neocortex added
1 to 3 months	1 month: active signs of pleasure and displeasure in response to immediate external world. 1 to 3 months: vocalizations become more differentiated, reflecting inner states more accurately. 3rd month: cooing, babbling, vocalizing one syllable.	The foregoing "foundation circuit" becomes part of Intraorganismic short circuit as it emerges.
3 to 6 months	Vocalization is more frequent and still more differentiated and reflective of inner feelings. Sounds basic to speech and two syllables emerge, in addition to cooing and babbling.	Layer 4 of primary motor-speech area added.
6 to 12 months	6–7 months: Vocalizes pleasure with crowing and cooing; tends to use a low throaty sound; may coo to music. 7–8 months: Vocalizes satisfaction on attaining a desired object; emits singing tones. Back consonants begin to appear, and two-syllable words (in which the second syllable is a repetition of the first) emerge. 8–9 months: Interjection vocalized. 6–12 months: Mutually facilitating interaction between vocalization and motor activity.	Layer 3c of Broca's area plus thalamus and lower layers of the gyrus cinguli added.

92

	9–12 months: More differentiated use of vocalization to express inner feelings. Utters first clearly intelligible word between 10 and 13 months. Rhythmic vocal accompaniment to physical activity is typical from 9 months to 3 years.	
1 to 2 years	13–17 months: Expressive jargon is common. Consonants appear in greater variety. 18–24 months: Spurt in vocabulary. Much of child's speech is emotionally toned during the second year, with a peak in speech problems at 21 months.	Layer 3b in Broca's area and Layer 3c in secondary motor-speech area are added.
2 to 4 years	18–30 months: Large percentage of emotionally toned verbalizations—commands, requests, desires, threats. 1½ to 3 years is a high-stress period (in our culture, at least) and much of this stress/anxiety is reflected in the child's speech. Physical means of aggression decline and verbal means increase among girls during this period. Rhythmic vocalization and verbalization are common and clearly enjoyable. Postulated emergence of awareness of one's inner world of feeling by the end of period.	All of Layer 3 in frontal speech areas added. Intraorganismic long circuit is tentatively established and as it is, the basic speech circuit is incorporated in it.
4 to 6 years	Steady increase in accuracy of articulation and in addition (or substitution) of verbal means of expressing strong feelings for the earlier physical means.	Stabilization of Intraorganismic long circuit and of its functional incorporation of speech-related centers
5 to 9 years	Especially among boys, a vocabulary of scatology and obscenity is acquired as a means of expressing strong feeling, especially strong negative feelings.	

TABLE 12 Speech-Language Neural System C (for Intentionally Communicative Speech and Language)

Age range	Behavioral events	Postulated associated CNS mechanisms
1 to 9 months	3–4 months: emits low throaty sounds to social stimulation. 4–5 months: turns head at sound of another's voice and responds to another's voice by making sounds. Is more discriminating of another's tones and expressions than earlier. Early evidences of denotation—from turning toward, to touching, to reaching towards—emerge parallel with babbling and call-sounds.[a] By 6 months is highly responsive vocally to social stimulation. Between 6 and 7 months, is able to distinguish between others' friendly and angry talking. Between 7 and 8 months, vocalizes recognition of another. Between 8 and 9 months, attends to familiar words; repeats a word or sentence, imitating sounds without understanding their meaning; understands another's gestures and adjusts to sounds. 4–5 months to 9 months, forms objects of contemplation.[a]	1–9 months: gradual establishment of Phase 1 of the Transactional subsystem (see Table 10), and S–L System C is included in it as it does. Layer 4 of Broca's area and the temporal primary speech-comprehension area are added to the System C circuit from 3 to 6 months.
6 to 12 months	9–12 months: responds to another's gestures and to "bye-bye." At 12 months, waves bye-bye and often says it. Responds to commands of various sorts from 10 to 12 months. In general, between 6 and 13 months, the speech rhythms and intonations of the infant's mother tongue, as well as accommodations to another's verbal communications emerge; social development and speech development appear to be mutually facilitating during this period. Depictive vocal imitation emerges between 8 and 9 months; attitudinal expressions through intonation and gesture show up towards the end of the first year.[a]	Layer 3c of the primary frontal and temporal speech-associated areas is added from 6 to 12 months. From 9 to 18 months, Layer 3b in the primary frontal temporal areas plus the neocellebullum are added Phase 2 of the Transactional subsystem (see Table 10) emerges, and as it does, System C is included in it.

94

Age		
12 to 18 months	Vocabulary increases slowly from 13 to 18 months (from 3–4 to 5–22 words). From 9 to 18 months, the infant progresses from earlier styles of denotation to pointing; physiognomic vocal depiction is common between 12 and 24 months.[a]	
18 to 24 months	1–2 years: practice of rhythms and intonations of mother tongue, comprehensibility of speech, understanding of words, intentional use of language to communicate, all increase. Vocabulary jumps markedly between 18 and 21 months. Integration of referents emerges between 20 and 24 months; predicative sentences emerge between 12 and 24 months.[a]	Phase 3 of the Transactional subsystem (the long circuit) is initiated, and System C is included in this development.
2 to 6 years	Marked increase in accuracy of articulation occurs between 2 and 3 years. Conventional vocal representation emerges between 21 and 30 months.[a] The largest increase in verbalization (number of words spoken per time period) occurs between 2½ and 3 years. Complete sentences emerge at 4 years. (Girls are ahead of boys in all phases of speech and language development during this period.) Language becomes simultaneously a tool for relating more adequately to one's physical and social environments and a means of self-regulation: from 3 to 5 years, 10–15% of all conversation is questions; from 3 to 4 years, the child regulates her behavior with overt, self-instructive speech; between 4½ and 5 years, such speech becomes internal.	All of Layer 3 in frontal and temporal speech areas is added. Continuation and stabilization of development of the Transactional long circuit.
5 to 20 years	The focus of speech and language development shifts from acquisition of basic skills to making language an increasingly accurate and effective means for communicating with others.	From 5 to 12 years, more central parts of the T–O–P area and additional sections of the frontal lobe become functional. From 12 to 20 years, there is continuing T–O–P area and PF area development.

[a]Werner and Kaplan (1963).

95

TABLE 13 Speech-Language Neural System S (for Symbolizing Language and Language-Mediated Mentation)

Age range	Behavioral events	Postulated associated CNS mechanisms
6 to 12 months	The first evidences of ideational activity—intention, memory, rudimentary imagery, reasoning—emerge, especially between 9 and 12 months.	From 8 to 24 months, CI Branches 3 and 4 (see p. 67) are added to the earlier-established CI
1 to 2 years	A few words are acquired from 12 to 18 months. Vocabulary size jumps sharply between 18 and 21 months, but speech is highly subject to temporary emotional states. Linguistic expressions of coordination and of sequence emerge during the second year.[a]	Branches 1 and 2, and co-ordinated functioning of CI Branches 1, 2, 3, and 4 (which include S–L systems E and C feed-ins) is initiated.
1½ to 4 years	Perception is chiefly physiognomic during this period. Linguistic expressions of simultaneity, of antithesis, of dependency begin during the third year; formation of derivatives begins between 2 and 3 years, of composites between 3 and 4 years.[a]	Additional CI Branch 4 tracts are added, plus CI Branch 5.
4 to 6 years	Complete sentences emerge at 4 years. Overt self-instructive speech becomes internal between 4½ and 5½ years. Visual and auditory perceptual errors are frequent until about 6 years; thereafter perceptual discrimination begins to improve. Problem-solving reasoning shifts from an original whole-body approach to a more ideational one between 3 and 6 years. Beginning about 5 years, the earlier tendency to perseverate within one perceptual or memory system starts to give way to the ability to shift to other perceptual and memory systems. Intellectual functioning begins to approximate at 5 years what IQ tests later test.	CI Branches 1–5 join in an unstable functional unity (= initiation of the CI short circuit) from 3 to 6 years.

5 to 14 years	Between 5 and 9 years, there is a shift from physiognomic and global perception toward more qualitative and individualized discriminations. Ideationally, there is a shift from concrete body manipulations and operations to mental manipulations and operations, and the ability to symbolize consciously, i.e., to grasp that a word or number stands for an entity or concept, develops. The ability to conceptualize—to form generalizations from specific instances—increases markedly from 6 to 11 years, when it reaches the subadult level. Beginning at 9½ years, there is a marked falling-off in the proportion of questions in conversation. Lexicalization of words begins about 10½ years.[a]	Stably coordinated functioning of the CI short circuit is established.
13 to 16 years	Verbal mediation (both recognition and use-vocabulary) continues to increase (2½ times between 10 and 20). Ideational memory continues to increase until at least the mid-20s. Cognitive and ideational processes, including word lexicalization, reach mature levels at mid- to late adolescence.[a]	Restabilization of Transactional, Intraorganismic, and CI circuits after the 11 to 14 years shake-ups. Initiation of the still unstable CI long circuit. Onset of functioning in lower layers of PF area.

[a]Werner and Kaplan (1963).

1. the prelanguage, imagery, and adaptive-behavior stage, from 6 to 18 months;
2. transition-stage I, the self-centered phase, from 18 months to 4 to 5 years;
3. transition-stage II, the awareness-of-others'-perspective phase, from 4 to 11 years;
4. the language as mental-tool stage, 9–11 years on.

The mechanisms mediating each stage do not replace the previous stage's mechanisms; rather, each stage's mechanisms continue to function throughout life as discrete subcomponents within a larger unity. It may be that beginning in mid-adolescence among persons of high intellectual ability, the subcortical as well as other directly speech-associated components of System S are bypassed during problem-solving mentation.

S–L System S may be seen as an extension of Myers' perspicacious statement that each functional sector of the cortex makes its own separate contribution to speech and language functions, and that (paraphrasing Penfield & Roberts, 1959) the expression of language as organized within the several sectors of the cortex is likely to occur through vertically oriented projection systems extending down to brainstem centers for speech production (Myers, 1967, p. 68).

The third and fourth stages in the Werner–Kaplan theory are explicitly included in the behavioral column of Table 13, which delineates S–L System S.

The foregoing triple-system formulation does not, admittedly, provide specific answers to the sorts of specialized and specific issues raised in a volume such as *Brain mechanisms underlying speech and language* (Darley, 1967). But it does provide a delimited yet holistic, basic framework within which future research on linguistically related issues can and should proceed.

EPILOGUE

The delimited character of the writer's assignment for this volume, together with her conscious effort to stay within its implied boundaries, seem to her to have left the impression of her adherence to a narrowly mechanistic perspective on the acquisition of speech and language despite earlier disclaimers. To counter this impression, the author would have liked to include, as a postscript to this chapter, a series of excerpts from E. Milner (1967) which would serve to document her previously stated recognitions that there is a close and reciprocal relationship between speech and language development and social, emotional, perceptual, and self development, and that the time-graded interaction of individual-experiential influences with biological potentialities is the fundamentally significant dimension in our species' development of the higher, uniquely human abilities.

Space limitations permit the inclusion of only one such excerpt, drawn from the closing analysis (E. Milner, 1967). Other numerous discussions that also document the foregoing points, some explicitly related to speech and language development, can be found in context throughout the original monograph.

Human Development Principle 1 concerns the consequences of the way in which our species' dual genetic endowment—a human principle superimposed on a mammalian foundation—expresses itself in ontogenesis. The neural and the behavioral data indicate that:

1. At birth, man is functionally a decorticate mammal; his humanity is present entirely as potential.
2. The development and expression of that potential is dependent upon the growing normal individual human organism's suitably enabling transactions with its environment.
3. The 'suitability' of these transactions is a function of each unfolding stage of development.

These interrelated species circumstances jointly comprise the first developmental principle; they make human development a very complicated and hazardous enterprise indeed. . . .

Circumstance 2 may be termed the 'if-then' or 'open system' subprinciple. It stems from the character of human postnatal nervous system development, which *allows* the individual member of the human species to express the behaviors associated with each succeeding developmental stage but does *not ensure* their provision. *If* at a particular stage of neural maturation, the environment provides one with the sorts of experiences one requires in order to go on to the next developmental stage, *then* the integrative apparati of the nervous system can perform their coordinating job and move the organism on to its next higher level of development. If these 'enabling' experiences are not available to the growing individual, the integrative processes will have incomplete or distorted sub-processes to coordinate—and the next functional stage does not emerge at all or does so in incomplete or distorted form. If the environment continues to be nonenabling, the distortions may become cumulative to the point of *later* arrest in psychological development; at the least, inappropriate handling of the early, mammalian-principle-dominated period of human development creates an underlying vulnerability to later stress.

The expression of this contingency principle is analogous to that of the physical mechanisms which implement genetic inheritance: these develop in a chain of successive links, the emergence of the last link dependent upon the one just prior to it; if one link should fail to develop or be defective, all subsequent links are in some way defective.

Here the idea of an 'enabling environment,' that is, one which supplies the experiences most appropriate to each human-developmental stage and so fosters integrated progression to the next stage—Circumstance 3, suggests itself and raises the possibility of rating cultures and subcultures according to the *species-appropriateness* of their child-rearing practices, relationships, values, secondary institutions [E. Milner, 1967, pp. 278–280] .

REFERENCES

Adrian, Lord 1959. Sensory mechanisms—an introduction. In H. W. Magoun (Ed.), *Handbook of physiology*. Vol. 1. Washington, D.C.: American Physiological Society, Pp. 365–367.

Arey, L. B. 1954. *Developmental anatomy.* (6th ed.) Philadelphia: Saunders.

Ariëns-Kappers, C. U., Huber, G. C., & Crosby, E. C. 1936. *The comparative anatomy of the nervous system of vertebrates including man.* Vol. II. New York: Macmillan.

Arieti, S. 1955. *Interpretation of schizophrenia.* New York: Robert Brunner & Basic Books.

Bailey, P., & Von Bonin, G. 1951. *The isocortex of man.* Urbana: Illinois Monographs in the Medical Sciences, University of Illinois Press.

Barcroft, J. 1938. *The brain and its environment.* New Haven: Yale University Press.

Bishop, G. H. 1956. Natural history of the nerve impulse. *Physiological Review, 36*(3), 376–399.

Brodal, A. 1957. *The reticular formation of the brain stem.* London: Oliver & Boyd.

Carmichael, L. 1951. Ontogenetic development. In S. S. Stevens (Ed.), *Handbook of experimental psychology.* New York: Wiley.

Cobb, S. 1950. *Emotions and clinical medicine.* New York: Norton.

Conel, J. L. 1939–1967. *The postnatal development of the human cerebral cortex.* Cambridge, Mass.: Harvard University Press. 8 vols.

Darley, F. C. (Ed.) 1967. *Brain mechanisms underlying speech and language.* New York: Grune & Stratton.

Denny-Brown, D. 1960. Motor mechanisms: general principles of motor integration. In H. W. Magoun (Ed.), *Handbook of physiology.* Vol. 2. Washington, D.C.: American Physiological Society. Pp. 781–796.

Dreyfus-Brisac, C., Samson, D., Blanc, C., & Monod, D. 1958. L'electroencephalogramme de l'enfant normale de moins de trois ans. *Études Neo-Natales, 7*(4), 143–175.

Eiseley, L. C. 1955. Fossil man and human evolution. *Yearbook of Anthropology,* pp. 61–78.

Falconer, M. A. 1967. Brain mechanisms suggested by neurophysiologic studies. In F. C. Darley (Ed.), *Brain mechanisms underlying speech and language.* New York: Grune & Stratton. Pp. 185–196.

Fois, A. 1961. *The electroencephalogram of the normal child.* Springfield: Charles C Thomas.

Fulton, J. F. 1955. *A textbook of physiology.* (17th ed.) Philadelphia: Saunders.

Gardner, E. 1963. *Fundamentals of neurology.* (4th ed.) Philadelphia: Saunders.

Gellhorn, E. 1953. *Physiological foundations of neurology and psychiatry.* Minneapolis: University of Minnesota Press.

Gerard, R. W. 1960. Neurophysiology: an integration. In H. W. Magoun (Ed.), *Handbook of physiology.* Vol. 3. Wshington, D.C.: American Physiological Society. Pp. 1919–1965.

Gibbs, F. A., & Gibbs, E. L. 1950. *Atlas of encephalography.* Vol. 1. (2nd ed.) Reading, Mass.: Addison-Wesley.

Gooddy, W. 1956. Cerebral representation. *Brain, 79,* 167–187.

Granit, R. 1955. *Receptors and sensory perception.* New Haven, Conn.: Yale University Press.

Hamilton, W. J., Boyd, J. D., & Mossman, H. W. 1952. *Human embryology.* (2nd ed.) Baltimore: Williams & Wilkins.

Harlow, H. F. 1962. The heterosexual affectional system in monkeys. *American Psychologist, 17,* 1–9.

Hebb, D. O. 1949. *The organization of behavior.* New York: Wiley.

Hebb, D. O. 1958. *A textbook of psychology.* Philadelphia: Saunders.

Hécaen, H. 1967. Brain mechanisms suggested by studies of perietal lobes. In F. C. Darley (Ed.), *Brain mechanisms underlying speech and language.* New York: Grune & Stratton. Pp. 146–166.

Henry, C. E. 1944. Electroencephalograms of normal children. *Child Development Monographs, 9*(3).

Herrick, C. J. 1956. *The evolution of human nature.* Austin: University of Texas Press.

Himwich, H. E. 1951. *Brain metabolism and cerebral disorders.* Baltimore: Williams & Wilkins.

Himwich, H. E., & Himwich, W. A. 1957. General neurophysiology. *Progress in Neurology and Psychiatry, 12,* 18–42.

Jackson, J. H. 1882. *Medical Press and Circular, 2,* 34–42.

Jackson, J. H. 1884. Croonian lectures. In *Lancet* (i, 535, 649, 739), *British Medical Journal* (i, 951, 660, 703), *Medical Times and Gazette* (i, 411, 445, 485).

Jasper, H. H. 1952. Thamalocortical integrating mechanisms. *Research Publications, Association for Research in Nervous and Mental Disease.* Vol. 30. Pp. 493–512. (Ch. 23).

Langworthy, O. R. 1933. Development of myelinization of the nervous system in the human fetus and infant. *Contributions to Embryology, 24*(39).

Lansdell, H. C. 1964. Sex differences in hemispheric asymmetries of the human brain. *Nature (London), 203,* 550.

Lashley, K. 1951. The problem of serial order in behavior. In L. A. Jeffress (Ed.), *Cerebral mechanisms in behavior.* Hixon Symposium. New York: Wiley. Pp. 529–552.

Lenneberg, E. H. 1967. *Bilological foundations of language.* New York: Wiley.

Levy, S., & Kennard, M. A. 1953. The EEG patterns of patients with psychologic disorders of various ages. *Journal of Nervous and Mental Disease, 118*(5), 416–428.

Lindsley, D. B. 1939. A longitudinal study of the occipital alpha rhythm in normal children. *Journal of Genetic Psychology, 55,* 197–213.

Livingston, R. B. 1959. Central control of receptors and sensory transmission systems. In H. W. Magoun (Ed.), *Handbook of physiology.* Vol. 1. Washington, D.C.: American Physiological Society. Pp. 741–760.

Magoun, H. W. 1967. In F. C. Darley (Ed.), *Brain mechanisms underlying speech and language.* New York: Grune & Stratton. P. 18.

Milner, B. 1954. Intellectual functions of the temporal lobes. *Psychological Bulletin, 51,* 42–62.

Milner, E. 1967. *Human neural and behavioral development: A relational inquiry (with implications for personality).* Springfield, Ill.: Charles C Thomas.

Monnier, M. 1957. Plan d'organisation, continuité, et stades du developpement des activitiés electrique cerebrales. *Dialectica, II*(1–2), 167–178.

Myers, R. E. 1967. Cerebral connectionism and brain function. In F. C. Darley (Ed.), *Brain mechanisms underlying speech and language.* New York: Grune & Stratton. Pp. 61–69.

Nissen, H. W. 1951. Phylogenetic comparison. In S. S. Stevens (Ed.), *Handbook of experimental psychology.* New York: Wiley. Pp. 346–385.

Novikoff, A. B. 1945. The concept of integrative levels and biology. *Science, 101,* 209–215.

Olds, J., & Milner, P. M. 1954. Positive reinforcement produced by electrical stimulation of . . . regions of the rat brain. *Journal of Comparative and Physiological Psychology, 47,* 419–427.

Patten, B. M. 1953. *Human embryology.* (2nd ed.) New York: McGraw-Hill.

Penfield, W. 1952a. Epileptic automatism and the centrencephalic integrating system. *Research Publications, Association for Research in Nervous and Mental Disease,* Vol. 30. Pp. 513–528.

Penfield, W. 1952b. Memory mechanisms. *AMA Archives of Neurology and Psychiatry, 67,* 178–191.

Penfield, W., & Rasmussen, T. 1952. *The cerebral cortex of man.* New York: Macmillan.

Penfield, W., & Roberts, L. 1959. *Speech and brain mechanisms.* Princeton, N.J.: Princeton University Press.

Piaget, J. 1952. *The origins of intelligence in children.* New York: Basic Books.

Pond, D. A. 1963. The development of normal EEG rhythms. *In* J. D. N. Hill & G. Parr (Eds.), *Electroencephalography.* (2nd ed.) New York: Macmillan. Pp. 193–206 (Ch.6).

Romer, A. S. 1958. Phylogeny and behavior. In A. Roe and G. G. Simpson (Eds.), *Behavior and evolution*. New Haven, Conn.: Yale University Press. Pp. 48–75 (Ch. 3).

Ruch, T. C. 1951. Motor systems. In S. S. Stevens (Ed.), *Handbook of experimental psychology*. New York: Wiley. Ch. 5.

Ruch, T. C., & Fulton, J. F. (Eds.) 1960. *Medical physiology and biophysics*. Philadelphia: Saunders.

Schneirla, T. C. 1957. The concept of development in comparative psychology. In D. B. Harris (Ed.), *The concept of development*. Minneapolis: University of Minnesota Press. Pp. 78–108.

Sellars, R. W. 1938. An analytic approach to the mind-body problem. *Philosophical Review, 47*, 461–487.

Sholl, D. A. 1956. *The organization of the cerebral cortex*. New York: Wiley.

Smith, J. R. 1938. The EEG during normal infancy and childhood, II. The nature of the growth of alpha waves. *Journal of Genetic Psychology, 53*, 471–482.

Tilney, F. 1934. Comparative ontogeny of the cerebral cortex in four mammals. *Research Publications, Association for Research in Nervous and Mental Disease, 13*, 49–82.

Tinbergen, N. 1951. *The study of instinct*. New York: Oxford University Press.

Turner, O. A. 1948. Growth and development of cerebral cortical pattern in man. *Archives of Neurology and Psychiatry, 59*, 1–12.

Turner, O. A. 1950. Postnatal growth changes in the cortical surface area. *Archives of Neurology and Psychiatry, 64*, 378–84.

Walter, W. G. 1953. *The living brain*. New York: Norton.

Werner, H., & Kaplan, B. 1963. *Symbol formation*. New York: Wiley.

Whitaker, H. A. 1975. Neurobiology of language. In E. C. Carterette & M. P. Friedman (Eds.), *Handbook of perception*. Vol. 7. *Language and speech*. New York: Academic Press.

Zubek, J. P., & Solberg, P. A. 1954. *Human development*. New York: McGraw-Hill.

3 Subcortical Language Mechanisms[1]

George A. Ojemann

UNIVERSITY OF WASHINGTON, SEATTLE

In a subject as diverse as neurolinguistics, the reader seems entitled to a preview of a chapter's contents. This chapter reviews evidence on the relationship between thalamus and adjacent subcortical structures and language function. Articulatory changes in speech production follow lesions in some of the subcortical sites whose relation to language will be considered here, for example lesions in the genu of the internal capsule (Hermann, Turner, Gillingham, & Gaze, 1966) and ventrolateral thalamus (Bell, 1968; Riklan, Levita, Zimmerman, & Cooper, 1969), but will not be further considered. Nor is this chapter concerned with classical subcortical aphasia, a language disturbance associated with white-matter lesions immediately beneath the classical speech areas of cortex. Rather, interest is centered on evidence relating some of the nuclear masses deep in the cerebral hemispheres (the thalamus and adjacent structures, including globus pallidus, immediate subthalamus, and adjoining internal capsule) to language. Figures 1 and 2 show the location of these structures, and the subdivisions of thalamus that are discussed in the following review.

This chapter assumes that language function can be localized in the human brain. This does not necessarily imply the discrete detail localization of the *diagram makers* (Head, 1926), but rather a larger-scale localization, to the extent that particular groups of cortical gyri or subcortical nuclei are concerned

[1] The author's research reported in this chapter is supported in part by grant NS 04053 from National Institutes of Health, U.S. Public Health Service. The procedures for obtaining informed consent in this research received the prior approval of the University of Washington Biomedical Sciences Review Committee in accordance with the currently applicable Public Health Service guidelines for human experimentation.

103

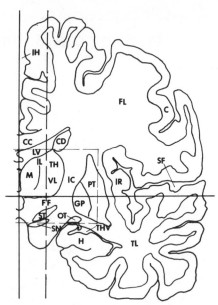

Figure 1 Line drawing of coronal section of cerebral hemisphere. Plane of this section is indicated by vertical dashed line on Figure 2. On this figure, vertical solid line is midline of brain, horizontal solid line the intercommissural plane. Vertical dashed line is the plane of the parasaggital section in Figure 2, 1 cm lateral to the midline. Dashed box is the approximate area of the sections in Figure 5. C—cortex (on parasaggital section in post central gyrus); CC—corpus callosum; CD—caudate; CF—calcarine fissure; CM—centrum medianum nucleus of thalamus; F—fornix; FF—Fields of Forel; FL—frontal lobe white matter; GP—globus pallidus; H—hippocampus; IC—internal capsule; IH—interhemispheric fissure; IL—intralaminar nucleus of thalamus; IR—Island of Reil; LC—lateral ventricle; M—dorsomedial nucleus of thalamus; OL—occipital lobe white matter; ON, OT—optic tract; PL—parietal lobe white matter; POF—parieto-occipital fissure; PT—putamen; PUL—pulvinar; SF—Sylvian fissure; SN—substantia nigra; ST—subthalamic nucleus; TH—thalamus; THV—temporal horn of lateral ventricle; TL—Temporal lobe white matter. (Adapted from Schaltenbrand & Bailey, 1959.)

generally with language function, while others are not. From the standpoint of the cerebral cortex it is quite clear that such localization exists. For most people, language functions in terms of gross deficits following lesions are lateralized to the left cerebral hemisphere and are not present on the right. Within the left cerebral hemisphere, cortical language function is localized to the parietal temporal junction (so-called *Wernicke speech area*), the posterior inferior portion of the third frontal convolution (the so-called *Broca speech area*), and the supplementary motor area on the medial face of the left hemisphere (Penfield & Roberts, 1959). These cortical areas are listed in decreasing order of apparent importance, to the extent that lesions are likely to result in permanent language deficits, though temporary language deficits seem to follow disruption of function in all three areas.

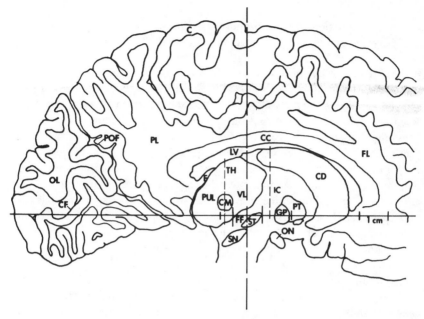

Figure 2 Line drawing of parasaggital section of cerebral hemisphere 1 cm lateral to midline. Solid horizontal line is the intercommissural plane of brain. Short crosslines on this are location of anterior (to right) and posterior commissures. Short dashed lines enclose the area represented on sections in Figure 5. C—cortex (on parasaggital section in post central gyrus); CC—corpus callosum; CD—caudate; CF—calcarine fissure; CM—centrum medianum nucleus of thalamus; F—fornix; FF—Fields of Forel; FL—frontal lobe white matter; GP—globus pallidus; H—hippocampus; IC—internal capsule; IH—interhemispheric fissure; IL—intralaminar nucleus of thalamus; IR—Island of Reil; LV—lateral ventricle; M—dorsomedial nucleus of thalamus; OL—occipital lobe white matter; ON, OT—optic tract; PL—parietal lobe white matter; POF—parieto-occipital fissure; PT—putamen; PUL—pulvinar; SF—Sylvian fissure; SN—substantia nigra; ST—subthalamic nucleus; TH—thalamus; THV—temporal horn of lateral ventricle; TL—Temporal lobe white matter. (Adapted from Schaltenbrand & Bailey, 1959.)

There are distinct limitations in efforts to localize language function. Such efforts must be considered on a population basis, since individual exception to the general rule of left-brain language lateralization (at least in right-handed patients) in these areas have been clearly identified and frequently reported (i.e., Boller, 1973). Some left-handed patients seem to have less strongly lateralized language organization, or occasionally language function in right brain. Damage in early life to the portions of the cortex usually concerned with language (likely before the age of 5) may result in a different pattern of organization of language function (Penfield & Roberts, 1959).

It would appear that no one of these cortical areas is invariably indispensible for language function. A degree of "functional plasticity" seems to exist in these areas so that the long-term language deficit following a lesion may to some extent be a function of what proportion of those parts of the brain concerned with language function remain intact rather than the result of a specific deficit in one site. Roberts (1958) suggests that even serial lesions in the region of the left parietal temporal junction may be placed without permanent language deficits. Several cases reported by Mohr (1973) suggest that permanent language deficits do not invariably follow the massive destruction of the Broca speech area. Recovery of language following supplementary motor lesions in the dominant hemisphere is almost the rule (Penfield & Roberts, 1959). Thus, in the evaluation of the effects of subcortical lesions on language function, the intactness of the remainder of brain concerned with language, such as cortical language areas, may be important in determining whether a disturbance of language will occur, and whether it will be permanent. The size of individual lesions may also be of importance, both in terms of the proportion of areas concerned with language destroyed, and in terms of the suddeness of the lesion: A general property of brain damage appears to be that lesions of a particular size achieved serially are associated with significantly less functional deficit than those of the same size achieved abruptly (Finger, Walbran, & Stein, 1973). Youth also predisposes to recovery of function. Indeed, some degree of recovery follows almost all static cerebral lesions, over a period of 6 months to a year or more.

The classical view of "localization" of language function has not included subcortical structures at the level of the thalamus, but rather includes only cortex and the immediately subcortical white matter (Head, 1926, p. 537). Nielsen (1946) felt that thalamic lesions affected language only "pari passu" with general deterioration, a view reiterated by Geschwind (1967, 1970) and Brown (1972). Within the limitations of localization of language function briefly discussed above and so eloquently presented in the first portion of Volume I of Sir Henry Head's *Aphasia* (1926), this chapter will review the evidence relating language to the thalamus and immediate adjacent subcortical structures, including some evidence that is contrary to the classical view.

Information on this relation of subcortical sites in the region of the thalamus to language is available from two general sources: the effect of lesions, and the effect of focal stimulation. We will first consider the evidence derived from the study of lesions. This category includes studies of language changes in patients with spontaneous lesions, tumors in the region of the thalamus and surrounding structures, hemorrhage into these areas, and with more discrete surgical lesions placed stereotaxically in these subcortical structures for the treatment of a number of conditions, particularly dyskinesias.

SPONTANEOUS THALAMIC LESIONS

Language disturbances have been reported with thalamic tumors, especially in the dominant hemisphere (Cheek & Taveras, 1966; Smyth & Stern, 1938) but whether due to local damage, or to secondary distal effects of tumor extension (edema or increased intracranial pressure) is unknown.

Thalamic hemorrhages may be considerably more focal in their extent than tumors, and produce fewer distant effects. Fisher (1958) in an early review of the clinical syndrome associated with thalamic hemorrhage pointed out that it was "surprising to find that on the dominant side global dysphasia is usually present." He felt that this was especially true of hemorrhages situated superiorly in the middle third of the thalamus. Penfield and Roberts (1959, p. 215) reported a case of thalamic hemorrhage in the left hemisphere diagnosed by arteriography, in a patient who was said to be aphasic.

More recently Ciemins (1970) presented two cases of pathologically verified thalamic hemorrhage that exhibited clear language disturbances. In the first case the patient had a sudden insult, after which he had a speech disturbance characterized by jargon and a tendency to perseverate and understand commands with difficulty, though with some insight into his language disturbance. Over the next several days a picture emerged of little spontaneous speech and fragmentary sentences—though with the correct syntax. The patient was able to carry out simple but not complex commands, could read, but could not follow written commands. There was notable perseveration on writing and naming. The syndrome was present at least to the twelfth day. At the patient's death on the twenty-second day there was a left thalamic hemorrhage extending from the region of the anterior nucleus and involving all nuclei but not the internal capsule. There was also an old, small, cystic lesion in the right thalamus, involving the medial portions of ventrolateral nucleus and anterior pulvinar. Ciemins' second case also had sudden onset of an aphasia, not otherwise well described, which was present as a "slight expressive aphasia" $1^1/_3$ years later. Autopsy demonstrated an old hemorrhage involving the left posterior thalamus, including the lateral aspects of ventro-posterior and lateralis posterior nuclei, and obliterating the medial third of the left pulvinar. Fazio, Sacco, and Bugiani (1973) also recorded a series of thalamic hemorrhages with pathologic verification, some with language disturbance. In their first case, in which the entire left thalamus had been destroyed by a hemorrhage, the patient was described as having been in a stupor, exhibiting "muddled utterances" though he was able to follow simple commands. The third case had only a mild paresis and a mixed speech disturbance; the patient was further described as having little spontaneous speech, many syntactical errors, paraphasias, and stereotypic speech. Word repetition was intact, but the patient failed about half of the authors' test of speech comprehension. This deficit persisted for 13 days and at autopsy the entire left thalamus was involved by hemorrhage. Fazio *et al.* (1973) also reported another patient (Case 2) having no speech disturbance where there had been a rather similar hemorrhage, maximal in the middle third of the left thalamus including pulvinar.

The cases recorded above seem to indicate that hemorrhage into the thalamus of the dominant hemisphere is often but not invariably associated with a language disturbance and, in at least one case (Ciemins' Case 2), that language disturbance seems to be long lasting. But except for Ciemins' first case the nature of the language deficit in these cases is not well described.

We have had the opportunity to obtain some further information on the nature of these language deficits in a relatively small left-thalamic hemorrhage. The patient, a 26-year-old right-handed male, was under the care of my colleague, A. Basil Harris. His premorbid intellectual function is not known formally, but he was functioning satisfactorily in graduate school at the time he had the sudden onset of severe headache, right-sided weakness, and difficulty speaking. Neurologic examination revealed a right hemiparesis, paralysis of upward gaze (Paranoud's syndrome), and a significant aphasia. Further workup revealed only a small angioma in the region of the left pulvinar, and a mass, impinging on the posterior portion of the third ventricle in the region of the left posterior thalamus. This mass did not seem to extend anterior to the Foramen of Monroe. Language testing was carried out on the second day following this event, and then repeated 18 days later. At the time of the second testing the patient felt that his speech and language deficits had largely cleared as had his hemiparesis. Repeat neuroradiologic studies at this time showed a reduction in size of the mass in the region of the third ventricle. Thus the presumptive diagnosis based on the neuroradiologic studies in this patient is a small angioma in the region of the pulvinar which bled, producing a small hematoma in the posterior portion of the left thalamus. No neuroradiologic or clinical evidence of dysfunction elsewhere was present in this case.

The language test administered to this patient was the same as that used by the author in evaluating patients undergoing stereotaxic thalamotomy and during the course of thalamic stimulation. The results under these different conditions will be presented throughout this chapter, so it seems appropriate at this point to describe the test in some detail. It is published in Ojemann, Blick, and Ward (1971a). It is designed as a test of object naming, mental arithmetic, and short-term verbal memory, using either cued recall or recognition as modes of retrieval. The test consists of 60 consecutive trials, each trial consisting of 4 achromatic slides that the patient successively views on a screen. The 4 slides in each trial are as follows: (1) The first, a test of object naming, is a slide picture of an object whose name is a common word of Thorndike–Lorge (Thorndike & Lorge, 1944), A or AA frequency. Above the picture of the object the words *This is a* are printed. The patient is trained to read the words *This is a* aloud and then give the name of the object pictured. (2) The second slide, a test of mental arithmetic, contains a picture of a randomly selected 2-digit number greater than 30. The patient is trained to read this number aloud and then to count backwards by threes aloud from it until the appearance of (3) the third slide, which is the retrieval part of a test of short-term verbal memory, patterned after the single-item tests of short-term memory of Peterson and Peterson (1959). This retrieval slide may take one of two forms. When retrieval is by cued recall, the slide has the word *recall* printed on it and the patient had been trained to give back the name of the object presented on this trial, before the mental arithmetic task, which acts as a standard distraction. The second mode of retrieval is by recognition of one of four words, one of which is the name of the object pictured on this trial, one the name of the object pictured on the previous trial, and the other two names of objects appearing elsewhere in the test. (4) The fourth slide in each trial is the other mode of retrieval, recognition or cued recall, whichever did not appear as the third slide.

As used in testing Harris' patient, the object-naming slide and each retrieval slide were presented for 5-sec intervals, and the duration of the mental arithmetic task was varied randomly at 3-, 6-, 10-, 15-, or 21-sec intervals.

At initial testing (2 days following hemorrhage), the patient was able to understand the instruction for the test, and follow them for the entire sequence—suggesting that little if any confusion was present. However, object-naming performance was notably impaired: 30.7% of the 49 objects presented were erroneously named. By 18 days this deficit has entirely cleared and no errors were made in the naming of 57 objects. This object-naming task is quite easy, and the most errors that any of the patients with dyskinesias have made on their initial exposure to it is 8%. Thus, this patient appeared to have a significant deficit in object naming that cleared in a few weeks.

Only one of the acute object-naming errors was an omission; the remaining 14 were misnaming errors. Nine of these wrong names were names of objects pictured elsewhere on the test. The remainder were quite extraneous to the list—including the most dramatic error, perseveration on the phrase *affirmative action*. There were two instances of perseveration on a wrong object name covering 2 successive objects and this third where perseveration covered 3 successive objects. The patient was able to correctly recognize 6 of the 14 objects that he could not name. On no occasion however, was he able to correctly recall the name of an object that he could not name. (Though on 4 of the 14 occasions he accurately recalled the wrong name that he had used.)

Performance on the mental arithmetic task was determined by matching the trials of the acute and delayed testing for the last three trials in which the mental arithmetic task was at 10-, 15-, or 21-sec duration and object naming was correct. These criteria were introduced to avoid encroachment of object naming onto the time available for the mental arithmetic task, and to minimize any practice effects, by choosing the last trials where counting backwards by threes is an overlearned task for most patients. Mental arithmetic performance was compared in terms of the accuracy of identification of the pictured number, the number of numbers enunciated during the available time, the accuracy of these calculations, and whether errors made involved the one's place or the ten's place.

Performance on the test of mental arithmetic also markedly improved at the 18-day testing compared to the 2-day testing. The rate of counting backwards by threes had increased 145%, and no identification errors were made at the time of the later testing, compared to one such error on the nine trials during acute testing. Calculation errors in counting backwards by threes decreased from 40½% of the calculations made during acute testing to 10.8% of the more frequent calculations made in the later testing. Calculation errors involving the ten's place decreased from 41.7% of the decade transitions (i.e., going from 62–59) to 5.3%; calculation errors involving the ones place decreased from 28.6% of calculations to 9.2%. Presumably those functions showing the most recovery as the thalamic hemorrhage diminished may be the ones related to left thalamus. Thus, these changes in mental arithmetic, accompanying a left thalamic hemorrhage seem to show involvement of this subcortical structure in rate of counting, calculations, and particularly calculations involving the ten's place. Generally similar changes were found in a study of the effect of left thalamic stimulation on mental arithmetic (Ojemann, 1974a).

Retrieval performance from short-term verbal memory was measured over variable distractions (the mental arithmetic task) from 3 to 21 sec. In a test of this nature, lesions interfering with short-term memory would be expected to have a greater effect on the longer-duration distraction than on the shorter, while deficits unrelated to memory, such as difficulty with speech, should be distributed uniformly across the different distraction intervals (Melton, 1963). Neither pattern of errors related to the distraction interval was seen in the acute testing of this patient; rather the maximal number of errors on both cued recall and recognition modes of retrieval occurred at the 6-sec distraction interval. Fewer errors occurred at both shorter and longer intervals. This is perhaps best explained as a problem in perseveration, with a lack of flexibility in mental processes.

Thus, from a review of the effects of spontaneous lesions on language, both those reported in the literature and tests on the author's patient, it would appear that hemorrhages into the dominant thalamus can be associated with language disturbances, which though often transitory, can occasionally be long lasting (Ciemen's Case 2). This language disturbance typically exhibits generally intact comprehension, but major deficits in expression, particularly in naming objects where wrong names, rather than omissions predominate, with frequent perseveration. These deficits may involve not only spoken speech, but also reading, writing, and arithmetic operations.

STEREOTAXIC VENTROLATERAL THALAMIC LESIONS

Much of the interest in the relationship between thalamus and adjacent structures and language has been an outgrowth of the development of techniques for treating a variety of dyskinesias with stereotaxically placed lesions in these *Stereotaxic technique* structures (Ojemann & Ward, 1973). Stereotaxic techniques allow the placement of lesions of relatively predictable size in fairly discrete and predictable locations with the use of radiologic landmarks supplemented by physiologic corrections. Although the use of anatomic landmarks alone suffers from the problems of a very high degree of variation around even nearby radiologically demonstrable landmarks (Van Buren & Borke, 1972), modern stereotaxic lesions that have come to later autopsy examination seem to be surprisingly reliably placed in the desired target (Harmann-Von Monakow, 1972). These lesions are sufficiently discrete so that one can now deal not with damage to the entire thalamus, but with lesions confined to a segment of it, limited at least to lateral or medial, anterior or posterior, and in many cases to a single nuclear mass. Thus it is now possible to compare the results of lesions in different portions of thalamus, as well as lesions reasonably well confined to adjacent structures, on various tests of language function.

However, another problem arises. The vast majority of these lesions have been *Parkinsonism* carried out in a single disease state, Parkinsonism. Hence, the effects of the lesions are confounded with effects of that dyskinesia. Formal tests of language function in Parkinsonism patients similar to those who would be candidates for thalamic surgery, including the Weschler Adult Intelligence Scale (WAIS) and object naming, have shown no deficits compared to intact individuals (Asso, 1969; Loranger, Goodell, McDowell, Lee, & Sweet, 1972). Nevertheless the possibility remains that there may be a particular synergism between the thalamic lesion and the Parkinson pathophysiology that is responsible for some of the language disturbances reported with thalamotomy (Shapiro, Sadowsky, Henderson, & Van Buren, 1973). The occurrence of similar language disturbance in dystonic patients undergoing thalamotomy is evidence against such an interaction between disease and lesion.

The following discussion will first consider the effect on language of stereotaxic lesions in the ventrolateral thalamus, as this represents the bulk of available studies. Then the effects of lesions in other thalamic nuclei and nearby structures will be mentioned.

Dysphasia is rather frequently mentioned as a complication of ventrolateral thalamotomy in the reports of the procedure's efficacy in Parkinsonism. This complication, somewhat to the surprise of the surgeons, seems to be related to the side on which the thalamotomy is performed, occurring almost exclusively *42% of left thalamotomies show dysphasia* after left thalamotomy, at least in right-handed patients. Dysphasia has been seen in as high as 42% of the left thalamotomies in one series (Selby, 1967). It was noted that this symptom, in general, tended to subside over 10 to 14 days, only rarely persisting as a recognizable language disturbance. The occurrence of this complication seemed to be totally unrelated to the patient's preoperative speech status.

Bell (1968) identified dysphasic responses following 9 of 31 left thalmotomies and 0 of 22 right thalamotomies in right-handed patients, a significant tendency to lateralization. Dysphasia was described as varying from a mild difficulty in finding words and in naming objects to a much more severe disorder that rendered the patient's speech almost incomprehensible. Verbal output was reduced and there were disturbances of rhythm and modulation of speech, but even in the most severely involved, comprehension of speech was relatively preserved. Repetition of speech was normal. In the most mild cases speech was laconic and hesitant and the patient claimed he knew what he wanted to say, but would misname objects occasionally; one patient shows some impairment of grammar. The more severe cases demonstrated the uses of paraphasias and faulty grammar with perseveration in both spoken and written speech. The most severe cases, on the other hand, also showed additional disabilities including hemiplegia and disturbances of consciousness. Dysphasic responses cleared within a few weeks in six of the patients but persisted in 4; in 2 of these for 32 and 28 months, respectively, at last record. Bell considers a variety of the features of a stereotaxic operation that might be responsible for the dysphasia other than the ventrolateral thalamic lesion itself. In his series the burr holes through the skull was made a week early in a group of cases and no aphasia followed this procedure. Needling the brain alone has not produced aphasia, the language disturbance appearing only after creation of a lateral thalamic lesion (Riklan & Levita, 1969, pp. 136–137; Sem-Jacobsen, 1965). Bell concludes that the dysphasic disorder appears similar to the dysphasias of frontal lesions.

Further evidence associating this language disturbance to the ventrolateral thalamic lesion has come from post mortem studies of patients who demonstrated dysphasia acutely following thalamotomy. The report of Samra, Riklan, Levita, Zimmerman, Waltz, Bergmann, and Cooper (1969) histologically demonstrates lesions, acutely associated with dysphasia, that are clearly confined to ventrolateral thalamus. In the study of Hermann *et al.* (1966) the centers of the lesions associated with dysphasia are associated with ventrolateral thalamus or globus pallidus and rather conspicuously spare the intervening portion of internal capsule.

Another example of a lesion that is associated with language disturbance clearly localized to lateral thalamus and sparing internal cpasule is seen in Figure 3 (Ojemann, Blick, & Ward, 1969). This patient,[2] a middle-aged female, had had a right thalamotomy 3 years previously with no speech disturbance. She had a left thalamotomy 17 days before death from a pulmonary embolus. During those 17 days she was mildly dysnomic. This example of a ventrolateral thalamic

[2] I thank Arthur Ward, E. C. Alvord, and James Haynes of the Department of Neurosurgery and the Neuropathology Laboratory of the University of Washington for this material.

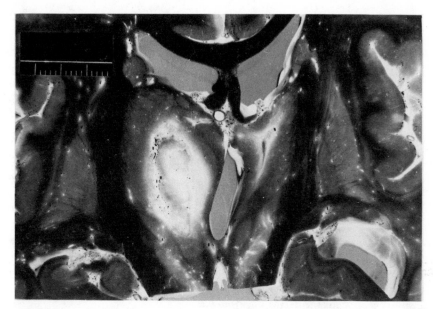

Figure 3 Coronal section of thalamus showing extent of a stereotaxic thalamic lesion associated with acute dysnomia. Lesion on right placed 3 years previously without language disturbance. Lesion on left placed 17 days before the right-handed patient succumbed to pulmonary embolus. Mild dysnomia persisted during those 17 days.

lesion actually producing dysnomia at the time of the patient's death, with the lesion histologically confined to thalamus, further supports the view that the language disturbance is related to lateral thalamus and not to immediately adjacent structures, especially internal capsule.

The language changes recorded on formal psychological tests, before and after stereotaxic ventrolateral thalamotomy, have been the subject of some controversy: Do any changes occur at all? And if they do occur, is there a differential effect of left from right thalamic lesions? The reported results on the verbal measures from the WAIS or its equivalent can be summarized as follows: No change in these measures could be detected in late testing (4 or more months after operation) in the reports of Christiensen, Juul-Jensen, Malmros, and Harmsen (1970) and Shut (1970), while Jurko and Andy (1964) found only a late decline in verbal IQ a year and a half after operation, unrelated to lateralization of the thalamotomy and not present on acute testing.

Deterioration of verbal performance following thalamotomy has been more frequently reported. Some studies have shown only early deterioration, others persisting deficits. Several studies found equivalent deficits after right or left thalamotomy, others differential deficits more marked after left thalamotomy. (There are no studies showing significantly greater verbal deficits on the WAIS following right thalamotomy.) Studies showing relatively equivalent changes after right or left thalamotomy include those of Asso, Crown, Russell, and Logue (1969) who compared the performance with a matched parkinsonian control group and at 3 weeks noted deterioration in comprehension, digit span, and picture arrangement for the operated group. These deficits had cleared by the time of late assessment, an average of 10 months following thalamotomy. Perret, Kohenof, and Siegfried (1969) have also reported a decrease in both verbal and performance IQ following right and left thalamotomy though not to a statistically significant extent. Their earliest testing, however, was at 6 months; the deficits persisted out to late testing, 18 months after operation. Riklan and Levita (1969) report extensive evaluation of thalamotomy patients using the WAIS and similar tests and have generally interpreted their data as showing acute deficits following thalamotomy but equivalent for the two hemispheres, although in an early study (Riklan, Diller, Weiner, & Cooper, 1960) they noted particular declines in digit span and arithmetic subtest scores for the left and not right brain, and on the subsequent factorial study (Riklan & Levita, 1964) they noted that "greater verbal weight occurred for left brain operants and great nonverbal weight occurred for right brain operants" although similar factors seem to account for the decrement from either side.

On the other hand several studies have found rather strongly lateralized decrements in the verbal performance measures of these psychologic tests. Krayenbuhl, Siegfried, Kohenof, and Yasargil (1965), testing at 4–6 days after operation, found a notable decrease in verbal memory following left and not right thalamotomy. No late testing is reported in this paper. Shapiro *et al.* (1973), testing patients at 2 weeks and again at a mean of 17 months postoperatively, found a decrease in the verbal IQ following left thalamotomy particularly involving vocabulary, similarities, comprehension, and general information (similarities and general information as well as digit span, also being disturbed from the right thalamotomy). These deficits persisted, though to a somewhat diminished extent, in the late postoperative testing.

Aside from the variation due to different timing in administering the postoperative test, one gets the impression that the WAIS and similar tests are not very sensitive instruments for evaluating the kind of language deficits that seem to be associated with thalamic lesions, for when one turns to reports of testing the effects of thalamic lesions using other formal neuropsychological tests, much more clearcut results seem to be present. A few test results show equivalent deficits from right or left thalamic lesions. Thus, measures of immediate and delayed recall and learning of paired associates carried out by Perret *et al.* (1969), and testing of paired-associate and auditory verbal recall and recognition by Asso *et al.* (1969) showed results that were disturbed equally by lesions in either thalamus. Deficits on these tests persisted in late testing 10–18 months postoperatively. Perret *et al.* (1969) concluded that thalamic lesions interfered with the storage of information, irrespective of the type of information, or side of lesion.

On the other hand, Almgren, Andersson, and Kullberg (1969, 1972) show both an acute and late highly significant disturbance on the Stroop Color Word Test and a memory test of word pairs following left and not right thalamotomy. Hays, Krikler, Walsh, and Woolfson (1966) found that the practice effect that they could identify following right thalamic lesions was absent following left thalamic lesions on Ammons Full Range Picture Vocabulary Test, and Jurko and Andy (1964) found deficits on the trail making and memory for designs tests following left and not right thalamic lesions. Riklan *et al.* (1969) who were unable to show significant differences between left and right thalamus on standard intelligence tests showed very clearcut differences when tests of object naming were used. A significant disturbance of object naming occurred in patients with left thalamic lesions compared to patients with right thalamic lesions or to Parkinson patients who were not operated on; the disturbance seemed to be more severe for the more complicated object names and seemed to clear with time following surgery.

We have studied the effects of right or left thalamotomy on our standard test of object naming, mental arithmetic, and short-term verbal memory described previously. Object-naming and retrieval slides were shown for a period of 4 sec, while the duration of the mental arithmetic task varied randomly from 3, 6, 10, 15, or 21 sec. Performance on object naming was measured by comparing performance on trials without stimulation at the time of operation, and on those same trials on the second postoperative day. With this particular comparison, the control period is after the placement of the burr hole and insertion of the electrode into the target area of the brain so that any later changes principally result from effects of a lesion, rather than brain needling. Any practice effect (which seems to be quite small) from the initial preoperative exposure to the test is also taken into account, and confounding with trials where stimulation occurs at the time of operation, which, as discussed at the end of this chapter, seems to have an effect on performance several days after operation, is avoided. We have data on object-naming performance in 11 patients following left ventrolateral thalamic lesions; 8 of these patients made no object-naming errors on the test at the time of operation; the other 4 made 2–8% errors. Two days following the ventrolateral thalamic lesion, one patient was too confused to undertake the test, 7 showed an increase in object-naming errors, none a decrease, and 3 no change. The average increase in object-naming errors for the 7 was 13½% with a range of 4–33%. This increase following left ventrolateral thalamic lesion is statistically significant (*P* < .01, Wilcoxson Matched Pairs Signed-Rank Test, single-tailed, Siegel, 1956). Although several patients had had right thalamic lesions six or more months previously, there is no particular correlation between those showing an increase in object-naming errors following left ventrolateral thalamic lesion and the presence of the previous right-sided lesion.

Ten patients had postoperative testing after right thalamotomy. During control performance at the time of operation, four of these showed no object naming errors, the remaining six showed 2–7% errors. (This does not differ significantly from performance of patients with left thalamic lesions.) Two days following right ventrolateral thalamotomy, all patients could be tested; five showed no change in their object-naming rates, three showed an increase, and two a decrease. The average was a 2.3% increase with a range of 17% increase to a 3% decrease. This change in performance following right thalamotomy is not statistically significant, but does differ significantly from the change following left thalamotomy ($P < .05$, Mann–Whitney U Test, one tail, Siegel, 1956). Most of the errors that occurred in responses of patients whose error rate increased following thalamotomy were misnamings, rather than omissions. Several of the patients who had left thalamic lesions showed perseveration in their postoperative performance. This was not seen after right thalamotomy. A number of the objects that could not be correctly named could be correctly retrieved following the mental arithmetic task distraction. Three left-thalamotomy patients correctly retrieved an average of 31% of the items incorrectly named, and 2 right-thalamotomy patients correctly retrieved an average 27% of the items incorrectly named.

Thus left thalamotomy seems to be associated with significantly more object-naming errors than right. The errors that appear acutely following thalamotomy appear to be principally misnamings, with an element of perseveration. Since a proportion of incorrectly named objects could be later correctly retrieved, it appears that confusion, or disturbances of perception, are not responsible for this disturbance of language.

Short-term verbal memory, with retrieval by cued recall was analyzed by comparing pre- with postoperative performance on trials with correct object naming (Ojemann, Hoyenga, & Ward, 1971b). Short-term verbal memory was disturbed following left but not right thalamotomy as illustrated in Figure 4. Patients undergoing left thalamotomy did significantly less well than they had preoperatively ($P < .05$) for all durations of the distraction, and the performance following left thalamotomy was significantly poorer than that following right thalamotomy at every distraction duration except 10 sec. Even when cued recall performance is corrected for the same proportion of speech errors that occurred during object naming (though whether they would occur during cued recall is an open question) there is still a significant residual increase in recall errors at 21-sec distraction after left thalamotomy compared to preoperative performance, which is significantly worse than performance following right thalamot-

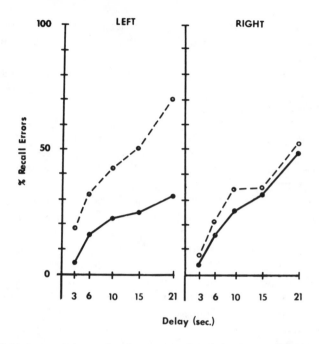

Figure 4 Short-term verbal memory disturbance after thalamotomy. Solid lines represent preoperative performance on cued recall of object names following a standard distraction (mental arithmetic) of 3 to 21 seconds duration (delay). Dashed lines are performance on second postoperative day. Performance after left thalamotomy is significantly poorer than before operation, or than after right thalamotomy. (Reprinted from Ojemann *et al.*, 1971b; by permission of the American Association of Neurological Surgeons on behalf of the *Journal of Neurosurgery*.)

omy. As one can note from Figure 4, the increase in recall errors following left thalamotomy appears to be related to the duration of the distraction, showing greater decrements in performance at the longer distractions. This data has been interpreted to suggest that left thalamic lesions not only interfere with object naming, but also with short-term verbal memory functions, at least on an acute basis (Ojemann *et al.*, 1971b).

STEREOTAXIC LESIONS OTHER THAN IN VENTROLATERAL THALAMUS

There is considerably less evidence concerning the changes in language function following the stereotaxic lesions in structures other than the ventrolateral nucleus. We have already mentioned the evidence that lesions centered in the internal capsule, immediately lateral to the lateral border of the thalamus do not seem to be associated with language disturbances (Hermann *et al.*, 1966).

In the early days of stereotaxic surgery for dyskinesias, medial globus pallidus was the preferred target rather than the ventrolateral thalamic nucleus. Thus, there is some evidence on the effects of pallidal lesions on language function. McFie (1960) using the Weschler–Bellevue Scale as well as a test of sentence learning and memory for designs, found decrements in digit span, arithmetic, similarities and vocabulary, and sentence learning following left and, except for arithmetic, not following right pallidal lesions; the same results occurred on testing a few patients with thalamic lesions within the first four weeks after operation. From inspection of his graphs, it would appear that the sentence-learning decrement involved exclusively cases of left pallidal lesions and digit-span decrement seemed to predominantly involve pallidal cases also, although the number of left thalamic cases in the entire series was very small. Svennilson, Torvik, Lowe, and Leksell (1960), in reviewing the effects of pallidal lesions on dyskinesias, noted dysphasia exclusively following lesions in the dominant hemisphere, present in 24% of the patients who had dilated ventricles and 7½% of patients with normal ventricles. The aphasia is described as a word-finding difficulty with paraphasias, indicating a lack of coordination between thought and speech. In every case, recovery was nearly complete within three months of operation. Christiensen *et al.* (1970) evaluated patients having both pallidal and thalamic lesions, but found no deficits in chronic WAIS testing with either type lesion although on Rorschach evaluation, it was thought that the pallidal group in particular had a diminished and more rigid activity in contrast to the patients who had undergone thalamotomy. In the study of Hermann *et al.* (1966) where lesions were placed in ventrolateral thalamus, globus pallidus, or the intervening capsule, dysphasic responses seemed to be present about equally for lesions centered in either ventrolateral thalamus or globus pallidus.

More recently, stereotaxic lesions for dyskinesias have often been placed immediately beneath the ventrolateral thalamus in the subthalamic region of the fields of Forel. Few comparisons have been made of the effects on language function of these often smaller lesions compared with lesions in ventrolateral thalamus. In evaluating the effects of a variety of subcortical lesions in the region of the thalamus on epilepsy, Mullan, Vailati, Karasick, and Mailis (1967) reported pre- and postoperative IQ testing, though the interval between operation and postoperative testing is not stated. Verbal IQ decrements were noted in some patients having left ventrolateral thalamic lesions, whereas these decrements did not seem to be present in patients having lesions in the fields of Forel on the same side. The number of cases is quite small, however, and some of them already had rather low preoperative IQ's. It should be noted that persisting deficits in Porteus Maze testing of visual spatial function have been noted from field-of-Forel lesions in the nondominant hemisphere (Meier & Story, 1967).

Spiegel and Wycis (1962) reported on the language changes following dorso-medial thalamic lesions. Dysphasic problems were rare postoperatively, being present in only 1 of 90 cases, while dysphasia was present in 3 of 16 ventro-lateral thalamotomies reported by the same author. (On the other hand, dys-arthria was quite apparent after dorsomedial thalamotomy.)

More recently, lesions have been placed in the inferior half of the pulvinar in the treatment of some dyskinesias, particularly dystonia and spasticity. Brown, Riklan, Waltz, Jackson, and Cooper (1971) and Brown (1974) studied the effects of these inferior pulvinar lesions on language. The language changes following these lesions are reported to be much like those accompanying ventrolateral thalamus lesions; that is, they appear only following dominant hemisphere lesions, and are relatively infrequent and transient. In Brown *et al.*'s (1971) case material, these language changes were present only when there was a previous deficit in language function. Then the pulvinar lesion sometimes exacer-bated the language deficit, producing an additional "anomic or misnaming state" without disturbing comprehension. Brown (1974) noted that there was an immediate postoperative decrement in verbal learning demonstrated by such tests as supra-span word recall and paired associates. The verbal IQ tends to be acutely diminished after left pulvinar lesions, rather similarly to that described by the same group following ventrolateral thalamic lesions. This deficit generally clears within 3 months.

We might briefly summarize the effects of the stereotaxic lesions in and around the thalamus on language function as follows, keeping in mind that the exact location of the stereotaxic lesions is not always precisely known. Internal capsule and medial thalamic lesions do not seem to be associated with language disturbance, and this may also be true of subthalamic lesions. Globus pallidus and pulvinar lesions resemble those in the ventrolateral thalamus in terms of the language disturbance obtained. The deficits following pallidal lesions perhaps are more marked, and those following inferior pulvinar lesions less marked than those from ventrolateral thalamus, although this observation is confounded by the fact that the pallidal lesions generally were made earlier in the history of stereotaxic surgery, during which time the accuracy and precision in lesion size have increased markedly. Ventrolateral thalamic lesions in the dominant hemi-sphere are sometimes (perhaps in as many as a third or more of cases) associated with a language disturbance that is usually transient but occasionally may persist (see for example Bell's two cases and the study of Shapiro). The language disturbance is usually expressive, with many misnamings and frequent persevera-tion, but little disturbance in comprehension. Occasionally it may appear after nondominant thalamotomy, but significantly less often than after dominant. It is associated with rather striking and persisting deficits in color-word naming, and with acute and sometimes persisting deficits in verbal memory function.

THALAMIC CHANGES ACCOMPANYING CORTICAL
LESIONS WITH LANGUAGE DEFICITS

Another approach to the role of thalamic structures in language function is to look at the anatomic status of the thalamus in patients having language deficits and cortical lesions. Two studies along this line are of interest. Van Buren and Borke (1969) assessed the degree of thalamic damage in patients having rather sparsely described language disturbances following cerebral lesions. Cerebral lesions predominantly involved temporal and parietal lobes. Thus, such a study seems to shed most light on the anatomic basis for interaction between cortical speech areas and the thalamic structures. These investigators found that the severity of the language defect seemed to parallel the degree of degeneration of the pulvinar, that speech is not supported in an essential fashion by the posteriolateral quadrant of the pulvinar, that preservation of the posterior pole and much of the medial pulvinar did not prevent the speech defect, but that there is an area of overlap apparently significant to speech loss or retention located in the anterior superior pulvinar and particularly in its more lateral aspects.

Another kind of suggestive data comes from the cases reported by Mohr (1973). In these three cases, infarcts that destroyed the left inferior frontal area and immediately underlying subcortical white matter, were followed only by a transient motor aphasia that rapidly cleared. Mohr (personal communication) indicates that the thalamus in these patients was histologically intact. Thus, the intactness of those portions of dominant thalamus concerned with language function would be one hypothesis that might explain the rapid regression of the motor aphasia in these patients.

STIMULATION OF SUBCORTICAL SITES DURING
LANGUAGE TESTS

Electrical stimulation provides another technique for studying the relationship between a particular subcortical site and language function. This technique yields a somewhat different type of information than that obtained from the study of static lesions. Application of an electric current across a group of neurons elicits both excitatory and inhibitory effects, usually a central excitation with an inhibitory surround. Such a current will also alter function in "en passage" fibers.

Vocalization can be evoked by electrical stimulation of the motor strip, but these vocalizations are never words. Spontaneous language has not been evoked from cortical stimulation. Rather cortical stimulation seems to act on such complex behavior as language as though it were introducing noise into the system, effectively creating a temporary lesion during stimulation. The brain apparently does not have time to compensate for this sudden burst of noise, so its introduction at any point in the complex system involved in language production may interfere with ultimate performance. Thus, the anatomic picture that comes from the study of the effects of stimulation on language would seem to indicate the full extent of brain structures concerned with language at a given time, both those essential for the maintenance of language, and those areas for which alternative pathways would be readily available, given sufficient time.

The use of stimulation as a technique for studying language has one great advantage over the use of lesions. The period of disruption of function is, in large measure, temporary, and thus such questions as how well the intact brain can use information introduced during the time language systems are disrupted can be studied (Ojemann & Ward, 1971). However, a number of special problems are present when stimulation is used, for which controls are necessary. The first of these is spread of the stimulating current widely beyond the electrode. Near the thalamus, controls for spread of current are relatively easily obtained. Immediately lateral to thalamus is the internal capsule, a structure having a very low threshold for contralateral motor movements in response to electrical stimulation. If one restricts the stimulating currents to those below the threshold for evoking motor movement, there is achieved a fair degree of confidence that current has not spread to the capsule. Similarly, the sensory relay nuclei (ventro-posterior-medial and lateral nuclei) in the human thalamus have a very low threshold for evoked sensations when electrically stimulated. These sensations are a very localized contralateral dysesthesia. Again, restricting stimulating currents to those below the threshold for sensation would seem to indicate that current spread to this quite sensitive structure has not occurred.

Additional problems center around localizing the stimulating electrode in the absence of histologic confirmation of its position. This problem has been handled in our data by plotting the location of the electrode in relation to reference points, usually the anterior and posterior commissure, that can be identified on X-rays taken at the time of the stereotaxic operation. These measurements, after correction for X-ray magnification, are then transferred to charts showing the mean location of the thalamus and the range of variation of its borders about the same X-ray reference points. Such charts have been prepared from meticulous histologic studies (cf. Van Buren & Borke, 1972). From such charts one can then make a statistical statement about the probability that a particular electrode is or is not in thalamus or in one of the subgroups of thalamus. We have had only a single occasion in which we could check the location of an electrode by later histologic examination. This case has been published (Ojemann, Fedio, & Van Buren, 1968) and seems to provide good correlation between the electrode location inferred by the above method and its actual location histologically.

Before considering the effects of subcortical stimulation on language, it seems appropriate to review the effects of cortical stimulation on language. Penfield and Roberts (1959) have reported an extensive experience on the language changes associated with cortical stimulation, principally using tests of object naming. In their data, an arrest of speech for the duration of the stimulus could be evoked, especially from right or left motor strip, and to a lesser extent, from the supplementary motor area, the parietal temporal junction, and the inferior frontal operculum on the left side. Such an arrest of speech seemed to be the most nonspecific language response evoked, in terms of localization. What Penfield and Roberts (1959) defined as *repetitions* (and what we shall call *perseverations*) were evoked from the left side in the inferior frontal operculum, the parietal temporal junction, the supplementary motor area, and in a single instance from the medial face of the right cerebral hemisphere. What Penfield and Roberts (1959) defined as *anomia*, i.e., the inability to name objects but with retained ability to speak, was the most localized language change evoked; this response was evoked only from the left side in the region of the inferior frontal operculum, in the parietal temporal junction, and in the supplementary motor area, the three cortical areas usually considered to subserve language function. Thus, from the observed effects of cortical stimulation on language function, one would not expect an arrest of speech to be a sign of involvement of a particular subcortical site in language functions, while the presence of anomia especially might well be. Indeed, arrests of speech have been reported following stimulation of either thalamus (Guiot, Hertzog, Rondot, & Molina, 1961; Sem-Jacobsen, 1968, pp. 96–97) and from the frontal striate areas of both cerebral hemispheres including the heads of the caudate nuclei (Van Buren, 1963; Van Buren, Li, & Ojemann, 1966).

VENTROLATERAL THALAMIC STIMULATION

Stimulation, including stimulation during tests of language, is part of the standard techniques involved in ventrolateral thalamotomy, as an aid in accurate lesion placement, and in minimizing complications of the procedure (Ojemann & Ward, 1973; Ward & Stern, 1963). The test of object naming, mental arithmetic, and short-term verbal memory described earlier in this chapter has been used in place of informal testing of language function during thalamic stimulation. In the following studies, objects are presented for a 4-sec period, the mental arithmetic task lasts 6 sec, and retrieval slides 4 sec each. Testing is carried out immediately after initial insertion of the 1 X 5 mm thalamic electrode into the target area. For a test of object naming, stimulation is applied during the 4 sec that an object is pictured on the screen on randomly selected trials. Monopolar stimulation uses 60 Hz, 2.5-msec biphasic square wave pulses delivered by a constant current stimulator. All stimulation currents are below the threshold for sensation or motor responses. Further check on the localization of the electrode is provided by responses that are considered to be local to the ventrolateral thalamus: the driving of the dyskinetic process, and inhibition of the gamma loop (Ward & Stern, 1963). Both of these local effects are evoked at thresholds that are approximately the same as those that elicit language changes.

Satisfactory data on the effect of stimulation on object naming has been obtained from 17 right-handed patients undergoing left thalamotomy and 20 undergoing right thalamotomy. Most patients suffered from Parkinson's disease, but 6 of the group had other dyskinesias, and in 2, intractible pain was the indication for thalamotomy. Some of these patients had had previous thala-motomies, but none performed less than six months before. Any apparent relation between the previous lesions and the stimulation results is mentioned below. Only 6 of these patients were female. There are no significant differences between patients undergoing right or left thalamotomy as to age or preoperative performance on the object-naming task.

The locations of the centers of electrodes are plotted in Figure 5, indicated by symbols (see legend, Figure 5) showing whether any alteration in language occurred upon stimulation. An arrest of speech, i.e., inability to speak at all during the stimulation was evoked from three patients with right-brain elec-trodes and one with left (identified on Figure 5 as "N"). Arrest responses were evoked from electrodes in right brain that had a high probability of being in internal capsule, lateral to the mean location, indeed in some cases even lateral to the extreme lateral range of variation of the lateral thalamic border. This would seem to fit rather well with observation that arrest responses can be evoked from the motor strip and frontostriate white matter of right as well as left brain.

The one patient exhibiting an arrest response from stimulation of left brain had an electrode located either in superior lateral thalamus or in the adjacent capsule. Because of the nonspecific relationship of the arrest response to lan-guage function at cortical levels, it will not be considered further in the following discussion of the language changes accompanying ventrolateral thalam-ic stimulation.

Three other types of errors were evoked on the object-naming task. One, we have called *anomia* ("A" on Figure 5), i.e., the patient was unable to name the object correctly but demonstrated his ability to speak, either by saying *this is a* but omitting the name during the time available, or by giving a wrong object name. The second type of error we have called perseveration ("P" on Figure 5), repetition of the first syllable of the correct object name during the duration of stimulation. The third type of error, which seems to be unique to the thalamus, we have called repetition, ("R" on Figure 5),[3] the frequent repeated use of a particular wrong word each time stimulation currents above threshold are

---

[3] In a previous report on speech representation in the thalamus (Ojemann & Ward, 1971) the one case of a *repetition* error (as now defined) then present in our data was not distinguished from other anomic errors.

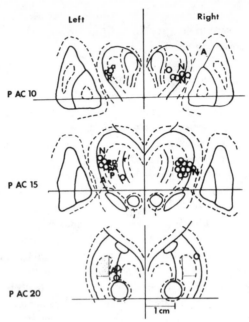

Figure 5 Object-naming errors accompanying thalamic stimulation. The mean location and range of variation of the border of thalamus and globus pallidus are shown on sections 10, 15, and 20 mm posterior to the anterior commissure. The center of each electrode included in this study is plotted on the nearest section. The changes in object naming during formal testing evoked from each electrode is indicated by the following symbols: O, no change; N, arrest of speech; A, anomia; P, perseveration; R, repetition. ⊠ marks the site of the electrode in a case where repetition errors were evoked at stimulating current above the threshold for sensation. "r" marks the site of the electrode in a case where repetition errors were evoked on informal testing. The shaded area in the section 20 mm posterior to anterior commissure is the most anterior extent of the "pulvinar" electrodes in the study of Ojemann *et al.* (1968). Anomia was evoked from left- but not right-brain electrodes in this area. The site of all other object-naming errors evoked from left thalamus in that study are also indicated, by "a" for anomic and "p" for perseveration errors. (Mean location and range of variation adapted from Van Buren & Borke, 1972.)

applied. Object-naming errors of these three types were evoked only from left brain in these right-handed patients except for one right-brain electrode clearly in internal capsule, from which an anomic response was evoked.

Statistical comparison of the effect of stimulation of right and left brain on object naming runs into the difficulty that the sensory threshold in the region of ventrolateral thalamus is lower in right than in left brain (Fedio, Van Buren, & Ojemann, unpublished data). In order to avoid confounding results with this factor, we can consider only those patients who were stimulated at current levels above the lowest current eliciting an object-naming error. This procedure and the exclusion of patients showing the arrest response reduced the sample size to 14 left-brain patients and 14 right. One patient with a right-brain electrode made an anomic error, while 7 of the left made anomic, perseverative, and repetition errors. This difference is significant, at a *P* value of .025 (Fisher's exact probability).

These types of language errors seem to be evoked from different parts of left lateral thalamus. The anomic type of error was evoked principally from posterior central portions of ventrolateral thalamus. These anomic errors appeared at an average threshold of 8mA[4] (range 6–10 mA) and were predominantly omissions of the object name (In two patients only omissions were seen, while the third made half omission and half misnaming errors.) They could be reproduced an average of 42% of the time, with subsequent stimulation at or above threshold current. In the two patients in which anomic errors were omissions, the correct object name could not be recalled, while in the third the omissions were recalled correctly while the misnamings were recalled as the erroneous word.

Perseverative errors cluster in a very discrete area in the central portion of the ventrolateral thalamus. Both the two patients in this series, and the only patient from the earlier series of Ojemann *et al.* (1968) who showed perseverative errors have electrodes located in this quite discrete area. Perseverative errors appeared with an average threshold of 5.5 mA (range 5–6 mA). These errors were repetitions of the first syllable of the correct object name lasting the duration of stimulation. For example, in response to a picture of a telephone the patient would say *This is a tele-tele-tele* (the current was then turned off)—*a telephone*. Perseverative errors or other language errors appeared on 50–60% of the ensuing trials at or above the threshold stimulating current. The two patients showing perseverative errors in our series were also the only patients who showed evoked errors of another class, in each case a single jargon misnaming of an object.

The two patients showing repetition errors had electrodes clustered together more anteriorly in lateral thalamus. The first of these two patients repeated the word *ace* on 3 out of 4 occasions when the stimulation current, above 8 mA, was applied during object naming. On the fourth occasion, he gave a different wrong word. The word *ace* does not appear as an object on the test. On two of these four occasions he was able to retrieve correctly the object for which he used the term *ace*. The word *ace* appeared on 1 of 4 stimulations at or above the 8-mA threshold at the time of recall for correct object names. The other patient used *boat* as an incorrect name for 2 of 4 objects above the 10-mA threshold. *Boat* is the name of an object on the list. Indeed it was the last object picture correctly named at a 9-mA current, just below the threshold for object-naming errors. Recall was for the incorrect object name, and when stimulation currents were

---

[4] Current levels are measured between peaks of the biphasic pulses. These threshold current levels are in the same range as those recently reported for evoking phosphenes from human cortex (Dobelle, Mladejovsky, & Girvin, 1974).

applied at the time of recall for correct object names *boat* appeared incorrectly on 2 of 6 trials.

We have seen a somewhat similar phenomenon in two other patients with left-brain electrodes, identified on Figure 5 by "r" and the shaded "R". The small "r" marks the location of an electrode in a woman suffering from Parkinsonism who was not formally tested because of her advanced age. When initially stimulated at this site at 8 V the patient said *that's goofy*. On repeating the stimulation the second time the patient said *twinky*. This same word was evoked promptly with the third and fourth stimulation, the last applied when the patient was instructed to remain quiet beforehand. On the fifth stimulation the patient was actively counting and the evoked word interrupted the counting, following which counting was immediately resumed where it had left off. On the seventh stimulation the patient changed her phrase to *you just made the shuck go* and when the eighth stimulation occurred a similar phrase, *shucks once in a while* appeared. Stimulations at the same current levels but at a location 2 mm more lateral or 2 mm more anterior did not alter language function. Thus, this patient shows a repeated evoked wrong word, which appaears to be spontaneously evoked by stimulation even when she was instructed to be quiet, a determination that could not be made in the other patients because of the constraints of formal testing.

The patient identified by the shaded "R" had evoked sensation at 8 mA. When he was instructed to ignore the sensation and the current was increased to 10 mA, the word *fish*, the name of the last object correctly named during stimulation at 8 mA, was used incorrectly on each of the two objects presented at this larger current. No similar language error has been evoked in this series of patients by stimulating currents above threshold for sensation, although such currents are sometimes associated with an omission of an object name, a phenomenon that we have generally ascribed to the distraction of the evoked sensation. Since rather wide current spread may be present with stimulating currents above sensory threshold, the location of this patient's electrode provides less indication of the area where repetition can be evoked in left thalamus than do the other cases.

Evoked disturbance of language with left thalamic stimulation seems to be somewhat more likely in the presence of a previous right thalamotomy. All patients showing evoked repetition errors (except the elderly lady), none of those showing anomic errors, and one of the patients showing perseverative errors had previous contralateral lesions. Thus the presence of a contralateral thalamic lesion is not an essential condition for evoking language disturbance from left thalamus.

The latency for correct object naming has also been determined. Left thalamic stimulation tends to decrease this latency (a mean decrease of 3½%); 12 of the 17 patients showed a decrease and 5 an increase, not a statistically significant change. Latencies for evoked anomic misnaming errors are generally longer than the latency for correct object naming on the interspersed trials without stimulation.

As described above, the test of language function used in these patients also provides a measure of performance on short-term verbal memory tests with a standard distraction, the 6 sec of the mental arithmetic task. Analysis of performance on short-term verbal memory tests was restricted to stimulating currents below the threshold, not only for sensation, but also for any object-naming errors. The stimulating currents were applied either during the presentation of the material to be recalled (the object-naming task), during the standard distraction (the mental arithmetic task), during retrieval by cued recall, or during both presentation and retrieval on the same trial. Randomly interspersed between trials with these stimulations were trials without stimulation, which provided the measure of control performance.

Ojemann *et al*. (1971a) describe the following changes in short-term verbal memory with this test. Stimulation during presentation significantly decreases the number of recall errors compared to control trials. Stimulation in the same locations with the same currents, but applied at the time of retrieval by cued recall, significantly increases the number of recall errors. Pairing the stimulation on the same trial at both the time of presentation and the time of retrieval results in the algebraic sum of these two effects and cannot be distinguished from control performance. The latency for correct recall responses is significantly shortened by stimulation during recall (Ojemann, 1974a). Right ventrolateral thalamic stimulation differs significantly from left thalamic stimulation, in that many of these changes in either short-term verbal memory errors or latency are absent.[5] The model proposed as an explanation of these findings was that stimulation of left ventrolateral thalamus evokes a "specific (or focal) alerting response" labeling verbal material in the external environment so that its subsequent retrieval is enhanced, while at the same time inhibiting the retrieval of material already internalized. This specific alerting response may act as a gate determining what enters or leaves short-term verbal memory at a given time. The shortening of retrieval latency is part of this specific alerting response, as is the tendency to decrease latency in object naming with left thalamic stimulation.[6]

[5] Patients with right or left thalamic electrodes included in these comparisons do not differ significantly as to recall performance on trials without stimulation, number of trials with stimulation, or maximum stimulating currents. Mean threshold for recall error with left-brain stimulation during recall was 4.1 mA (Ojemann *et al.*, 1971a).

[6] This specific alerting response does not seem to be generalized arousal. It does not involve number reading (Ojemann, 1974a) as would be expected if it were part of generalized arousal, but rather seems to be most marked for internal processes involving memory. The specific alerting response seems more focal, but somewhat similar to the "directed activation" of Riklan and Levita (1969). Those authors suggested that diminished "directed activation" after pallidotomy and thalamotomy was responsible for the language changes they observed.

Study of the effect of left thalamic stimulation on the mental arithmetic portion of the test described above has also been carried out (Ojemann, 1974a). Left thalamic stimulation accelerated the rate of counting, while right thalamic stimulation tended to slow the rate of counting. This acceleration of counting backwards by three's was not due to faster identification of the initial number, but rather seemed to be an acceleration of the mental calculations involved in that task. This change also has been ascribed to a specific alerting response resulting from left thalamic stimulation. The thalamocortical activating system, mediated through the intralaminar and reticular nuclei of the thalamus (Jasper, 1960) that have extensive interactions with ventrolateral thalamic nucleus (Purpura, 1969; Scheibel & Scheibel, 1967), has been proposed as the anatomic base for this specific, or focal, alerting response.

There seems to be an interaction between this specific alerting response and language functions in the dominant ventrolateral thalamus. Correlations between some of the effects of stimulation and the acute postoperative anomia following left thalamotomy described above were sought. A statistic measuring the specific alerting response, generated by summing the increase in recall errors with stimulation during recall, minus the change in recall errors with stimulation during presentation, and minus the change in latency of correct recall responses with stimulation during recall has a Spearman Rank Order correlation (Siegel, 1956) with the degree of postoperative anomia of $-.799$ ($p < .01$). This correlation seems to suggest that the greater the effects of the specific alerting response on the short-term memory and latency, the less likely is a postoperative anomia. Thus, the thalamic role in language may be related to an interaction with mechanisms involved in the maintenance of focal attention to specific and perhaps specifically verbal aspects of the external environment, mechanisms that are also important in at least short-term memory function.[7]

Another possible function of the left thalamus in language comes from study of the autonomic changes associated with thalamic stimulation. Thalamic stimulation, particularly medial thalamic stimulation, is known to produce an inhibition of respiration with prolonged expiration (Schaltenbrand, 1965). In a study of these effects, Ojemann and Van Buren (1967) found that this respiratory inhibition has a significantly lower threshold from left than right thalamus and seems to localize to the medial central portion of the ventrolateral thalamus, and superior parts of pulvinar (which are also the location of electrodes where language effects can be evoked from the human thalamus). Thus, an interface

---

[7] Correlations of such significance do not exist between the degree of postoperative anomia and: any single part of the specific alerting response statistic, or the magnitude of the short-term verbal memory disturbance after thalamotomy. [However, the magnitude of the evoked specific alerting effect seems to predict the severity of the short-term memory disturbance (Ojemann *et al.*, 1971b).]

with the respiratory mechanism, providing prolonged expiration, the necessary respiratory substrate for speech production, may also be located in the lateral thalamus.

PULVINAR

Ojemann *et al.* (1968) studied the effects of stimulation of chronically implanted multicontact electrodes on performance on an object-naming task somewhat similar to the one described in this chapter. They found that at stimulating currents that evoked no sensation or after discharge, anomic responses were evoked when electrodes were located in a discrete area bounded by a coronal plane 3 mm in front of the posterior commissure, horizontal plane 7½ mm superior to the intercommissural plane, and parasaggital plane 12½ mm lateral to the midline in all but one case. In 13 right-handed patients having electrodes within this area of left posterior superior lateral thalamus, anomia was evoked in 10, while in 12 similar patients with electrodes in the same area on the right side no anomia was evoked (Ojemann, 1974b).[8] The average threshold current for this effect was 7.6 mA with a range of 4–14 mA. About half of these errors were misnamings, the remainder omissions. Anomia could be evoked on about three-quarters of successive stimulations of the same pair of contacts, at the same or larger currents. When the arbitrary borders delimiting this area are compared to the average anterior border of the pulvinar (Ojemann *et al.*, 1968; Van Buren & Borke, 1972) these two areas seemed to show a remarkable correspondence. Thus it appears that anomia can also be evoked from the anterior superior portion of the left pulvinar. The anterior limit of the superior pulvinar is indicated in Figure 5. Anomic responses evoked from ventrolateral thalamus appear to be an anterior extension of this same area.

The latency for correct object naming at stimulation currents below the threshold for anomia or sensation was found to be prolonged with left pulvinar stimulation, and not with right (Ojemann *et al.*, 1968). This can be contrasted with the tendency for left ventrolateral thalamic stimulation to shorten the latency of correct object naming.

Short-term verbal memory function was also studied with left pulvinar stimulation (Ojemann & Fedio, 1968; Ojemann, 1974b). The test used to measure short-term verbal memory in those studies differs some from the one described previously, and has been published in detail in Fedio and Weinberg (1971), and Ojemann and Fedio (1968). Retrieval is cued by the picture of the succeeding object, after a 4-sec distraction occupied by reading the word *and* pictured on the screen. Performance was determined for trials with stimulating currents

---

[8] These patients were matched as to age, IQ, memory quotient, average stimulating current, and number of trials on the two sides.

below the threshold for anomia, and where the latency of response was such that at least half of the 4 sec that the cueing object was on the screen were available for a short-term memory response. The ability to recall information presented prior to stimulation was found to be markedly impaired with left and not right pulvinar stimulation below the threshold for anomia, while the ability to retrieve during stimulation information presented earlier in the same stimulation, or to retrieve after stimulation information presented during stimulation was found to be appreciably less impaired. However, the ability to retrieve information presented during stimulation was still more impaired than the ability to retrieve information presented and retrieved under nonstimulation conditions. We can now interpret this data as suggesting that the pulvinar stimulation too shows some effect of the specific alerting response, so that information presented during stimulation is retrieved more accurately than that presented prior to stimulation, but retrieved during stimulation. However, the specific alerting response seems to be less intense with pulvinar than with ventrolateral thalamic stimulation, since performance does not reach control levels, while control levels are exceeded with ventrolateral thalamic stimulation. This data would suggest that the specific alerting response is related more to anterior thalamic structures.[9]

OTHER SUBCORTICAL SITES

The multicontact electrodes used in the study of Ojemann *et al.* (1968) also place some contacts in the subcortical white matter just lateral to the splenium of the corpus callosum. Anomic errors were evoked from this subcortical white matter of both left and right brains. (6 of 11 patients showed anomia from the left and 4 of 9 from the right.) The ability to reproduce the anomia with the same or larger currents was appreciably less in the right parietal white matter than in the left [39% right versus 79% left (*P* of difference = .024)]. Anomic errors in the parietal white matter tended to be of the omission type rather than approximately half misnamings as seen with thalamic stimulation. In addition the patients were generally unable to recall the objects that were incorrectly

---

[9] We have considered the disturbance of recall, when stimulation occurs during recall, to be part of the specific alerting response, because the effect is seen in the same electrode sites and at the same stimulating currents as is the improvement in performance when stimulation occurs during presentation. However, the disturbance of recall seems to be of greater magnitude at electrode sites more posterior in lateral thalamus, in pulvinar, and in posterior ventrolateral nucleus, while the improvement in performance with stimulation during presentation is more intense with anterior ventrolateral-nucleus stimulation. Magnitude of the improvement in recall performance after stimulation during presentation does not correlate significantly with disturbance in recall when stimulation occurs during recall, nor with the degree of shortening of latency for correct recall responses, either.

named with parietal white matter stimulation, in contrast to thalamic stimulation, where recall of misnamed objects is as accurate as that for correctly named objects. These data were interpreted to suggest that stimulation altered function in a condensation of fibers passing from the right parietal cortex to the language area on the left parietal cortex.

The results from the studies reviewed above on the effects of thalamic stimulation on object naming may be summarized as follows. There seems to be an area in left lateral thalamus encompassing the anterior superior portion of the pulvinar, and the central portions of ventrolateral thalamus from which the same kind of object-naming errors can be evoked as those that are evoked with stimulation of the cortical surface in those areas considered to be related to language function. Just anterior to the area of central ventrolateral thalamus where these anomic errors can be evoked, perseverative errors occur. With stimulation anterior to that, a type of error, seemingly unique to thalamus, is evoked in which there is repetition of the same wrong word, that wrong word representing a kind of spontaneous speech, in that it appears on occasions when the current is applied even when the patient has been instructed not to speak. These studies also suggest that anterior parts of dominant lateral thalamus are the site of an interface between language functions and a specific alerting response for verbal material in the external environment.

Aphasic disturbances with dominant thalamic stimulation have been described (Ramamurti, 1967; Sem-Jacobsen, 1968, p. 141; Toth, 1972). Arrest of speech with ventrolateral thalamic stimulation of only dominant hemisphere has been mentioned by Krayenbuhl *et al.* (1965). Guiot *et al.* (1961) and Sem-Jacobsen (1968, pp. 96–97) evoked speech arrest from either ventrolateral thalamus. The phenomenon of evoked spontaneous speech was initially described by Schaltenbrand (1965; Schaltenbrand, Spuler, Wahrens, & Rumler, 1971; Doty (1969)), resulting from stimulation of the dominant ventral oral thalamus and is mentioned in passing by Toth (1972). (Ventral oral thalamus corresponds to the anterior part of ventrolateral nucleus in the nomenclature we have used here.) On the other hand Bertrand (1966) and Hermann *et al.* (1966) were unable to evoke any alterations in speech by stimulating the ventrolateral thalamus. Disturbance of short-term memory with stimulation of anterior thalamus and caudate has been reported by Bechtereva, Genkin, Morseeva, and Smirnov (1967). Schaltebrand, Spuler, and Wahrens (1972) has also observed an inhibitory effect on speech function with stimulation in a rather discrete area in the corpus callosum.

CONCLUSIONS

The data cited above, from the study of spontaneous and stereotaxic lesions, and with stimulation of thalamus and adjacent structures, all seem to point in the same direction. An area of dominant lateral thalamus involving the ventro-lateral nucleus and a corner of the pulvinar is a site where object naming can be disturbed in a rather stereotyped way. The patient retains intact comprehension and remains fluent, but is often unable to name objects and frequently per-severates. The defect extends across modalities and involves arithmetic informa-tion. This language defect, resulting from alteration of dominant lateral thalamus function, is usually more transitory than language defects resulting from al-tered function of the cortical speech areas.

What function can be proposed for the dominant thalamus in language? Penfield and Roberts (1959) suggest that it is major integrating center between the frontal and parietal cortical language areas. Anatomically this seems reason-able (Ojemann & Ward, 1971; Penfield & Roberts, 1959) but one would expect more profound language disturbances from lesions in these areas were it such an integrating structure. Rather, the thalamus may provide an interaction with mechanisms involved in highly specific focal alerting, and directing of attention—mechanisms that are also important in short-term (and perhaps long-term, see the following) memory. Indeed these thalamic mechanisms may be the site of an important interaction between language and memory. We have also presented data suggesting that dominant lateral thalamus may be an interface between language processes and respiratory function. Interaction between language and specific alerting or respiration are functions that could likely be eventually subsumed by other areas of the brain, since both the central autonomic system and central alerting mechanism are generally systems with bilateral and rather widespread representation.

Thus, it seems likely that parts of the language function are performed in dominant lateral thalamus, but this structure usually is not an indispensable part of the language system.

EFFECTS OF THALAMIC STIMULATION ON APHASIA

The evidence that dominant thalamic stimulation at the time of input of material enhances later retrieval, so that the material is recalled more accurately than under nonstimulation control conditions has been previously mentioned. In order to determine whether this effect might extend into long-term memory, and also to see if it might be of some therapeutic benefit in patients having language disorders, the effect of intraoperative stimulation on postoperative testing (on the second day after operation) for patients showing postoperative anomia has been analyzed.[10] For these patients the number of object-naming

---

[10] Patients who demonstrated no postoperative dysnomia showed no consistent effect of lateral thalamic stimulation on later object naming. Analyzed in the manner described here the three nonanomic patients having left-brain electrodes showed, respectively, more, fewer,

errors occurring on nonstimulation trials at the time of operation was determined, and then the change in number of object-naming errors on these nonstimulation trials on second postoperative-day testing was determined. The patients who showed an increase in object-naming errors on second day after operation were considered to demonstrate an anomia (as discussed previously) and they are the subjects of this study. Of 10 testable left-thalamotomy patients, 7 showed such an increase, as did 3 of 10 following right thalamotomy. Each of these patients' average postoperative performance per nonstimulation trial was then used to determine the expected number of object-naming errors at postoperative testing on trials where stimulation during object naming had occurred at operation. This expected number was compared with the actual number of errors made at postoperative testing on these same trials. Fewer errors actually occurred in postoperative performance in the trials where stimulation during object naming had occurred at operation, than would be expected from the performance on trials without stimulation at operation, in 6 of the 7 patients who showed anomia on nonstimulation trials after left thalamotomy. [Mean expected number of errors 2.3, mean observed number of errors 1.3, a 43.4% decrease from the expected error rate ($P = .016$ Wilcoxson Matched Pairs Sign-Ranked Test, single-tailed, Siegel, 1956).] Of the three right-thalamotomy patients who showed anomia on nonstimulation trials postoperatively, the observed number of errors at the time of second postoperative-day testing on trials where stimulation occurred at the time of operation was also less than the expected number in all three (mean expected number 1.87, mean observed number 1.0, a 44.4% decrease from expected error rates). The only patient actually making more errors than expected following left thalamic lesions was the only patient who did not show a specific alerting response with left thalamic stimulation. One of the three right-thalamotomy patients showing a decrease was the only one of all patients studied who showed the specific alerting response with right thalamic stimulation. Stimulation is randomly dispersed across all trials of the test on these patients, so differential difficulty of stimulation items will not explain these results. Rather, these data suggest that the specific alerting response with thalamic stimulation extends to long-term memory, and that it might be useful in some patients having language disorders, insofar as the transient anomia following thalamotomy is a model of a language disorder.

Further opportunity to test this hypothesis was possible in a patient having a preexisting anomia following a left-hemisphere cerebrovascular accident several years previously. In this patient, suffering from spasticity, the inferior pulvinar

---

and the same number of observed errors postoperatively on trials with stimulation at the time of operation as would have been expected from performance on nonstimulation trials. Of seven patients with right-brain electrodes, no errors were expected in five and none seen. Of the other two, one showed more, and one fewer errors than expected.

was the target for the lesions (Cooper, Amin, Chandra, & Waltz, 1973). Prior to placement of the lesion, ventrolateral thalamic nucleus and superior pulvinar were stimulated during object naming as described previously, using 4-sec trains of 10 mA, 60 Hz, 2.5 msec total duration biphasic squarewave pulses. On trials without stimulation during object naming at operation, this patient made 20.8% errors in object naming, on both preoperative and intraoperative testing. He showed no change in performance on these trials on testing on the fourth postoperative day. On 14 trials randomly interspersed among the nonstimulation trials, stimulation during object naming had been undertaken at the time of operation. Based on performance on nonstimulation trials, 2.9 errors would be expected on those trials at the time of postoperative testing, but only a single object-naming error was observed. We have not had any additional therapeutic opportunities to test this hypothesis in patients with preexisting anomia, but this one experience, coupled with the experience in patients showing anomia following ventrolateral thalamotomy, suggests that stimulation of lateral thalamus at the time of input of verbal material is likely to be associated with improved performance on that same material at least several days later. The limitations of this study to date are obvious, in that only visually presented nominal material, and verbal mode of retrieval have been tested. The ultimate duration of the effect and ultimate limitations are as yet unknown, but these data seem to provide a direction for future studies in the role of lateral thalamus and language processes.[11]

REFERENCES

Almgren, P.-E., Andersson, A. L., & Kullberg, G. 1969. Differences in verbally expressed cognition following left and right ventrolateral thalamotomy. *Scandinavian Journal of Psychology, 10*, 243–249.

Almgren, P.-E., Andersson, A. L., & Kullberg, G. 1972. Long-term effects on verbally expressed cognition following left and right ventrolateral thalamotomy. *Confinia Neurologica, 34*, 162–168.

Asso, D. 1969. W.A.I.S. scores in a group of Parkinson patients. *British Journal of Psychiatry, 115*, 555–556.

Asso, D., Crown, S., Russell, J., & Logue, V. 1969. Psychological aspects of the stereotactic treatment of Parkinsonism. *British Journal of Psychiatry, 115*, 541–553.

Bechtereva, N. P., Genkin, A., Morseeva, N., & Smirnov, V. 1967. Electrographic evidence of participation of deep structures of the human brain in certain mental processes. *Electroencephalography and Clinical Neurophysiology, Supplement, 25*, 153–166.

Bell, D. S. 1968. Speech functions of the thalamus inferred from the effects of thalamotomy. *Brain, 91*, 619–638.

[11] Subsequent to the preparation of this chapter, an additional review of the thalamus and language including several papers on language changes with thalamic lesions, and with thalamic stimulation appeared in *Brain and Language, 2*(1), 1975.

Bertrand, C. 1966. Functional localization with monopolar stimulation. *Journal of Neurosurgery, 24,* 403–409.

Boller, F. 1973. Destruction of Wernicke's area without language disturbance. A fresh look at crossed aphasia. *Neuropsychologia, 11,* 243–246.

Brown, J. 1972. *Aphasia, apraxia and agnosia, clinical and theoretical aspects.* Springfield, Ill.: Charles C Thomas. Pp. 144–147.

Brown, J. 1974. Observations on language following cryopulvinectomy. In I. S. Cooper, M. Riklan, & P. T. Rakic (Eds.), *The pulvinar-LP complex.* Springfield, Ill.: Charles C Thomas. Pp. 186–191.

Brown, J., Riklan, M., Waltz, J., Jackson, S., & Cooper, I. S. 1971. Preliminary studies of language and cognition following surgical lesions of the pulvinar in man. *International Journal of Neurology, 8,* 276–299.

Cheek, W. R., & Taveras, J. 1966. Thalamic tumors. *Journal of Neurosurgery, 24,* 505–513.

Christiensen, A.-L., Juul-Jensen, P., Malmros, R., & Harmsen, A. 1970. Psychological evaluation of intelligence and personality in Parkinsonism before and after stereotaxic surgery. *Acta Neurologica Scandinavica, 46,* 527–537.

Ciemins, V. 1970. Localized thalamic hemorrhage. A cause of aphasia. *Neurology, 20,* 776–782.

Cooper, I. S., Amin, I., Chandra, R., & Waltz, J. 1973. A surgical investigation of the clinical physiology of the LP-Pulvinar complex in man. *Journal of Neurological Science, 18,* 89–110.

Dobelle, W., Mladejovsky, M., & Girvin, J. 1974. Artificial vision for the blind: electrical stimulation of visual cortex offers hope for a functional prosthesis. *Science, 183,* 440–444.

Doty, R. 1969. Electrical stimulation of the brain in behavioral context. *Annual Review of Psychology, 20,* 289–320.

Fazio, C., Sacco, G., & Bugiani, O. 1973. The thalamic hemorrhage. *European Neurology, 9,* 30–43.

Fedio, P., & Weinberg, L. 1971. Dysnomia and impairment of verbal memory following intracarotid injection of sodium amytal. *Brain Research, 31,* 159–168.

Finger, S., Walbran, B., & Stein, D. 1973. Brain damage and behavioral recovery: serial lesion phenomena. *Brain Research, 63,* 1–18.

Fisher, C. M. 1958. Clinical syndrome in cerebral hemorrhage. In W. S. Fields (Ed.), *Pathogenesis and treatment of cerebrovascular disease.* Springfeld, Ill.: Charles C Thomas. Pp. 318–342.

Geschwind, N. 1967. Discussion on cerebral connectionism and brain function. In C. H. Millikan & F. L. Darley (Eds.), *Brain mechanism underlying speech and language.* New York: Grune & Stratton. Pp. 71–72.

Geschwind, N. 1970. The organization of language and the brain. *Science, 170,* 940–944.

Guiot, G., Hertzog, E., Rondot, P., & Molina, P. 1961. Arrest or acceleration of speech evoked by thalamic stimulation in the course of stereotaxic procedures for Parkinsonism. *Brain, 84,* 363–379.

Hartmann-Von Monakow, K. 1972. Histological and clinical correlations in 29 Parkinson patients with stereotaxic surgery. *Confinia Neurologica, 34,* 210–217.

Hays, P., Krikler, B., Walsh, L., & Woolfson, G. 1966. Psychological changes following surgical treatment of Parkinsonism. *American Journal of Psychiatry, 123,* 657–663.

Head, H. 1926. *Aphasia and kindred disorders of speech.* Vol. I. Cambridge, Eng.: Cambridge University Press.

Hermann, K., Turner, J., Gillingham, F., & Gaze, R. 1966. The effect of destructive lesions and stimulation of the basal ganglia on speech mechanisms. *Confinia Neurologica, 27,* 197–207.

Jasper, H. H. 1960. Unspecific thalamocortical relations. In J. Field, H. W. Magoun, & V. E. Hall (Eds.), *Handbook of physiology*. Sect. I. *Neurophysiology*. Vol. 2. Washington, D.C.: American Physiological Society. Pp. 1553–1593.

Jurko, M. F., & Andy, O. J. 1964. Psychological aspects of diencephalotomy. *Journal of Neurology, Neurosurgery, and Psychiatry, 27*, 516–521.

Krayenbuhl, H., Siegfried, J., Kohenof, M., & Yasargil, M. 1965. Is there a dominant thalamus? *Confinia Neurologica, 26*, 246–249.

Loranger, A., Goodell, H., McDowell, F., Lee, J., & Sweet, R. 1972. Intellectual impairment in Parkinson's syndrome. *Brain, 95*, 405–412.

McFie, J. 1960. Psychological effects of stereotaxic operations for the relief of Parkinsonian symptoms. *Journal of Mental Science, 106*, 512–517.

Meier, M., & Story, J. 1967. Selective impairment of Porteus Maze test performance after right subthalamotomy. *Neuropsychologia, 5*, 181–190.

Melton, A. W. 1963. Implications of short-term memory for a general theory of memory. *Journal of Verbal Learning and Verbal Behavior, 2*, 1–21.

Mohr, J. P. 1973. Rapid amelioration of motor aphasia. *Archives of Neurology, 28*, 77–82.

Mullan, S., Vailati, G., Karasick, J., & Mailis, M. 1967. Thalamic lesions for the control of epilepsy. *Archives of Neurology, 16*, 277–285.

Nielsen, J. M. 1946. *Agnosia, apraxia, aphasia: Their value in cerebral localization*. (2nd ed.) New York: Hoeber.

Ojemann, G. A. 1974a. Mental arithmetic during human thalamic stimulation. *Neuropsychologia, 12*, 1–10.

Ojemann, G. A. 1974b. Speech and short-term verbal memory alterations evoked from stimulation in pulvinar. In I. S. Cooper, M. Riklan, & P. T. Rakic (Eds.), *The pulvinar-lp complex*. Springfield, Ill.: Charles C Thomas. Pp. 173–184.

Ojemann, G. A., Blick, K., & Ward, A. A., Jr. 1969. Improvement and disturbance of short-term verbal memory during human ventrolateral thalamic stimulation. *Transactions of the American Neurological Association, 94*, 72–75.

Ojemann, G. A., Blick, K., & Ward, A. A., Jr. 1971a. Improvement and disturbance of short-term memory with human ventrolateral thalamic stimulation. *Brain, 94*, 225–240.

Ojemann, G. A., & Fedio, P. 1968. Effect of stimulation of the human thalamus and parietal and temporal white matter on short-term memory. *Journal of Neurosurgery, 29*, 51–59.

Ojemann, G. A., Fedio, P., & Van Buren, J. 1968. Anomia from pulvinar and subcortical parietal stimulation. *Brain, 91*, 99–116.

Ojemann, G. A., Hoyenga, K., & Ward, A. A., Jr. 1971b. Prediction of short-term verbal memory disturbance after ventrolateral thalamotomy. *Journal of Neurosurgery, 35*, 203–210.

Ojemann, G. A., & Van Buren, J. 1967. Respiratory, heart rate and GSR responses from human diencephalon. *Archives of Neurology, 16*, 74–88.

Ojemann, G. A., & Ward, A. A., Jr. 1971. Speech representation in ventrolateral thalamus. *Brain, 94*, 669–680.

Ojemann, G. A., & Ward, A. A., Jr. 1973. Abnormal movement disorders. In J. Youmans (Ed.), *Neurological surgery*. Vol. 3. Philadelphia: Saunders. Pp. 1829–1867.

Penfield, W., & Roberts, L. 1959. *Speech and brain mechanisms*. Princeton, N.J.: Princeton University Press.

Perret, E., Kohenof, M., & Siegfried, J. 1969. Influences de lesions thalamiques unilaterales sur les fonctions intellectuelles, mnesiques et d'apprentissage de malades Parkinsoniens. *Neuropsychologia, 7*, 79–88.

Peterson, L. R., & Peterson, M. J. 1959. Short-term retention of individual verbal items. *Journal of Experimental Psychology, 58*, 193–198.

Purpura, D. P. 1969. Mechanisms of propagation: Intracellular studies. In H. H. Jasper, A. A. Ward, Jr., & A. Pope (Eds.), *Basic mechanisms of the epilepsies*. Boston: Little, Brown. Pp. 441–451.

Ramamurti, B. 1967. Stimulation responses in the diencephalon. *Neurology (Bombay), 15,* 123–126.

Riklan, M., Diller, L., Weiner, H., & Cooper, I. 1960. Psychological studies on effects of chemosurgery of the basal ganglia in Parkinsonism. I. Intellectual functioning. *Archives of General Psychiatry, 2,* 22–31.

Riklan, M., & Levita, E. 1964. Psychological effects of lateralized basal ganglia lesions: a factorial study. *Journal of Nervous and Mental Disease, 138,* 233–240.

Riklan, M., & Levita, E. 1969. *Subcortical correlates of human behavior*. Baltimore: Williams & Wilkins.

Riklan, M., Levita, E., Zimmerman, J., & Cooper, I. 1969. Thalamic correlates of language and speech. *Journal of Neurological Science, 8,* 307–328.

Roberts, L. 1958. Functional plasticity in cortical speech areas and the integration of speech. *Research Publications, Association for Research in Nervous and Mental Disease, 36,* 449–466.

Samra, K., Riklan, M., Levita, E., Zimmerman, J., Waltz, J., Bergmann, L., and Cooper, I. 1969. Language and speech correlates of anatomically verified lesions in thalamic surgery for Parkinsonism. *Journal of Speech and Hearing Research, 12,* 510–540.

Schaltenbrand, G. 1965. The effects of stereotaxic electrical stimulation in the depth of the brain. *Brain, 88,* 835–840.

Schaltenbrand, G., & Bailey, P. 1959. *Introduction to stereotaxis with an atlas of the human brain*. Vol. 2. New York: Grune & Stratton.

Schaltenbrand, G., Spuler, H., & Wahrens, W. 1972. The anatomy of the corpus callosum determined electrically during stereotactic stimulation in man. *Confinia Neurologica, 34,* 169–172.

Schaltenbrand, G., Spuler, H., Wahrens, W., & Rumler, B. 1971. Electroanatomy of the thalamic ventro-oral nucleus based on stereotaxic stimulation in man. *Zeitschrift für Neurologie, 199,* 259–276.

Scheibel, M. E., & Scheibel, A. B. 1967. Structural organization of nonspecific thalamic nuclei and their projection toward cortex. *Brain Research, 6,* 60–93.

Selby, G. 1967. Stereotaxic surgery for the relief of Parkinson's disease. II. An analysis of the results of a series of 303 patients (413 operations). *Journal of Neurological Science, 5,* 343–375.

Sem-Jacobsen, C. W. 1965. Depth-electrographic stimulation and treatment of patients with Parkinson's disease including neurosurgical techniques. *Acta Neurologica Scandinavica, Supplement, 13,* 365–377.

Sem-Jacobsen, C. W. 1968. *Depth-electrographic stimulation of the human brain and behavior*. Springfield, Ill.: Charles C Thomas.

Shapiro, D. Y., Sadowsky, D., Henderson, W., & Van Buren, J. 1973. An assessment of cognition function in post thalamotomy Parkinson patients. *Confinia Neurologica, 35,* 144–166.

Shut, D. 1970. Psychological examination before and after stereotactic operations in Parkinson patients. *Psychiatria, Neurologia, Neurochirurgia, 73,* 375–386.

Siegel, S. 1956. *Nonparametric statistics for the behavioral sciences*. New York: McGraw-Hill.

Smyth, G. E., & Stern, K. 1938. Tumors of the thalamus—a clinico-pathological study. *Brain, 61,* 339–374.

Spiegel, E., & Wycis, H. 1962. *Stereoencephalotomy*. Part 2. New York: Grune & Stratton.

Svennilson, E., Torvik, A., Lowe, R., & Leksell, L. 1960. Treatment of Parkinsonism by stereotactic thermolesions in the pallidal region. *Acta Psychiatrica et Neurologica Scandinavica, 35,* 358–377.

Thorndike, E. L., & Lorge, I. 1944. *The teacher's word book of 30,000 words.* New York: Teacher's College, Columbia University.

Toth, S. 1972. Effect of electrical stimulation of subcortical sites on speech and consciousness. In G. Somjen (Ed.), *Neurophysiology studied in man.* Amsterdam: Excerpta Medica Foundation. Pp. 40–46.

Van Buren, J. 1963. Confusion and disturbance of speech from stimulation in vicinity of the head of the caudate nucleus. *Journal of Neurosurgery, 20,* 148–157.

Van Buren, J., & Borke, R. C. 1969. Alterations in speech and the pulvinar. *Brain, 92,* 255–284.

Van Buren, J., & Borke, R. C. 1972. *Variations and connections of the human thalamus.* Vol. 2. *Variations of the human diencephalon.* Berlin & New York: Springer-Verlag.

Van Buren, J., Li, C.-L., Ojemann, G. 1966. The fronto-striatal arrest response in man. *Electroencephalography and Clinical Neurophysiology, 21,* 114–130.

Ward, A. A., Jr., & Stern, J. 1963. Thalamic inhibitions of the myotatic reflex in man. *Journal of Neurosurgery, 20,* 1033–1039.

4

The Role of Phonology in Linguistic Communication: Some Neurolinguistic Considerations

Marc L. Schnitzer

PENNSYLVANIA STATE UNIVERSITY

INTRODUCTION

Linguistic communication takes place in the context of a communicator and a receiver of the communication. In most cases, when the medium by which such communication takes place is sound waves, we call the one who encodes and transmits the communication the *speaker* and we call the one who decodes and comprehends the communication the *hearer*. What are generally communicated are sentences in the form of linearized surface structures consisting of lexical and grammatical formatives.

According to current linguistic theory, these surface structures are derived from abstract nonlinear underlying structures by means of a system of rules. The rules that determine the form of underlying structures, along with those that relate the underlying structures to the surface structures constitute a major part of a competence grammar (i.e., a system that represents the linguistic knowledge of an idealized native speaker of a language).[1]

Another part of the grammar is called the phonological component. This component maps the surface representations onto phonetic forms. The grammatical and lexical formatives of the surface structure, which have phonological features associated with them, are converted into phonetic form by means of the rules of the phonological component.

---

[1] See Chomsky (1957, 1965), Chomsky and Halle (1968), Fodor and Katz (1964), Katz and Postal (1964), Bach and Harms (1968), Katz (1972), and Jackendoff (1972), for example.

139

The question to which this paper addresses itself is whether this phonological component should be a component of the grammar (i.e., the representation of the speaker's knowledge of his language), or whether it should be part, not of the grammar itself, but of a larger theory of communication in which the grammar plays a part.

MESOTICS

The most common context for linguistic communication is the one described above, involving a *speaker* and a *hearer*. In this context, the encoded linguistic form is carried from encoder to decoder by means of sound waves.

But sound waves are not a necessary part of linguistic communication. Much communication takes place by the written and printed word by means of phonemic, morphophonemic, syllabic, and ideographic writing systems. When linguistic communication occurs in this sort of context, we speak of a *writer* and a *reader* rather than of a *speaker* and a *hearer*.

I use the term *mesotic*[2] to refer to the means by which linguistic communication is transmitted from encoder to decoder. Hence the speaker–hearer situation defines what I call the *articulatory–auditory mesotic*. The situation in which the encoder uses a phonemic writing system and the decoder reads what is written is called the *phonemic writing–reading mesotic,* and so forth. There are many mesotics possible for linguistic communication. Finger spelling and "finger reading" constitute a mesotic used by the deaf, as do articulation and lip reading.[3] Reading and writing braille constitute yet another mesotic.

Various comments can be made regarding the formal properties of different mesotics and how those of one differ from those of another, e.g., that articulation–audition, finger spelling–finger reading, and articulation–lip reading contrast with the various writing–reading mesotics in that the encoded form is relatively ephemeral in the former and relatively permanent in the latter, or that certain mesotics demonstrate the presence of Hockett's (1958, 1963) notion of "duality" (e.g., articulatory–auditory), whereas others do not (e.g., ideographic writing–reading). But the property that is most relevant to the present chapter is one immediately discernible from Table 1.

What is of interest here is that the only mesotic involving auditory input is the articulatory–auditory one. One of the fundamental assumptions inherent in nearly all discussions of the phonological component of a grammar is that the abstract phonological representation of lexical and grammatical formatives consists of matrices of *phonetic* features chosen from a set claimed to be universal.

---

[2] I am indebted to the late Larry Grandin for his suggestion of this term.
[3] I have not mentioned the "sign language" of the deaf since it is unclear that it constitutes a mesotic for communication of natural language. There is some evidence that it is a different sort of semiotic from ordinary language. See, for example, MacLeod (1973).

TABLE 1 Mesotics

Mesotic	Modality of encoding	Modality of decoding
1) Articulatory–auditory	articulatory	auditory
2) Phonemic writing–reading	tactile	visual
3) Morphophonemic writing–reading	tactile	visual
4) Syllabic writing–reading	tactile	visual
5) Ideographic writing–reading	tactile	visual
6) Finger spelling–finger reading	tactile	visual
7) Articulatory–lip reading	articulatory	visual
8) Braille writing–braille reading	tactile	tactile

That is, part of the representation of lexical and grammatical formatives is related to sound.

What is also of interest is that the only mesotics involving articulatory output are the articulatory–auditory and articulatory–lip reading mesotics (the latter being identical in all respects to the former from the standpoint of the encoder). But the phonetic features in the universal set are for the most part articulatory in nature and conform to what are believed to be the limits of possible human speech articulation.

It is clear that were articulation–audition the only mesotic available for linguistic communication, the presence of a phonological component of the type mentioned as an inherent part of a grammar would be well motivated. That is, the articulatory and acoustic properties of lexical and grammatical formatives would in all likelihood constitute part of the *system* of the language internalized by native speakers.

But what of the other mesotics? Is the phonological component necessary for the encoding and decoding of language when mesotics other than articulation–audition (and articulation–lip reading—for the encoder only) are used? Or do encoders and decoders using non-articulatory–auditory mesotics have direct access to the syntactic and semantic properties of the linguistic form communicated without requiring any mediation by a phonological component. That is, do encoders of natural language have to encode phonologically interpreted surface structures when they are not speaking?; do decoders of natural language have to decode phonologically interpreted surface structures when they are not "hearing"?

Four possible answers come to mind:

1. Phonological mediation is required for linguistic encoding and decoding regardless of the mesotic used. Demonstration of the validity of this hypothesis would constitute evidence that the phonological component is in fact a proper part of the grammar, an aspect of a speaker's knowledge of his language.

2. Phonological mediation is used only in the articulatory–auditory mesotic (and in the encoding side of the articulatory–lip reading mesotic). Access to the linguistic forms communicated in non-articulatory–auditory mesotics is provided by various systems for each mesotic. The phonological component would then constitute a particular mediation system between the grammar and the auditory–articulatory mesotic. Other mediation systems would parallel the phonological component for each mesotic known by the encoder–decoder.

3. (1) is correct for some encoder–decoders. (2) is correct for others. Different people organize their linguistic communication systems differently.

4. Linguistic communication in mesotics other than the articulatory–auditory can occur either with phonological mediation or without it. That is, encoder–decoders have both types of organization available and use one or the other depending on various factors (e.g., encoding versus decoding, type of task involved, familiarity with the mesotic used, and so forth). Sometimes phonological mediation is employed in non-articulatory–auditory communication, and other times it is not.

THE RELATION OF MESOTICS TO LINGUISTIC COMMUNICATION

Most discussion in the literature has tended to favor the "primacy" of the articulatory–auditory mesotic. For example, Whitaker (1971) states:

> On neuropsychological criteria then we may wish to consider the reading and writing systems one step removed in some sense from the speaking and listening systems. . . . One might propose a primary level of production and recognition systems—the vocal tract and the auditory pathways; a secondary level of production and recognition systems would be the arm/hand musculature and the visual pathways. The secondary level, however, can be extrapolated from its normal systems and be adapted to general motor and sensory systems in man [p. 39; reprinted by permission of Linguistic Research Inc.] .

Weigl and Bierwisch's (1970) discussion is aimed more directly at the point being considered here:

> (i) Is the concrete graphic structure assigned to written utterances derived by graphemic rules from the already established phonemic structure P or is there a separate underlying graphemic structure G?
>
> (ii) Assume that there is an autonomous graphemic structure G. Is this G derived by certain orthographic rules from the phonemic structure P based on the dictionary entries, or is there a particular storage of the graphemic structure for each individual dictionary entry? [p. 8; by permission of Reidel Publishing Co.] .

They come to the following tentative conclusion:

With respect to the system of performance components this leads to the question of whether dictionary entries are accessible by means of independent phonemic and graphemic structures, or whether their identification converges at an earlier stage. Some experiences gained in the 'Arbeitsgruppe für Sprachpathologie' provide evidence in favor of the latter possibility. In a large variety of (pathological) cases it has been possible to deblock graphemic structures by means of phonemic ones and vice versa, even in the case of nonsense syllables and words. Since in this case the possibility of lexical storage and hence of separately stored phonemic and graphemic patterns is to be excluded, the existence of one underlying level of abstract internal representation or at least of correspondence rules mediating between two forms of representation seems plausible [pp. 8–9; by permission of Reidel Publishing Co.].

In the following sections of this chapter, various reports of cases of neuropathology that bear on the issue of whether the articulatory–auditory mesotic is primary, whether phonology is used as a mediating system in language communication regardless of what mesotic is employed, will be considered.

NEUROLINGUISTIC EVIDENCE

Evidence from Japanese Aphasics

The Japanese language is represented in three different writing systems. Two of them, the *kanas* (*hiragana* and *katakana*) are basically syllabic and are a kind of phonemic writing. Each kana character represents a Japanese syllable, or mora. Hiragana is used for native words; katakana is used for non-Chinese imported words. Figure 1 (from Nelson, 1962, pp. 1013–1014) contains a list of the 46 basic symbols in each of the hiragana and katakana syllabaries, with romanized equivalents.

The third system, called *kanji*, is basically ideographic. Although educated Japanese can often determine the pronunciation of unfamiliar kanji symbols by inspection, in general kanji writing does not follow the phonemic principle. There are about 10,000 basic kanji (probably over 40,000 including compounds); however, since World War II, the Education Ministry has officially limited the number to be taught in mass education and the number to be used in newspapers, magazines, etc., to 1800. The average adult Japanese probably knows about 2000 basic kanji.

Sasanuma and Fujimura (1971) performed some interesting tests on two groups of native Japanese aphasics—Group A aphasics, who were "characterized by reduced efficiency in the processing of linguistic units in all modalities, without any specific perceptual, apraxic or dysarthic disabilities" (p. 3), and Group B aphasics, who exhibited, in addition to general aphasic disabilities, "a problem of apraxia of speech . . . with no demonstrable paralysis, weakness, or incoordination of the speech musculature" (p. 3). The following characteristics of Group B patients constitute the basis for their special classification:

THE HIRAGANA A–I–U–E–O ARRANGEMENT

あ a	か ka	さ sa	た ta	な na	は ha	ま ma	や ya	ら ra	わ wa	
い i	き ki	し shi	ち chi	に ni	ひ hi	み mi	い (y)i	り ri	ゐ (w)i	
う u	く ku	す su	つ tsu	ぬ nu	ふ fu	む mu	ゆ yu	る ru	う (w)u	
え e	け ke	せ se	て te	ね ne	へ he	め me	え (y)e	れ re	ゑ (w)e	
お o	こ ko	そ so	と to	の no	ほ ho	も mo	よ yo	ろ ro	を (w)o	ん n

THE KATAKANA A–I–U–E–O ARRANGEMENT

ア a	カ ka	サ sa	タ ta	ナ na	ハ ha	マ ma	ヤ ya	ラ ra	ワ wa	
イ i	キ ki	シ shi	チ chi	ニ ni	ヒ hi	ミ mi	イ (y)i	リ ri	ヰ (w)i	
ウ u	ク ku	ス su	ツ tsu	ヌ nu	フ fu	ム mu	ユ yu	ル ru	ウ (w)u	
エ e	ケ ke	セ se	テ te	ネ ne	ヘ he	メ me	エ (y)e	レ re	ヱ (w)e	
オ o	コ ko	ソ so	ト to	ノ no	ホ ho	モ mo	ヨ yo	ロ ro	ヲ (w)o	ン n

Figure 1 The syllabaries of Japanese. (From A. N. Nelson, *The modern reader's Japanese–English character dictionary* [rev. ed.] (Tokyo: Tuttle, 1962), pp. 1013–1014. By permission of Charles E. Tuttle Co.)

1) errors in phoneme-sequencing, such as non-systematic substitutions, metatheses, repetitions, additions, and omissions of phonemes and syllables, some of them being perseverative or anticipatory, 2) errors in producing isolated phonemes or syllables, usually distortions in their phonetic actualization, accompanied by an apparent groping behavior for the correct articulatory posturing, and 3) prosodic disturbances consisting of reduced rate of speech, monotonous stress or pitch distribution and lack of adequate phrasing [Sasanuma & Fujimura, 1971, p. 3].

Note that these disturbances are all of a phonological nature.

Two nonaphasic control groups (C and D) were used in the tests. Among the tests performed were a visual recognition test and two writing tests.

In the visual test, 30 common nouns were used as transcriptional stimuli. These consisted of non-Chinese imported words transcribed in katakana, 10 native words, normally written in kanji, transcribed in kanji, and the latter 10 words transcribed also in hiragana. Each subject was shown each item for one tenth of a second and then asked to match the transcription with a picture of the object corresponding to it from a display of four.

There were two writing tests. In the *picture-to-transcription conversion task*, each *S* was instructed to look at 20 pictures corresponding to the 20 words used in the visual task and to write the word for what was presented in each picture. For the 10 nonimported (i.e., native) words, *S* was instructed to write both the kanji and the hiragana form. In the *speech-to-transcription conversion task*, each *S* was instructed to transcribe each of the words upon oral presentation by the examiner. Once again, each *S* was told to write both the kanji and the hiragana form for the nonimported words.

The results of these tests, shown in Figure 2 (from Sasanauma & Fujimura, 1971, p. 9), are interesting in a number of ways. The control groups made virtually no errors in the visual recognition task. They did make some errors in writing kanji words. This is expected since memorization of each character is involved here. Kanji writing does not follow the phonemic principle. The control subjects did not make errors in writing katakana or hiragana however. Since these systems of writing are essentially phonemic, the subjects could use their phonological competence to mediate their transcription. Memorization of each word was not necessary.

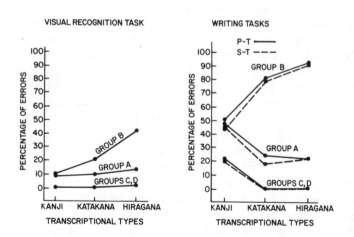

Figure 2 The error responses (in percentages) made by two aphasic and two nonaphasic subgroups on the visual recognition task (1/10-sec exposure) and on the two writing tasks (picture-to-transcription conversion, P-T; speech-to-transcription conversion, S-T). (From S. Sasanuma & O. Fujimura, "Selective impairment of phonetic and nonphonetic transcriptions of words in Japanese aphasic patients: Kana vs. Kanji in visual recognition and writing," *Cortex*, 1971, *7*, 9. By permission of La Tipografica Varese.)

Group A aphasics' performance on the visual and writing tasks was significantly worse than that of the control group. What is interesting is that their performance on each word class parallels that of the control groups. They scored approximately the same on the visual task for kanji, katakana, and hiragana words. On the writing tasks, they scored the worse on kanji words, and significantly better on kana words. Recall that this group did not have any particular phonological difficulty in addition to general transmodal aphasia. Hence they were still able to use what was intact of their phonological competence to mediate their transcriptions on the kana writing tasks.

Group B scored as poorly as Group A on all three tests involving kanji words. But on both the visual and the writing tasks, they scored significantly *worse* on kana words than on kanji words. Recall that this is the group that demonstrated particular phonological difficulties beyond the general aphasic syndromes of Group A. If the phonological competence of members of this group was sufficiently impaired, they would not have been able to use it to mediate their transcriptions in the writing tasks or their word recognitions in the visual task.

There is additional evidence that this is in fact the case. Notice that Group B subjects scored significantly worse on both visual and writing tasks with hiragana words than with katakana words. The katakana words are normally written in Japanese using katakana. There is no kanji representation for them. Thus it is likely that the average Japanese has stored many katakana words ideographically,[4] just as he has stored *all* kanji words which he knows. (Since kanji are ideograms, there is no other way to store them.) But the hiragana words used in this study would never be written in hiragana unless a writer could not remember the correct kanji form. Thus it is unlikely that any subject would have any of the hiragana words used in this study stored ideographically. Hence, the only way a Japanese could write or read any of the hiragana words used in this study is by means of phonological mediation. Since there is evidence of phonological impairment among Group B aphasics, the hypothesis proposed would explain not only why they performed worse on kana than on kanji, and not only why they performed worse on kana than did Group A aphasics, but also why they performed worse on hiragana tasks than on katakana tasks: Some katakana words were ideographically stored, whereas no hiragana words were so stored; since Group B aphasics suffered from a disruption of that system which would allow for phonological mediation of reading and writing, they could not perform reading and writing tasks requiring such mediation.

A subsequent report by the same authors (Sasanuma & Fujimura, 1972) provides further evidence for the conclusions just stated. One of the major conclusions that the authors drew from the previous article was that kanji and

[4] See the section entitled "Evidence from Lexical Redundancy Disruption in Aphasia" for some discussion of ideographic storage of morphophonemic orthographic representations.

kana are processed in different ways, the latter utilizing a "phonological processor." In this latter study, the authors investigate the *types* of errors made by subjects in the previous study.

In Figure 1 were listed the symbols of the kanas with their phonetic significance given in roman form. There is no kanji alphabet or syllabary per se; the kanji consist of only certain strokes in certain combinations. In theory there are 9 such strokes, but in practice there are 17. These are shown in Figure 3 (from Wieger, 1965, p. 12).

The types of kanji errors made by both normals and aphasics were similar to each other, the most common being what the authors call "graphical confusions." These involved "compounding two or more units of a character, with at least one unit remaining correct" (Sasanuma & Fujimura, 1972, p. 270), "misarrangement of units within a character" (p. 270), and "metathesis of the two constitutent characters in a word" (p. 270). Other kanji errors were no response, incomplete response, and the substitution of another whole word or character of a word for the original word or character; in the latter case, the substituted word or character was always semantically related to the word or character substituted for. Among kanji errors, Sasanuma and Fujimura found no instances of phonologically related errors.

What is significant is that among kana errors (none of which were made by members of the control groups), the authors found that " 'phonological confusions' accounted for most of the errors, while there was only a negligible amount of 'graphical confusion'." (Sasanuma & Fujimura, 1972, pp. 281–282)

Hence kanji processing seems *not* to involve phonological mediation, whereas kana processing does. This is further evidence that the Group B aphasics' phonological difficulties bear a relationship to their inferior performance on kana tasks.

It is also evidence that phonology need not always perform a mediating role in linguistic communication.

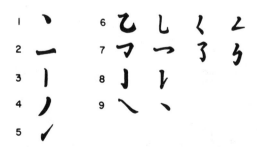

Figure 3 Basic strokes employed in Kanji. (From L. Wieger, *Chinese characters* [L. Dauret, translator] (New York: Dover, 1965), p. 12. By permission of Dover Publications.)

Evidence from Alexia

In two papers, Dubois-Charlier (1971, 1972) discusses the results of tests performed on so-called "pure alexics"—previously literate adults having no linguistic deficit other than a reading dysfunction. She considers the question of whether reading is mediated through an abstract phonological representation, or related directly to lexical items (in particular, their semantic properties—although one would assume, also their syntactic properties), without phonological mediation. She presents these hypotheses, represented herein by Figures 4 and 5 (from Dubois-Charlier, 1972, pp. 77–78). She then presents evidence relevant to these hypotheses.

On the basis of the results of a variety of reading tests, the author distinguishes three types of alexia: *alexie littérale, alexie verbale*, and *alexie phrastique*, of which only the first two are relevant to the present discussion. Comparing the group of literal alexics with the verbal alexics, the percentages of reading errors were as follows:

	Literal alexics	*Verbal alexics*
Letters	80%	0%
Words	70%	79%
Sentences	23%	50%

We see that although the verbal alexics had no difficulty in reading individual letters, they demonstrated greater difficulty in reading sentences than did the literal alexics.

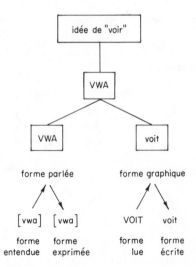

Figure 4 Model with mediation. (From F. Dubois-Charlier, "A propos de l'alexie pure," *Langages*, 1972, *25*, 77. By permission of Société Encyclopédique Universelle.)

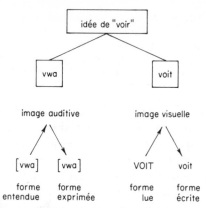

Figure 5 Model without mediation. (From F. Dubois-Charlier, "A propos de l'alexie pure," *Langages*, 1972, *25*, 78. By permission of Société Encyclopédique Universelle.)

Dubois-Charlier notes that for each kind of alexic there is a characteristic strategy employed in reading. Regarding literal alexics, she observes:

> —Chex les sujets atteints d'*alexie littérale*, la stratégie de la lecture est la *lecture globale*: les sujets ne cherchent pas à déchiffrer; ils «devinent» à partir de quelques éléments repérés, indices graphiques ou sémantiques; il n'y a pratiquement pas d'épellation ou de syllabation et les réponses données, quand elles sont fausses, sont significatives: ainsi, au niveau du mot, les lectures erronées sont des mots de la langue, qui présentent une certaine ressemblance graphique, phonique ou sémantique, avec l'item présenté; de même, au niveau de la phrase, le sujet peut faire des erreurs sur certains mots, mais ces erreurs ne l'arrêtent pas et en général il parvient à donner une phrase (ou un texte) qui a du sens et qu'il comprend [Dubois-Charlier, 1972, p. 88; reprinted by permission of Société Encyclopédique Universelle].[5]

Regarding verbal alexics, she observes:

> —Chez les sujets atteints d'*alexie verbale*, au contraire, la stratégie de la lecture est le *déchiffrement*; l'unité de déchiffrement peut être la lettre, il y a alors épellation systématique, ou la syllabe, mais, dans les deux cas, la caractéristique essentielle est qu'il n'y a pas d'appréhension globale de l'item—qu'il s'agisse d'un mot, d'une phrase ou du texte—et que le sujet ne cherche pas à deviner; en ce sens, même les éléments

---

[5] The subjects with literal alexia use a global reading strategy; they do not try to "decipher" (decode), but make "guesses" on the basis of graphically or semantically marked elements. There are practically no attempts at spelling or syllabication, and the responses given, when they are wrong, are quite interesting: At the level of the word, the reading errors are words in the language that have a certain (orthographic or semantic) similarity to the item presented. Similarly, at the level of the sentence, the subject may make errors with some words, but these errors do not make him stop, and in general he succeeds in producing a sentence (or a text) which makes sense, and which he understands.

correctement identifiés ne l'aident pas puisque chaque élément est déchiffré indi-
viduellement; parfois cette épellation ou syllabation est suivie d'une tentative de
reconstruction (qui peut être totalement erronée), mais parfois aussi il n'y a aucune
tentative d'assemblage: les différentes composantes ne constituent pas un tout;
l'unité du mot est perdue [Dubois-Charlier, 1972, pp. 88; Reprinted by permission of
Société Encyclopédique Universelle] .[6]

What is interesting here is that the literal alexics do not try to employ any kind
of phonological mediation in their attempts to cope with their reading difficulties. They seem to try to guess words, based on the parts of the graphic
representation that they recognize, either along semantic lines or along lines of
partial recognition of words that partially resemble orthographic forms that they
know. That is, the approach to the words tends to be ideographic rather than
phonological. There is no attempt to use phonological correspondences to
alphabetic representations as a mediator between the disrupted reading mesotic
and the language.

On the other hand, the verbal alexics (who have no trouble with component
graphemes of lexical items) do not try to guess the word, based on the part of
the word they recognize. Since they recognize all the parts, they attempt to
combine them using the phonemic principle (which is to a large degree possible
in French, the language of the subjects involved, since French orthography is in
part phonemic and in part morphophonemic). They usually fail in such attempts
since they are generally able to decipher only the individual graphemes. What is
significant is that the approach to reading of this group of alexics seems to be
one in which a strategy of phonological mediation is attempted.

These results provide evidence that alphabetic writing–reading may function as
a language mesotic either directly or through phonological mediation.

Evidence from Aphasia in Deaf Mutes

Among the four major papers reported in the literature that deal with aphasia
in deaf mutes (Critchley, 1938; Douglass & Richardson, 1959; Sarno, Swisher, &
Sarno, 1969; Tureen, Smolik, & Tritt, 1951), the ones by Critchley and by
Douglass and Richardson are directly relevant to the present discussion.

The Douglass and Richardson (1959) paper concerns a woman who was deaf
from birth and who developed aphasic symptoms at age twenty-one. She

---

[6] The subjects with verbal alexia, on the other hand, use a reading strategy characterized
by deciphering. The unit of this deciphering may be the letter, there is thus systematic
spelling, or the syllable. In both cases, the important characteristic is that there is no
understanding of the item as a whole—whether it concerns a word, a sentence, or a text—and
that the subject does not try to guess. In this way, even the elements that are correctly
identified do not help, since each element is individually deciphered. Sometimes the spelling
or syllabication is followed by an attempt at reconstruction (which may be totally wrong),
but sometimes there is no attempt to assemble the units: The different components do not
constitute a whole; the unity of the word is lost.

suffered impairment of her ability to read and write, her ability to converse in sign language, and her ability to use finger spelling both productively and receptively. It is the latter dysfunctions that are of interest here.

Receptively, she could read individual finger-spelled letters, but was unable to read finger-spelled words even when they were presented slowly. In this respect her performance paralleled that of the verbal alexics discussed by Dubois-Charlier.

Productively, she made errors in finger spelling characteristic of the kinds of errors made in speech by motor aphasics who hear, e.g., substitutions, perseverations (e.g., *h-o-u-u-u-s-e* for *house*, *a-b-c-d-e-d-e*, for the recitation of the alphabet), and abbreviations (e.g., *h-o-u* for *house*). With respect to substitutions, Douglass and Richardson note that "when the patient made errors in her attempts at expression by finger spelling, she frequently substituted a wrong letter which was clearly related in *digital articulation* to the correct letter" (p. 75, emphasis mine).

For example, she confused *d* with *f*, *s* with *o*, and *h* with *u*. See Figure 6 (from Douglass & Richardson, 1959, p. 76).

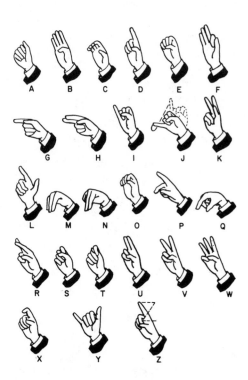

Figure 6 Finger spelling chart. (From E. Douglass & J. C. Richardson, "Aphasia in a congenital deaf-mute," *Brain*, 1959, *82*, 76. By permission of Macmillan Journals Ltd.)

The errors were thus related to the forms of the medium of representation (tactile and perhaps visual) rather than to forms in any abstract phonological system. This is no surprise, of course, since the patient was a deaf mute from birth.

These results contrast with those reported by Critchley (1938). Critchley's patient could hear until the age of seven, at which point he gradually began to lose his hearing. He was stone deaf by the age of fourteen. The aphasia patient's finger spelling was also full of mistakes characteristic of the speech of motor aphasics who can hear. His finger speech was "telelgrammatic": Words were omitted, wrong words were used, and so forth. What is significant is that his segmental errors are described as "confusion of the vowels, viz., he might point to 'A' instead of 'E'." (Critchley, 1938, p. 166). That is, the segmental errors seem to be related to segments that were phonologically similar, but not necessarily dactylologically similar. Thus, there was evidently some sort of phonological mediation occurring in this patient's attempts at communication via finger spelling. Since this patient had not been deaf from birth, it is conceivable that some sort of abstract phonological competence remained and that it was used by him even in linguistic communication that did not involve sound.

Thus, in these two cases of aphasia in deaf mutes, we find evidence that for one patient the (tactile) performance of finger spelling was mediated phonologically, whereas in the other, there was no such mediation, i.e., the visuotactile mesotic of finger spelling–finger reading was directly related to the rest of the language system, without phonological mediation.

Evidence from Braille Alexia

Gloning, Gloning, Weingarten, and Berner (1954) present a case report on a blind alexic. The patient was not congenitally blind, but lost his sight due to injury in World War I. Many years later he developed an alexia of his braille reading. Two aspects of his dysfunction are significant.

First of all, at the segmental level, the patient made errors that involved the confusion of orthographic representations. For example, he would confuse *Q* with *St* and *Y* with *N*. The way these letters are written in braille is as follows:

$$Q \qquad St \qquad Y \qquad N$$

Thus the confusions were unrelated to the phonological correlates of these German letters. There is no evidence of phonologically mediated confusion: It was not similar sounds that were confused, but graphically similar braille representations.

Secondly, and even more interestingly, it seems that there was an attempt when reading words to employ both the strategy characteristic of literal alexics and that of verbal alexics, reported in the paper by Dubois-Charlier discussed previously. In the data quoted (following), we see evidence that the patient first attempted to apply the literal alexic strategy, i.e., make a guess at the word, based on the part recognized, without any attempt at decipherment via phonological mediation. In the examples cited, we then find some evidence of the use of the verbal alexic strategy, i.e., attempting to find the phonetic value of each segment, and then combining them:

W   IE   N

Der Pat. liest hier: ,,W . . . ,
Wir? . . . , nein Wie . . . Wien.

A   N

Pat. liest: ,,Aber, Nicht. . . . Nein
das sind die Kürzungen in der Kurzschrift
. . . A . . . , N . . . , An [Gloning *et al.*, 1954, p. 265] .

Hence we find in braille reading, an activity using the tactile modality, that a patient may attempt to process information directly, without recourse to phonological mediation, or may resort to phonological mediation. The evidence here closely parallels that reported in the case of the French alexics, reading via the visual modality.

Evidence from Lexical Redundancy Disruption in Aphasia

It has long been observed that native speakers can distinguish between "systematic" and "accidental" lexical gaps. As Chomsky and Halle (1968, *The sound pattern of English*) note,

> speakers can distinguish in various ways among items that are not in their lexicon. Certain "nonsense" forms are so close to English that they might be taken by the speaker to be accidental gaps in his knowledge of the language: e.g., brillig, karulize, thode. Other forms, such as gnip, rtut, or psik, will almost certainly be ruled out as "not English." To account for these and other facts, we must assume that there is more structure to the internalized lexicon than merely the list of known items [p. 380; reprinted by permission of Harper and Row] .

Thus a native speaker of English knows that although *spen* is not part of the English lexicon, it is a "possible" form, whereas he knows that *zpen* is not. In order to capture such knowledge, Chomsky and Halle propose certain rules, called "lexical redundancy" or "morpheme structure" rules, to be included in their readjustment component. Such rules fill in redundant phonological features in lexical items. Some of these rules are context free (that is, they fill in redundant features in particular segments regardless of the environment of the segment involved), whereas others are context sensitive (that is, they fill in features that are redundant for a given segment only by virtue of the segment's position relative to surrounding segments).

> each language places certain conditions on the form of phonetic matrices and hence on the configurations of pluses and minuses (indicating membership in one of a pair of complementary categories) that may appear as entries in the classificatory matrices of the lexicon. These constraints make it possible to predict, in a given language, the specification of features in particular segments. Such predictability applies to segments in isolation (e.g., in Finnish, all obstruents are voiceless) as well as to segments in particular contexts (e.g., in English /s/ is the only true consonant admissible before a true consonant in word-initial position). Rules describing these constraints can readily be formulated within our framework, and can be interpreted as specifying the coefficients of particular features in particular environments. It is therefore natural to propose that such rules be incorporated in the grammar and that the features that are predictable be left unspecified in lexical entries [Chomsky & Halle, 1968, p. 381; reprinted by permission of Harper and Row].

Rules of the context-free type are known as "segment structure" rules or "blank filling" rules; those of the context-sensitive type are known as "sequence structure" rules or "sequential constraint" rules.

There is abundant evidence from normal speakers that lexical redundancy rules account for psychologically real knowledge or processes: viz., normal speakers can distinguish possible from impossible lexical items. However, thus far there is little evidence that there is a psychologically real lexical-redundancy subcomponent per se that functions as a distinguishable functional unit for speakers.

In Schnitzer and Martin (1974) we present evidence obtained from an aphasic that there is a subcomponent involving sequential constraint rules that has psychological as well as neuropsychological reality. The test performed was roughly as follows: The patient was asked to repeat various sound sequences, which included real English lexical items (*R*s), possible but nonexistent English words (*P*s), and impossible English sequences (*I*s). No non-English phones were included in any of the impossible "words". The impossibility of these sequences was due solely to disallowed segment sequencing. The subject performed significantly better in repeating *R*s than in repeating *P*s and *I*s, and significantly better in repeating *P*s than in repeating *I*s.

Generative phonological theory would predict that native speakers should be able to repeat *P*s with no more difficulty than *R*s. A nonaphasic control group bore out this prediction: They repeated *P*s no worse than *R*s; however, they repeated both *P*s and *R*s better than *I*s.

In an attempt to control for modality of presentation, we had the aphasic and the control subjects *read* the list of sequences used in the repetition task. On this task, the patient scored significantly better on *R*s than on *P*s and *I*s, but did *not* perform significantly better on *P*s than on *I*s. The theory would predict better performance with *R*s and *P*s than with *I*s, and no significant difference between performances with *R*s and with *P*s. We subjected the control group to the reading task and found them to perform in accordance with the theoretical prediction. Quantitative results are indicated in Table 2.

One of the more puzzling aspects of the data presented in this study is as follows: For repetition, although the aphasic performs worse than normals on *P*s, he is able to repeat some *P*s; however, he is virtually incapable of *reading P*s at all. Why is this so?

From the fact that the aphasic can repeat some *P*s, it is clear that his lexical redundancy system is merely impaired, not destroyed. However, from the fact that the aphasic cannot read *P*s, it appears that he cannot apply whatever is intact of this system to input from the reading modality.

We propose the following hypothesis to account for this discrepancy between the aphasic's repetition and reading performances: Reading nonexistent lexical items may be an inherently more complicated task than repeating them. As Head (1963, *Aphasia and kindred disorders of speech*) notes:

> most persons, when reading to themselves, skim over the words without becoming acutely aware of their actual structure and arrangement. But, should any difficulty arise, the doubtful word or phrase must be analysed and dissected into its constituent parts; although an educated man does not habitually "spell out" what he reads, he must always be able to do so, should the combination of symbols appear in any way unfamiliar or their meaning obscure [p. 312. Reprinted by permission of Cambridge University Press].

Luria (1970) notes the following:

> The experienced reader ceases to extract individual letters or syllables. He quickly learns to recognize words "as individuals;" words are transformed into visual

TABLE 2 Aphasic and Normal Responses to R, P, and I Tasks

Subject		R		P		I	
		Number right	Number wrong	Number right	Number wrong	Number right	Number wrong
Aphasic	rep.	58	3	24	33	0	26
	read.	45	14	1	58	0	26
Control 1	rep.	61	0	55	2	19	7
	read.	59	0	55	4	9	17
Control 2	rep.	61	0	53	4	3	23
	read.	54	5	36	23	2	24
Control 3	rep.	61	0	55	2	4	22
	read.	59	0	52	7	4	22

ideograms. Recognition of the meanings of words may occur with no reference to their sound structure [p. 348].

Thus a familiar word (e.g., most of the *R*s on the list) is processed directly as an ideogram. An unfamiliar word, however, such as all of the *P*s, must first be converted to phonological form by means of the graphophonological principles used in the reading of English. According to Head and Luria, the latter principles would be used less and less as a reader became more experienced. However, even an experienced reader would have to use them for unfamiliar words. All of the *P*s are, of course, unfamiliar words.

The aphasic may, therefore, have been required to perform a more complex task when reading *P*s than when he was required to: (*1*) read *R*s (since he may have processed these directly as ideograms), or (*2*) repeat *P*s (since there is no involvment of graphophonological principles in this task).

Thus there is evidence that for the reading of *P*s, the aphasic must make use of phonological mediation (which is impaired), just as the Japanese aphasics must do for kana words. There is evidence from both studies that failure in the performance of these tasks is due to failure to successfully perform this phonological mediation. But most of the *R* words used in the Schnitzer and Martin study are quite common and are therefore probably stored ideographically, as are kanji words for literate native speakers of Japanese. Evidently, for the majority of *R* words, the aphasic was not required to employ principles or strategies of phonological mediation.

DISCUSSION

Summary

In five different studies involving aphasics and alexics, evidence was adduced which indicated that phonological mediation is sometimes employed in linguistic performance involving mesotics other than articulation–audition. In these same studies, other evidence was adduced which indicated that linguistic performance involving non-articulatory–auditory mesotics sometimes occurs in the absence of phonological mediation.

1. In the discussion of the Japanese aphasics, it was argued that phonological mediation takes place in reading–writing tasks involving hiragana, whereas for tasks involving kanji, phonological mediation appears to be absent. Katakana tasks seem to represent an intermediate phenomenon in which phonological mediation may or may not take place, depending upon whether the subject has learned a particular katakana representation ideographically or not.

2. The discussion of the performances of the French alexics indicates that there are (at least) two types of alexia. One type of alexic (literal) attempts to read by guessing at ideograms, some of which are poorly known, and does not

attempt to relate individual letters to sounds. Another type of alexic (verbal) tries to "sound out" words he is reading, thereby attempting to mediate his impaired reading ability through his knowledge of correspondences between letters and phonological segments.

3. The case of the blind alexic suggests that this patient first attempts to read ideographically (employing the strategy of the literal alexic), and upon failure, then proceeds to use phonological mediation to successfully read the word being attempted (employing the verbal alexic strategy).

4. The discussion of aphasic deaf mutes tentatively suggests (on the basis of only two cases) that whereas those having congenital deafness employ no phonological mediation in finger-spelling tasks, those with acquired deafness may mediate finger-spelling performance through a phonological system acquired prior to the onset of deafness.

5. Finally, the discussion of the aphasic with the impaired lexical redundancy system suggests that familiar words are read ideographically without phonological mediation, whereas unfamiliar words (or possible but nonexistent words) are read by means of mediation through the phonological system. Since this system was impaired in the aphasic discussed, he could not read unfamiliar words.

Conclusion

From the data presented and discussed herein, what can be suggested in answer to the initial question, viz.: What is the role of phonology in linguistic communication? I propose the following:

1. Normal speakers have access to a phonological system which is used in linguistic communication in the articulatory–auditory mesotic.

2. Normal speakers can use this system for language performance involving other mesotics as well. Since for normal speakers the articulatory–auditory mesotic is developmentally prior to any others, it is likely that at early stages of acquisition of proficiency in other mesotics, phonological mediation occurs in performance in all mesotics.

3. Once proficiency in non-articulatory–auditory mesotics is attained, it is sometimes possible to engage successfully in linguistic communication by means of these mesotics, *by-passing* phonological mediation. There is evidence for this from the fact that the aphasic with lexical redundancy impairment could read familiar words but not unfamiliar ones, from the fact that Type B Japanese aphasics could process kanji words better than kana words, and from the fact that the French literal alexics gave evidence of a reading strategy involving no phonological mediation.

4. In the event of brain damage, two kinds of symptomology may arise that relate to the question at issue:

a. In the first case, the ability to use a non-articulatory–auditory mesotic may be impaired, in which case it may be possible to perform in that mesotic by relying on phonological mediation (even if such mediation had not been required prior to the onset of pathology). There is evidence for this from the fact that Type A Japanese aphasics performed better than Type B aphasics on hiragana tasks, and from the fact that the braille alexic was able to read if he were given the opportunity to "sound out" the words.

b. In the second case, it is the system of phonological mediation that is disrupted. In this case, the phonological system cannot be relied upon for mediation in the use of a non-articulatory–auditory mesotic. We find evidence for this in the fact that the aphasic having lexical redundancy impairment could read real words (for which there was no need for phonological mediation), but could not read nonexistent possible words, in the fact that Type B aphasics performed no worse than Type A aphasics on kanji tasks—tasks involving no phonological mediation—but did perform worse on kana tasks, and in the fact that the deaf mute having noncongenital (acquired) deafness, who became aphasic, made dactylological errors that seemed to be phonological. In at least the first two of these cases there is independent evidence that the phonological system of these patients was imparied: Thus they could not successfully employ it for mediation of linguistic performance in the writing–reading mesotics.

c. We find evidence for the impairment of *both* specific mesotics *and* phonological mediation in the case of the verbal alexics, who could not read very well and who tried to mediate their reading tasks phonologically: They were unsuccessful at such mediation. We also find such evidence in the case of Type B aphasics, since, in addition to their special phonological deficit just noted, they also performed worse than normals on kanji tasks; for kanji tasks they had as much difficulty as did Type A aphasics (those with no special phonological difficulties). In the case of the congenital deaf mute, the dactylological errors showed no evidence of phonological mediation. In this case it is not that brain damage disrupted the system of phonological mediation, but rather, that no such system ever developed: The patient was deaf from birth.

With respect to the more general question of whether the phonological component is a proper part of a grammar, or whether it is rather a part of a larger communication system in which it serves (in some cases) or does not serve (in other cases) as a mediating system between the language system and the various mesotics, it seems that it is mainly a matter of definition. It depends on what one expects a grammar to do. It depends on if and how and where one makes the competence–performance distinction. It depends on how one defines or conceives of language.

One thing is clear. It makes sense to speak of coherent, functional linguistic communication in the absence of phonological mediation. It does not make sense to speak of linguistic communication in the absense of syntax or semantics. Language without syntax or semantics is not language. Language without phonology *is* language.

ACKNOWLEDGMENTS

I am indebted to Bill Walsh, Susan Belmore, John Zavacki, Ken Shields, Peggy Kowing, and Margie Marshall for their comments on an earlier version of this paper. I am grateful to Kat Momoi for discussing various aspects of the Japanese writing systems with me.

REFERENCES

Bach, E., & Harms, R. T. (Eds.) 1968. *Universals in linguistic theory*. New York: Holt.
Chomsky, N. 1957. *Syntactic structures*. The Hague: Mouton.
Chomsky, N. 1965. *Aspects of the theory of syntax*. Cambridge, Mass.: MIT Press.
Chomsky, N., & Halle, M. 1968. *The sound pattern of English*. New York: Harper.
Critchley, MacD. 1938. "Aphasia" in a partial deaf-mute. *Brain, 61*, 163–169.
Douglass, E., & Richardson, J. C. 1959. Aphaisa in a congenital deaf-mute. *Brain, 82*, 68–80.
Dubois-Charlier, F. 1971. Approche neurolinguistique du problème de l'alexie pure. *Journal de Psychologie*, Jan.-Mar., 39–67.
Dubois-Charlier, F. 1972. A propos de l'alexie pure. *Langages, 25*, 76–94.
Fodor, J. A., & Katz, J. J. (Eds.) 1964. *The structure of language*. Englewood Cliffs, N.J.: Prentice-Hall.
Gloning, I., K. Gloning, K. Weingarten, and P. Berner. Über einen Fall mit Alexie der Brailleschrift, *Wiener Zeitschrift für Nervenheilkunde und deren Grenzgebiete, 10*, 260–273.
Head, H. 1963. *Aphasia and kindred disorders of speech*. New York: Hafner. Reprinted by permission of Cambridge University Press.
Hockett, C. F. 1958. *A course in modern linguistics*. New York: Macmillan.
Hockett, C. F. 1963. The problem of universals in language. In J. H. Greenburg (Ed.), *Universals of language*. Cambridge, Mass.: MIT Press. Pp. 1–29.
Jackendoff, R. S. 1972. *Semantic interpretation in generative grammar*. Cambridge, Mass.: MIT Press.
Katz, J. J.1972. *Semantic theory*. New York: Harper.
Katz, J. J., & Postal, P. M. 1964. *An integrated theory of linguistic descriptions*. Cambridge, Mass.: MIT Press.
Luria, A. R. 1970. *Traumatic aphasia*. (D. Bowder, translator) The Hague: Mouton.
MacLeod, C. 1973. A deaf man's sign language—Its nature and position relative to spoken languages. *Linguistics, 101*, 72–88.
Nelson, A. N. 1962. *The modern reader's Japanese-English character dictionary*. (rev. ed.) Tokyo: Tuttle.
Sarno, J. E., Swisher, L. P., & Sarno, M. T. 1969. Aphasia in a congenitally deaf man. *Cortex, 5*, 398–414.
Sasanuma, S., & Fujimura, O. 1971. Selective impairment of phonetic and non-phonetic transcriptions of words in Japanese aphasic patients: Kana vs. kanji in visual recognition and writing. *Cortex, 7*, 1–18.

Sasanuma, S., & Fujimura, O. 1972. An analysis of writing errors in Japanese aphasic patients: Kanji versus kana words, *Cortex, 8,* 265–282.

Schnitzer, M. L., & Martin, J. E. 1974. Sequential constraint impairment in aphasia: A case study. *Brain and Language, 1,* 283–292.

Tureen, L. L., Smolik, E. A., & Tritt, J. H. 1951. Aphasia in a deaf mute. *Neurology, 1,* 237–244.

Weigl, E., & Bierwisch, M. 1970. Neuropsychology and linguistics: Topics of common research. *Foundations of Language, 6,* 1–18.

Whitaker, H. A. 1971. *On the representation of language in the human brain.* Edmonton, Alta, Can.: Linguistic Research.

Wieger, L. 1965. *Chinese characters.* (L. Daurout, translator) New York: Dover.

5

Neurogenic Disorders of Output Processing: Apraxia of Speech

Donnell F. Johns

UNIVERSITY OF TEXAS
HEALTH SCIENCE CENTER AT DALLAS
SOUTHWESTERN MEDICAL SCHOOL

Leonard L. LaPointe

VETERANS ADMINISTRATION HOSPITAL,
GAINESVILLE, FLORIDA

INTRODUCTION

Controversy concerning articulation disturbances associated with cortical lesions is generously reflected in the neurological literature of the past century. The nature and indeed the existence of motor speech disorders of an apraxic nature have been the subjects of considerable discussion, some acrimonious and it would appear mostly semantic.

This chapter is concerned with a neurologically based motor speech disorder that has been recognized for over 100 years, and yet today is scarcely recognized by many clinicians. It is a disorder that has gone by more different names than perhaps any other disorder, the nomenclature having occasioned perhaps more confusion than that occasioned by any other disorder. This disorder has been identified variously as motor aphasia, Broca's aphasia, expressive aphasia, dyspraxic dysarthria, cortical dysarthria, and more. However, many investigators question the adequacy of these terms in describing the true nature of articulatory disturbances of cortical origin.

Reviewing the literature describing speech deficits associated with focal lesions reveals many attempts to characterize the clinical features of this disorder, primarily by presentation of single-case reports. However, such a review also reveals a paucity of systematic research designed to increase understanding of motor speech deficits associated with cortical lesions. Obviously such systematic study would make possible a better understanding of those disorders, by facilitating their differentiation from other speech deficits. A better differentiation would provide the basis for rational therapy.

REVIEW OF THE LITERATURE

At a meeting of the recently formed (at that time) Société d'Anthropologie de Paris, Auburtin (1861) presented a report of a patient who suffered hemorrhage into both frontal lobes, resulting in loss of speech but no other symptoms. He reported another case in which he described immediate loss of speech when a surgical spatula was placed upon the exposed frontal lobe. He localized the frontal lobes as being responsible for "the faculty of coordinating the movements peculiar to language" (p. 217). As it happened, Paul Broca had under his care a patient named Leborgne, who later became well-known in neurological literature as "Tan." Broca reported that this patient was suffering from loss of speech, all other behavior appearing essentially normal. His hearing retained its acuity, his tongue moved perfectly in every direction and did not deviate on protrusion, and he understood all that was said to him. However, this patient answered questions asked him by saying "Tan, tan," accompanied by appropriate gestures and in this manner succeeded in expressing himself. Broca asked Auburtin to see this patient in the surgical wards of the Bicêtre. Within a week after Auburtin and Broca had jointly examined the patient, he died.

Broca (1861) presented his findings at the next meeting of the Society. He reported his observations of the patient and described the pathological changes of the brain in the *Bulletin of the Societe d'Anthropologie de Paris*, concluding that "the lesion in the frontal lobe was the cause of the loss of speech" (p. 237).

A month later a similar case came under Broca's care. This patient, Lelong, was described as having good sight and hearing; sensation was unaffected. The tongue was not paralyzed and did not deviate on protrusion. His gestures were expressive and he apparently understood everything that was said to him. His articulated speech, however, was confined to the French words *oui, non, tois (trois)*, and *toujours*, spoken quickly but with effort.

Broca coined the term *aphemia* to describe the speech deficits that he had observed in these patients. Writing of his second patient (Lelong) he is quoted by Brain (1965) as stating, "in this patient, therefore, the aphemia was the result of a profound, but accurately circumscribed lesion of the posterior third of the second and third frontal convolutions" (p. 34). Broca's views aroused a good deal of interest and a great deal of controversy regarding neurologically based speech disorders, cerebral localization, and disorders of language.

Lord Brain (1965) relates that "some years later Broca distinguished two main groups of speech disturbances resulting from a cerebral lesion—aphemia, and verbal amnesia—in which the patient lost the memory not only of spoken but also written words, but he did not localize the lesion responsible for verbal amnesia" (p. 35).

Thus, to Broca *amnesie verbale* was an impairment of the *general faculty of language*. Broca did not attempt to localize the lesion or lesions responsible for this deficit. It was *aphemie*, a disorder of the faculty of articulated language, for which he localized the neurological deficit.

Critchley (1967) notes that it was Trousseau, in 1864, who introduced the term *aphasia* and particularly rejected Broca's preferred term *aphemia*. Critchley relates that "Broca prided himself as an etymologist, but he pleaded in vain for the rejection of *aphasia* in favor of *aphemia*" (p. 12). He points out that this expression *aphemia* is now virtually dead in neurological literature "despite Bastian's attempts in the nineteenth century to keep it in currency, and more recently Symonds' plea for its restoration" (Critchley, 1967, p. 12).

Luria (1966) succinctly summarized Broca's observations concerning the salient features of aphemia:

> The basis of this defect (aphemia) is a disturbance of the "ability to articulate" or, the "ability to produce coordinated motor acts . . . constituting articulated speech." According to Broca's description, the patient with "aphemia" retains the relationships between thoughts and words extremely well but has lost the ability to express these relationships by the coordinated movements that have been formed and consolidated during long practice. He loses the "special type of memory—not memory for words, but memory for the movements essential for the articulation of words" [p. 184].

Luria (1966) also notes that Broca localized the area responsible for this memory for motor images of words at the base of the third frontal gyrus of the left hemisphere. "Subsequently, this area of the brain came to be regarded as the 'center for motor speech' or 'Broca's center' " (p. 184).

It is interesting to note the agreement of subsequent writers as to the speech behavior described in relation to lesions of *Broca's motor speech area*. Although their descriptions of the resultant speech problems are strikingly consistent, the labels they attached to their descriptions tend to be confusing and obscure. Table 1 traces the evolution of the different terms used by some of the major writers concerned with speech deficits associated with circumscribed cortical lesions. The table indicates that generally good clinical agreement has existed in describing the salient features of nonlinguistic cortically based motor disorders of speech. It also demonstrates the resultant chaos that has evolved due to the complex, varied, and equivocal terminology used to designate the observed behavior of these patients. It can be seen that terms such as aphemia, Broca's aphasia, motor aphasia, predominantly expressive aphasia, subcortical motor aphasia, anarthria, verbal aphasia, phonetic disintegration of speech, apraxia, apraxic dysarthria, cortical dysarthria, and oral verbal apraxia, while attempting to describe a particular set of speech behaviors, can be extremely confusing and bewildering to the clinician who is faced with designing appropriate therapeutic procedures for such a patient. Hardy (1967) has pointed out that the literature shows a "relative paucity of systemic research" (p. 131) in this area, and that

TABLE 1 Different Terms Used by Writers Concerned with Speech Deficits

Author and year	Descriptive terms	Clinical description
Auburtin (1861)	"No symptoms beyond loss of speech"	Auburtin felt that frontal-lobe damage was responsible for the "faculty coordinating the movements peculiar to language."[a]
Broca (1861)	Aphemia	Broca defined a "circumscribed lesion of the posterior third of the second and third convolutions . . . caused a disturbance of the ability to articulate . . . to produce coordinated motor acts constituting articulated speech."[b] Lesion at the base of the third frontal gyrus of the left hemisphere . . . "A loss of the faculty of articulated speech in the absence of paralysis of the tongue, impairment of comprehension, or loss of intelligence."[c]
Trousseau (1864)	Aphasia	Trousseau objected to the use of the term *aphemia* and replaced it with *aphasia*, "a term of his own invention, which unfortunately gained uniform acceptance . . . such fictitious classification of disease is one of the familiar methods adopted by popular teachers for stamping their image on the history of medicine. He added nothing that deserves to be remembered. Broca's letter of protest is a model of respectful irony and he justly complained that Trousseau had 'brought back into pathology the very confusion I thought to dissipate.' "[d] Trousseau "used the word aphasia to replace aphemia."[e] Trousseau "introduced the word 'aphasia' and particularly rejected Broca's preferred term 'aphemia.' "[f]
Jackson (1866)	Speechlessness	"Jackson believed that the destruction of Broca's are produced aphasia. . . . He thought the nervous arrangement of Broca's region represented movements of tongue, palate, lips, larynx and pharynx."[g] "The anterior lobe of the left hemisphere is particularly important for voluntary speech. . . . The speechless patient is able to think."[h] "In all this, Jackson was considering the form of aphasia which was later called 'motor' or 'verbal' and it is to this that he applied the term speechlessness."[i]

TABLE 1 (Continued)

Author and year	Descriptive terms	Clinical description
Wernicke (1874)	Motor aphasia	Head writes that Wernicke acknowledged the existence of a motor aphasia that was "equivalent to the aphemia of Broca, due to the destruction of the third frontal convolution. The patient can utter at most a few words only, but can understand all forms of speech."[j] Wernicke located "the conceptual basis of articulated speech in Broca's area. Destruction of the third frontal convolution led to motor aphasia, with loss of the images for articulated speech."[k]
Liepmann (1900)	Apraxia	Head relates that Liepmann was first to subject the clinical manifestations of neurologically based speech disorders to "comprehensive analysis and classify them under the term 'apraxia.' "[l] Head continues by stating that "Apraxia has been described as an inability to perform certain purposive movements or complex actions, although motion, sensation and coordination are preserved. Such a definition would include many morbid manifestations usually classed under aphasia, particularly its 'motor' forms, and in 1900 Liepmann spoke of the aphasia of his Regierungsrat as 'apraxia of the speech muscles.' Aphasic disorders, in as far as they assume an expressive form, are of an apraxic nature in the wide sense of the term. For instance, motor aphasia is a particular form of apraxia of the glossolabio-pharyngeal apparatus; the unparalyzed muscles cannot be innervated in such a manner that the sounds of speech come into being."[m]
Marie (1906)	Anarthria	"A lesion of Broca's area, in his (Marie's) view, caused anarthria, a disturbance of speech as a motor activity without any impairment of its intellectual basis. Anarthria could exist alone, and then internal speech and the comprehension of speech were unaffected."[n] ". . . the expressive defect of these patients does not belong to aphasia, because it concerns merely the motor mechanism of articulation . . . 'loss or disturbance of

Continued

TABLE 1 (Continued)

Author and year	Descriptive terms	Clinical description
Marie (cont.) (1906)	Anarthria	articulated speech, with more or less complete preservation of inner speech' . . . 'a defect in the coordination of the movements of phonation.' He (Marie) denied that it (anarthria) was due to paralysis of the oral muscles."[o]
Wilson (1908)	Apraxia	". . . We have in Broca's area a centre for the coordination of movements requisite for speech: in the area movements of tongue, throat, palate, larynx, etc., are combined prior to the actual innervation of the corticomuscular apparatus . . . In motor aphasia we have a form of apraxia, viz., apraxia of the speech musculature."[p] Wilson stated that, " 'Since the articulatory muscles are not paralyzed in motor aphasia, the symptom may legitimately be called an apraxia of the speech musculature."[q]
Henschen (1920)	Aphemia	"Henschen found that a lesion of the left third frontal gyrus caused aphasia owing to the inability of the patient to produce word forms. Henschen preferred to call this disorder 'aphemia.' "[r] According to Head, Henschen concluded that although the first and second frontal convolutions play no important part in the mechanism of articulated speech, the third frontal convolution plays a very important part, forming "a physical center for these movements. . . . Thus, a lesion of cortex in the third frontal region produces want to power of coordinating letters and syllables to form words; the patient knows what he wants to say, but cannot find the suitable forms of verbal expression. He has forgotten the movements of speech; to this high-grade motor loss of function, Henschen prefers to apply the term 'aphemia.' "[s]
Head (1926)	Verbal aphasia	In Chapter six, entitled, "Chaos," of his 1926 volume, Henry Head reviewed the history of motor speech disorders associated with neurological lesions. He, like Liepmann, apparently believed that there are three different forms of executive speech disorders, (including

TABLE 1 (Continued)

Author and year	Descriptive terms	Clinical description
Head (cont.) (1926)	Verbal aphasia	what he called but put into quotation marks, "motor" aphasia). He stated that "Anarthria, verbal apraxia and 'motor' aphasia are purely descriptive terms for three different forms of abnormal speech, which can occur separately or in combination. . . . Each set of clinical manifestations must be carefully scanned and investigated to discover to which class they rightly belong . . . there are regions where a lesion of sufficient extent and severity can disturb normal sets of speech in a way that can be designated 'apraxia' or 'aphasia.' "[t] Head, however, had a category which he called "verbal aphasia." Patients in this category could follow oral or written commands but had executive disorders of speech. Alajouanine writes, "Does not Head himself point out that certain of his patients had such difficult oral expression that they constantly used pencil and paper. This type of disorder, in which articulatory disturbances are predominant, forms an important category within the group of Broca's aphasia . . . Head reserved for such facts the name of verbal aphasia."[u]
Kleist (1934)	Aphasic Anarthria Speech-sound-muteness Word-muteness	"Speech-sound-muteness, or aphasia anarthria, is attributed by Kleist to an innervating apraxia of speech-sound formation resulting from a lesion at the base of the left precentral convolution. Word-muteness due to a lesion of Broca's area is characterized by defective production of verbal sounds."[v]
Weisenberg and McBride (1935)	Predominantly expressive aphasia	"The predominantly expressive group, the largest, is comprised of patients who show defects in the articulation and formation of words. . . . In some cases speaking is slurred as if the mechanisms of speech production were not carried through with sufficient precision. Usually, instead of poor quality of the sound in their combination, or perhaps in addition to this defect, there are actual errors in articulation where one sound is substituted for another . . . a sound badly failed in one setting may be well

Continued

TABLE 1 (Continued)

Author and year	Descriptive terms	Clinical description
Weisenberg and McBride (cont.) (1935)	Predominantly expressive aphasia	articulated in another. . . . After producing a sound or word badly, a patient of the predominantly expressive type often realizes there has been an error and attempts to improve his performance."[w] In this "predominantly expressive" group "receptive functions are relatively satisfactory."[x] "This system of classification has been criticized for being too vague and noncommital. . . . It also contains an even more dangerous implication . . . namely the tacit assumption that all morbid symptoms in the patients concerned belong to the realm of aphasia. This is by no means obvious."[y]
Alajouanine et al. (1939)	Phonetic disintegration of speech	". . . they concluded that it was possible to isolate a 'syndrome of phonetic disintegration' . . . certain phonemes were found to be impossible .,. . other phonemes suffered when occurring in sequence."[z] "Unfortunately, the results of their phonetic studies are not presented in such a way that the reader can make his own evaluation of their findings. The work also suffers from failure to provide the necessary controls."[aa] Writing on subject of "Aphasia and Physiology of Speech" Alajouanine and Lhermitte described associated articulatory disturbances of neurologically damaged adults and stated that "a point of primary importance, the occurrence of distortions which appear to reproduce the various types of accommodation observable in the speech of the child. One of us has proposed to group all of these features under the heading 'phonetic disintegration of speech.' "[bb]
Nathan (1947)	Apraxic dysarthria	"These cases of aphasia conspicuously lack a disturbed auditory component; this suggests that the temporal love is not involved. From the anatomical and physiological evidence, the site of lesion . . . is seen to be the lower part of the pre-central gyrus or the region deep to this area."[cc] "He (Nathan) emphasized that 'apraxia' was the cortical motor function *par excellence* and

TABLE 1 (Continued)

Author and year	Descriptive terms	Clinical description
Nathan (cont.) (1947)	Apraxic dysarthria	suggested that apraxia was in fact the basic lesion in many cases of motor aphasia."[dd]
Goldstein (1948)	Peripheral motor aphasia	"*Spontaneous speech* is severely diminished, but intention to speak great. The patient *tries* to speak, even though the words he utters are motorically defective. Sounds and words show severe motor defects. *Voluntary effort* improves speech. Voluntary movements show 'trial and error.' Repetition is sometimes better than spontaneous speech, but in principle the same defect."[ee] Goldstein equates his term "Peripheral motor aphasia," with "Broca's aphasia" as being expressive disorders due to cortical lesions.[ff]
Critchley (1952)	Articulatory dyspraxia	In his summary Critchley states that "(1) many patients with aphasia show disorders of articulate speech, which are both varied and variable in their character; (2) dysarthria and dysphasia, though often occurring in combination, are actually separate phenomena; (3) articulatory dyspraxia is also an independent entity, although it may co-exist with an aphasia and contribute to a defect of articulation."[gg]
Russell and Espir (1961)	Motor aphasia	"Motor aphasia—a category in which they (Russell and Espir) appear to include both Broca's aphasia and subcortical motor aphasia. This type of aphasia is closely associated with lesions involving the lower part of the Rolandic area."[hh]
Bay (1962)	Cortical dysarthria	Bay writes that "The 'motor' defect of these patients arises from a disturbance in the movement of the articulatory muscles . . . generally connected with a damage to the lower part of the central region. Therefore, we named it cortical dysarthria."[ii] however, it is combined with real aphasia and then represents the major part of the so-called 'cortical motor' or Broca aphasia."[jj] "A well-defined and frequent group of speech disorders is marked by a distinct apraxia of the

Continued

TABLE 1 (Continued)

Author and year	Descriptive terms	Clinical description
Bay (cont.) (1962)	Cortical dysarthria	articulatory muscles and impaired tongue movement in the glossogram test . . . these patients show practically no receptive disorders but uniform disturbance of the expressive speech performance . . . this group with predominantly expressive disorders represents the bulk of cases with so-called motor aphasia."[kk]
Mayo Clinic (1963)	Apraxia of speech sounds	"Although the disorder manifests itself as an articulatory defect, the fact that volition is the important factor identifies the deficit as an *apraxia of speech sounds*"[ll]
Whitty (1964)	Cortical dysarthria	Whitty reports a case with a lesion "at the base of the fissure of the Rolando (thus undermining part of the third and probably second frontal convolutions) causing transient cortical dysarthria and dysprosody. The case is taken as evidence in support of the occurrence of a cortical dysarthria, basically dyspraxic in nature and due to a strictly frontal lesion."[mm]
Denny-Brown (1965)	Apraxia of vocal expression	Denny-Brown makes a sharp distinction between speech deficits associated with focal neurological lesions, noting that "the subcortical disorder (dysarthria) is fixed, whereas the cortical disturbance (apraxia) is greatly variable. . . . It is characteristically a variable difficulty in beginning a word, with special difficulty in making some types of syllables. . . . We find no objection to the view that such (phonemic) disintegration is a special and complex type of apraxia of vocal expression."[nn] Denny-Brown reports that an autopsy on apraxic patient's brain showed "a discrete cortical lesion cutting across the third and second frontal convolutions, without involvement of the underlying white matter."[oo]
DeRenzi et al. (1966)	Oral apraxia (O.A.) Phonemic-articulatory disorders	"Within the left brain damaged group, O.A. and phonemic-articulatory disorders appeared together very often, and this is a fact which, whatever its possible interpretations, cannot be ignored. . . . As a rule, the severity of O.A. is also directly propotional to the severity of phonemic-articulatory disorders. Exceptions are

TABLE 1 (Continued)

Author and year	Descriptive terms	Clinical description
DeRenzi et al. (cont.) (1966)	Oral apraxia (O.A.) Phonemic-articulatory disorders	represented mainly by those subjects (N=28) in whom the verbal disturbance is more severe than the nonverbal one . . . when severe phonemic-articulatory errors appear in a setting of virtually normal oral apraxias."[pp]
Shankweiler and Harris (1968)	Phonetic disintegration	"Articulatory defects, rather than reduced vocabulary and errors of syntax, constitute the chief residual impairment in many cases of cortical lesion due to stroke in the left cerebral hemisphere. . . . Speech is extremely effortful and slow, not because the patient cannot retrieve the word he needs, but because the machinery for producing sounds no longer functions properly. . . . This condition, which is sometimes called 'cortical dysarthria' and 'apraxia dysarthria' must be distinguished from dysarthric disorders arising from damage restricted to lower levels of the motor system. We have chosen to call the syndrome 'phonetic disintegration'. . . . The disorder is familiar to everyone concerned with rehabilitation of stroke patients, yet remarkably little is known about it."[qq]

[a] Brain (1965, p. 34).
[b] Luria (1966, p. 184).
[c] Schuell, Jenkins, and Jimenez-Pakon (1964, p. 12).
[d] Head (1926, p. 27).
[e] Brain (1965, p. 35).
[f] Critchley (1967, p. 12).
[g] Penfield and Roberts (1959, p. 64).
[h] Brain (1965, p. 36).
[i] Brain (1965, p. 36).
[j] Head (1926, p. 62).
[k] Brain (1965, p. 39).
[l] Head (1926, p. 94).
[m] Head (1926, p. 98).
[n] Brain (1965, p. 42).
[o] DeRenzi et al. (1966, p. 50).
[p] Wilson (1908, p. 199).
[q] Brain (1965, p. 52).
[r] Brain (1965, p. 25).
[s] Head (1926, p. 81).
[t] Head (1926, pp. 101–103).
[u] Alajouanine (1956, p. 20).

[v] Brain (1965, p. 46).
[w] Weisenberg and McBride (1935, p. 147).
[x] Weisenberg adn McBride (1935, p. 148).
[y] Bay (1964, p. 123).
[z] Critchley (1952, p. 11).
[aa] Shankweiler and Harris (1966, p. 278).
[bb] Alajouanine and Lhermitte (1964, p. 213).
[cc] Nathan (1947, p. 465).
[dd] Whitty (1964, p. 509).
[ee] Goldstein (1948, p. 80).
[ff] Goldstein (1948, p. 151).
[gg] Critchley (1952, p. 17).
[hh] Brain (1965, p. 61).
[ii] Bay (1962, p. 214).
[jj] Bay (1962, p. 415).
[kk] Bay (1964, p. 126).
[ll] Mayo Clinic (1963, p. 255).
[mm] Whitty (1964, p. 510).
[nn] Denny-Brown (1965, p. 462).
[oo] Denny-Brown (1965, p. 464).
[pp] DeRenzi et al. (1966, p. 68).
[qq] Shankweiler and Harris (1968, p. 1).

"the confusion in the literature regarding the latter two areas [apraxia of speech and motor aphasia] seems overwhelming" (p. 131). The enhancement of the most efficient methods of clinical management of these patients' speech disorders is not fostered by nondescriptive and bewildering nomenclature nor by vague clinical descriptions of "stroke cases." Therefore, it is thought that a descriptive label, evolving from systematic investigations designed to increase the understanding of these articulation problems associated with cortical lesions, is clearly needed. The descriptive term to be used in this chapter is *apraxia of speech.*

The terms *aphasia* or *dysphasia* have long been used to indicate a linguistic deficit that includes problems of symbolic and integrative functioning that cross all language modalities.

The term *dysarthria* is commonly used to refer to defective motor control due to impaired innervation of speech musculatures resulting in imperfect coordination of these musculatures in speech acts. Other terms have been used to describe a motor speech disorder that is neither of the above.

The phrase *phonetic disintegration of speech*, offered by Alajouanine, Ombredane, and Durand (1939), or the shortened version of *phonetic disintegration* preferred by Shankweiler and Harris (1966; Shankweiler, Harris, & Taylor, 1968) only designates the acoustic end-results of these patients' speech deficits. Since the term phonetic disintegration limits itself to the acoustic end-products of speech, the characteristic speech patterns of patients with pseudobulbar palsy, amyotrophic lateral sclerosis, or parkinsonism might be lumped together, as it were, under this "descriptive" label. The various dysarthrias, exacerbated states of stuttering, and cluttering could be called conditions of phonetic disintegration. However, this term lacks the essential feature of identifying the dynamics of the disorder, thereby rendering its meaning at best equivocal.

The phrase *apraxia of speech*, on the other hand, focuses on the underlying dynamics of the disorder. Apraxia of speech explicitly (*1*) directs one's attention to the motor aspects of speech; (*2*) emphasizes the volitional execution of articulation; (*3*) excludes significant weakness, paralysis, and incoordination of the speech musculature; and (*4*) indicates a discrepancy between execution of the speech act and relative linguistic intactness.

Apraxia of speech, therefore, will be the phrase used in this chapter. The *severity of the acoustic end-result* will refer to the extent of impairment of volitional phonemic execution specific to transmissive rather than integrative problems—nonsymbolic rather than symbolic in nature—a discrepancy between impairment due to motor control of the speech musculature and performance, and a discrepancy between reflexive and voluntary muscle and speech activities. Quite simply then, in the absence of any problem of symbolic nature or paralysis or incoordination of the speech musculature adequate to account for the speech disorder, a patient with a "pure" apraxia of speech knows exactly what he wishes to say but he cannot say it.

The following review further emphasizes the distinguishing features between apraxia of speech and aphasia, and apraxia of speech and dysarthria.

NECESSARY DIAGNOSTIC DIFFERENTIATIONS

Darley (in a 1967 personal communication) stated that he had had "contact with a significant number of patients who present this problem of articulatory difficulty associated with aphasia (or independent of aphasia)," which led him and his colleagues to make a "rather careful scrutiny of the problem." He and his associates at the Mayo Clinic feel that "The identification of this disorder (apraxia of speech) as distinct from dysarthria and aphasia is extremely important, both for the neurologist and the speech pathologist but especially for the speech pathologist since the management of the disorder is quite different from the management for aphasia" Darley, 1967 personal communication.

Contributions to the study of apraxia were made as early as 1908 by Wilson, who reviewed the early literature pertaining to apraxic symptomatology. Wilson (1908) defined apraxia as "inability to perform certain subjectively purposive movements or movement complexes, with conservation of motility, of sensation and coordination" (p. 163). This definition appears to be essentially the same as that held by most modern investigators including DeJong (1958), Brain (1965), Denny-Brown (1965), and Luria (1966).

Confusion between apraxia and aphasia and between apraxia and dysarthria is replete in the literature pertaining to expressive communicative disorders associated with neurological impairment. Darley (1964), in describing patterns of articulatory errors, recognized this confusion and emphasized that "the speech pathologist must differentiate the problems of motor speech production displayed by patients who have suffered strokes, undergone surgery for brain tumor, suffered an infectious process involving the cerebral hemispheres, or experienced cerebral trauma. He must differentiate aphasic symptoms from dysarthria and dysarthria from apraxia" (p. 69).

Apraxia of Speech versus Aphasia

In earlier accounts of so-called *motor types of aphasia* in association with apraxia of the lips, tongue, and sometimes the pharynx and larynx has been noted. Nathan (1947) reviewed six such cases in great detail and used the term *apraxic dysarthria* to describe them. He emphasized that praxis was the cortical motor function *par excellence* and suggested that apraxia was in fact the basic problem in many cases of so-called *motor aphasia*. He considered the localization of lesions associated with apraxia and apraxic dysarthria to be in the "lower part of the pre-central gyrus or the region deep to this area," the former being synonymous with the face area, and the latter with Marie's lenticular zone.

Wepman (1955) is of the opinion that there has been general acceptance of the term *aphasia* as meaning a problem of symbolic formulation, but the label *aphasia* has been inappropriately applied in cases of nonlinguistic motor speech disorders of cortical origin. He has stated: "Over the years, however, this specific meaning has been lost as the term aphasia has been loosely applied to almost all language problems subsequent to cortical lesions. Studies of so-called aphasic patients during therapy show that in many instances no problem of symbolic formulation seems to be present" (p. 223).

In concluding his discussion of aphasia, DeJong (1958) states: "Oral expressive aphasia and other varieties of expressive aphasia are in reality apractic defects" (p. 82).

Critchley (1952, 1960) also discussed aspects of "so-called aphasia" but concluded that articulatory dyspraxia was an independent entity, though it might coexist with a true aphasia.

Bay (1962) emphasized the need for evaluation of empirical data in the field of aphasia to differentiate disturbances in speech production that may be distinct from or associated with aphasia. He wrote: "We must first solve the question which symptoms of the different speech disorders are really of an aphasic nature and which may be due to the occurrence of non-linguistic factors" (p. 411).

Bay continued by stating: "If, for instance, we do not consider a possible existence of non-aphasic disturbances in a case of aphasia we surely will not find such disturbances" (p. 412). In reporting the results of his study based on the examination of 80 unselected patients having various aphasic speech disorders, Bay identified a well-defined group having expressive speech disturbances and exhibiting difficulty in the movement of the articulatory muscles. Bay described this group as having *cortical dysarthria*. (The term *cortical dysarthria* will be dealt with in some detail in the section dealing with apraxia of speech versus dysarthric disturbances.) The point being emphasized in this section is the differentiation made by Bay between motor speech disturbances and aphasia. He further reported that this well-defined and frequently found group of speech disordered, neurologically impaired patients showed "practically no receptive disorders, whereas the expressive speech disorders were uniformly disturbed" (p. 414). He continued by stating that "this group with predominantly expressive disorders represents the bulk of the so-called motor aphasia" (p. 414).

In 1964, Whitty repeatedly emphasized the need to distinguish motor speech disturbances from aphasia. Whitty (1964) agrees with Marie that "dysphasia must by definition entail some lack of comprehension of the meaning of words" (p. 509). His opinion is that obscurity may result if the term *motor aphasia* is retained: "It is the retention of this anomalous use of dysphasia that is confusing" (p. 509). He continues:

> Anatomically speaking, if the cortical apparatus of speech is at fault, wrong words as well as mispronounced words may be expected, but as long as their fault is

recognized no comprehension difficulty need be postulated. Thus, what at first glance appears to be an anmesic or receptive dysphasia may in fact be a purely motor one. . . . It is the inability to recognize the error that makes it a true defect of comprehension [p. 509].

Whitty feels that the segregation of aphasia and motor speech disturbances is essential and that

the recognition by the subject in mistakes in words should be regarded as crucial distinction. . . . It illustrates once more the need for segregating the motor speech abnormalities in cortical lesions from those involving comprehension. Such a segregation should be maintained in the terminology . . . the term motor dysphasia is best avoided as its past usage renders its meaning equivocal [p. 509].

Along the same lines, Bay (1964) relates:

For the handling of any larger number of facts, such as the manifold types of aphasic disorders, it is essential to divide them into smaller and uniform groups, that is to say, to classify the whole body of experience according to certain principles. This is necessary for any scientific analysis as well as for mutual communication . . . neglect of this problem has had a disastrous influence on the evolution of aphasiology for nearly a century [p. 122].

Bay cites the study done by Weisenberg and McBride (1935), who confined their classification to *receptive* and *expressive* aphasias. Bay notes that this system of classification has been criticized for being too vague and noncommittal while still maintaining an essential item of the classical doctrine, "namely the strictly symmetrical organization of speech from *motor* and *sensory* elements. It also contains an even more dangerous implication of the classical theory, namely the tacit assumption that all morbid symptoms in the patients concerned belong to the realm of aphasia" (1964, p. 124). He feels that this is by no means obvious.

Bay (1964) continues:

If we want to maintain the concept of aphasia as a pathogenically uniform disorder we can consider only part of the speech disorder as being aphasic in nature; we must eliminate from consideration the non-linguistic disturbances of speech. This is impossible with a classification which regards every disorder as a subgroup of aphasia [p. 124].

In short, Bay stressed that it is essential to separate cortical motor disorders of speech from "the *linguistic* disorder we call aphasia" (p. 128).

DeRenzi, Pieczuro, and Vignolo (1966) in their study of "Oral Apraxia and Aphasia," reported cases of severe oral apraxia in two nonaphasic, left-brain-damaged patients. They reviewed the literature, emphasizing Marie's views and definition of "anarthria." They note that Marie "never precisely defined the nature of anarthria. He merely denied that it was due to paralysis of the oral muscles. Indeed he did once define it as a 'defect in the coordination of the movements of phonation' and on another occasion (1908) he accepted Ballet's suggestion that it might be an apraxic disorder" (p. 51).

In 1966, DeRenzi and his colleagues expressed the opinion that only recently had the significance of motor speech defects and nonverbal oral movements in "motor" aphasia been grasped by some investigators. These authors report that many writers up to and including Nielsen (1946) failed to grasp the significance and implications of articulatory disturbances that are extraneous to specific language disorders. DeRenzi *et al.* (1966) state, "Thus, whether the speech disorders in these patients should be defined as 'aphasic' or 'apraxic' was merely a terminological question" (p. 51).

Luria (1966) feels that the identification of apraxia of speech as an independent entity by investigating parameters of motor speech functions "must be regarded as a giant step forward, opening the way to further scientific study of this complex phenomenon". He continues by stating that "This tendency to bring the analysis of motor aphasia closer to the analysis of other motor disorders, and thus include aphasia among the apraxias, is undoubtedly one of the progressive tendencies in modern neurology" (p. 186).

Shankweiler and Harris (1966) report what appears to be the first experimental attempt to investigate apraxia of speech. The experiment deals exclusively with the "nature of the articulatory disturbance which is often associated with so-called 'motor' aphasia" (p. 279). It is limited to the aspect of articulatory function that is expressed in phonetic terms in an attempt to "gain an accurate picture of the dimensions of phonemic error which occur in the syndrome of phonetic disintegration associated with 'motor' aphasia" (p. 279).

In discussing physiological aspects of speech disturbances, Denny-Brown presents autopsy findings to support the notion that nonsymbolic motor speech disorders can result from discrete cortical lesions and maintains that an apraxia of speech can be readily distinguished. Denny-Brown (1965) applies several traditional terms in an attempt to describe the symptomatology of apraxic speech:

> The next grade of disorder to which I would draw your attention is what I believe is truly "Broca's aphemia" and is identical with Head's verbal aphasia—and Alajouanine's (1939) "Phonetic Disintegration of Speech." It can be truly a cortical disorder of a quite localized kind . . . though it can also be combined with dysarthria or perceptive defect, or both [p. 462].

Denny-Brown finds no objection to the view that an apraxia of speech is a "special and complex type of apraxia of vocal expression . . . but the disorder itself is not propositional" (p. 464). He concludes this by succinctly stating that "the expressive part of the mechanism can be separately disordered, then producing apraxia of speech" (p. 474).

Wepman and his associates have drawn upon their therapeutic experiences with many patients who presented apraxic speech disorders in an attempt to bring order out of the existing terminological confusion in their formulation published in 1955 (Wepman & Van Pelt, 1955) and revised in 1960 (Wepman, Bock, Jones, & Van Pelt, 1960). They demonstrated that some behavior of so-called *aphasic patients* does not involve problems in symbolic formulation.

The term *verbal apraxia*, as used by Darley (1964), refers to a "specific difficulty in performing the oral acts in articulating speech sounds and ordering them sequentially into words, although understanding of speech is adequate . . ." (p. 32). Darley (1964) points out that these are not merely armchair distinctions but that they "emerge from patient performance and have profound implications for the selection of remedial procedures . . . apraxias respond to direct training procedures whereas aphasia proves unamenable to drill and responds rather to general language stimulation procedures" (p. 32).

In summary, the importance of differentiating neurologically based speech disturbances that are of an aphasic nature from those that present themselves independent of comprehension, formulative, or perceptual difficulties has been recognized by numerous modern investigators. Neglect of this problem has had a deleterious effect, both in the choice of treatment of patients who present such disorders and on scientific communication. Moreover, numerous writers have indicated a need for the identification of articulatory disturbances associated with cortical lesions based on empirical data.

Apraxia of Speech versus Dysarthria

Although some writers include the dysarthrias as varieties of apraxia (dyspraxic dysarthria, cortical dysarthria, anarthric dysarthria), a distinction has been made in the majority of neurological texts and current medical dictionaries.

A distinction between apraxic and dysarthric disorders, based on Darley's (1964) differentiations, will be made here. "The term *dysarthria* will refer to an impairment of motor control due to faulty innervation of speech musculatures in complex acts. The term *apraxia* will refer to difficulties in the voluntary control in the absence of paresis or incoordination" (p. 37).

A common distinction made by neurologists in patient examinations is that of comparing reflex muscle activities and voluntary muscle activities. Darley (1964) notes that, "If the patient can smile at a joke and chew and swallow during eating but demonstrates difficulty in retraction or pursing of lips, elevation of tongue tip, or repetition of syllables on command, the discrepancy in performance suggests an oral apraxia" (p. 37).

Thus, a critical differentiation arises from the consistency of given oral acts. The dysarthric patient is typically consistent both in articulatory errors and in voluntary and reflexive motor acts. As an example, if the dysarthric patient is unable to produce a correct phoneme in isolation, it is predictable that he will be unable to produce it in a word, regardless of whether the act is volitional or a reactive automatic speech production. If the dysarthric patient cannot lick his lips upon request, it is to be expected that he will be unable to perform this motor act in an attempt to remove food or lick his lips after drinking water. On the other hand, a patient with an apraxia of speech might demonstrate an inability to perform a motor sequence on request but do so reflexively. The apraxic patient unable to produce the /sh/ phoneme in the word *ship* may produce a perfectly acceptable /sh/ in an emotional response such as cursing.

Another such example is found in *Clinical Examinations in Neurology*:

> Thus, the patient who is unable voluntarily to articulate a word beginning with the sound "S" may be able to curse with complete clarity. Although the disorder manifests itself as an articulatory defect, the fact that volition is the important factor identifies the deficit as an *apraxia of speech sounds*. In contrast with this, in pseudobulbar palsy the articulatory defect is present in both volitional and emotional speech [Mayo Clinic, 1963, p. 255].

In reporting her clinical observations on aphasia, Schuell (1954) made the following distinctions between dysarthric and apraxic speech production: "In dysarthria, articulation errors tend to be consistent; some speech sounds are impaired more than others, and these are impaired whenever they occur. When the problem is due to an apraxia . . . errors tend to be inconsistent; sounds are used incorrectly at times but not at others" (p. 183). Shankweiler and Harris (1966) state "This condition, which is sometimes called cortical dysarthria (Bay, 1962) and apraxic dysarthria (Nathan, 1947), must be distinguished from dysarthric disorders arising from damage restricted to lower levels of the motor system. In the latter, articulatory movements are impaired in a more stereotyped and regular fashion . . ." (p. 277).

In their group of neurologically impaired patients, Shankweiler and Harris (1966) reported a common inconsistency that one would not associate with dysarthric patients. They stated, "Particularly common were the substitution of consonant clusters for single consonants" (p. 288).

Darley (1964) reported Schuell's observations in this respect: "In dysarthria, some sounds requiring more complex positioning and consonant combinations are impaired more than sounds with uncomplicated movement patterns. In apraxia . . . the patient sometimes pronounces difficult words effortlessly and makes errors on easy ones" (p. 38).

In describing some of the salient feature differentiating dysarthria from apraxia of speech, Luria (1966) states,

> The disturbance [apraxia of speech] is distinguished from dysarthria by the fact
> that sometimes the required sounds are pronounced clearly enough, the patient
> showing none of that slurring and monotony of speech characteristic of bulbar or
> pseudobulbar dysarthria. As a rule, such a patient does not exhibit the dysphonic
> disorders of speech usually produced by bilateral lesions of this region. The principle
> defect that can be found in disturbances of the kinesthetic basis of speech consists
> of substitutions for individual articulations [p. 187].

In summary, it seems that a major distinction that can be made between the
apraxic patient and the dysarthric patient is that of volitional, purposive movement versus reflexive or emotional responses in motor speech acts. Another is
that of consistency versus inconsistency, the former being associated with
certain types of dysarthria, the latter with apraxia.

Numerous references have been made to the importance of identifying, describing, and differentiating apraxia of speech as a disorder distinct from dysarthria and aphasia. It has been pointed out that the identification of apraxia of
speech is extremely important both for the neurologist and the speech pathologist: for the neurologist, for diagnostic and referral purposes; and for the speech
pathologist, for the selection and application of appropriate and specific remedial procedures.

Critchley (1960) stated that "the conception of any such pure entity as motor
aphasia is out of favor. Correlation of cerebral dysarthria—that is, a disorder due
to cortico-subcortical lesion, with an articulatory apraxia—is, however, still
conceded. Further than that modern neurologists are unwilling to go" (p. 11). A
review of the literature reveals that those speech pathologists who have concerned themselves with articulatory disturbances of neurologically impaired
patients take essentially the same position as that which Critchley attributes to
the neurologists.

Bay (1967) in discussing the confusion that exists in classifying the disorders
of speech, writes "The current classification comprises so many biased and
inconsistent features that it must lead to misunderstandings and embarrass-
ment. . . . If we could only eliminate some of its errors and inconsistencies, we
should at least be able to agree upon certain generalities and fundamentals of
classification, in order to reduce the level of misunderstanding" (p. 26).

An extensive review of the literature reveals that probably the first experimental investigation of this problem is that of Shankweiler and Harris (1966).
They studied a group of five patients presenting major residual deficits in
articulation following lesions of vascular origin. These lesions were presumably
confined to the left cerebral hemisphere. A "rhyme" test was administered to
their subjects in order to be reasonably certain "that the errors in articulation
occur on the basis of impaired motor organization, rather than on the basis of
perceptual impairment" (p. 280). Each subject was requested to repeat 200
monosyllabic words. Verbal responses were tape-recorded and phonetically ana-

lyzed. The transcribed results were presented as confusion matrices to indicate the incidence and types of errors made. These data were summarized to indicate the incidence of difficulty with regard to consonants, consonant clusters, and vowels. The authors found that, for these patients, initial sounds were harder than final sounds, that fricatives and affricates and certain consonant clusters were the classes of speech sounds most consistently misarticulated, that unrelated substitutions and omissions were the most common errors, that substitutions of consonant clusters for single consonants were particularly common, and that these articulatory problems were not attributable to specific muscles or muscle groups.

The Shankweiler and Harris study was just a beginning and provided the impetus for other investigations that were expanded in terms of the number of patients studied, the types of stimuli presented, the modes of response involved, and the data concerning associated abilities.

In discussing the confusion that exists in differentiating apraxia of speech from dysarthria and aphasia, Bay (1967) states that "This question can only be answered by further investigations which have never been made, as far as I know. Instead, the problem is allegedly solved on the basis of preconceived theoretical assumptions" (p. 28).

Subsequent research has specified the articulatory characteristics of apraxia of speech (Darley, 1967; Johns, 1968a; Johns & Darley, 1970; LaPointe, 1969; La-Pointe & Johns, 1975; Shankweiler & Harris, 1966) and has differentiated it from other output disorders such as the dysarthrias and aphasias (Darley, Aronson & Brown, 1969; Halpren, Darley, & Brown, 1973; Johns & Darley, 1970; Trost, 1970). Other studies have concentrated on input or sensory deficits in apraxia of speech (Aten, Johns, & Darley, 1971; Guilford & Hawk, 1968; Larimore, 1970; Rosenbek, Wertz, & Darley, 1973c) and on the influence of linguistic and situational variables as they affect phonemic accuracy in patients having apraxia of speech (Deal & Darley, 1972). The differential effects of apraxia of speech and aphasia on visual recognition tasks and writing errors in Japanese patients has recently been reported and appears to be another area of study that offers a step forward toward our understanding of the complexity of verbal impairments (Sasanuma & Fujimura, 1971, 1972). Based on experimental data, studies directed toward the application of therapeutic techniques have been reported by Johns (1970), Johns and Macaluso (1972), and Yoss (1972, 1973). The foregoing studies, dealing with patients having neurogenic speech and language disorders directly related to known lesions, are representative of an effort to describe and better understand the communication disorders and to study which therapies might be more efficient and efficacious.

It would appear that further sutdies designed to identify and describe the entity apraxia of speech, based on empirically derived data, are both justifiable and indicated. Such studies could offer substantial contributions to the understanding of articulatory disturbances found in populations with certain neurological disorders and may provide answers to some of the questions concerning the syndrome of apraxia of speech as a disorder distinct from dysarthria and aphasia.

PHONOLOGICAL CHARACTERISTICS

The lack of standardization and apparent confusion of teminology surrounding research into neurogenic phonological impairment makes it difficult to interpret some of the findings in various reports. Not all reports provide detailed descriptions of the verbal performance of subjects, and a reader cannot be confident of the homogeneity of subjects across studies. Several reports, however, have focused on the phonological aspects of verbal impairment and have given us a clearer understanding of this area.

In one of the earliest detailed reports of phonological impairment accompanying aphasia, Fry (1959) demonstrated a systematic method of analysis of some of the articulatory characteristics of such subjects. He examined the phonemic substitutions of an aphasic patient by phonetic analysis of tape-recorded utterances. A confusion matrix used for tabulation of responses then permitted the classification of all substituted phonemes according to the distinctive features of place and manner of articulation. As Shankweiler and Harris (1966) have noted, "Fry's paper demonstrates the relevance to aphasia studies of a powerful method for discovering the dimensions of a phonological disturbance" (p. 278).

This strategy of tabulation on confusion matrices and subsequent classification and analysis of responses, adopted by several researchers in the 1960s, permits a degree of order and understanding to emerge from the morass of phonological impairment in these patients.

In 1966, Shankweiler and Harris described some of the dimensions of phonemic error in five patients who presented the syndrome of "phonetic disintegration" associated with "motor aphasia." Patients who exhibit this syndrome, according to Shankweiler and Harris (1966) "articulate slowly, hesitantly, with extrinsic facial movements and with many substitutions of one phoneme for another" (p. 277). These researchers found that subjects had maximal difficulty in articulation at the beginning portion of words. Consonant sounds were much more frequently misarticulated than vowel sounds and fricative, affricate, and certain linked groups of consonants were most frequently affected. An important conclusion of Shankweiler and Harris was that no particular region or structure could be implicated to the exclusion of other parts of the articulatory apparatus. The frequency of errors of voicing, nasalization, and consonant clusters, and the relative integrity of vowels, all seemed to indicate a disturbance of coordinated sequencing of several articulators.

In a related study (Shankweiler *et al.*, 1968), surface electromyography was used to investigate disordered articulatory movement of two patients. This study revealed that: (*1*) traces for both patients having phonetic disintegration were grossly abnormal in form; (2) repeated utterances of the same word showed great variability in the timing of sequential movements; (3) vowels were prolonged and variable in length; and (4) labial consonants in the initial position were more defectively formed than those in the terminal position in one patient. Also, the occurrence of simultaneous peaks from all electrode locations showed a "striking reduction of the capacity for independent movement of the articulators" (Shankweiler *et al.*, 1968, p. 8). This study contributed valuable information about the temporal and spatial organization of defective speech gestures, though the sample studied was very limited.

The termination of the 1960s brought a wave of interest in the study of neurogenic phonological impairment and doctoral dissertations by Johns (1968b), LaPointe (1969), Trost (1970), and Larimore(1970) highlighted much of what is currently known in the area. These studies were subsequently published in the *Journal of Speech and Hearing Research* (Johns & Darley, 1970), the *Journal of Communication Disorders* (LaPointe & Johns, 1975), and *Brain and Language* (Trost & Canter, 1974).

The Johns and Darley (1970) study provides information on several phonological characteristics in apraxia of speech and contrasts these with the performance of dysarthric patients. The speech productions of apraxic subjects is characterized by a high degree of variability. This inconsistency is evident from sound to sound, from word to word, across different modes of stimulus presentation, and between contextual and conversational speech. For example, a typical apraxic subject might insert a *schwa* in a three-element consonant cluster on his first attempt, say the cluster correctly the second time, repeat and block on the third attempt, produce an apparently unrelated substitution on the fourth attempt, emit an additive substitution the fifth time, and then say the target word with the precision of a normal speaker.

The total number of errors and the phonemes on which they were made failed to differentiate the apraxic from the dysarthric groups, but the types of errors differentiated them clearly. Apraxic subjects presented predominantly substitutions, repetition, and addition errors as opposed to the predominance of distortion errors of the dysarthrics. Additive substitutions, such as /pl/ for /p/ and /spl/ for /pl/ were common in apraxic productions.

Disturbed prosody and inflectional patterns were also evident, and as Johns and Darley (1970) reported "In contextual speech apraxic subjects seemed to be tip-toeing through their words. They appeared to be—and they reported they were—attempting to slow down and approach articulatory adjustments cautiously. . . . Their rate tended to be slow, even, and hesitant . . . and whatever partial success may be attributed to these compensatory adjustments to gain articulatory control, prosody and inflectional patterns suffered" (p. 581).

Though clinical impressions of disturbed prosody in apraxia of speech are apparently widespread, to date no study of the dimensions and severity of prosodic alterations has been reported.

Trost (1970) studied a clinical population comprised of 10 patients having "Broca's aphasia" who exhibited articulatory defects in their verbal productions. She reported high error rates on the phonemes /dʒ/ and /θ/, which supported previous reports that fricatives and affricates are the most impaired classes. Trost suggested a tendency for final consonants to have lower error rates than initial consonants but her reported *t* test of differences in error rates between the two positions is not statistically significant. This reported tendency for more errors on initial than final consonants apparently has been interpreted by some as a characteristic of apraxic speech when the actual evidence to date is indicative of no differences.

Trost found substitutions to comprise 78% of the articulatory errors of her subjects. She also reported three types of errors on consonant clusters, which included: (*1*) simplification by omission and/or substitutions, (*2*) additive substitutions, and (*3*) transitional pauses.

Trost reported five types of "inadequate responses" that could not be evaluated phonetically. These responses included "random phonemes," where phoneme strings failed to yield word approximations; "perseverative responses" of either phonemic and/or linguistic repetition from a prior test word; "paraphasic responses," which were semantically related words (*bat* for *coat*); "recurrent utterances," and "no response." These "inadequate responses" were not included in Trost's phonetic analysis.

In another study, LaPointe (1969) investigated the articulatory productions and the nonverbal oral movement abilities of 28 subjects who sustained left-hemisphere cortical damage. The phonological characteristics of 13 of these subjects who met criteria indicative of apraxia of speech were studied in some detail and reported in a subsequent article (LaPointe & Johns, 1975). Analysis of errors plotted on confusion matrices revealed significantly more errors on consonants than vowels ($p < .001$) and significantly more errors on consonant clusters than single consonants ($p < .001$).

Analysis of the position of errors has resulted in different interpretations, as previously cited in this chapter. Some authors (Shankweiler & Harris, 1966; Trost, 1970) have suggested that initial consonants are more susceptible to error than final consonants. LaPointe and Johns (1975), however, found error percentages for initial, medial, and final positions to be nearly equal. (Mean error percentages for initial, medial, and final positions were 27%, 25%, and 26%, respectively.) These results support the finding of Johns and Darley (1970) that "no single position in the word emerged as characteristically more difficult" (p. 578). Lack of agreement on this issue may be partly definitional, however, depending on whether retrials and repetitions (the difficulty in getting started presented by many subjects having apraxia of speech) are tallied as a separate type of error, or are added to those errors made on the initial phoneme of words. LaPointe and Johns (1975) cataloged initiation errors (retrials and repetitions) separately from errors made on the initial phoneme.

LaPointe and Johns (1975) also reported error percentages relative to manner and place of production. They found significantly more errors on affricatives than on fricatives, nasals, glides, or plosives. Fricatives were more frequently in error than all others except affricatives, and no other significant differences among manner categories existed. Similarly, an analysis of error percentages according to place of production revealed significant differences among categories. Palatal and dental phonemes were significantly more susceptible to error than all other categories. No significant differences in voiced or unvoiced phonemes were found in this study.

Another analysis of the phonemic production of these 13 speech apraxic subjects concerned the sequential nature of their articulatory errors. Lashley (1951) in his classical work on serial order, postulated that the realization of linguistic sequences requires the interplay of at least three relatively independent neurophysiological mechanisms:

1. The "determining tendency" or "idea."
2. A mechanism of "primary" or "arousal of expressive units."
3. A mechanism having to deal specifically with serial ordering of preactivated units.

Lecours and Lhermitte (1969) reviewed some of Lashley's theories and suggested that many of the phonemic errors made by brain-damaged patients are sequential in nature. Johns and Darley (1970) suggested that these sequential errors are "anticipatory" or "perseverative." In apraxic subjects, sequential error becomes apparent by analyzing only two categories of error—phoneme substitution and initiation errors (difficulty in getting started). In the LaPointe and Johns study (1975) when initiation errors and substitution errors were analyzed relative to the target word, three types of sequential error became evident: "anticipatory" (prepositioning), "reiterative" (postpositioning), and "metathesis" (two phonemes in which order was reversed). All subjects in this study produced some sequential errors, but the percentage of these errors relative to total substitution and initiation errors was small (seven percent). Anticipatory or prepositioning errors outnumbered postpositioning errors by a ratio of 6 to 1, but metathesis of phonemes was not prevalent. Sequential errors did exist as defined in this study, but did not account for a significant proportion of the phonemic errors in this particular sample of subjects.

The question of the relationship of substituted phonemes to the target sound has been discussed by some researchers (Johns & Darley, 1970; Trost, 1970). Substitutions of speech apraxics have been characterized by some as being quite unrelated to the replaced sound. LaPointe and Johns (1975) determined whether substitutions of their 13 apraxics were errors of placement alone, of manner, of voicing, or combinations of these. Of the substitution errors in their sample, 38% were defective in two or more features and "bore little acoustic resemblance to the target sound." Conclusions regarding distance between error and target sound are dependent upon the number of features used in the analysis, however.

Further distinctive-feature analysis of errors in apraxia of speech appears to be a fruitful area for additional research. For example, one of the problems studied at the University of Florida and the Gainesville Veterans Administration Hospital involves determining movement toward or away from the target sound in the repetitions and retrials of apraxic patients.

Characteristics of apraxia of speech as reflected on the Porch Index of Communicative Ability and other specific tests for apraxia of speech have been reported by Wertz, Rosenbek, and Collins (1972).

Another study of phonological impairment in aphasia was reported by Martin (1974) who contends that impaired phonemic production involves many levels of linguistic processing and presents some objections to the use of the term *apraxia of speech*.

NONVERBAL APRAXIA OF THE ORAL MECHANISM

Brain-injured patients are frequently seen who present disturbed voluntary movements of the jaw, lips, face, and tongue in addition to phonemic selection and sequencing impairment. This condition, which is now most frequently called *oral nonverbal apraxia* (Rosenbek, Deal, & LaPointe, 1973a) was observed and reported as early as 1866 by Hughlings Jackson. Wilson (1908) reports that Jackson stated: "In some cases of defect of speech the patient seems to have lost much of his power to do anything he is told to do, even with those muscles that are not paralyzed. Thus a patient will be unable to put his tongue out when we ask him, although he will use it well in semi-involuntary actions—for example, eating and swallowing" (p. 168).

The relationship of oral nonverbal apraxia to articulatory impairment in the brain injured is unclear at this time. It seems intuitive to some that if a patient presented disturbed volitional movement of nonspeech oral movements, then he would also exhibit disturbances when similar movements were used in speech. Thus Nathan (1947) stated, "It is obvious that if there is apraxia for those movements needed for speaking, a dysarthria due to apraxia will result" (p. 3).

On the other hand, Goldstein (1948) suggested the opposite when he indicated: "Other patients are unable voluntarily to produce non-language movements, e.g., screwing up the mouth, closing the lips (as in pronouncing the letter "m"), moving the tongue voluntarily, puckering, etc., while they *can* produce these movements as language performances" (p. 81).

DeRenzi *et al.* (1966) investigated the relationships between oral apraxia and certain clinical syndromes in aphasia; between oral apraxia and "phonemic-articulatory" disorders; and between oral apraxia and limb apraxia. They found a strong correlation between oral apraxia and severity of phonemic-articulatory disorder. Four patients in this study were found whose phonemic-articulatory impairment of speech was not accompanied by oral apraxia and seven patients were discovered whose oral apraxia was more severe than their articulatory disorder.

To explain their finding that some patients have an oral apraxia but no speech defect, and that patients with different apraxic syndromes may have an oral apraxia, DeRenzi *et al.* (1966) formulated two hypotheses. The first is that oral nonverbal movements and speech movements may be subserved by two discrete cortical association areas and, therefore, lesions may produce impairment of one but not the other.

Their second hypothesis is that apraxia from commands can result from lesions to pathways connecting frontal and temporal lobes; and apraxia from imitation can result from lesions disrupting occipital and frontal fasciculi.

Alajouanine and Lhermitte (1960) maintained that nonverbal oral apraxia is common in Broca's aphasia and suggested that nonspeech oral movements are less complex than articulatory movements involving speech and, therefore, may recover more rapidly.

Geschwind (1965) stated that facial apraxia was commonly found in patients having conduction aphasia. Similarly to DeRenzi's hypothesis, Geschwind also suggested that facial apraxia may be specific to a stimulus mode, and that a lesion, for example, to the neural pathway connecting the visual centers with the

TABLE 2 Tests of Isolated Oral Movement [a]

Test	Structure tested	Task description
A	Tongue	1. Protrusion–retraction
		2. Lateral movement
		3. Upper lip center
		4. Lower lip center
		5. Licking lips
B	Jaw	1. Lateral movement
		2. Open and close mouth
C	Teeth	1. Click (three times)
		2. Bite lower lip
D	Lips	1. Protrude lips (pucker)
		2. Show teeth (spread lips)
		3. Smile (without showing teeth)
E	Other	1. Puff out cheeks
		2. Whistle (one note)
		3. Cough (nonreflexively)

[a] LaPointe and Wertz (1974).

TABLE 3 Tests of Oral Motor Sequencing[a]

Test	Number in sequence	Movements
A	2	Tongue (upper lip center), jaw (lower–raise)
B	2	Teeth (click once), lips (protrude)
C	3	jaw (lateral), teeth (bite lower lip), lips (show teeth)
D	3	Tongue (lower lip center), lips (protrude), tongue (lick lips)
E	4	Lips (show teeth), teeth (bite lower lip), jaw (lateral), tongue (lick lips
F	4	Cheeks (puff out), lips (protrude), jaw (lower–raise), tongue (lick lips)
G	5	Teeth (click once), lips (protrude), jaw (lateral) teeth (bite lower lip), jaw (lower–raise)
H	5	Lips (protrude), tongue (lick lips), teeth (click once), cheeks (puff out), tongue (upper lip center)

[a] LaPointe and Wertz (1974).

motor cortex in the area of the supramarginal gyrus, could produce a facial apraxia to visual stimulation.

LaPointe (1969) assembled a number of cited clinical suggestions for assessing nonverbal oral apraxia and designed tasks for evaluating isolated oral movements and oral motor sequencing ability of brain-injured patients.

The results of this study have been reported in the literature (LaPointe & Wertz, 1974) and Tables 2 and 3 present the tasks used for isolated and sequenced oral movement.

These tasks were scored using a system adapted from that of DeRenzi *et al.* (1966) as can be seen in Table 4. LaPointe and Wertz (1974) reported the performances on these tasks by 28 cortically damaged, articulatorily impaired subjects and 28 matched controls. Of the 28 brain-injured patients, 17 had difficulty making isolated oral movements and 21 displayed problems in oral motor sequencing. Not all of the patients who displayed oral-movement deficits could be considered to have a nonverbal oral apraxia, however. Some gave responses that were defective in speech or symmetry; and these patients, typically presenting an accompanying dysarthria or mixed apraxia of speech and dysarthria, invariably demonstrated a lower facial paralysis or lingual paresis. Other patients, however, made random, bizarre, irrelevant movements including vocal overflow, and displayed what DeRenzi *et al.* (1966) described as "oral apraxia." Of the brain-injured subjects (14 of 28), 50% presented this nonverbal

**TABLE 4 Scoring System Used for Isolated
Oral Movement Tests**[a]

Response definition	Observed behavior	Score
Correct	Accurate response immediately follows presentation of test item.	4
	Accurate response is preceded by pauses, during which unsuccessful movements may be present.	3
Crude	Overall pattern of movement is acceptable though movements are defective in amplitude, accuracy, or speed.	2
Partial	Some important part of the movement is lacking, though the rest is performed correctly.	1
Perserveration	Movements elicited by preceding items are performed.	0
Irrelevant	Some other incorrect oral performance (including speech sounds) is produced.	0
Nil	No oral performance is produced.	0

[a] LaPointe and Wertz (1974).

oral apraxia and the condition was most frequently present in patients who also demonstrated the phonological characteristics of apraxia of speech.

The groping, bizarre movement patterns characteristic of nonverbal oral apraxia are typified in several descriptions of patient behavior presented by LaPointe (1969). One subject who was attempting to puff out his cheeks moved his tongue laterally while opening and closing his mouth. The same subject could not cough voluntarily when asked to do so, and exclaimed, "I guess I just can't do it." Many of these subjects also produced "vocal overflow" while attempting movements. One subject vocalized a prolonged /ɑ/ while clicking her teeth and moving her jaw. She also presented many searching, random movements while attempting to show her teeth, and made a prolonged, distorted /s/ throughout her attempts on this item. Another subject, in attempting to place his tongue on the center of his lower lip, made circular tongue movements and attempted to "help out" his tongue with his thumb and index finger. In attempting to cough volitionally, this subject puckered his lips and vocalized /hu/ several times in succession.

The tasks that appear to be the most susceptible to oral apraxia movement are those that demand the coordination of the breath stream and/or phonation with some isolated oral movement, i.e., commands such as *Cough, Clear your throat, Blow*, or *Whistle*.

The diagnostic and therapeutic implications of oral nonverbal movement testing are provocative. As Rosenbek *et al.* (1973a) point out, however, the burdens of hypothesis testing in this area are great, and the need for more sophisticated and standardized assessment strategies is obvious. Until now, tests have been too little standardized and too idiosyncratically conceived to be of general use. Further conceptual considerations such as similarity to speech movements, stimulus length and type, and refinement of scoring systems will no doubt bring about modifications that will make these tests more attractive and useful to persons interested in brain function. Research underway in 1975 at the University of Colorado (see Moore, 1975) addressed many of these issues. In addition the inter-relationships of severity levels of speech and nonspeech movement disturbance must be clarified, as well as the relationship of nonverbal, oral apraxia to jargon aphasia.

Refinement in instrumental procedures, including cineradiography, electro-myography, and the development of miniature strain gauge transducers for measuring articulatory contact pressures and displacement have now provided researchers with improved potential for studying the dynamics of speech and nonspeech movements. Instrumentation must be designed or adapted that will allow precise measurement of disturbances of range, duration, sequencing, and timing of lingual movements.

DEVELOPMENTS IN THE STUDY
OF APRAXIA OF SPEECH

Perhaps the most intensive recognition given the disorder of apraxia of speech on any one occasion thus far, occurred on 20 November 1970 at the annual convention of the American Speech and Hearing Association in New York. The condition was afforded the status of a separate and distinctive disorder of speech by virtue of its placement on this convention's program in a three-hour dual session entitled: "Apraxia of Speech: Description, Diagnosis and Treatment." Approximately 1500 people heard papers and discussion on the topic by Frederic Darley, Robert T. Wertz, John Rosenbek, Leonard L. LaPointe, Jon Deal, and Donnell F. Johns; and this event seemed to serve as a catalyst for a surge of interest in the disorder in the early 1970s.

Since then, several studies on apraxia of speech have been published that have both furthered our understanding of the condition and raised compelling questions about it.

Linguistic and Situational Variables

One such study, by Deal and Darley (1972), investigated the influence of several linguistic and situational variables on phonetic accuracy in apraxia of speech. In this study, 12 subjects were tested under four different experimental conditions: (*1*) the effects of instructions, (*2*) the effect of three experimentally imposed response-delay intervals on word repetition, (*3*) the effect of noise, and (*4*) the effect of visual monitoring. These authors also studied the loci of errors in oral reading, the subjects' ability to predict and recognize their errors, and the nature of the errors. Deal and Darley found that different instructions, response-delay intervals, noise, and visual monitoring had no significant influence on phonemic accuracy. Subjects had significantly more difficulty with three-syllable than with one-syllable words, and grammatical class also appeared to be an important characteristic influencing increases in numbers of errors. The ability of apraxia subjects to predict errors appeared to be an individual, rather than a group characteristic, but subjects were aware of their errors and could recognize them. The authors concluded that apraxia of speech appears to be essentially a motor speech disorder not significantly influenced by auditory or visual variables. It might well be, however, that future studies will find visual or auditory variables not studied by Deal and Darley that do in fact influence apraxia of speech. Nevertheless, this study provided significant new information about the condition.

Perceptual Factors

Apraxia of speech has been traditionally viewed as a disturbance of encoding, essentially free of perceptual decoding impairment, though few studies have reported on the perceptual abilities of apraxics.

Sasanuma and Fujimura (1971), in an interesting investigation that considered communicative differences in the Japanese language, studied the abilities of two group of aphasics (with and without apraxia of speech) to deal with ideograms (kanjis) and phonograms (kanas) on visual recognition and writing tasks. They concluded that the selective impairment of kana processing exhibited by some of their patients was associated not only with overall severity, but with a specific syndrome of apraxia of speech superimposed on aphasia. Further, they hypothesized that a "phonological processor" exists as an independent subsystem that is involved in retrieving phonetic specifications for lexical codes.

Recently, Aten *et al.* (1971) reported on the auditory perception of phonemes in sequenced words in 10 patients suffering from apraxia of speech and 10 matched normal control subjects. The test items were 190 sequences of two and three words having minimal variation of initial consonant, final consonant, medial vowel, or multiple phonemes. The apraxic patients made significantly more perceptual errors as a group, but varied considerably in their level of performance. Three patients performed within the range established by the control subjects. The remaining seven apraxic subjects made inferior scores, although three of these performed at intermediate levels. The major deficit in the apraxic group appeared to be in the ability to retain second- and third-syllable consonant elements in three-word sequences. Aten and his colleagues (1971) concluded that, despite the significant mean differences between the apraxic and control groups, the appearance of no auditory perceptual difficulty by some apraxics fails to support a hypothesis that identifies anticipatory auditory feedback problems as the cause of apraxia of speech. It would appear, however, that the evidence is not unequivocal, and that perhaps more sensitive tests of phoneme discrimination and sequential storage might alter our concept of the relationship between auditory perception and phonemic sequencing in apraxia.

In addition to auditory factors, tactile-kinesthetic feedback has been long recognized as important to normal speech production and maintenance. The possibility that impaired tactile-kinesthetic input might influence or even cause the production problems seen in apraxia patients, however, received relatively little attention until Rosenbek *et al.* (1973c) reported the results of a quite significant study. They investigated the performances of 30 patients suffering from apraxia of speech, 10 patients having aphasia and no apraxia of speech, and 30 normal subjects on three oral sensory-perceptual measurements: oral form identification, two-point discrimination, and mandibular kinesthesia. These researchers reported that:

1. As a group, patients with apraxia of speech showed significant oral sensory-perceptual deficit on the three measures.
2. The errors of apraxic patients on sensory tests, while more numerous than those of both normals and aphasics, do not differ in type from those of the latter two groups. This finding suggests a true oral sensory-perceptual deficit rather than the influence of perseveration, decreased auditory memory span, or confusion about instructions.
3. Severity of apraxia of speech and oral sensory-perceptual deficit are interdependent.

These authors further concluded that patients having apraxia of speech are not homogeneous in oral sensory-perceptual ability. Two groups, one with oral sensory-perceptual deficit and one without, were identified. Lack of homogeneity in the apraxic group appeared to be more closely related to severity of apraxic symptoms than to the existence of different types of apraxia of speech, however. The existence of two types of apraxia of speech, differing in both symptoms and in locus of lesion has been an attractive speculation for several authors including Luria (1966) and Canter (1969). While Rosenbek *et al.* (1973c) believe that severity levels adequately explain their finding of apraxics with and without oral sensory-perceptual deficit, perhaps further study will indeed lead to the discovery of discrete patterns or types of apraxic speech behavior. At any rate, Rosenbek *et al.* (1973c) raised some compelling theoretical and clinical questions, and they have revised the concept of apraxia of speech to include sensory-perceptual influences rather than the traditional view of it as strictly a motor, or output, speech disorder. Refinements in measuring oral sensory-perceptual integrity may clarify these relationships even further.

Apraxia in Children

The surge of research interest in apraxia of speech in adults has apparently served to pique the curiosity of several investigators about the existence of an analagous condition in the so-called *functional* articulation disorders of children.

Descriptions of articulatory behavior in children seem to parallel those of speech-apraxic adults, although labels and terminology vary widely. Yoss (1972) compared the results of several speech and nonspeech tests of 30 articulatory defective children between the ages of five and nine years with matched controls who had never been enrolled or recommended for speech therapy. 16 subjects were identified whose articulation and nonspeech behavior combined to distinguish them from other subjects with defective articulation. Yoss (1972) stated that their behaviors could be characterized as "developmental apraxia of speech." These children presented slower than normal oral diadochokinesis rates of /pʌ/, /tʌ/, /kʌ/, and /pʌ tə kə/; omission, revision, or addition of syllables in polysyllabic words; and some prosodic alteration. They also exhibited difficulty in performing volitional oral movements of the articulators, a high incidence of "soft" neurological signs, and difficulty in sequencing volitional oral movements.

Fifteen of these 16 children with developmental apraxia of speech were retested 12 to 16 months after initial testing (Yoss, 1973). Performance on isolated volitional oral movements was unchanged, but diadochokinetic rates, total number of phonemic errors, and ratings of overall intelligibility were significantly improved at follow-up testing in 10 of the 15 children who had been enrolled in speech therapy. The 5 children who were not enrolled in speech therapy failed to show these changes.

In another study of apraxia in children, Kools, Williams, Vickers, and Caell (1971) adapted the DeRenzi, Pieczuro, and Vignolo Test for Oral and Limb Apraxia and administered it to 33 children of normal intelligence who had articulatory disorders and 30 retarded children and adults who had defective articulation and were matched in mental age with the nonretardates. The retarded group was also divided into two etiological categories, organic and nonorganic, and the results indicated that the organic retardates exhibited significant degrees of apraxia. Nonorganic retardates showed significant apraxia, also, but less severity than the organic group. Correlation techniques revealed no significant association of apraxia with defective articulation but an association of apraxia with vocabulary mental age and intelligence. Kools *et al.* (1971) speculated that their finding of no correlation between articulatory ability and oral apraxia might be due to the lack of sensitivity of their articulatory tests to rate, effort, fluency, juncture, and other characteristics frequently associated with apraxia of speech in adults.

Clinical Treatment of Apraxia of Speech

Since many speech pathologists, who are vitally concerned with communicative rehabilitative strategies, will no doubt be interested in this chapter on apraxia of speech, it would appear to us to be an oversight to exclude some recent findings on management. The field of aphasiology and neurogenic output disturbances of speech, it would seem to some observers, has been preoccupied for a century with localization of lesion issues, neuroanatomical correlates of speech behavior, and neuropsychological concerns, with subsequent neglect of focus on clinical rehabilitative procedures. Many speech pathologists view the continuing pursuit of "Lesion, lesion, where is the lesion?" with the attitude of "So what?" The continuing importance of neuropsychological and neurolinguistic issues is recognized as vital to understanding neurogenic speech and language impairment, but it now seems that clinical management issues are on the threshold of receiving long-neglected equal attention.

Recent developments in treatment and refinements of therapeutic strategies have improved our ability to play the relevant game, which is, as Darley (1972) urges, to "restore the patient to communicative efficiency" (p. 4).

Johns (1970) outlined treatment suggestions, based on research findings, that include emphasis on stimulus delivery in the combined auditory and visual modes, and repetitive articulation drill by such direct techniques as phonetic placement, phonetic approximation and progression techniques, and mirror work.

Another report, which is a major contribution to the synthesis and amplification of therapeutic principles relevent to apraxia of speech, was presented by Rosenbek, Lemme, Ahearn, Harris, and Wertz (1973b). These principles include attention to the preparation of stimulus materials that systematically increase speech-sound difficulty, response length, and articulatory distance between successive sounds. An eight-step task continuum based on these principles was then constructed to establish predictable, volitional control of selected utterances. This task continuum is based heavily on integral stimulation (*Watch me. Listen to me.*), simultaneous production by the patient and clinician, and the gradual fading of first auditory then visual cues. Rosenbek *et al.* (1973b) present the results of this strategy, used in treating three adults suffering from severe apraxia of speech of longer than one year's duration. Each patient demonstrated the ability to move from imitative productions to volitional, purposive control on a limited number of utterances.

Another trend in the treatment of neurogenic speech and language disorders has been the adaptation of certain principles of operant conditioning and programmed learning. Programmed–operant approaches emphasize stimulus definition and control, the meticulous plotting of session-by-session performance on clearly specified tasks, and the definition of criterion, or acceptable terminal behavior, on a speech or language task.

These principles have been adapted into a treatment strategy called "Base 10 Programmed Speech–Language Stimulation" (LaPointe, 1973). In this approach speech or language material is organized into segments containing 10 stimulus items per task, which are scored and plotted over 16 sessions. The Base 10 Response Form (LaPointe, 1973) is used in this strategy; and it permits specification of the task to be worked upon, permits a definition of terminal behavior performance levels (criterion), allows for listing of the exact stimulus items used within a task, and provides space for scoring patient response on each item during every session. The form also permits patient performance levels to be converted to a graphic percentage display of progress or lack of progress over 10 sessions.

These trends of careful construction of task continuua and specification, scoring, and plotting of patient behavior over time have contributed to a more systematized and organized approach to remediation of neurogenic speech and language problems. No doubt such approaches will add to the mounting evidence regarding the efficacy and necessity of treatment and will aid in shifting emphasis to vital clinical issues within the area of neurogenic communicative handicaps.

SUMMARY

The subject of output processing disorders of speech associated with cortical lesions has proved to be a fertile area for controversy for more than a century. Theoretical and interpretative arguments have abounded, resulting in biased and inconsistent terminology which, for the most part, has reflected preconceived theoretical assumptions.

The paucity of systematic research in the area of neurogenic speech disorders appears to be largely responsible for the misunderstandings and confusions of past and contemporary researchers and clinicians alike. The terminological confusion, which leads to confused diagnostic classification, often results in uncertain, unspecified, and uncalled-for "shotgun" approaches to therapy. A better understanding of neurogenic disorders of speech is best brought about by clear differentiation (by specifying and validating distinctive characteristic patterns of certain disorders from other disorders) based upon empirical data and not drawn from "armchair" speculations. Likewise, clinical management consisting of appropriate and specific remedial procedures that have emerged from empirical data is more likely to be efficacious than theoretically derived modes of management or procedures applied automatically in response to a traditional label. Although these issues involve semantics, they are not *just* a matter of semantics. If we continue to apply unclear labels and let our language do our thinking for us, we will continue to mistreat the patients who present specific neurogenic speech disorders, a procedure that results in frustration to clinician and patient alike.

Thus, the importance of identifying and describing apraxia of speech in an attempt to better understand and separate this disorder from other deficits of output processing can be appreciated for the following reasons:

a. For mutual scientific communication (including the teaching of students and training of professional personnel).

b. For defining discrete populations so as to permit strategies to be designed for the establishment of treatment approaches and implementation of specific therapeutic procedures in a systematic and rational manner.

Based on present information, we simply do not have the basic understanding of how motoric speech is organized and programmed in time. Our knowledge of the complex neural patterns that underlie the over-learned acts of phonemic production (the substrate or substrates of speech) is far from satisfactory. It seems obvious that there is an overriding need to study the basic neurophysiological correlates that relate to output processing and disorders of output processing and to relate the output process to the "central process" of human communicative behavior. Instead of trying to resolve these problems on the basis of preconceived theoretical assumptions, it would appear both justifiable and necessary to consider the objective measurement of relevant aspects of behavioral change by collecting reliable quantitative data of a physiological nature. Such information would be extremely useful in the development of improved treatment procedures and would be significant as well because of what it would reveal concerning the nature and cause of these disorders.

We believe that apraxia of speech, associated with focal lesions in the dominant hemisphere, constitutes an example of an output processing disorder. Also, that apraxia of speech is a diagnostically definable entity that can be specified in quantitative terms and described qualitatively by certain clinical features.

The peculiarities in the speech of apraxic patients—variability of phonemic production; unrelated and additive substitutions, repetitions, and blocks; groping through repeated efforts toward right production; disturbances of prosody; and perservative and anticipatory errors (more evident in tasks of reading and repeating than in spontaneous conversation)—are alterations of volitional articulation, which fit well within the generic term *apraxia*. As stated by Johns and Darley (1970):

> Despite a difference between volitional-purposive and spontaneous-reflexive performance, these complex and variable errors do not have their basis in perceptual

impairment (aphasia), for visual and auditory perception of speech stimuli generally is much better than the oral reproduction of them. But also, the errors occur in the absence of significant weakness, slowness, or incoordination of the speech muscula-ture which would signify impairment of the lower levels of the speech motor system (dysarthria). Therefore, their identification by the term *apraxia of speech* seems appropriate [p. 582].

We have found that the most potent differentiating characteristics of apraxic speech to be: (*a*) additive substitutions superimposed on other substitutions; (*b*) problems of initiating the speech act; (*c*) stuttering-like repetitions of phonemes; and (*d*) error-type changes in repeated utterances. Such aberations in program-ming of articulatory movements in volitional speech in the absence of significant impairment of language comprehension, and which cannot be attributed to loss of motor power, warrant a therapeutic approach distinct from approaches effective in aphasia and dysarthria.

REFERENCES

Alajouanine, T. 1956. Verbal realization in aphasia. *Brain, 79,* 1–28.

Alajouanine, T., & Lhermitte, F. 1960. Les troubles des activités expressives du langage dan l'aphasie. Leur relations avec les apraxies. *Revue Neurologique, 102,* 604–633.

Alajouanine, T., & Lhermitte, F. 1964. Aphasia and physiology of speech. In D. M. Rioch & E. A. Weinstein (Eds.), *Disorders of communication.* Baltimore: Williams & Wilkins. Pp. 204–219.

Alajouanine, T., Ombredane, A., & Durand, M. 1939. *Le syndrome de désintegration phonétique dans l'aphasie.* Paris: Masson.

Aten, J. L., Johns, D. F., & Darley, F. L. 1971. Auditory perception of sequenced words in apraxia of speech. *Journal of Speech and Hearing Research, 14,* 131–143.

Auburtin. 1861. Sur la forme et la volume du cerveau: Sur le siége de la faculté du langage. *Bulletin de la Sociéte d'Anthropologie, Paris, 2,* 214–233.

Bay, E. 1962. Aphasia and non-verbal disorders of language. *Brain, 85,* 412–426.

Bay, E. 1964. Principles of classification and their influence on our concepts of aphasia. In A. V. DeRueck & M. O'Connor (Eds.), *Disorders of language.* Boston: Little, Brown. Pp. 122–139.

Bay, E. 1967. The classification of disorders of speech. *Cortex, 3,* 26–37.

Brain, W. R. 1965. *Speech disorders.* London: Butterworth.

Broca, P. 1861. Remarques sur la siège de la faculté du langage articulé suives d'une observation d'aphémie. *Bulletin de la Société d'Anthropologie, Paris, 2,* 235–257.

Canter, G. J. 1969. The influence of primary and secondary verbal apraxia upon output disturbances in aphasic syndromes. Paper presented at the Annual Convention of the American Speech and Hearing Association, Chicago, November.

Critchley, MacD. 1952. Articulatory defects in aphasia. *Journal of Laryngology and Otolo-gy, 66,* 1–17.

Critchley, MacD. 1960. Jacksonian ideas and the future with special reference to aphasia. *British Medical Journal, ii,* 6–12.

Critchley, MacD. 1967. Aphasiological nomenclature and definitions. *Cortex, 3,* 3–25.

Darley, F. L. 1964. *Diagnosis and appraisal of communication disorders.* Englewood Cliffs, N.J.: Prentice-Hall.

Darley, F. L. 1967. Unpublished paper presented to a joint meeting of the Montreal and Quebec Speech and Hearing Associations, Montreal, May.

Darley, F. L. 1972. The efficacy of language rehabilitation in aphasia. *Journal of Speech and Hearing Disorders, 37,* 3–21.

Darley, F. L., Aronson, A. E., & Brown, J. R. 1969. Differential diagnostic patterns of dysarthria. *Journal of Speech and Hearing Research, 12,* 246–270.

Deal, J. L., & Darley, F. L. 1972. The influence of linguistic and situational variables on phonemic accuracy in apraxia of speech. *Journal of Speech and Hearing Research, 15,* 639–653.

DeJong, R. N. 1958. *The neurologic examination.* New York: Hoeber.

Denny-Brown, D. 1965. Physiological aspects of disturbances of speech. *Australian Journal of Experimental Biology and Medical Science, 43,* 455–474.

DeRenzi, E., Pieczuro, A., & Vignolo, L. A. 1966. Oral apraxia and aphasia. *Cortex, 2,* 50–73.

Fry, D. B. 1959. Phonemic substitutions in an aphasic patient. *Language and Speech, 2,* 52–60.

Geschwind, N. 1965. Disconnection syndromes in animals and man. *Brain, 88,* 237–294.

Goldstein, K. 1948. *Language and language disturbances.* New York: Grune & Stratton.

Guilford, A. M., & Hawk, A. M. 1968. A comparative study of form identification in neurologically impaired and normal adult subjects. *Speech and Hearing Science Research Reports.* Ann Arbor: University of Michigan.

Halpern, H., Darley, F. L., & Brown, J. R. 1973. Differential language and neurologic characteristics in cerebral involvement. *Journal of Speech and Hearing Disorders, 38,* 162–173.

Hardy, J. C. 1967. Suggestions for physiological research in dysarthria. *Cortex, 3,* 128–156.

Head, H. 1926 *Aphasia and kindred disorders of speech.* London: Cambridge University Press.

Johns, D. F. 1968a. Phonemic variability in apraxia of speech: A disorder distinct from dysarthria and aphasia. Paper presented at the annual convention of the American Speech and Hearing Association, Denver, November.

Johns, D. F. 1968b. A systematic study of phonemic variability in apraxia of speech. Unpublished doctoral dissertation, Florida State University.

Johns, D. F. 1970. Treatment of apraxia of speech. Paper presented at the Annual Convention of the American Speech and Hearing Association, New York, November.

Johns, D. F., & Darley, F. L. 1970. Phonemic variability in apraxia of speech. *Journal of Speech and Hearing Research, 13,* 556–583.

Johns, D. F., & Macaluso, S. 1972. Profile of aphasia and apraxia: Onset through recovery: A case study. Paper presented at the Second Annual Conference on Clinical Aphasiology. Albuquerque, February.

Kools, J. A., Williams, A. F., Vickers, M. J. & Caell, A. 1971. Oral and limb apraxia in mentally retarded children with deviant articulation. *Cortex, 7,* 387–400.

LaPointe, L. L. 1969. An investigation of isolated oral movements, oral motor sequencing abilities, and articulation of brain-injured adults. Unpublished doctoral dissertation, University of Colorado.

LaPointe, L. L. 1973. Rehabilitation of adult aphasics: Therapy, referral, counselling. Short course presented at the Southeastern Regional Conference of the American Speech and Hearing Association, Atlanta, May.

LaPointe, L. L., & Johns, D. F. 1975. Some phonemic characteristics in apraxia of speech. *Journal of Communication Disorders, 8,* 259–269.

LaPointe, L. L., & Wertz, R. T. 1974. Oral-movement abilities and articulatory character-istics of brain-injured adults. *Perceptual and Motor Skills, 39*, 39–46.

Larimore, H. W. 1970. An analysis of phonemic variability in apraxia of speech. Unpub-lished doctoral dissertation, University of Denver.

Lashley, K. S. 1951. The problem of serial order in behavior. In L. A. Jeffress (Ed.), *Cerebral mechanisms in behavior.* New York: Wiley. Pp. 112–136.

Lecours, A. R., & Lhermitte, F. 1969. Phonemic paraphasias: Linguistic structures and tentative hypotheses. *Cortex, 5*, 193–228.

Luria, A. R. 1966. *Higher cortical functions in man.* New York: Basic Books.

Martin, A. 1974. Some objections to the term apraxia of speech. *Journal of Speech and Hearing Disorders, 39*, 53–64.

Mayo Clinic, Sections of Neurology. 1963. *Clinical examinations in neurology.* Philadelphia: Saunders.

Moore, W. McN. 1975. Assessment of oral, nonverbal movement in normal and brain-dam-aged populations. Unpublished doctoral dissertation, University of Colorado.

Nathan, P. W. 1947. Facial apraxia and apraxic dysarthria. *Brain, 70*, 449–478.

Nielsen, J. M. 1946. *Agnosia, apraxia, aphasia: Their value in cerebral localization.* 2nd ed. New York: Hoeber.

Penfield, W., & Roberts, L. 1959. *Speech and brain mechanisms.* Princeton, New Jersey: Princeton University Press.

Rosenbek, J., Deal, J. L., LaPointe, L. L. 1973a. Perspectives in oral, nonverbal movement testing. Paper presented at the Third Conference on Clinical Aphasiology, Albuquerque, March.

Rosenbek, J., Lemme, M. L., Ahearn, M. B., Harris, E. H., & Wertz, R. T. 1973b. A treatment for apraxia of speech in adults. *Journal of Speech and Hearing Disorders, 38*, 462–472.

Rosenbek, J., Wertz, R. T., & Darley, F. L. 1973c. Oral sensation and perception in apraxia of speech and aphasia. *Journal of Speech and Hearing Research, 16*, 22–36.

Sasanuma, S., & Fujimura, O. 1971. Selective impairment of phonetic and non-phonetic transcription of words in Japanese aphasic patients: Kana vs. kanji in visual recognition and writing. *Cortex, 7*, 1–18.

Sasanuma, S., & Fujimura, O. 1972. An analysis of writing errors in Japanese aphasic patients: Kanji versus kana words. *Cortex, 8*, 265–283.

Schuell, H. 1954. Clinical observations on aphasia. *Neurology, 4*, 178–189.

Schuell, H., Jenkins, J. J., & Jiménez-Pabon, E. 1964. *Aphasia in adults.* New York: Harper.

Shankweiler, D., & Harris, K. S. 1966. An experimental approach to the problem of articulation in aphasia. *Cortex, 2*, 277–292.

Shankweiler, D., Harris, K. S., & Taylor, M. L. 1968. Electromyographic studies of articulation in aphasia. *Archives of Physical Medicine and Rehabilitation, 48*, 1–8.

Trost, J. E. 1970. A descriptive study of verbal apraxia in patients with Broca's aphasia. Unpublished doctoral dissertation, Northwestern University, Evanston, Ill.

Trost, J. E., & Canter, G. J. 1974. Apraxia of speech in patients with Broca's aphasia: A study of phoneme production accuracy and error patterns. *Brain and Lanuage, 1*, 63–79.

Weisenberg, T. H., & McBride, K. E. 1935. *Aphasia.* New York: Commonwealth Fund.

Wepman, J. M., Bock, R. D., Jones, L. V., & Van Pelt, D. 1960. Studies in aphasia: Background and theoretical formulations. *Journal of Speech and Hearing Disorders, 25*, 323–332.

Wepman, J. M., & Van Pelt, D. 1955. A theory of cerebral language disorders based on therapy. *Folia Phoniatrica, 7*, 223–235.

Wertz, R. T., Rosenbek, J., & Collins, M. J. 1972. Idenficiation of apraxia of speech from PICA verbal tests and selected oral-verbal apraxia tests. Paper presented at the Second Conference on Clinical Aphasiology, Albuquerque, February.

Whitty, C. W. M. 1964. Cortical dysarthria and dysprosody of speech. *Journal of Neurology, Neurosurgery and Psychiatry, 27,* 507–510.

Wilson, S. A. 1908. A contribution to the study of apraxia with a review of the literature. *Brain, 31,* 163–216.

Yoss, K. A. 1972. Developmental apraxia of speech in children with defective articulation. Paper presented at the Annual Convention of the American Speech and Hearing Association, San Francisco, November.

Yoss, K. A. 1973. What Happens to Children with Developmental Apraxia of Speech? A Follow-up of Fifteen Cases. Paper presented at the Annual Convention of the American Speech and Hearing Association, Detroit, October.

6

Broca's Area and Broca's Aphasia[1]

J. P. Mohr

MASSACHUSETTS GENERAL HOSPITAL
AND HARVARD MEDICAL SCHOOL, BOSTON

INTRODUCTION

Broca's aphasia, a clinical and clinicopathologic entity, has persisted for over a century as one of the cornerstones in the litany of aphasiology. It was the first cluster of symptoms and signs to achieve the status of a syndrome in aphasia, and the first aphasic syndrome to be attributed to a focal injury (lesion) of the brain. It was successfully defended as a clinical entity by the discoverer himself in written and spoken debates against his leading contemporaries, including Hughlings Jackson, Trousseau, Bouchard, Vulpian, and Charcot. It endured vigorous assaults a half century later by critics such as Pierre Marie (Cole & Cole, 1971). As a term, *Broca's aphasia* has outlasted a whole host of more mechanistic substitutes, including Broca's (1861) own term, *aphemia, pictorial motor aphasia* (Wyllie, 1894), *cortical motor aphasia* (Déjerine & Mirallié, 1896), *verbal aphasia* (Head, 1926), *verbal dyspraxia* (Nielsen, 1962), and *efferent motor aphasia* (Luria, 1966). Enjoying the advantages of historical and eponymic precedent, the term *Broca's aphasia* has the additional advantage of ambiguity, since its use conveys no implicit commitment to any given cerebral mechanisms (Goodglass, Quadfasel, & Timberlake, 1964). It has received repeated treatment in reviews, monographs, and textbooks, to a degree rendering wholly inappropriate another recitation of the details of Broca's cases, the classical features, the presumed pathologic lesion(s), and the traditional brief sketch of the disturbed

[1] This paper was supported by grants HL 14888-02, NS 10828-01A1, and HS 00188.

cerebral mechanisms as individually envisioned by the great and the not so great who have written on the subject of aphasia.

The present review makes an attempt, instead, to approach the subject as if no such litany existed; to review the basic data available in personal and published cases; to derive a syndrome formulation based on the case material for which some direct assessment of lesion topography is available; and to take into account the effects played by time on both the quantitative and qualitative features of the deficit. As a background to the clinical material in naturally occurring brain lesions (usually caused by strokes) the gross, microscopic, and traditional functional neuroanatomic features of Broca's area are first reviewed, followed by a brief section dealing with the various technical means of assessing lesion topography and etiology. The detailed case material review that then follows requires separation into two categories: the clinical deficit associated with a Broca's-area lesion, and the brain lesion found in association with the syndrome referred to as Broca's aphasia. The historical views are then reviewed from this perspective.

These studies, taken together with a review of the literature, suggest that destruction of Broca's area and its immediate surround, even deep into the brain, does not reliably produce the protracted mutism, later emerging dyspraxic speaking, and condensed simplified grammatical language functions currently envisioned as characteristic of the syndrome of Broca's aphasia. Instead, little persisting deficit in articulation seems to occur, and frequently no significant persisting disturbance in language function is present. The syndrome currently referred to as Broca's aphasia arises instead from a considerably larger brain injury that encompasses most of the operculum, insula, and subjacent white matter, far exceeding Broca's area. It conforms more to the large zone of damaged brain actually present in Broca's original cases.

A final ironic note is evident since Broca was well aware of the much greater extent of the lesion, but disregarded it in favor of the more circumscribed component in the inferior frontal region. He did so not through gross neglect, but in obedience to the mechanisms of stroke then current (Marie, 1906b) that large strokes always began as a smaller focus, and spread slowly outward. Had Broca confined himself to the observations, emphasized the entire extent of the lesion, and correlated it with the major syndrome he uncovered, subsequent developments in the history of aphasia might have been much different.

GROSS, MICROSCOPIC, AND FUNCTIONAL PATHOANATOMY

Broca's area is currently thought of as the pars opercularis of the third frontal convolution (Bailey & von Bonin, 1951). The ease with which it is demonstrated varies considerably from brain to brain. Usually, a variety of neighboring landmarks can be utilized singly or in combination to fix its position (Figure 1). The usual procedure is to locate the Rolandic (central) fissure and follow it to the Sylvian fissure, counting one gyrus forward; seek the characteristically shaped pars triangularis on the operculum just at the anterior end of the Sylvian fissure, thus locating the pars opercularis immediately behind; count down from the first to the third convolution, using the superior frontal sulcus as the marker between the first and second.

Histologically, the pars opercularis has few distinguishing features (Bailey & von Bonin, 1951). In the days of Brodmann (1909), the region was labeled "area #44," presumably based on a unique histology. The histological features were, however, never published by Brodmann in a human case. Indeed, among the many classifiers of cortical histology, only Bailey and von Bonin (1951) utilized a double blind method for histologic classification of cerebral cortical areas, and they were unable to detect unique histologic features for Broca's area or to distinguish it from other motor gyri on histologic grounds. At present, there are no active claims for a histologic appearance unique to the region to justify continued use of the Brodmann numerical nomenclature apart from its value as a convenient shorthand.

Notions concerning physiologic functions of Broca's area come largely from anatomic formulations concerning the general organization of the cerebral gray and white matter. These formulations have been partially corroborated by physiologic studies including neuropathology, electrical stimulation, and evoked potential EEG work. Flechsig's rule (Flechsig, 1901; Geschwind, 1965a) remains the major concept of cerebral organization. It was devised from studies of the anatomy of the cerebral white matter, and arose in part from speculations concerning the function of Broca's area. According to this rule, two types of

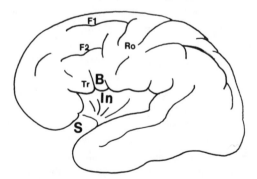

Figure 1 Lateral view of the left hemisphere illustrating the main landmarks: B = Broca's area; Tr = pars triangularis; Ro = Rolandic fissure; F_1 = first frontal convolution; F_2 = second frontal convolution; S = Sylvian fissure; In = insula. The operculum constitutes the entire upper rim of the Sylvian fissure; its anterior aspect including the pars triangularis, Broca's area, and the adjacent motor strip.

white matter fibers from two types of cortex gray matter were envisioned. One type of gray matter (primary receiving or sending cortex) was thought to have long white-matter fibers projecting to systems outside the cerebrum (cortico-fugal fibers). These included the visual (visual radiation), motor (corticospinal tracts), and sensory pathways (thalamocortical projections). This primary cortex was thought also to have short white-matter fibers projecting to the immediately adjacent second type of gray matter, association cortex. Association cortex was envisioned as the recipient of the short white-matter fibers from primary cortex. It gave rise to long white-matter fibers that projected to other areas of associa-tion cortex in the same hemisphere (intrahemispheral fibers) or opposite hemi-sphere (transcallosal fibers). According to this theory the primary cortex related the brain to the periphery by the major motor and sensory pathways. The association cortex, by contrast, served to relate these primary regions with each other, in both general and specific ways. Through action of the association system, to give a crudely simplified example, visual word stimuli discriminated as forms by the primary visual (calcarine) cortex could be associated with their auditory equivalents in the auditory regions and these equivalents related to the association system adjacent to the motor cortex, which would mediate the articulatory efforts so that the words could be spoken aloud; in this way reading aloud could occur. The implications of this view included the further specializa-tion of function in the various types of association cortex. Broca's area, which appears to be part of the association cortex adjacent to the portion of the motor cortex subserving the lips, tongue, palate, pharynx, and respiratory apparatus, was easily envisioned as mediating and later acquiring the "memory for move-ments" (Liepmann, 1915) of articulation. In principle, this region originated—or at least had routed through it—all aspects of motor behavior unique to speech.

The Flechsig thesis of cerebral white matter provided the main theoretical framework for, and derived some of its impetus from, the classical aphasia syndromes described 15 years earlier (Lichtheim, 1885). These syndromes were envisioned as reflecting lesions of the cortex itself or interruptions of the intrahemispheral and/or transcallosal association pathways. The most elaborate (Lichtheim, 1885; Liepmann, 1915) of the classical theories of aphasia postu-lated three forms of the disorder, applying to the various motor speech func-tions: a cortical motor aphasia (Broca's aphasia) in which the gray matter of Broca's area—presumed the seat of organization of articulatory movements—was destroyed, depriving the patient of articulatory speech function; a subcortical motor aphasia (pure word mutism) in which the fibers projecting to the bulbar apparatus were destroyed, producing in essence a disconnection syndrome in which the patient failed to speak because of failure to activate the peripheral speech organs; and a transcortical motor aphasia envisioned (but never docu-mented) as a more diffusely spread white-matter injury in which the elementary motor function was unimpaired (the patient could pronounce words), but the products of "thought" would not reach the speech center for spontaneous speech. In this situation, the patient could repeat aloud but could produce no spontaneous speech.

Broca's thesis that his patients had lost the memory for the movements involved in speech (Broca, 1861), and that this loss was caused by a brain lesion in the inferior frontal region, helped pave the way for the region to be viewed by later authors as the association cortex containing mnemic images for motor speech function (Liepmann, 1915). This view was incorporated into the early schemes of aphasic syndromes. It has been powerfully reiterated on the resurrected concepts of disconnection syndromes (Geschwind, 1965b). Electrical stimulation research has corroborated the principal of intrahemispheral and transcallosal pathways (Bailey & von Bonin, 1951). And, finally, recent studies of the evoked potentials of electrophysiologic activity of this region in the milliseconds before actual articulation begins lend support to these views (McAdam & Whitaker, 1971).

The validity of the thesis built by the synergistic interaction of clinical syndromes (including Broca's aphasia) and Flechsig's larger theory of cerebral organization has been subject to criticism from several sides. These criticisms included other views of anatomic organization, the experimental results of cerebral stimulation, and—the subject of the bulk of this paper—the findings in the very cases studied clinically and pathologically that test the thesis.

The opposing views on the anatomic organization of the cerebral white matter are most represented in the opinions of Yakovlev (1970 personal communication). This author argues that the intrahemispheral fibers (the association fibers of Flechsig's view) are not functional pathways in the same sense that the corticofugal pathways (connecting the cerebrum to the peripheral organs) are. Instead, any structure resembling a pathway in the hemispheral white matter, exclusive of cortifugal pathways, is incidental to the folding of the cerebrum during embryologic development. Instead of functioning as discrete tracts, the intrahemispheral pathways are broadly distributed, anatomically and functionally, and not sharply separable on functional grounds.

Cerebral cortical electrical stimulation involves transiently placing an electrode on the exposed cortex surface at operation, and passing a tiny current sufficient to generate a clinical response, without harming the brain. Vocalization has resulted from stimulation along the central (Rolandic) fissure and also separately from stimulation of the supplementary motor area on the medial surface of the hemisphere (Penfield, 1958). In 206 operations, 51 vocalizations were produced by Penfield and Rasmussen (1968); three-quarters were from the precentral and the rest from the postcentral gyrus, stimulated at points as high as half way up the central fissure. The vocalizations usually took the form of a single vowel monotone cry, whose pitch at times could be made to vary by minor changes in the exact site of stimulation. Repetitive vocalizations (*te, te, te, te, te, te*) were demonstrated by these workers on continuous stimulation high on the frontal lobe near the peak of the convexity, and on the lateral and medial surface in both left and right hemispheres. Speech arrest—sudden cessation of vocalization coincident with stimulation begun without warning the patient—was reported by Penfield and Rasmussen (1968) 74 times in 35 operations. Speech arrest was four times more frequent in precentral stimulation than in postcentral, but occurred in either hemisphere: In two-thirds of the cases, the arrest in speech was unaccompanied by observed, or retrospectively reported, motor or sensory effects. Arrest of speech could also be produced by stimulation forward of the lower sensorimotor cortex, approximately in Broca's area. Stronger stimulation was required, but similar arrest in speech, or failure at self-initiated efforts to begin speaking, occurred in parietal- and temporal-lobe stimulations. The investigators were unable to detect a qualitative difference in effects on speech from stimulation separately applied to Broca's, supplementary motor, or parieto-temporal regions (Penfield & Roberts, 1959). These findings have provided evidence supporting the importance of the Sylvian region for speech functions, but not a qualitative clarification of the role played by Broca's area.

Clarity and ease of comprehension are prime virtues of the hypothesis begun by Broca, and solidified by the implications of Flechsig's rule. The clinical and pathologic case material, reviewed next, is the major source material against which this hypothesis can be tested.

METHODS USED TO DETERMINE BRAIN-LESION TOPOGRAPHY

Only those cases in which the topography of the brain lesion is known can serve to study the relationship between a behavioral deficit and a brain lesion. As a means of establishing lesion topography, the autopsy study remains the least disputed. But this source of information is only infrequently available: Happily, the clinical outcome in cases of aphasia is rarely fatal in the short run; families of the unfortunate deceased vary considerably in their interest in an autopsy; and death often occurs when the opportunity to seek permission for autopsy does not arise or is missed. Even in the autopsied cases, the nature of the brain lesion frequently proves unsuitable for clear correlations: Tumors, hemorrhages, trauma, and infections often injure or distort the brain at great distances from the primary site of the lesion. In general, the most suitable material for study is the focal lesion resulting from blockage of a branch or trunk of a cerebral surface artery. The region relatively deprived of blood is referred to as suffering from *ischemia*, and the destroyed brain tissue that results from the ischemia is described as having undergone *infarction*. Cases featuring ischemic infarction always have been the preferred material for autopsy correlations of aphasic syndromes.

Ironically, the most common cause of unsatisfactory clinicopathologic correlation is insufficient clinical study of a case later autopsied. Those interested in such correlations must be prepared for detailed study of many clinical cases from which the rare subsequently autopsied case(s) will arise unpredictably over the years. Given the wide range of fascinating clinical syndromes that await detailed elucidation on clinical grounds alone, it is little wonder that the method of clinicopathologic correlation is more praised than practiced.

In Broca's time, only gross (as opposed to microscopic) pathologic description was made of autopsy specimens. Up to the turn of this century, the pia arachnoid, which contains the blood vessels, was usually stripped away to expose the naked brain surface. Inspection of the naked surface and description of the damaged regions found were the extent of autopsy reports. Broca's original cases were described in this manner, and remained intact as late as 1906 (Marie, 1906b); as far as the present author can determine, they have never been sectioned (Cole, 1974 personal communication).

Brain sectioning was developed in the late 19th century. The plane of the face—coronal, frontal—has proved most popular. Most textbooks show the brain in coronal sections that are suitable for demonstrating a portion of the convex surface, the operculum, insula, and deep white matter in the same section. The horizontal section, popularized by Pierre Marie, permits a view of the entire length of the operculum in a single section, which runs at right angles to the coronal. Sagittal section, in which the cutting edge is oriented from front to back in the vertical plane, offers no advantages in the study of aphasia and is used chiefly in specialized anatomy books (Singer & Yakovlev, 1954).

Histologic material supplements gross autopsy studies. The method of choice is one that permits the entire brain to be embedded intact and sectioned in serial fashion (Yakovlev, 1970). The sections are stained to show changes that might be easily overlooked on gross pathologic inspection, including cell loss, degeneration in white matter tracts, extent of infarction into subcortical structures, and so forth. Although expensive, this method affords the most thorough study of the brain for the purposes of clinical correlations (Mohr, Leicester, Stoddard, & Sidman, 1971; Mohr, 1973).

Modern technology has provided a variety of new methods, applicable to the living patient, that are becoming a useful, if not equivalent, substitute for the autopsy. The information gained has the obvious advantage of selecting those cases for which efforts at study in life can be profitably redoubled. In addition, the cases studied by these methods can be used to supplement those also studied by autopsy. Electroencephalography was the first such technique to be developed, but has not proved entirely reliable as a method of inferring the location of a focal lesion affecting the cerebral surface, such as an ischemic infarct (Kugler, 1964). Cerebral arteriography (Taveras & Wood, 1964) is useful in those cases where a blocked artery is found, but whether the brain tissue beyond that blocked branch is healthy, ischemic, or infarcted, in part or entirely, is an issue left unsettled. Radioactive isotope brain scanning (Ojemann, Aronow, & Sweet, 1966) has become an increasingly popular method of localizing ischemic infarction, and is especially suitable for the larger infarcts after the initial days and weeks; unfortunately, many smaller infarcts escape detection. Computerized axial tomography (CT scan), in use in America only since mid-1973 (New, Scott, Schnur, Davis, & Taveras, 1974), has already proven itself of enormous value in localizing focal infarction, even of small size, especially in the more chronically established cases; infarcts as small as several millimeters have been demonstrated.

Sufficient methodology exists at present to warrant the current active renaissance of interest in clinical and inferred-pathologic correlations in living cases. It appears likely that many of the traditional aphasic syndromes may be as subject to revision, as is Broca's aphasia.

CASE MATERIAL

For reasons documented in detail in the sections that follow, it is necessary to consider the relevant case material from two separate viewpoints: One is the clinical syndrome associated with documented infarction in Broca's area of the dominant hemisphere; the other is the documented infarction that is associated with the clinical syndrome currently referred to as Broca's aphasia. The two are not equivalent.

Broca's-Area Infarction and Its Clinical Aspects

PERSONAL OBSERVATIONS

Mohr (1968, 1973) and colleagues (Mohr, Funkenstein, Finkelstein, Pessin, Duncan, & Davis, 1975) have studied the clinical effects of documented infarction affecting Broca's area in cases gathered from three sources: a personal series of cases; cases found in a review of the autopsy population from a 10-year period at a large hospital (Massachusetts General Hospital); and finally, a full-scale review of the documented-autopsy cases published in the literature since 1861. The effort was prompted by experience with several cases whose clinical impairment was unpredicted by textbook descriptions of Broca's aphasia. The observations corroborated many of those traditionally described but, extended over time, produced a formulation of the syndrome rather different from the litany.

Personal experience with cases suffering from Broca's-area infarction include 13 cases shown by autopsy, technesium brain scan (Tc scan), computerized axial tomography (CT scan), or arteriogram to have focal infarction affecting the left-third-frontal convolution, either alone or including immediately adjacent areas, encompassed anatomically by the territory of supply of the anterior branch(es) of the upper division of the left middle cerebral artery. Figure 2 documents by Venn diagram the topography of the surface lesions in these cases.

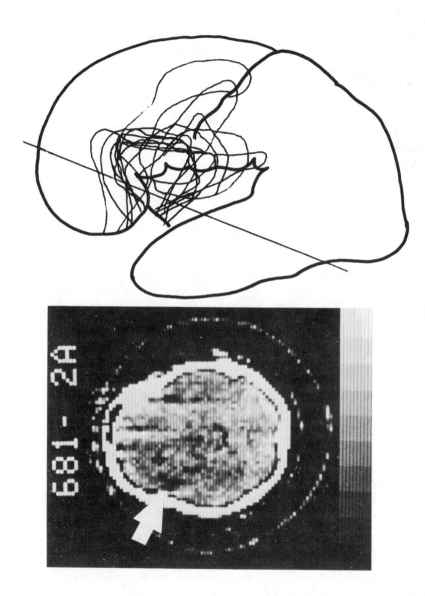

Figure 2 Topography of lesions in personal cases showing syndrome of Broca's-area infarction. (top) Projected on a lateral view of the left hemisphere; (bottom) an example of a CT scan with the lesion indicated by the arrow. The plane of section for the CT scan is indicated by the line drawn through the top diagram.

Access to these cases resulted from the author's role on the Stroke Service at the Massachusetts General Hospital. The clinical responsibilities of the Stroke Service occasioned clinical observation and often direct personal management of these cases from their arrival in the Emergency Ward, through hospitalization, and into long-term outpatient follow-up. Those with fatal outcome were autopsied personally in all but one instance, and several brains were sectioned, using the whole-brain serial sectioning method of Yakovlev (1970). The remainder were personally processed by more conventional neuropathologic methods (Mohr, 1973). All cases were of embolic origin, documented or presumed. All patients were right-handed, confirmed by the patient, the family, and friends. The youngest was age 28, the oldest 83.

Four cases were autopsied (Mohr, 1973). The first case, initially reported as a clinicopathologic exercise (Friedlich, Castleman, & Mohr, 1968) was considered unusual in view of the great depth of the lesion and rapid improvement in her initial mutism and in other language deficits. Within a year, two other cases were observed and autopsied, suggesting that the first case was not rare in occurrence, merely rarely described and analyzed clinicopathologically. Each case showed right-sided motor deficit, ideomotor dyspraxia, mild language deficit and initial mutism followed by rapidly emerging spoken speech (or only dysarthria from the beginning). Little evidence was found for condensed sentence structure (agrammatism) at any time during the course of improvement. The only case surviving beyond two years yielded no evidence of motor aphasia when examined in detail seven years later. A brief sketch of each case follows:

Case 1. A 57-year-old right-handed woman suffered sudden mutism accompanied by a right hemiparesis, hemisensory syndrome, and homonymous hemianopia. She obeyed no dictated or printed commands. Four days later she matched short dictated words to printed word choices by pointing with the left hand. By the twelfth day, she repeated aloud and read aloud short words, and performed a few dictated commands using the eyes, lips, tongue, neck, and left hand. She died on the sixteenth day.

At autopsy, a large, deep infarct was found to involve the pars triangularis and opercularis (Broca's area), anterior insula, inferior and pre- and postcentral gyri, subcortical white matter; and more deeply situated claustrum putamen, caudate, and extreme and internal capsules.

Case 2. An 84-year-old right-handed woman suffered suden inability to speak aloud accompanied by a dense right-central weakness of the face and tongue, hemiparesis, hemisensory syndrome, and homonymous hemianopia. By day four she still struggled unsuccessfully to vocalize, made illegible marks on paper with either hand when attempting to write, yet moved the tongue, and individual fingers and arms to dictated command. On day six she repeated aloud a few short words. Tests on day eight yielded a few laconic spontaneous sentences spoken in a halting dysarthria with some simplification of grammatical forms in sentences. Repeating from dictation was correct for short words, poor for longer words or syllable sets. She recited familar sequences poorly. She read aloud short words and many single letters. The next day the word–letter comparisons were further tested; the patient read aloud 16 short words but only 2 of 10 single letters. Writing was confined to clumsy copy and slow but correct writing to dictation.

As late as five months after her stroke, her facial weakness, dysphagia, and mild dyspraxia remained little changed; yet she spoke more clearly and showed no grammatical abnormalities in spontaneous speech. Following a generalized seizure at sixteen months, the entire deficit relapsed, then remitted over the succeeding month. Right arm and face weakness remained. The visual fields were full and sensation normal.

Autopsy at twenty-two months revealed the residue of ischemic infarction involving the left pars triangularis and opercularis, pre- and postcentral gyri, anterior portion of the insula, and subcortical white matter as deep as the lateral edge of the putamen.

Case 3. A 77-year-old right-handed man was hospitalized for evaluation of mental slowing and a right grasp reflex. During hospitalization, he awoke with a severe right facial and arm weakness, hemisensory syndrome, and severe dysarthria. Reading aloud and description of pictures showed paraphasic substitutive errors compared with his performance just two days before the stroke. Although he spoke aloud with dysarthria, tests for praxic function on day two demonstrated an almost amorphous ideomotor dyspraxia for movements of the left arm, and he was only slightly better with orofacial movements. Language tests showed improved scores. By the forty-fifth day, his dyspraxia and language deficits had faded.

Autopsy on the sixty-seventh day revealed ischemic infarction involving the pars triangularis and opercularis, entire lower half of the precentral gyrus, anterior half of the insula, and subcortical white matter to the edge of the putamen, plus a small band extending through the centrum semiovale to the anterior parietal area.

Case 4. At age 28, after eight years of symptomatic rheumatic mitral valvular disease, this right-handed married woman was hospitalized following sudden inability to speak clearly, associated with numbness of the right arm and hand, and tingling of the right foot. Few details of language deficit were described during this hospitalization. When first admitted to the Massachusetts General Hospital seven years later, extensive language and praxia evaluation demonstrated speech syntactically correct without omission, normal repeating from dictation, with no evidence of dysphonia, dysarthria, or dysmelodic impairments. Autopsy six years later revealed an old infarct, confined to the cortical surface and immediately subjacent white matter, involving LF3, inferior motor cortex, and anterior insula.

Mohr and colleagues (1975) have also studied eight additional cases at the Massachusetts General Hospital during an 18-month period since January 1973.

These cases have corroborated and extended the findings in the autopsied group.

The eight cases were all right handed, with a clinical course consistent with cerebral embolism. Six were seen from the day of onset and followed through their course of amelioration and beyond, the longest over a year. The age of the patients varied from 25 to 87 years, averaging 64. Five were men. Educational level and occupations ranged from Italian-American matriarch and homemaker to multilingual archeology professor and museum director. All patients suffered an initial linguofacial paresis ranging from mild to severe and a moderate right-arm weakness; all patients could support the weight with the right leg within a few days at least. Tonic head and eye deviation was not a feature of the syndrome. Sensory and visual-field defects were short-lived if present.

All patients seen on day one of the illness demonstrated facial, oral, respiratory, and left-arm ideomotor dyspraxia to varying degree. Most improved to quite satisfactory performances within a week, although three persisted several weeks. Deficits in writing were evident in all cases tested within the first week of illness, characterized by misspelling and incomplete short words in written naming tests, in addition to the expected poor morphology of the clumsily executed left-handed efforts. Mild impairment in matching dictated to visual stimuli was evident in three patients tested the first day, but all had improved to satisfactory levels on tests involving grammatical contingencies, Marie's three-paper test, and naming of dictated spelled short words, within two weeks. Two cases had no such deficits when tested the first day of illness; the other three were not examined until later in their course.

Six patients were struck mute at onset. Emergence of articulation from mutism occurred in one day in the earliest case, 14 days in the latest. The remaining two continued to speak. All cases spoke with noticeable effort, but varied considerably in their individual deficit features, from respiratory-vocal dyspraxia to stereotypic syllabic echoes. Only one case showed any elements of grammatical condensation and simplified sentence structure at any time, although all patients agreed that they preferred to say less than formerly because of the effort involved in speaking. Within two weeks five spoke smoothly enough that no difficulties arose in slow conversation. Within a month or two, examiners previously unfamiliar with the individual patients were prepared to guess that these patients' individual speech patterns might have predated the stroke. At three months, three patients, all having been mute for at least several days, still spoke laborously, but even these often spoke smoothly when in familiar company. Evidence of linguofacial paresis improved but was the most striking persistent feature of the deficit. Disordered language function in conversational, written, and reading tests was no longer evident except on extremely complex tests. Spoken speech was not agrammatic.

In each case, the topography of the lesion was established by arteriogram, technesium brain scan, or computerized axial tomogram. The estimated topography of the lesions so established is summarized in Figure 2.

Other cases have also been encountered through two additional sources. The first source comes from a cooperative venture, in which the Massachusetts General, Beth Israel, and Peter Bent Brigham Hospitals have undertaken a prospective study of stroke in a computer registry since January 1973. As of December 1974, over 670 cases had been observed. These cases include those discussed above, as well as other personal cases in which the lesion topography could not be successfully corroborated. These data were reviewed in hopes of demonstrating some indication of the clinical frequency of such cases in a stroke population.

To date, 193 of 670 cases of stroke suffered some form of aphasia; 49 of these have been recorded as *anterior* (motor, Broca) aphasia. 38 of these cases were patients at the Massachusetts General Hospital. They ranged in age from 25 to 94, averaging 67 years. Where documented, 27 were right handed. All cases had an accompanying right-sided motor deficit, many severe. Fully 25 were considered to have strokes of embolic origin, and in 23 of the cases the diagnosis was corroborated by arteriogram, operation, CT scan, or autopsy. Of particular interest, and reflecting the experience detailed above, of 38 cases where information was available, most were discharged from the initial hospitalization with little deficit: five were free of deficit; sixteen were mild, eight moderate, five severe, and four died from the stroke or other cause. The findings are considered preliminary, since only 49 cases provide the data base. However, they suggest considerable improvement is common, perhaps expected, in a short time.

The second source of cases comes from a retrospective study of autopsy records for a 10-year period (1963–1973) at the Massachusetts General Hospital. In this review, 69 cases (0.43%) in over 16,000 general autopsies were found to have left cerebral infarction involving the frontal operculum and inferior frontal regions, territories supplied by the anterior branches of the upper division of the left-middle cerebral artery. The case records of all 69 were examined, and 36 were judged uninterpretable due to inadquacy of the clinical data, other coexisting disease, other signs including obtundation, or prompt death after stroke. Of the remaining 39, 13 appear to have undergone rapid amelioration of a documented motor aphasia or contain no evidence of a disturbance in spoken speech when initially examined at some time after the clinical stroke; 11 cases had insufficient data with which to make a judgment. Reference is made later to the remaining 15 cases. These findings support a thesis that rapid amelioration and little persisting deficit in speech or language occurs in cases of infarction confined to the inferior frontal region of the dominant hemisphere.

LITERATURE SURVEY OF AUTOPSIED CASES
WITH LF3 LESIONS

A second line of approach to test these findings involved a review of the clinical features in the reported autopsied cases in which a lesion involved LF3

TABLE 1 Autopsy Documented Cases of Broca's or Total Aphasia Found in the Literature[a]

*F3 B 51 Broca (case Leborgne)
SYL T 23 Dejerine (Moutier 70)
SYL T . . Moutier (case Maillard)
SYL B . . Bastian (Moutier 98)
OI T . . Mills (Henschen 1069)
FOI B 45 Bernard (Moutier 84)
SYL B 59 Moutier (case Chissadon)
FOI B 55 Preston (Moutier 96)
FOI B . . Broadbent (Moutier 51)
SYL T . . Vulpian & Mongie (Moutier 40)
SYL T 80 Bernard (Moutier 86)
SYL T 54 Bernheim (Moutier 90)
SYL T . . Comte
*F3 B . . Broca (case Lelong)
SYL T 39 Giraud (Moutier 64)
SYL B . . Archambault (Moutier 31)
FOI T 43 Pitres (Moutier 74)
FOI B 25 Lange (Moutier 52)
SYL T . . Bleuler (Moutier 92)
EN B . . Ballet (Moutier 132)
FOI T 80 Moutier (case Fauchier)
SYL B 56 Skwotzoff (Moutier 78)
F3 B 25 Baldisseri (Henschen 719)
SYL T 39 Rosenthal (Moutier 78)
F3 B 25 Böe (Henschen 779)
F3 B 43 Ballet & Boix (Moutier 130)

F3 B . . Rosenstein (Wyllie 3)
F3 B 45 Atkins
F3 B . . Magnan
F3 B 61 Chauffard & Rathery (Henschen 849)
F3 B . . Malicherg (Henschen 1052)
FOI T 69 Demange (Moutier 80)
F3 B . . Ogle
F3 B . . Sheinker & Kuhr
F3 B . . Magnan
F3 B 55 Nielsen (case Lulu)
F3 B 50 Hervey (Moutier 127)
F3 B . . Banti (Bastian 7)
F3 B 68 Nielsen (case Ingols)

10	20 30	10 20	30	10	20 30		10	20	30
	Days		Weeks		Months			Years	

(Time after onset when the last or only examination was described in the Case Report)

[a]Key:	F3	Broca's area (3rd Frontal),
	FOI	frontal operculum and anterior insula,
	OI	operculum and insula,
	SYL	Sylvian region,
	EN	encephalitis,
	B	Broca's aphasia,
	T	total aphasia,
	. .	age not stated,
	PH	putaminal hemorrhage.

alone or in addition to the immediately adjacent regions. This survey might be considered somewhat unrepresentative since there are very few such reports found in the twentieth-century literature. Perhaps the lesion and its clinical consequences had been thought sufficiently well established to offset the need for any further demonstrations. In any case, the reports surveyed have been the source material for most of the large reviews published throughout this century. In that sense, at least, they were considered representative of the available literature.

This literature survey was taken beyond the usual correlation of pathologic findings with clinical deficit. The time after ictus, when the deficit was described, was a third variable especially sought in view of the findings in our own studies.

When the data from the literature were arranged taking this third variable into account by using time on the abscissa (Table 1), virtually no cases were found showing left inferior frontal infarction with motor or Broca's aphasia, whose deficit was clinically described beyond a few days or weeks following the ictus. The literature cases establish only the initial occurrence of the deficit. Whether this initial deficit was permanent or transient, and, if transient, to what degree and what elements of the deficit underwent improvement, are matters not settled by the classical literature.

A few cases were described in which subsequent examinations were performed. Considerable improvement had occurred in most cases (Table 2). In general, these findings corroborate Mohr (1973; Mohr, Funkenstein, Finkelstein, Pessin, Duncan, & Davis, 1975) regarding the time course of improvement.

Very few cases were found in the literature showing persisting and severe motor, or Broca's aphasia, with autopsy showing a lesion limited to Broca's area, LF3. Moutier (1908) surveyed the 304 reported cases of aphasia autopsied from 1861 to 1906, and found only 108 cases with localized lesion; 84 experienced some form of aphasia with intact LF3 or an LF3 lesion with no Broca's aphasia; 19 suffered aphasia with an LF3 lesion. The data on fully 14 of these cases either contain no reference to the time course (four cases), indicate the patient survived less than two weeks, or describe an initial deficit with survival up to three months, but no statement of subsequent changes, if any. In only five cases was long survival recorded and some statement made concerning the persisting deficit: Moutier case 130—6 weeks, 132—10 months, 139—3 years, 145—3 years, 146—10 years. Even in these cases, re-examinations are not recorded, and there is no statement of when, after onset, the findings were described. Two of these cases (Moutier 145, 146) were described by Déjerine, who provided the most forceful textbook descriptions of the syndrome. Language deficits were said not to be present; the absolute failure to speak aloud was accompanied by vocal-cord paralysis. One of Déjerine's cases was subject to severe criticism by Marie (1907) as factually inaccurate, based on Marie's independent inquiries into the case.

TABLE 2 Autosopy Documental Cases of Broca's Aphasia Considered Ameliorated Found in Literature

```
                                          OI B 32 Monakow (Henschen 1113)
                                  OI T 57 Improved Monakow (Henschen 1114)
                                   OI T 45 Improved Dejerine (Henschen 866)
                            F3 B 20 Disappeared Luys (Henschen 1031)
                            F3 B . . Recovered Wadham
                         F3 B 20 Recovered Dejerine (Henschen 865)
                    FOI B 61 Ameliorated Leva (Moutier 95)
                   OI T 25 Recovered Lange (Henschen 986)
                  F3 B 25 Improved DeFont (Henschen 905)
              F3 B . . None Bourneville
              PH B 61 Improved Nielsen
              OI B 62 Improved . . . Cured DuFour (Henschen 885)
        F3 B 20 Rapid Foulis (Henschen 908)
        OI B 38 Later DuFour (Henschen 883)
      F3 B 32 Rapidly Dejerine (Henschen 871)
    F3 B 70 Cleared Bramwell
   F3 B Transient Tuke
F3 B 65 Improving . . . . Normal Simon (Henschen 1240)
F3 B . . 10 Days Barlow
F3 B 49 Cleared Monokow (Henschen 1116)
```

10	20	30	10	20	30		12	15	25	35	5	10	15	20
	Days			Weeks					Months				Years	

(Time after onset when initial examination was described, followed by repeat examination or comment regarding outcome)

[a]Key	F3	Broca's area (3rd Frontal),
	FOI	frontal operculum and anterior insula,
	OI	operculum and insula,
	SYL	Sylvian region,
	EN	encephalitis,
	B	Broca's aphasia,
	T	total aphasia,
	. .	age not stated,
	PH	putaminal hemorrhage.

Henschen (1925) surveyed 85 cases, including tumors and bilateral lesions, but provided virtually no information regarding the time course of the deficit. Nielsen (1962) drew largely on Henschen for his literature material, much of which is represented in Table 1 of this chapter. The survey to date does not contradict Kleist's (1934, pp. 929–930) long-overlooked conclusion that persisting and severe motor aphasia is not the result of infarction limited to LF3 and its adjacent white matter. Instead, the literature appears to show merely that an initial deficit in speaking aloud occurs, with no clear indications of the expected outcome over time.

PREVIOUS CRITICISMS OF BROCA'S APHASIA
RESULTING FROM A BROCA'S-AREA LESION

The current thesis is the most recent in a long history of attacks on the role played by the LF3 lesion in the initial and/or persisting symptoms of aphasia. Despite many persuasive features, all previous attacks have failed to dislodge the notion of Broca's aphasia, and most are currently ignored or forgotten. When reviewed in detail, most of the attacks appear to have failed for reasons other than the arguments against the LF3 lesion itself. Most of the criticisms leveled against Broca's aphasia are based on observations of cases showing no impairment in speaking despite an LF3 lesion. But each attack has some flaw sufficient to permit the data to be incorporated as legitimate exceptions to the litany.

These critics can be grouped under five headings as follows.

Opponents in Broca's time. Broca did not lack contemporary critics. As lucidly reviewed by Marie (1906b; Cole & Cole, 1971), numerous observations of aphasia cases were reported without the finding of lesions in the inferior frontal region. Some of the cases were even autopsied in Broca's presence. These critics included some of the foremost authorities of the time, such as Hughlings Jackson, Vulpian, Trousseau, and Charcot, the last of whom changed his position to full support of Broca within 10 years. Despite the critics, several sources of support played major roles in the acceptance of Broca's tenets: Bouillaud, a respected physician senior to Broca, had espoused the thesis that articulation was a function of the frontal lobes, and lent his weight to Broca's interpretation, considering Broca's findings merely documentation of his (Bouillaud's) own views; Wernicke, in his own thesis concerning the aphasic syndromes of posterior Sylvian lesions (later to bear Wernicke's name), contrasted his syndrome with Broca's; early electrophysiologic studies supported an idea that the brain contained a topographic homunculus whose face region corresponded closely to Broca's area; and, finally, other cases independently reported by other authors broadly corroborated Broca's basic view. Within 15 years after Broca's first reports, despite the critics, the notion of Broca's aphasia was fully established.

Individual case reports. A number of spectacular cases have been reported that appear to contradict Broca's views. Each author clearly emphasized the features of the case that contradicted Broca's ideas, but much of the force of the argument was diminished by deference to Broca, emphasis on the rarity of the case, or excessive reliance on a single case report.

At least seven cases showing no aphasia from onset have shown a documented LF3 lesion at autopsy (Bruandet, 1900; Chouppe, 1870; Foulis, 1879; Moutier, 1908, cases 1–3, pp. 384–414; Simpson, 1867).

Two remarkable additional cases were described in which the authors showed quite clearly how the case contradicted the dogma. In each case an initial deficit faded rapidly and a focal LF3 infarct was found at autopsy. In one of these,

Tuke and Fraser (1872) described their case as critical to Broca's view by saying "not a loophole for escape is left" (for Broca's theory). In the other case, a 70-year-old businessman, Bramwell (1898) took pains to note: "the point I wish to emphasize, for it seems to me to be of supreme interest and importance, is that in this patient, who was a right-handed man and in no sense more left-handed than the majority of right-handed persons, acute and complete destruction of the left motor–vocal speech centre (Broca's convolution) and of the anterior end of the left island of Reil, merely produced a very temporary motor aphasia and did not produce, as would have been expected, complete and persisting motor aphasia".

Marie. Marie and his pupils (Cole & Cole, 1971) mounted a respectful, thoughtful, but forceful attack on the basic tenets of Broca's aphasia in a series of papers. Several autopsied cases were reported (Marie & Moutier, 1906a, 1906b, 1906c, 1906d) with varying thoroughness of clinical description showing what was referred to as *l'Aphasie de Broca* without a lesion of the third left frontal region, or vice versa, left third frontal lesion without l'Aphasie de Broca. These sharply worded papers aroused considerable controversy, featuring as they did such provocative titles as "The Third Left Frontal Convolution Plays No Special Role in the Function of Language" (Marie, 1906b), "What to Think About Subcortical Aphasias" (Marie, 1906c), and "Rectifications Concerning the Question of Aphasia" (Marie, 1907). Marie carefully summarized the evolution of the litany (Marie, 1906a), and his students further buttressed his argument with thesis volumes (Moutier, 1908).

In retrospect, his attacks lost much of their force due to his lack of a suitable hypothesis to substitute for Broca's. Further, his substitution of *anarthria* as a term for Broca's aphasia provided little improvement over the subsyndromes of Broca's aphasia then current. More important, and more damaging to his overall position, he equated the language deficit in Broca's aphasia with that seen in Wernicke's aphasia, and maintained that Broca's aphasia was merely Wernicke's aphasia plus anarthria. Finally, and unfortunately, many of his arguments appeared merely a personal quarrel with Dejerine, the then-current espouser of the litany, who vigorously defended the traditions of Broca's aphasia. The debates between these two [so faithfully and painstakingly translated along with Marie's other works by Cole and Cole (1971)] were inconclusive for both Marie and Déjerine.

Cortical resections. Robb (1948), Mettler (1949), Jefferson (1950), and Penfield and Roberts (1959) laid stress on the transient effects of cortical surgical removals, including Broca's area, in cases where the remainder of the hemisphere could be considered intact. The importance of these observations was considerably diminished, however, since normally the areas subject to cortical excisions were chronic scars. The possibility could not be excluded that prior reorganization of cerebral function had already rendered the scar tissue functionally inert, and no longer crucial for continued speech function.

Refinements of Broca's aphasia. Kleist (1934, pp. 929–930) accounted for many criticisms by envisioning two types of deficits resulting from a Broca's-area lesion. Basing his views on experiences with war injuries and cerebral infarcts, he considered that "severe and persisting word mutism" ("Schwere and anhaltende Wortstummheit") did not result from a lesion of the cortex and subjacent white matter of LF3. Persisting deficits always reflected involvement of the deeper white matter, which included the projection, association, and transcallosal fiber systems. He believed the deficits in language function resulting from such disruption were clearly separable from other cerebral syndromes of temporal- or parietal-lobe origin, and he specifically rejected Marie's notion that Broca's aphasia was Wernicke's aphasia plus anarthria. Kleist's views broadly support those independently reached by Mohr (1968, 1973; Mohr *et al.*, 1975) although Kleist did not predict the improvement in the cases with deep white-matter infarction.

Goldstein (1948, pp. 190–216), without reference to Kleist, and citing no cases of his own, also noted that cases in which the lesion was limited to LF3 might have no aphasia or only a transient deficit. He attributed such prompt improvement to preservation of the major intrahemispheral and transcallosal pathways, or to surviving portions of the LF3 itself, both proposals echoing those of Kleist. He differed from Kleist in his use of the term *peripheral motor aphasia* to characterize these cases. Such cases showed no deficits in language function as tested by writing, comprehension, and so forth; their entire deficit was confined to an inability to articulate. This view appears to align Goldstein's peripheral motor aphasia with the syndrome referred to by Marie as *anarthria,* and by the classicists as *pure word mutism* or *subcortical motor aphasia.* Goldstein further stated that the lesion could be cortical or subcortical. To the extent that this interpretation of Goldstein's views is accurate, his peripheral motor aphasia is different from that proposed by Kleist and demonstrated by Mohr *et al.* Later in his discussion, Goldstein noted that "in some individuals with *extensive lesion of the left Broca's area* . . . good *language* returns very rapidly" (emphasis Goldstein). He attributed this rapid improvement to preservation of "the connections through the corpus callosum between the operculum Rolandi and the central speech mechanisms of both hemispheres" (Goldstein, 1948, p. 204). However applicable this view might be in some cases, others exist (Mohr, 1968, 1973) in which the extent of cerebral destruction precludes this mechanism. Nielsen (1962) independently echoed both authors in proposing the possibility of prompt recovery from aphasia. The means by which such improvements occurred was only broadly suggested.

Modern workers. Many modern workers appear to show limited interest in the subject of anatomic correlations. Their faint enthusiasm has precedent in Head's

(1926) sarcastic criticisms of "diagram-makers," and in Brain's (1962) more recent chiding of the "naive psychoanatomical" approach. Bruyn and Gathier (1970) described in detail the clinical effects of anterior inferior frontal infarction under the label *operculum syndrome,* with only a passing reference to "aphasia (or Pierre Marie's anarthria)." Critchley (1970), in reviewing the issues of Broca's *aphemia,* made no reference to pathoanatomic aspects. Other authors have been concerned with the larger syndrome currently referred to as Broca's aphasia.

FORMULATION OF THE SYNDROME
OF BROCA'S-AREA INFARCTION

The results of the personal observations and the literature review prompt a formulation of the syndrome of Broca's-area infarction that agrees in part with the traditional views, but differs on several fundamental points sufficient to suggest basically different mechanisms of cerebral function.

Autopsy-documented Broca's-area infarction is not associated with severe and persisting motor aphasia. *Broca's-area infarction* refers to embolic ischemic infarction involving the left third (inferior) frontal convolution (LF3) and/or the neighboring anterior insula, below LF3, including the white matter subjacent to these regions. *Severe and persisting* is meant to imply a deficit incapacitating or at least significantly disruptive to the patient, continuing over months and years with little change, so that examination at such later time regularly yields findings qualitatively similar, if quantitatively less evident. *Motor aphasia* broadly refers to deficient communication by speaking aloud, due to defects in phonation; articulation; melodic line (conveying dialect, intonation, phrasing, emphasis on individual words, and syllable stress), grammatical usage, and/or completeness of sentence formulation.

A wide clinical spectrum occurs in the acute stage. At one end is a barely detectable alteration in melodic line. At the other is complete mutism; dyspraxia of the upper extremities, oral, and respiratory apparatus; and deficit in language-based tasks other than speaking, such as tests of writing and matching individual test stimuli to choice stimuli.

Neither the rate nor the extent of subsequent improvement in cases studied thus far has been predicted by age, handedness, sex, educational level, or associated motor, sensory, or praxic deficits. Lack of demonstrable language deficit on tasks of writing and matching has been a helpful sign that rapid and essentially complete amelioration of the speech deficit will occur. Improvement may begin in hours, days, or weeks. Evidence of language deficit, as reflected in nonspeaking tasks, fades rapidly, as does most evidence of dyspraxia for limb, oral, and respiratory apparatus. Spontaneous speech may yield slight evidence of stereotypes and agrammatism but these deficits also fade quickly as spontaneous speech emerges from mutism. The rate and extent of improvement in the mechanical features of spoken speech vary considerably: Some patients pass for normal on all but the most complex speaking tasks within days or weeks, while others become sufficiently fluent after a few months so that only those familiar with their premorbid speaking are aware of a deficit. Most continue with individual or combined deficits in the smoothness with which vocalization of one phoneme in a series can be ceased and changed to the next, in precise control of the respiratory component of vocalization, and/or in precise positioning of the oral cavity to produce desired phonemes. The degree of deficit is often increased by the artificial test setting, and by increased speed and complexity of the required utterance.

If the syndrome of Broca's-area infarction is overdescribed by the features encompassed by current definitions of Broca's aphasia, it is also very different from those referred to by the terms *anarthria, subcortical motor aphasia, pure word mutism,* and so forth. In these essentially identical syndromes, the patient is rendered mute by paralysis of the vocal apparatus, demonstrates no dyspraxia of parts able to move, shows excellent language function by writing, and undergoes slow and incomplete emergence from mutism to heavy dysarthria and dysphonia without dyspraxia of the vocal apparatus. While Broca's-area infarction approximates these syndromes, these latter reflect an elemental damage to motor pathways to the bulbar apparatus per se, in the form of motor cortex embolus, capsular infarction on each side of the brain, or the like, not primarily disease of Broca's area.

The disorder observed in Broca's-area infarction is rarely accounted for by elemental weakness of muscles serving articulation and phonation. Instead, it seems better explained by inadequacy in skilled execution of movements, an apraxia in speaking, such as initially suggested by Broca (1861), but not an associated disorder in language usage.

The improvements in many cases follow a timetable that precedes improvements that would be predicted from the gradual fading of edema and of other obvious neuropathologic sequelae of ischemic infarction, or those that would result from rehabilitative therapy. Instead, the improvement suggests that basic cerebral mechanisms are undergoing rapid reorganization.

The posterior Sylvian regions appear to survive the infarct intact, giving rise to the suggestion that these areas promptly seek access to the opposite (nondominant) inferior frontal region for mediation of vocalization. This view does not imply fundamental reorganization of language mechanisms but rather a shift in the side of the brain primarily responsible for articulation. The presumed coordinative effort of both inferior frontal regions in ordinary speaking might set the stage for easy emergence of the nondominant inferior frontal region as the sole mediator of speaking aloud when the left (dominant) side is injured. The anatomic pathways over which this relation between the dominant posterior

Sylvian and nondominant inferior regions is achieved remain speculative at present and still await documented cases of multiple lesions (Mohr, 1973).

This speculation regarding cerebral organization runs counter to some current views (Benson & Geschwind, 1971; Goodglass & Kaplan, 1972, pp. 54–55; Goodglass *et al.*, 1964) that considerably more than skilled motor movements for speaking are subsumed in Broca's area. If language mechanisms sufficient to produce condensed grammatical speech, dysgraphia, dyslexia, and other features currently encompassed by definitions of Broca's aphasia were mediated by Broca's area, rapid amelioration of the deficit, and the mechanisms of such amelioration proposed above, could scarcely be envisioned as feasible. Such improvements would imply interhemispheral shifts of major functions, which the present thesis does not. The present thesis envisions Broca's area as mediating a more traditionally postulated role as a pre-motor association cortex region concerned with acquired skilled oral, pharyngeal, and respiratory movements, involving speaking as well as other behaviors, but not essentially language or graphic behavior per se. These latter behaviors seem to involve the entire cerebral operculum, including insula, supramarginal gyrus, and deeper white matter. This larger syndrome, currently referred to as Broca's aphasia, is due to a lesion involving this broad region, far exceeding the confines of Broca's area.

THE CLINICAL SYNDROME OF BROCA'S APHASIA AND ITS ANATOMIC FOUNDATION

The literature contains a long list of articles concerning a syndrome referred to as Broca's aphasia. In most of these articles, primary emphasis has been placed on the description of the clinical features, with much less effort devoted to autopsy correlation of the clinical syndrome with the lesion topography.

The clinical features of the syndrome that have evolved in the literature over the past 110 years are more complex, involve more evidence of deficit in language usage, including easily documented deficits in "comprehension," appear more severe, and are much more thoroughly described than those met in the older literature, which presents autopsy data showing infarction limited to LF3 and its immediate surroundings. However, the uncomfortable possibility suggested by the more complex clinical syndrome is that the underlying lesion far exceeds that of LF3 and adjacent structures.

Despite the impressive list of authors who have written on Broca's aphasia, many have not cited personal cases that document their views, and few have provided autopsy or other laboratory evidence corroborating the lesion topography. In some, even the etiology of the case material has been unclear. Vascular material appears to have been the source material for Broca, Wernicke, Déjerine, Marie, Liepmann, Alajouanine, Nielsen, Kreindler and Fradis, and Goodglass, Quadfasel, and Timberlake. War material was used by Head, Kleist, Goldstein,

Conrad, Russell and Espir, and Luria. Weisenburg and McBride, and deAjuria-guerra and Hécaen, used a wide etiologic spectrum of cases. Brown presented an abscess case. Textbook authors usually have not specified their material. Included in this group are Brain, Critchley, Lhermitte and Gautier, Benson and Geschwind, and Adams and Mohr.

Perhaps as troublesome has been the frequently unstated time course over which the syndrome changed from or to the state described as Broca's aphasia. In the few cases reported, the late description of a deficit referred to as Broca's aphasia is better correlated with a lesion far larger than Broca's area, as illustrated in Tables 1 and 2. The two notable exceptions were Broca's own cases, further described at the end of this review.

Traditional Formulations of Broca's Aphasia

Wernicke (1874) might be credited with the first textbook characterization of Broca's aphasia. In 1874, he confined his remarks to a few simple features without citing actual cases: following "destruction of the speech movement images . . . the patient understands everything but has either suddenly become mute or has at most a few simple words at his disposal" (p. 57).

By 1908 (Wernicke, 1908, pp. 272–273) his description had enlarged considerably under the term *motor aphasia*, which he equated with *Broca's aphemia*, due to involvement of Broca's convolution. Still without cited cases, Wernicke described three main features:

1. "The power of articulate speech is wanting. The patients have forgotten the process, the mechanism, which they formerly called into action to produce its sounds." He considered the patients mute or at best minimally able to speak, using "senseless syllables," short words or phrases, profane expressions. Dyspraxia of bulbar musculature for other movements, right lower facial and tongue weakness, but no elementary weakness of the bulbar musculature were also described.

2. "In the main, the power of understanding speech is retained; at least this appears to be the case on ordinary tests. . . . There is almost invariably a certain inability to understand complicated constructions and the finer differentiations of speech. . . . I no longer am of the opinion that in pure motor aphasia the ability to understand speech always remains unimpaired." Here Wernicke considerably modified his earlier views, but did not indicate whether he considered this wider deficit to reflect a lesion larger than Broca's area.

3. "Written language . . . is lost simultaneously with articulate speech." This statement is the first of a long series of opinions concerning the intimate relationship between written and spoken speech stemming from Broca's original cases.

Wernicke considered the prognosis "generally unfavorable" for restoration of speech function.

This complex, severe, and persisting syndrome, together with the inference that Broca's area is the site of the responsible lesion, has persisted largely unchanged over the years under the label motor or Broca's aphasia (Adams & Mohr, 1974; Bastian, 1897; Benson & Geschwind, 1971; Brain, 1962; Brown, 1972; Déjerine & Mirallié, 1896; Hécaen, 1972; Heilbronner, 1910; Kreindler & Fradis, 1968; Lhermitte & Gautier, 1969; Lichtheim, 1885; Liepmann, 1915; Nielsen, 1962; Weisenburg & McBride, 1964; Wyllie, 1894). This description has also found application in war-injury studies where efforts have been made to correlate the clinical deficit with the skull defect or operative findings (Conrad, 1954; Goldstein, 1948; Head, 1926; Russell & Espir, 1961).

Several earlier authors took the trouble to present exemplary personal case reports and/or excerpted cases from the literature (Lichtheim, Wyllie, Bastian, Weisenburg and McBride, Nielsen), but only Dejerine appears to have published autopsied case reports.

Remarkably, despite the paucity of autopsy material for this larger syndrome, most of the differences of opinion revolve around individual features of the syndrome, in particular the explanations for deficits in behavior apart from disordered speaking. Disturbance in silent reading "comprehension" has been noted since the earliest reviews (Bastian, 1897; Wyllie, 1894). The explanations of dyslexia are typified by Bastian (1897):

> In reading, a proper comprehension of the meaning of the text requires a conjoint revival of the words in the visual and the auditory word-centres, but that for this mere comprehension it is not necessary for the stimulus to pass on also to the glosso-kinesthetic (Broca's) centre, as it must do in reading aloud. It may, however, be freely admitted that if the way is open, and this latter centre is in a healthy condition, it does commonly receive in reading to one's self a slight stimulus from the auditory word-centre, a fact which is often enough shown by the occurrence of involuntary half-whispered mutterings when reading. It may also be admitted that the rousing of all three centres does give assistance in the comprehension of anything difficult, as is shown by the common practice of reading aloud any passage the meaning of which may be at all obscure [p. 1009].

This principle has remained the explanation offered into modern times (Luria, 1966, p. 190).

Auditory comprehension and other disturbances in language formulations have been less easily explained. Opinion has been divided as to whether or not such disturbances even occur. Lichtheim (1885, p. 471), Wyllie (1894, pp. 318–319), Bastian (1897, p. 1005), and Liepmann (1915, pp. 526–527) considered motor aphasia to be free of such deficits. Others concurred with Wernicke's views (Déjerine & Mirallié, 1896, pp. 102–105; Heilbronner, 1910, pp. 1021–1028). Marie (1906b) took the extreme position that Broca's aphasia represents Wernicke's aphasia plus anarthria. Modern authors' views on this point are less clearly stated, partially because the current, revised syndrome lays stress on different features of the deficit (as will be explained further).

Writing disturbances have been explained by citing two separate mechanisms. Bastian (1897), almost alone in his opinion, maintained that any dysgraphia is secondary to involvement outside Broca's area, usually affecting the second frontal gyrus, so-called "Exner's writing center." A few subsequent authors (Brain, 1962; Henschen, 1925) have entertained these views, while others (Mohr *et al.*, 1973) have been content to indicate a certain degree of independence between writing and speaking performances without making anatomic inferences. The overwhelming weight of opinion has favored a coexisting deficit in writing and speaking. Where anatomic comments are included, the lesion is considered to involve Broca's area and need be no larger. The opinions of Jackson (1932) typify most authors: "speaking is propositionizing . . . that the speechless patient cannot propositionize *aloud* is obvious—he never does. But this is only the superficial part of the truth. He cannot propositionize internally . . . the proof that he does not speak internally is that he cannot express himself in writing. . . . He can say nothing to himself, and therefore has nothing to write." Given such reasoning, little additional explanation was required to account for the easily observed deficits in auditory comprehension noted by all authors, including Liepmann (1915), Pick (1973), Isserlin (1936), Lhermitte and Gautier (1969), Brown (1972), and others. None—as best can be determined by the present reviewer—based their views on personal cases with pathoanatomic correlation of the clinical deficits. Yet none expressed disagreement that the lesion lay in Broca's area.

Of the many features of this larger syndrome referred to as Broca's aphasia, the deficit in spoken speech has received the greatest attention. Broca (1861) has described the recurrent utterances and partial syllables that characterized the limited speaking behavior of his two patients. Jackson (1932), Wernicke (1908), Liepmann (1915), Pick (1973), Kleist (1934), Alajouanine, Ombrédane, and Durand (1939), Goodglass *et al.* (1964), and Brown (1972) have written and rewritten the basic features of verbal stereotypes, recurrent utterances, and condensed grammatical sentence structure that characterize speaking in cases of Broca's aphasia. Save for Kleist (1934), none have described clinical cases with individual pathologic correlation, although all authors have stated or implied that the lesion lies in Broca's area or immediately surrounding regions or needs to involve no additional areas for this characteristic speaking performance. In modern times, the work of Goodglass *et al.* (1964) provides an exemplary documentation of the clinical and linguistic features in clinical cases referred to as Broca's aphasia. Twenty-two of 53 patients studied with the Boston Veterans Administration Diagnostic Aphasia Test were characterized as cases of Broca's aphasia. They showed poor scores on melodic line, length of uninterrupted word groups, verbal agility in articulation, and correct grammatical form. Virtually no jargon in connected speech, impaired auditory comprehension, or problems in naming objects were found. The cases studied were all allowed at least two months after stroke onset before they were studied. Of particular interest to the present reviewer was the remark that "It appeared that most Broca's aphasics either remained grossly impaired or quickly attained a level of residual aphasia in which the classical features of agrammatism, telegraphic speech, and laborious articulation were no longer apparent." (Goodglass et al., 1964). These observations corroborate those of the present review (Mohr et al., 1975) that rapid amelioration of speech deficit occurs (in the local Broca's-area infarct), or when persisting, severe deficit is found in which disturbed language function is easily demonstrated (in the larger syndrome of Sylvian operculum infarction). Like most other authors, Goodglass et al. (1964) had no autopsy correlation in their clinical cases, but they appeared to consider that the presumed infarction involved Broca's area, since they speculated that "Broca's area contains critical structures which are so concentrated that a direct injury is likely to be permanently and severely damaging to speech." This speculation, based as it was on the litany, and not on the personal autopsy experience of the authors, is representative of the degrees to which this larger syndrome has been considered to reflect Broca's-area infarction by most authors.

Several authors have been impressed with the deficits in language behavior other than speaking to a degree that serious doubts were raised as to whether the term *motor aphasia* is appropriate for such cases. The painstaking work of Weisenburg and McBride (1964) represents some of the most detailed documentation of this larger deficit. Their criticisms of the concept of motor aphasia were based on a thorough literature review and 42 personal cases of "expressive" or "expressive–receptive" aphasia. Their efforts clearly documented the larger deficit and their reasons for objecting to motor aphasia as an inappropriate concept, but their case material could scarcely be considered an appropriate source for criticisms of the anatomic basis of the syndrome: Their 42 cases encompassed a broad etiologic spectrum including ischemic stroke, hemorrhage, tumor, cyst, gunshot wound, and subdural hematoma. None of the cases were autopsied, and in the early 1930s, save for the rare operated case, the topography of the lesion in each case was inferred on clinical criteria alone. The opportunity to relate the larger syndrome to a brain lesion far exceeding the confines of Broca's area and immediately adjacent brain tissue was not taken up by Weisenburg and McBride nor by a large number of other authors who also pointed out that the syndrome involved a deficit in language functions apart from that evident in speaking aloud. With few exceptions, Broca's-area lesion has been considered sufficient to cause this large deficit.

Kleist (1934, p. 930) considered the persisting and severe deficit to require infarction deep into the hemisphere, so as to disrupt the white matter fibers that served as projection and association pathways for Broca's area. By inference, these deeper lesions would mean a larger infarct, although Kleist did not specify the upper division of the left middle-cerebral artery as such. Foix (1928) earlier had made a similar inference by referring to deeper branches of the middle-cerebral artery. Goldstein (1948, pp. 204–205) made suggestions similar to those of Kleist, but also failed to specify the vascular territory involved in the larger lesion. Remarkably few cases of this larger syndrome have been autopsied and described in the literature (see Tables 1 and 2); those reported have proven difficult to classify simply as Broca's aphasia because they were examined only in the late stages, raising the possibility that they represented improved total aphasia.

The theoretic problems raised by the notions of total aphasia reflect sufficiently on those of Broca's aphasia to warrant further consideration of total aphasia. The term emerged in the late 19th century in the works of most textbook authors (Déjerine & Mirallié, 1896; Heilbronner, 1910; Liepmann, 1915; Wernicke, 1908). Liepmann's (1915) account is typical:

> More frequently than a lesion confined to the *frontal* or *temporal* speech region, we find, as a result of the arterial distribution bringing all the blood in the whole region of speech, through the *Art. foss. sylvii*, lesions, that affect both regions, and therefore causing *total* or almost total (motor and sensory) aphasia. Following the retrogression of the word-deafness, one sees, years later, a clinical picture, in which the symptoms of *motor* aphasia predominate. Word-dumbness conceals the paraphasia; the disturbance of speech understanding is no longer very serious. Writing and reading . . . are very poor. Hence it happens, that old cases, in which the lesions occur in both speech regions, are often classed clinically only as motor aphasia. *In these cases, disturbances in speaking, writing and reading, are particularly stable* [pp. 529–530]. (emphasis Liepmann)

This description by Liepmann bears a close resemblance to that currently referred to as Broca's aphasia in the later stages.

The existence of this syndrome prompts a detailed examination of the time-course data for published cases labeled as Broca's aphasia. Protocols for most of the wholly clinically described cases of Broca's aphasia usually show that the authors dealt with chronic cases, at least two months (Goodglass *et al.*, 1964), as long as six years (Alajouanine *et al.*, 1939), and ten years (Goldstein, 1948, case 6, pp. 208–245) after onset. The autopsy material (Tables 1 and 2) further reveals that the later a case labeled as Broca's aphasia is documented clinically, the greater the likelihood that a large lesion is found at autopsy. This material also documents the frequency with which cases quite similar in detailed clinical features are given the label total aphasia (Tables 1 and 2).

Personal Observations

Mohr *et al.* (1975) have succeeded in acquiring autopsy or other laboratory corroboration of lesion topography for ten cases suffering cerebral infarction, all of whom broadly satisfied the criteria currently used for Broca's aphasia months after their stroke. Seven were studied by computerized axial tomogram (CT scan), two by arteriogram, and one by autopsy. The lesion topography in each case far exceeded Broca's area. In most, the lesion was best explained by total or near-total infarction of the area of supply of the upper division of the left middle-cerebral artery, encompassing the operculum from anterior frontal through Broca's area (LF3) to anterior parietal regions, the insula, both banks of the central (Rolandic) fissure, the entire infarct usually extending deep into the hemisphere (Figure 3).

The initial deficit in these cases was uniformly severe, closely approximating Liepmann's (1915) descriptions of total aphasia. They later evolved, as described by Liepmann (1915), toward a state more or less conforming to current descriptions of Broca's aphasia. In all cases the later syndrome emerged from one more severe. Weeks, but usually months and occasionally years were required before this later state was fully established.

All cases experienced hemiplegia at onset. None were able to stand for over a week; all walked with a heavy circumducted gait, the arm essentially useless, the right lower face densely paretic. The six seen the day of onset experienced head and conjugate eye deviation to the side of the lesion, all six improving to full head and eye control within a week. Hemianopia was present for several days. After several months, a syndrome of spastic hemiparesis still disabled all patients although they achieved independence with a cane after prolonged physiotherapy.

Initially, all cases were mute and unable to write legibly with either hand; most graphic efforts were hopeless loops or marks without communicative value. Evidence of disturbed comprehension, for many complete, was present in auditory and visual language tasks. Two cases followed for years (Mohr *et al.*, 1973) underwent steady evolution toward much improved auditory comprehension, but began to speak only after ten months in one case, three years in the other. The most successful improvements occurred in two other cases, who performed Marie's three-paper test correctly at three months in the case of a 25-year-old left-handed man, and seven months in a 44-year-old right-handed man. Save for these two cases, deficits in language tasks were easily demonstrated months and even years after onset, if testing was carried beyond ordinary social conversation into more formal tests, particularly in spelling. All patients emerged from mutism into stereotype utterances, which soon became agrammatic laconic efforts at spontaneous speech; this difficulty was similarly reflected in misspelled dysgrammatic efforts at writing. Considerable variation in dyspraxia of the upper extremities, oral, and respiratory apparatus was observed.

Corroborative cases were culled from the retrospective autopsy series from the Massachusetts General Hospital for a 10-year period (mentioned previously). Fifteen of the 39 cases of left-cerebral infarction affecting the territory of

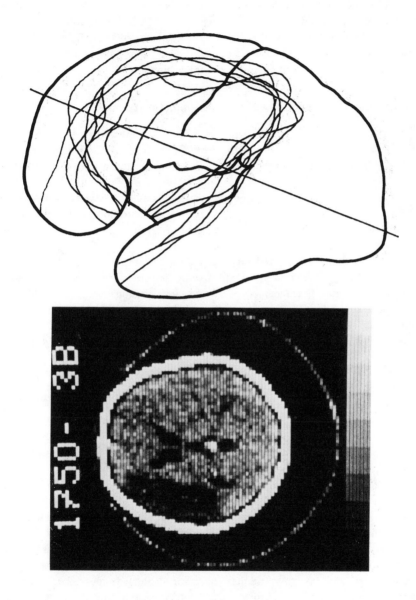

Figure 3 (top) Syndrome of infarction in the upper division of the middle-cerebral artery, projected on a lateral view of the left hemisphere. (bottom) An example of a CT scan with the large lesion evident. The plane of section for the CT scan is indicated by the line drawn through the top diagram.

supply of the upper division of the left middle-cerebral artery were described as having deficits in speaking and in language use persisting months and years, conforming (where data was available) to features broadly classifiable as Broca's aphasia. In all such cases, the lesion far exceeded Broca's area, usually involving the bulk of the territory of supply of the upper division.

Formulation of the Syndrome of Upper Division Infarction

These personal and retrospective autopsy cases, compared with the few described and the fewer autopsied cases in the literature, prompt a formulation of this syndrome that differs from the traditional and current notions of Broca's aphasia.

Broca's aphasia, as currently defined, is not a result of infarction of Broca's area and immediate surrounds. It reflects a major infarction involving most of the territory of supply of the upper division of the left middle-cerebral artery. As a clinical entity, the evidence to date suggests that the deficit profile known as Broca's aphasia is observed only later after the infarction. The initial syndrome is more severe, described traditionally as total aphasia. After weeks or months, the gradual emergence of stereotypes, agrammatism, and protracted dyspraxia in speaking evolves slowly toward the long-standing deficit profile of Broca's aphasia, which remains little changed after months and years.

Subsequent studies may reveal that the complex syndrome of Broca's aphasia can occur acutely, without evolving from the more obvious syndrome of total aphasia. But in such case, the prediction is made that a large lesion will be found, far exceeding Broca's area.

This formulation of the upper-division syndrome makes the terms *Broca's aphasia* and *total aphasia* seem inexact, even inappropriate in principle. Neither convey the anatomic or functional implications implicit in this new formulation. The upper-division syndrome is a complex, wide-ranging deficit profile, involving formulation and production of spoken and written communication, including "central" language functions as well as the more elemental organization of sensory, motor, and praxic skills for execution of such spoken and written efforts. The major disorganization of these systems is more easily understood when the great extent and depth of the lesion are appreciated. Less fanciful explanations are required to account for the deficit, and the long periods of time required for improvement are more easily accounted for than by traditional implications that all this complex behavior depended upon the herculean homuncular functions of Broca's area. Although much of the mystique of aphasiology might be lost by this formulations of the upper-division syndrome, a closer alignment with views of cerebral functions based on other physiologic studies might be the result.

BROCA'S CASES

In retrospect, had Broca emphasized the extent of the lesion topography in his two cases, he might have prevented over a century of controversy. When account is taken of lesion topography, Broca's cases appear relatively straightforward examples of the upper-division syndrome now referred to as Broca's aphasia: two chronic cases, seen 18 months and 10 years, respectively, after infarction, having severe speaking deficit confined to limited verbal stereotypes, conversationally satisfactory "comprehension," and, in the one case with autopsy findings, major infarction affecting the territory of supply of the upper division of the left middle-cerebral artery (Figure 4).

Broca saw neither case acutely. He used only conversational and not more formal grammatical tasks such as spelling, which might have shown a deficient performance sharply contrasting with the conversational evidence of good comprehension. In accordance with then-current ideas that stroke disease affected the brain in a slowly expanding fashion (Marie, 1906b), Broca understandably sought the site of "origin" of the stroke; he deliberately ignored the larger zone of infarction (which he considered the later spreading effect of the stroke) in favor of the portion involving the inferior frontal region, where he envisaged the stroke "began." By faithfully adhering to then-current notions of the pathophysiology of stroke, Broca missed the opportunity to formulate for all time the clinical, temporal, and pathologic features of the upper-division middle cerebral artery syndrome that should justifiably bear his name. Instead, his name came to be associated with a syndrome improperly correlated with brain infarct topography and with an area of the brain whose infarction produces only a modest long-term clinical deficit.

To avoid future ambiguities, the terms *Broca's aphasia, total aphasia,* and even *Broca's area* might preferably fall into disuse, in favor of other terms, such as the opercular syndromes, that better describe the spectrum observed, including that

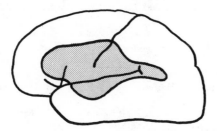

Figure 4 Topography of the infarct found in Broca's case Leborgne (drawing traced from Moutier).

end of the spectrum that Broca observed but did not interpret as such. Considering that Boulliaud gave Broca his original inspirations, the eclipse of Broca's epomyn seems a less than historic tragedy, since Boulliaud's own efforts have already largely passed into oblivion.

REFERENCES

Adams, R. D., Mohr, J. P. 1974. Affections of speech. In M. M. Wintrobe *et al.* (Eds.), , *Harrison's principles of internal medicine.* (7th ed.) New York: McGraw-Hill. Pp. 137–148.

Alajouanine, T., Ombrédane, A., & Durand, M. 1939. *Le syndrome de désintégration phonétique dans l'aphasie.* Paris: Masson.

Atkins, R. 1876. Case of sudden and complete aphasia and partial right hemiplegia, lesion of Broca's convolution, with a small haemorrhage in substance of corpus callosum &c. *Journal of Mental Science, 22,* 406–416.

Bailey, P., & von Bonin, G. 1951. *The isocortex of man.* Urbana: University of Illinois.

Bastian, H. C. 1897. Some problems in connexion with aphasia and other speech defects. *Lancet, 1,* 1005–1017, 1132–1137, 1187–1194.

Benson, D. F., & Geschwind, N. 1971. The aphasias and related disturbances. In A. B. Baker (Ed.), *Clinical neurology.* Vol. 1. New York: Harper. Pp. 1–25.

Bourneville. 1874a. Athérome généralisé: oblitérations multiples (aphasie; sphacèle du pied, etc.). *Progrès Médical, 2*(20), 278–280.

Bourneville. 1874b. Athérome généralisé: oblitérations multiples (aphasie; sphacèle du pied, etc.). *Progrès Médical, 2*(21), 296–298.

Brain, W. R. 1962. *Speech disorders.* London: Butterworths.

Bramwell, B. 1898. A remarkable case of aphasia. *Brain: A Journal of Neurology, 21,* 343–373.

Broca, P. 1861. Remarques sur le siége de la faculté du langage articulé, suivies d'une observation d'aphémie (perte de la parole). *Bulletins de la Société Anatomique de Paris, 6,* 330–357.

Brodmann, K. 1909. *Vergleichende Lokalisationslehre der Grosshirnrinde in ihren Prinzipien dargestellt auf Grund des Zellenbaues.* Leipzig: Barth.

Brown, J. W. 1972. *Aphasia, apraxia and agnosia.* Springfield, Ill.: Charles C Thomas.

Bruandet (Interne des hopitaux). 1900. Un cas d'hemispasme facial. *Revue Neurologique, 8,* 658–660.

Bruyn, G. W., and Gathier, J-C. 1970. The operculum syndrome. In P. J. Vinken & G. W. Bruyn (Eds.), *Handbook of clinical neurology.* Vol. 2. Amsterdam: North-Holland Publ. Pp. 776–783.

Chouppe. 1870. Ramollissement superficiel du cerveau intéressant surtout la troisième circonvolution frontale gauche, sans aphasie. *Bulletins de la Société Anatomique de Paris, 45,* 365–366.

Cole, M. F., & Cole, M. 1971. *Pierre Marie's papers on speech disorders.* New York: Hafner.

Comte, A. 1900. *Des paralysies pseudo-bulbaires.* (Thesis) 8°, No. 436. Paris: Steinheil.

Conrad, K. 1954. New problems of aphasia. *Brain: A Journal of Neurology, 77*(4), 491–509.

Critchley, MacD. 1970. *Aphasiology and other aspects of language.* London: Arnold.

DeAjuriaguerra, J., and Hécaen, H. 1964. *Le cortex cérébral.* Paris: Masson.

deBoyer, H. C. 1879. *Études topographiques sur les lésions corticales des hémisphères cérébraux.* (Thesis) Paris: Delahaye.

Déjerine, J. 1885. Étude sur l'aphasie dans lésions de l'insula de Reil. *Revue de Médecine (Paris), 5,* 174–191.

Déjerine, J. 1891. Contribution à l'étude de l'aphasie motrice sous corticale et de la localisation cérébrale des centres laryngés (muscles phonateures). *Comptes Rendus Hebdomadaires des Séances et Mémoires de la Société de Biologie, 3,* 155–162.

Déjerine, J. 1906. L'aphasie motrice. Sa localisation et sa physiologie pathologique. *Presse Medicale, 14*(57), 453–457.

Déjerine, J., & Mirallié, C. 1896. *L'aphasie sensorielle.* Paris: Steinheil.

Flechsig, P. 1901. Developmental (myelogenetic) Localisation of the cerebral cortex in the human subject. *Lancet, ii,* 1027–1029.

Foix, C. 1928. Aphasies. In G. H. Roger, F. Widal, & P. J. Teissier (Eds.), *Nouveau traité de médecine.* Vol. 18. P. 135. Paris: Masson et Cie.

Foulis, D. 1879. A case in which there was destruction of the third left frontal convolution without aphasia. *British Medical Journal, 1,* 383–384.

Friedlich, A. L., Castleman, B., & Mohr, J. P. 1968. Sudden stroke in a woman with dyspnea and anemia. *New England Journal of Medicine, 278,* 1109–1118.

Geschwind, N. 1965a. Disconnexion syndromes in animals and man: I. *Brain: A Journal of Neurology, 88,* 237–294.

Geschwind, N. 1965b. Disconnexion syndromes in animals and man: II. *Brain: A Journal of Neurology, 88,* 585–644.

Goldstein, K. 1948. *Language and language disturbances.* New York: Grune & Stratton.

Goodglass, H., & Kaplan, E. 1972. *The assessment of aphasia and related disorders.* Philadelphia: Lea & Febiger.

Goodglass, H., Quadfasel, F. A., & Timberlake, W. T. 1964. Phase length and type and severity of aphasia. *Cortex, 1,* 133–153.

Head, H. 1926. *Aphasia and kindred disorders of speech.* New York: Macmillan.

Hécaen, H. 1972. *Introduction à la neuropsychologie.* Paris: Larousse (Librairie).

Heilbronner, K. 1910. Die aphasischen, apraktischen und agnostischen Störungen. In M. Lewandowsky (Ed.), *Handbuch der Neurologie.* Vol. 1. Berlin: Springer-Verlag. Pp. 982–1093.

Henschen, S. E. 1922. *Klinische und pathologische Beiträge zur Pathologie des Gehirns.* Vol. VII. Stockholm: Nordiske Bokhandeln.

Henschen, S. E. 1925. Clinical and anatomical contributions on brain pathology; (Abstracts and comments by Walter F. Schaller); Fifth Part! Aphasia, amusia and akalkulia. *Archives of Neurology and Psychiatry, 13,* 226–249.

Isserlin, M. 1936. Aphasie. In O. Bumke and O. Foerster (Eds.), *Handbuch der Neurologie.* Vol. 6. Berlin: Springer-Verlag. Pp. 627–806.

Jackson, J. H. 1932. *Selected writings.* London: Hodder & Stoughton.

Jefferson, G. 1950. Localization of function in the cerebral cortex. *British Medical Bulletin, 6,* 333–340.

Kleist, K. 1934. *Gehirnpathologie.* Leipzig: Barth.

Kreindler, A., & Fradis, A. 1968. *Performances in aphasia.* Paris: Gauthier-Villars.

Kugler, J. 1964. *Electroencephalography in hospital and general consulting practice.* Amsterdam: Elsevier.

Lhermitte, F., & Gautier, J-C. 1969. Aphasia. In R. J. Vinken & G. W. Bruyn (Eds.), *Handbook of clinical neurology.* Vol. 4. Amsterdam: North-Holland Publ. Pp. 84–104.

Lichtheim, L. 1885. On aphasia. *Brain: A Journal of Neurology, 7,* 433–484.

234   *J. P. Mohr*

Liepmann, H. 1915. Diseases of the brain. In C. W. Barr (Ed.), *Curschmann's textbook on nervous diseases.* Vol. 1. Philadelphia: Blakiston. Pp. 467–551.

Luria, A. R. 1966. *Higher cortical functions in man.* New York: Basic Books.

McAdam, D. W., & Whitaker, H. A. 1971. Language production: Electroencephalographic localization in the normal human brain. *Science, 172,* 499–502.

Magnan. 1879. On simple aphasia, and aphasia with incoherence. *Brain: A Journal of Neurology, 2,* 112–123.

Marie, P. 1906a. Revision de la question de l'aphasie: L'aphasie de 1861 à 1866; essai de critique historique sur la genèse de la doctrine de Broca. *Semaine Médicale, 26,* 565–571.

Marie, P. 1906b. Revision de la question de l'aphasie: La troisième circonvolution frontale gauche ne joue aucun rôle spécial dans la fonction du langage. *Semaine Médicale, 26,* 241–247.

Marie, P. 1906c. Revision de la question de l'aphasie: Que faut-il penser des aphasies sous-corticales (aphasies pures)? *Semaine Médicale, 26,* 493–500.

Marie, P. 1907. Rectifications à propos de la question de L'aphasie. *Presse Medicale, 15*(4), 25–26.

Marie, P., & Moutier, F. 1906a. Examen du cerveau d'un cas d'aphasie de Broca. *Bulletins et Mémoires de la Société Médicale des Hopitaux de Paris, 23,* 743–744.

Marie, P., & Moutier, F. 1906b. Nouveau cas d'aphasie de Broca sans lésion de la troisième frontale gauche. *Bulletins et Mémoires de la Société Médicale des Hopitaux de Paris, 23,* 1180–1183.

Marie, P., & Moutier, F. 1906c. Nouveau cas de lésion corticale du pied de la 3e frontale gauche chez un droitier sans trouble du langage. *Bulletins et Mémoires de la Société Médicale des Hopitaux de Paris, 23,* 1295–1298.

Marie, P., & Moutier, F. 1906d. Sur un cas de ramollissement du pied de la 3e circonvolution frontale gauche chez un droitier, sans aphasie de Broca. *Bulletins et Mémoires de la Société Médicale des Hopitaux de Paris, 23,* 1152–1155.

Mettler, F. A. 1949. *Selective partial ablation of the frontal cortex: A correlative study of the effects on human psychotic subjects.* New York: Haeber.

Mohr, J. P. 1968. Cerebral control of speech. Letters to the Editor. *New England Journal of Medicine, 279,* 107.

Mohr, J. P. 1973. Rapid amelioration of motor aphasia. *Archives of Neurology, 28,* 77–82.

Mohr, J. P., Funkenstein, H., Finkelstein, S., Pessin, M., Duncan, G. W., & Davis, K. 1975. Broca's area infarction versus Broca's aphasia. *Neurology, 25,* 349.

Mohr, J. P., Leicester, J., Stoddard, L. T., & Sidman, M. 1971. Right hemianopia with memory and color deficits in circumscribed left posterior cerebral artery territory infarction. *Neurology, 21,* 1104–1113.

Mohr, J. P., Sidman, M., Stoddard, L. T., Leicester, J., & Rosenberger, P. B. 1973. Evolution of the deficit in total aphasia. *Neurology, 23,* 1302–1312.

Moutier, F. 1908. *L'aphasia de Broca.* (Thesis) Paris: Steinheil.

New, P. F. J., Scott, W. R., Schnur, J. A., Davis, K. R., & Taveras, J. M. 1974. Computerized axial tomography with the EMI scanner. *Radiology, 110,* 109–123.

Nielsen, J. M. 1962. *Agnosia, apraxia, aphasia.* New York: Hafner.

Ogle, W. 1867. Aphasia and agraphia. *St. George's Hospital Reports, 2,* 83–122.

Ojemann, R. G., Aronow, S., & Sweet, W. H. 1966. Scanning with positron-emitting isotopes in cerebrovascular diseases. *Acta Radiologica, 5,* 894–905.

Penfield, W. 1958. *The excitable cortex in conscious man.* Springfield, Ill.: Charles C Thomas.

Penfield, W., & Rasmussen, T. 1968. *The cerebral cortex of man.* New York: Hafner.

Penfield, W., & Roberts, L. 1959. *Speech and brain mechanisms.* Princeton, N.J.: Princeton University Press.

Pick, A. 1973. *Aphasia.* (Translated and edited by J. W. Brown) Springfield, Ill.: Charles C Thomas.

Robb, J. P. 1948. Effects of cortical excision and stimulation of the frontal lobe on speech. *Research Publications, Association for Research in Nervous and Mental Disease, 27,* 587–609.

Russell, W. R., & Espir, M. L. E. 1961. *Traumatic aphasia.* London: Oxford University Press.

Scheinker, I., & Kuhr, B. M. 1948. Motor aphasia and agraphia caused by small vascular lesion confined to third and second convolutions of left frontal lobe. *Research Publications, Association for Research in Nervous and Mental Disease, 27,* 582–586.

Simpson, J. H. 1867. On a case of extensive lesion of the left posterior frontal convolution of the cerebrum, without aphasia. *Medical Times and Gazette, 2,* 670.

Singer, M., & Yakovlev, P. I. 1954. *The human brain in sagittal section.* Springfield, Ill.: Charles C Thomas.

Taveras, J. M., & Wood, E. H. 1964. *Diagnostic neuroradiology.* Baltimore: Williams & Wilkins. Pp. 1.691–1.718.

Tuke, J. B., & Fraser, J. 1872. Case with a lesion involving Broca's convolution without Broca's aphasia. *Journal of Mental Science, 18,* 46–56.

Wadham, W. 1869. On aphasia. *St. George's Hospital Reports, 4,* 245–250.

Weisenburg, T., & McBride, K. E. 1964. *Aphasia.* New York: Hafner.

Wernicke, C. 1874. *Der Aphasische Symptomencomplex.* Breslau: Cohn & Weigert.

Wernicke, C. 1908. The symptomcomplex of aphasia. In A. Church (Ed.), *Modern clinical medicine. New York: Appleton.* Pp. 265–324.

Wyllie, J. 1894. *The disorders of speech.* Edinburgh: Oliver.

Yakovlev, P. I. 1970. Whole brain serial histological sections. In C. G. Tedeschi (Ed). *Neuropathology: Methods and diagnosis.* Boston: Little, Brown. Pp. 371–378.

7 Agrammatism[1]

Harold Goodglass

BOSTON VETERANS ADMINISTRATION HOSPITAL
AND BOSTON UNIVERSITY SCHOOL OF MEDICINE

CLINICAL AND ANATOMICAL DEFINITION

It was not until the nineteenth century that the clinically diverse forms of disturbance now labeled *aphasia* were universally recognized as being related by the concept *disorder of language* and by their dependence on lesions in a fairly well-defined zone of the left cerebral hemisphere. As clinicians began to observe the repeated occurrence of particular patterns of disturbance in speech output, they found that selective deficits at various linguistic levels of organization could be identified.

A selective disturbance at the *phonological* level is manifested in the patient who cannot recover the motor-articulatory code for his words, even though he can hear or read these words with good comprehension, and sometimes even write them correctly. A disturbance at the *lexical* level entails a loss of ability to evoke the contentives (nouns, verbs, adjectives) of normal discourse while preserving the sentence matrix in which these elements should be embedded. This chapter concerns the breakdown at the syntactical level, commonly referred to as *agrammatism*.

Grammatical disorders fall into two clinically opposite categories, both of which have been loosely termed "agrammatic" by some writers. The so-called *motor agrammatic* form of disorder entails the dropping out of articles, connective words, auxiliaries, and inflections, so that grammar may, in extreme cases, be reduced to rudimentary form—the juxtaposition of one- or two-word sen-

[1] This work was supported in part by USPHS grants NSO7615 to Clark University and NSO6209 to Boston University.

237

tences. The other, or _paragrammatic_ variety involves not so much the reduction of grammatical organization as the juxtaposition of unacceptable sequences: confusions of verb tense, errors in pronoun case and gender, and incorrect choice of prepositions. The clear separation of these two clinical varieties will be the first goal of this discussion, since we propose that they entail different mechanisms and that it is primarily the first of these that is properly referred to as _agrammatism_.

Disorders of grammar and syntax, while they are often conspicuous features of the patient's speech disorder, do not occur in isolation from other speech impairments. The motor agrammatic form appears as a frequent symptom of Broca's aphasia—the pattern of effortful, clumsily articulated speech, which is usually present with lesions of the anterior portion of the left-cerebral language zone. In the context of effortful, impoverished speech, the reduction of grammar has been interpreted by some writers (Isserlin, 1922) as economy of effort, much as economizing on cost motivates the terse wording of a telegram. Indeed, output of the partially recovered aphasic so much resembles the wording of a telegram that it is termed _telegraphic speech_.

The paragrammatic speech pattern, in contrast, is a common part of the syndrome of Wernicke's (or sensory) aphasia, and is associated with lesions involving the posterior third of the first temporal gyrus. This syndrome is marked by motorically facile, sometimes excessively rapid speech output. The chief defect is paraphasia, or the unwitting substitution of ill-chosen words and phrases in the stream of speech. Because of the patients' smooth delivery and natural sounding intonation, this speech may seem normal from a distance, where the incongruity of the verbal content may be missed. The misuse of inflections and prepositions and the juxtaposition of grammatically incongruous phrases strikes the listener as totally consistent with the paraphasic character of the patients' speech.

The following speech extracts illustrate the agrammatic and the paragrammatic styles. The first is from a young man of 28 who became aphasic following the ligation of his carotid artery, as treatment for an aneurysm. The prosodic quality of his speech, which can hardly be conveyed in written form, is notable. Each of the word groupings set off by a row of dots or by a period is spoken like a self-contained sentence unit, with a somewhat explosive attack and a falling intonation. In this extract the patient is explaining that he returned to the hospital to have work done on his gums.

> _Ah . . . Monday . . . ah, Dad and Paul Haney_ [referring to himself by his full name] _and Dad . . . hospital. Two . . . ah, doctors . . . , and ah . . . thirty minutes . . . and yes . . . ah . . . hospital. And, er Wednesday . . nine o'clock. And er Thursday, ten o'clock . . . doctors. Two doctors . . and ah . . . teeth. Yeah, . . . , fine._

An extract from a patient of Luria's shows a virtually identical pattern in translation. This patient has a motor aphasia following a bullet in the lower left prefrontal area. Telling about a moving picture, he says:

> *Ah! Policeman . . . ah . . I know! . . . cashier! . . . money . . . ah! cigarettes . . . I know . . . this guy . . . beer . . . mustache, etc.* [Luria, 1970, p. 196].

At a milder level of the same type of disturbance, we find longer word groupings and simple subject–verb–object sentences. In the next extract, a 22-year-old man with a frontoparietal shrapnel wound received in Vietnam is telling something of his past life.

> *My uh mother died . . . uh . . . me . . . uh fi'teen. Uh, oh, I guess six month . . . . my mother pass away. An' uh . . . an'en . . . uh . . . ah . . seventeen . . . seventeen . . . go . . uh High School. An uh . . . Christmas . . . well, uh, I uh . . . Pitt'burgh.*

As an example of paragrammatic speech, the following sample is that of a 70-year-old Wernicke aphasic, who has a thrombosis of a branch of the left middle cerebral artery. In spite of a dense comprehension defect, he responds freely to simple conversation with normal rate and rhythm and a very strong intonational pattern. Asked how he is feeling, he responds:

> *I feel very well. My hearing, writing been doing well, things that I couldn't hear from. In other words, I used to be able to work cigarettes I didn't know how . . . This year, the last three years, or perhaps a little more, I didn't know how to do me any able to.*

PREVIOUS VIEWS OF AGRAMMATISM

Pick (1913) is generally credited with being the first aphasiologist to make an effort to explain agrammatism as a specific disorder. He distinguished between motor agrammatism and the paragrammatism of sensory aphasia, calling the latter *pseudoagrammatism*. Pick viewed agrammatism as a breakdown in a middle phase of the development of a sentence. This development starts with a preverbal awareness of the general intent of the sentence, followed by a schematization of the sentence. This schema includes a vague sense of the melody and word order, although the precise choice of words is not yet made. At the next stage, the actual verbal content is adapted or grammatized to fit the sentence schema. The damaged organism, however, is governed by a "law of economy" that forces the use of "emergency language" (Notsprache) in which all the redundant elements, such as connectives and inflections, are dropped. Thus, for Pick, the economy of telegraphic speech is almost literally the same as that which dictates the abridged wording of a telegram.

Isserlin (1922) supports the view of Pick, holding that the abbreviated utterance of the agrammatic follows from his difficulty in uttering words which, in turn, brings about a basic change in his attitude toward expression. The result is the primitivization of speech, to a form resembling that of the young child, or the adult under great stress. (The hypothesis of economy of effort will be discussed later in this chapter, with contradicting evidence from this reviewer's laboratory.)

Kleist (1934) is the investigator responsible for introducing the term *paragrammatism*, in contrast to agrammatism. Kleist notes that the patient with motor output disorder can say the names of concepts but cannot link them into sentences with connecting words. His term *sentence-muteness* is synonymous with the usual agrammatism. The contrasting form of disorder, or paragrammatism, is marked by confusions in the choice and ordering of words and of grammatical forms, and is well illustrated by the last of the speech samples cited previously.

Goldstein (1948) describes agrammatism as a regular feature of motor aphasia, referring to the tendency of the motor aphasic to revert to the exclusive use of nouns and verbs. In inflected languages, like German, the verb tends to be spoken in the infinitive form. Goldstein recognizes that some agrammatic patients cannot find (or even read or repeat) the small grammatical words— pronouns and prepositions, despite concentrated effort. He does accept the Pick–Isserlin view as valid for a certain number of patients—i.e., that the patient concentrates on the words that are essential for carrying the meaning of the message.

Goldstein calls attention to another syndrome in which the inability to use the little words of grammar is attributed to a loss of abstract attitude. Here, the loss is specifically said to be in the ability to produce these words out of context, by repetition after the examiner. This symptom is characteristic of patients with *central aphasia* (also referred to as *conduction aphasia*).[2] Since the little words occur normally in the context of free speech, these patients do not show the features of motor agrammatism. Goldstein argues that the ability to understand or even repeat these words, isolated from a functional context, requires an abstract attitude. Whatever the merits of this argument, there is no doubt that

[2] Conduction (or "central") aphasia is a syndrome characterized by good auditory comprehension and relatively fluent speech output in which errors of phonemic tranposition or phoneme substitution predominate. Repetition of a spoken model is disproportionately difficult and results in increased effort, more severe phonemic substitution errors, and recourse to paraphrasing.

the fragility of the small words makes them vulnerable to disruption by different mechanisms.

Luria (1970) shares the view of agrammatism described by the preceding observers that this disorder is primarily associated with injury to the anterior speech zone, appearing in the context of *efferent motor aphasia*. This is the precise equivalent of Broca's aphasia, attributed by Luria to wounds in the inferior premotor area (Broca's area). His interpretation of agrammatism, however, introduces the linguistic opposition between nominative and predicative uses of language. Luria suggests that the motor agrammatic has a disturbance affecting the dynamic context of language, which prevents the arousal of the "dynamic schemata of sentences," even after the patient has recovered the ability to pronounce individual words. The linguistic units that are aroused during the patient's effort to speak are isolated words, used in their static, nominative function. The predicative use of language drops out. Consequently, the structure of agrammatic speech is in the form of a string of unrelated words—chiefly substantives, with few, if any, verbs. This difficulty appears even when the patient attempts to repeat sentences spoken for him by an examiner. Obviously Luria's formulation goes well beyond the simplistic idea that agrammatism represents an economy of effort.

Jakobson (1956) is the first linguist to have written extensively on aphasia and to have contributed influential ideas on the nature of agrammatism. Like Luria, Jakobson points to a fundamental opposition between two components of language—the paradigmatic and the syntagmatic. The former relates to the evocation of verbal symbols for specific referents (cf. the "nominative" use of language referred to previously); the latter refers to the sequential aspect of language, manifested in grammatical relationships. A breakdown in the word-finding (paradigmatic) aspect of language is referred to as *similarity disorder*, while a breakdown of the grammatical sequencing (syntagmatic) aspect is referred to as *contiguity disorder*. Thus the motor agrammatic has a contiguity disorder. Contiguity disorder is defined, however, in a sweeping and, probably, overinclusive fashion to include all acts of sequential programming of linguistic units, from the level of the phoneme upwards. In this way, Jakobson suggests, one can reconcile the difficulty that the motor agrammatic has in stringing phonemes together into words and stringing words together into grammatical units. This generalization would be more convincing if one found, clinically, that articulatory sequencing difficulties varied closely with grammatical ones. In terms of clinical fact, however, these two elements of Broca's aphasia have considerable autonomy from each other. It is probably safer to consider the articulatory and the grammatizing systems as independent, but both commonly vulnerable to a lesion in the anterior speech zone.

Treating contiguity disorder in its reference to the syntactic level, Jakobson proposes that rules governing relationships between words are lost, and with them those morphemes (e.g., prepositions, inflections, conjunctions, articles) whose functions depend on grammatical relationships. However, this breakdown does not apply uniformly to all grammatical elements, since some, e.g., terms of subordination, are more vulnerable than the simple coordinating conjunction *and*. As we saw in the first of the sample speeches cited earlier, *and* was the only surviving grammatical element, serving merely to string together the otherwise isolated substantives in the patient's message.

In a later work, Jakobson (1964) develops further the notion of a hierarchy in the resistance of grammatical structures to the effects of contiguity disorder. The fundamental syntactic relationship, he holds, is one of dependence. Grammatical *government* is a more fragile type of syntactic dependency than is grammatical *agreement*. Thus, one would predict more errors of case (e.g., possessive inflection) than of number.

PROBLEMS ENCOUNTERED IN EXPERIMENTAL STUDIES

The major outlines of the concept of agrammatism, as reviewed here, come primarily from clinical observation of free conversation, by neurologists of varying degrees of linguistic sophistication. In many instances, patients who displayed an agrammatic pattern in free conversation would be explored further with a series of grammatical questions improvised to bring out their deficits more dramatically. However, the concept of a controlled experiment to study the linguistic disorders of aphasia does not appear in the literature prior to 1958. Two types of variables need to be brought under control. By manipulating the stimulus variable, it is possible to define more precisely exactly what causes the patient to fail and what permits him to succeed. This approach can be applied to the study in depth of individuals or of small collections of individuals who appear to resemble each other clinically. Clear delineations of the gaps in capacity for linguistic processing and of the hierarchy of difficulty of linguistic operations is necessary to translate the disorder into psychological terms and perhaps, ultimately, into physiological terms.

On the other hand, manipulation of subject variables is equally important. It is not sufficient to demonstrate grammatical failures by experiments on patients who are clinically agrammatic. It is possible that under similar test conditions, failures would be observed in individuals whose spontaneous and reactive speech is grammatically intact. In fact, this latter consideration has proved to be a thorny methodological problem, not yet satisfactorily resolved. The mere fact of requiring a patient to listen to and react to a linguistic problem poses an artificial situation—often a metalinguistic problem. His performance under these conditions may bear little resemblance to what he produces in free conversation. It is easy to show that the agrammatic patient has difficulty in taking the active sentence *The policeman stopped the car* and transforming it into the passive *The car was stopped by the policeman.* It is quite another problem to take a subject with fluent paragrammatic speech and show that he can carry out the same task. In all probability, both patients will fail, and it is impossible to prove that they have failed for different reasons, even though we may have heard the latter patient use passive constructions in his free conversation. How do we know that the agrammatic patient may not have the construction at his disposal under some conditions, even though he does not use it spontaneously?

Thus, the design of structured tasks, aimed at exploring predetermined linguistic operations, is fraught with great difficulties. Often a slight change in wording makes the difference between success and failure. It is usually desirable to provide a framework in which the patient can complete an utterance, rather than pose the task as a point-blank question.

Thus, both the study of free conversation and the design of structured experimental tasks have their shortcomings and their advantages. Both methods have been used in the study of aphasic language.

REVIEW OF EXPERIMENTAL WORK FROM 1958 TO 1975

Studies of Free Conversation

Howes and Geschwind (1962) approached the analysis of aphasic language statistically, by examining the distribution of word frequencies in 5,000-word samples of free conversation, obtained with each of a large group of aphasic subjects. Although they approached the problem without preconceptions as to the existence of "agrammatism," they found it necessary, on both clinical and objective grounds to subdivide their subjects into two groups. *Standard aphasics* were those who had a markedly diminished rate of output. All the motor agrammatics in their sample fell into this group. The second group, *jargon aphasics* included all those with a high rate of output and fluent paraphasic speech. The authors' data permitted an objective comparison of the frequency of occurrence of grammatical function words (termed *interstitials*), which were operationally defined as the 50 most frequent words on the Thorndike–Lorge frequency count.

In a population of 29 standard aphasics and 11 jargon aphasics, there were none who were totally agrammatic, in the sense that they used no interstitial words. In fact, although interstitial words constitute at least 40% of the output of a normal speaker, the most impaired of the standard aphasics used 20% interstitial words in their speech. On the other hand, the jargon aphasics use a higher than normal percentage of interstitial words. In spite of a very large variance within the standard aphasic subgroup, there is a significant difference between the two categories of aphasia in the incidence of small grammatical words.

In spite of this evidence, the authors are very cautious in accepting the impairment of grammatical ability as being proven statistically. They point out that interstitial words may be important in strengthening and emphasizing relationships between contentive words, which may come too rapidly for the listener to grasp fully at normal rates of speech. Under the conditions of reduced rate, the need for relational words may drop out. The relationship between speech rate and incidence of interstitial words is seen in Figure 1.

A second interesting observation (Figure 2) is that when the incidence of personal pronouns is plotted against other interstitial words, there is a steep positive correlation among the more severely telegraphic subjects up to a given point (1400 interstitials/5000 words) after which there is a negative correlation. Most of the standard aphasics fall on the positive side of the slope; all of the jargon aphasics and normal controls fall on the negative side.

Interpreting such data is very difficult without observation of the actual speech context. Thus, the purely statistical approach must be supplemented by structured, process-oriented research. A recent study by Goodglass, Gleason, Ackerman, Hyde, and Green (unpublished) confirms the positive relationship and suggests a mechanism for it. Namely that severe agrammatism is marked by an inability to initiate sentences with unstressed functors, which are typically

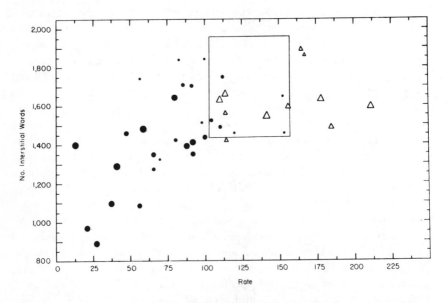

Figure 1 Relation between number of occurrences of interstitial words (ordinate) and average rate of speech (abscissa) for 41 aphasic patients. Jargon aphasics are indicated by open triangles, standard aphasics by solid circles. (From Howes & Geschwind, 1962; reproduced by permission of author.)

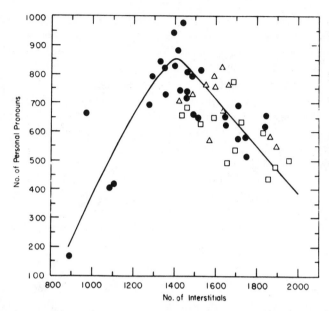

Figure 2 Relation between the number of occurrences of personal pronouns (ordinate) and of interstatial words (abscissa) among the 50 most frequent words in the Lorge Magazine Count. Data are shown for 12 normal subjects (open squares), 11 jargon aphasics (open triangles) and 29 standard aphasics (filled circles). (From Howes & Geschwind, 1962; reproduced by permission of author.)

personal pronouns. In compensation, severe agrammatics substitute noun subjects where the expected target utterance calls for a pronoun. This device disappears in milder forms of agrammatism and is totally absent in normals.

The negatively sloped portion of the curve probably reflects the fact that as sentences grow longer and more syntactically complex, the total number of interstitial words per sentence may increase. At the same time the number of newly started sentences, providing opportunities for personal pronouns, decreases.

Jones and Wepman (1965) applied a factor analytic approach to modified free-speech samples—Thematic Apperception Test stories. They found that the output of normal speakers could be characterized by six factors, based on combinations of word-frequency distribution and part of speech. Their factor *A* was particularly effective in distinguishing the output of agrammatics from that of fluent paragrammatic speakers. Positive scores on this factor are determined by a high incidence of nouns and adjectives and low incidence of subject pronouns, indefinite pronouns, and common verbs. The factor is considered to denote *descriptive specificity*. The agrammatics had relatively high scores, while the other patients had low scores on this factor. Here again, statistical analysis documents and confirms clinical observation. Agrammatic speech underrepresents those components (pronouns, auxiliary verbs) which serve as grammatical fillers, while overrepresenting words of high informational content.

Goodglass and Hyde (1969) took the analysis of free conversation one step beyond the labeling of parts of speech; they coded words for position and grammatical function in the sentence. They then compared 16 agrammatics, 17 fluent paraphasics, and 5 normal controls as to the first word in any utterance. The results strongly resemble those of Jones and Wepman (1965), which were obtained without taking sentence position into account. Severe agrammatics began more utterances with nouns, or with nouns preceded by adjectives or cardinal numbers, than did fluent aphasics. They used only a small fraction of the proportion of initial subject pronouns that are found in fluent aphasic speech. Further, each of these measures approached normal levels in subjects having milder degrees of agrammatism, but showed no variation in the fluent paragrammatic group as a function of severity of the disorder.

Comparison with Child Language

Brown and his associates (see Brown, 1973) found that the order of acquisition in child language was highly predictable for 14 English grammatical morphemes; progressive *ing* ending, third person singular—regular and irregular, copula and auxiliary uses of *be* (contractible and uncontractible), possessive *s*, regular plural *s*, the articles *a* and *the*, the prepositions *in* and *on*. De Villiers and De Villiers (1973) found that the same order that Brown reported on the basis of longitudinal samples of three children was obtained in a cross-sectional sample of 21 children. For any instance in which a morpheme was counted as "present" or "absent," an obligatory context requiring that phoneme had to be identified in the transcript.

De Villiers (1974) raised the question as to whether agrammatic speech might reflect a regression along the same path as the developmental data indicated. Her sample of agrammatic speech consisted of Howes' transcripts of 5000-word free-conversational samples from 14 standard aphasics. The requirement of at least 10 obligatory contexts reduced the number of scalable morphemes in the aphasic sample to 8. It is notable that the two most resistant morphemes, plural *s* and progressive *-ing*, are also the two earliest ones acquired by children. The most vulnerable, third person *s* also happens to be the latest acquired by children. However, between these extremes there are a number of conspicuous reversals in order of difficulty for agrammatics as compared to children. For example, the copula is more stable than the verbal past tense marker for aphasics. This is the reverse of the order of acquisition in children.

Brown had shown that the children's order of acquisition correlates highly with two theoretically derived rankings—one based on the semantic complexity and one on the transformational complexity of the morphemes. Neither of these rankings showed any significant relationship to the order of difficulty for agrammatic subjects. However, there is some indication that frequency of use is related to the order of availability of the morphemes for aphasics.

Criteria for Classification of Patients

The student of aphasic language must begin with the fact that among the syntactic failures said to be typical in agrammatism, some occur, at least occasionally, in all aphasics and even in normals. If we are to try to identify those gaps in syntactic ability which are most typical of agrammatics, we are faced with a circularity in experimental reasoning. The dependent variables are part of the definition of the independent variable. Nevertheless we can start by sorting patients, on the basis of clinical impression, into those who meet the general description of agrammatism and those—equally impaired in effective communication—who are clinically paragrammatic. By comparing their rate of success in individual grammatical operations, it should at least be possible to identify the features that chiefly determined the clinical impression.

Goodglass and Mayer (1958) adopted this approach in the comparison of five agrammatic and five paragrammatic patients, matched in severity, who were required to repeat after the examiner a battery of phrases and sentences, scaled in grammatical complexity. In addition, all subjects were tested with a 10-word synonym-finding test. The following error types discriminated best between the groups: inability to invert subject–verb order in interrogatives of the form, "*Is he here?*"; inability to reproduce a subordinating construction; abortive starts with sentence-opening formulas inappropriate to the target. Omissions and substitutions of grammatical morphemes were more frequent in the agrammatic group, but showed considerable overlap between subject groups. The results were interpreted as showing that the most discriminating feature was the tendency of the agrammatic patient to fall back on the most habituated simple sentence types and ignore those structures which represent more complex syntactic relations. It was felt that this molar level of interpretation was more useful than trying to determine which specific omissions and substitutions occurred more regularly in agrammatic than in paragrammatic speech.

An interesting incidental finding is that the agrammatics surpassed the non-agrammatics in synonym finding, an observation consistent with Jakobson's postulation of an inverse relationship between disorders affecting the syntagmatic and the paradigmatic dimensions of language.

Another approach to finding a criterion to identify the agrammatic subject is given in the work of Goodglass, Quadfasel, and Timberlake (1964). Instead of directly dealing with linguistic operations, they focussed on a byproduct of the syndrome of Broca's aphasia—the halting, effortful quality of the output. Two trained listeners transcribed tape-recorded conversations with 53 aphasic subjects, recording the number of words in each grouping spoken without a pause or hesitation. By tallying all occurrences of word groupings of one word to six or more words in length, they arrived at a plot of the distribution of length of word groups. In order to sharpen the discriminating power of this measure, they dropped out of consideration word groups of 3 or 4, which did not discriminate well, and dealt only with the ratio

$$\frac{\text{5-or-more-word groups}}{\text{1-word + 2-word groups}},$$

which they termed the phrase-length ratio. Figure 3 shows the bar graph resulting from grouping subjects by phrase-length ratios, with a class interval of .15. There is a distinctly bimodal distribution, with a large concentration (25 of 53 cases) falling in the phrase length interval of 0–.15, no cases in the interval .16–.30, and the balance of aphasic cases in the intervals representing phrase length ratios of .31 or more. Ten normal control subjects were also distributed across the class intervals above .31. The short-phrase dominant patients (i.e., those with phrase length ratios below .16) included all the patients in the sample who were clinically classified as Broca's aphasics with agrammatism. Only one paragrammatic patient fell into the short-phrase group. One of the practical

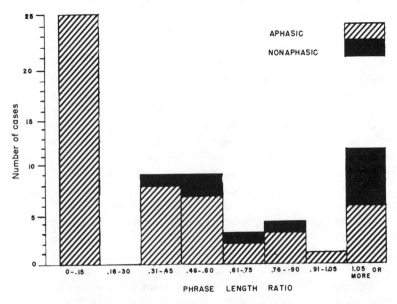

Figure 3 Distribution of 53 aphasic subjects and 10 normal subjects with respect to phrase-length ratio. Normals are represented by blackened portion of bars. (From Goodglass *et al.*, 1964, by permission of *Cortex*.)

benefits of this finding was to provide a simple and relatively objective criterion for classifying aphasics for further linguistic analysis, without the circularity entailed in the Goodglass–Mayer study. More important, however, is that the intimacy of the inverse relationship between utterance length and agrammatism raises the possibility that a common mechanism is responsible for both features. The implications of this relationship are discussed later.

Studies of Morphology

The first reported studies of inflectional endings were carried out on unselected aphasics. They bear indirectly on agrammatism as a selective deficit, to the extent that omissions of inflections are more frequent in agrammatic than in nonagrammatic patients. In the first of these studies Goodglass and Hunt (1958) tested a prediction based on Jakobson's notion concerning the order of stability of grammatical forms. This study is made possible by the fact that the final *s* in English plays three distinct grammatical functions: to indicate possession, to indicate plurality, and in the verb, to indicate the third person singular of the present tense. Moreover, the allomorphic variations /s, z, ə z/ are governed by the same phonological environments in all three functions.

The possessive *s*, as in *John's hat*, represents the syntactic relationship of government—theoretically the most vulnerable; while the plural *s* represents a purely semantic change in the noun, not syntactically dependent on another word in the sentence. Goodglass and Hunt elicited plurals and possessives by means of items of this type:

Examiner reads: *My sister lost her gloves.*
Question 1: *What did she lose?*
Question 2: *Whose gloves were they?*

Under these conditions, the possessive *s* was omitted twice as often as the plural, supporting Jakobson's position.

However, several alternative explanatory principles may be invoked. From the point of view of transformational grammar, formation of the possessive is more complex than that of the plural. Furthermore, the possessive is more redundant than the plural *s* in that its omission produces little or no ambiguity, while the plural *s* is redundant only when there is a preceding quantifier. Alternative explanations involve the sheer frequency of usage of the two forms and the age at which these inflections are acquired by children. Any one of these influences would lead to the prediction of the observed findings. Nothing in our data tells us whether a particular factor or the interaction of several factors accounts for the pattern of aphasic performance.

One of the special features of English inflectional morphology is the contrast between syllabic and nonsyllabic allomorphs of the final *s* /z vs. ə z/ and of the final *d* of the past tense /d vs. əd/. In each case, the syllabic form occurs when the stem ends with a sound identical with or closely related to the inflectional ending. Berko (1958) found that children between ages 4 and 7 often omitted the syllabic form of the inflection, while they had no difficulty with the simple nonsyllabic endings. For example, they were likely to complete an item like *Mother broke a dish and then she broke another one. She broke two . . .* by saying *dish* instead of *dishes*. They behaved as though the final sibilant of the stem gave them the feeling that it was already marked for plurality (or possession, or third-person singular as the case might be). Similarly, the final stop consonant of the verb stem seemed to be sufficient to mark it for past tense. This phenomenon, seen in children, offered the opportunity to test the notion that aphasia produces a regression to earlier modes of using language. Goodglass and Berko (1960) devised a test for inflectional endings that permitted comparison of the syllabic and nonsyllabic forms of all three uses of the final *s* and of the simple past. This test was administered to patients identified by the phrase-length criterion as agrammatic and nonagrammatic, with a curious result. The fluent, nonagrammatic subjects followed the pattern seen in young children, producing a greater number of errors in the more complex, syllabic allomorph of each of the inflections. The agrammatics, on the other hand, showed a paradoxical reversal in that the syllabic allomorphs were the more stable. This finding led to the conjecture that the saliency of the extra syllable provided a special facilitation for the agrammatic patient.

Aside from their differential response to syllabic inflectional endings, agrammatic and fluent aphasics showed the same hierarchy of difficulty among the English inflections: Plurals were again by far the easiest, possessives and third-person singular *s* the most difficult.

Prosody and Grammar

While the agrammatic patient makes more errors than the nonagrammatic on structured tasks, such as the Berko–Goodglass inflectional test, the order of difficulty of various constructions, as tested by sentence repetition, is precisely parallel in the two groups (Goodglass, 1968). Thus, it is particularly encouraging to discover a factor that appears to distinguish sharply between the two patterns. This factor, explored in a series of experiments by the writer and his associates, is the stress or saliency of the opening word in the utterance. A stressed opening word is highly facilitating for Broca's aphasics and of significantly less value for fluent aphasics, who have little difficulty with initial unstressed functors, such as auxiliaries and subject pronouns.

The first evidence in this direction came from an analysis of omissions of initial words in a 40-item sentence-repetition test (Goodglass, Fodor, & Schulhoff, 1967). Of the 40 items, 30 began with unstressed functors and 10 with stressed words. Omissions of unstressed opening words were proportionately more frequent than omissions of stressed words, and this inequality was overwhelmingly determined by the Broca's aphasics. Of the 27 Broca's aphasics, 70% (19) had one or more omissions (see Figure 4), while only 39% (9) of 23 fluent aphasics had any omissions. A Chi square test was significant beyond the .01 level. The two groups were closely equated on a test of repetition span for strings of disconnected words, whether these strings were composed of functors or nouns. Thus, the differential performance on initial functors in a sentence framework had to be attributed to the prosodic factor.

In order to explore further the relation of stress and sentence position to the production of function words, a battery of three-word test sentences was designed in which grammatical form, prosodic stress pattern, and initial versus medial position of the target grammatical function word were systematically varied. A series of 114 sentences administered for repetition was first given to a single patient who presented a severe and classical form of agrammatism.

The most dramatic finding is the omission rate of 70% (49/70) for initial functors versus 14% (6/44) for medial functors placed between two stressed words. The important thing to note is that this effect was virtually independent of grammatical complexity. Declaratives, interrogatives, imperatives, and conditional phrases showed no significant difference in success rates within a given

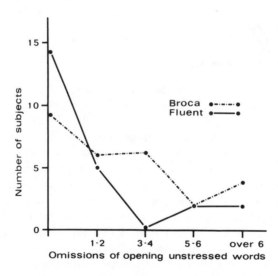

Figure 4 Distribution of Broca's and fluent aphasics with respect to number of omissions of initial unstressed functors in Sentence Repetition Test. (From Goodglass *et al.*, 1967, by permission of the American Speech and Hearing Association on behalf of the *Journal of Speech and Hearing Research*.)

prosodic framework. The one exception to this rule was the prepositional phrase (e.g., *in the house*), which was reproduced intact 5 of 7 times, in spite of the prosodic pattern of two initial unstressed words. Five of the grammatical words (*if, is, the, can, it*) occurred in both initial and medial positions. In 39 initial occurrences, these words were omitted 31 times; in 26 medial occurrences, there was but a single omission. Thus, it is clear that the observed effect cannot be explained by the use of different words in initial and medial positions.

An incidental but significant observation is that the stressed initial auxiliary of the negative interrogative (e.g., *Can't he dance?*) was retained more than half the time, while the corresponding unstressed form (*Can he dance?*) of the simple interrogative was omitted in 9 of 11 tries. Thus, it appears that the influence of prosody overrides that of grammatical complexity (negative vs. simple interrogative) insofar as the production of functors is concerned.

The assumption that all prosodic effects are confined to agrammatic patients proved incorrect when a similar but briefer battery of 48 sentences was administered for repetition to a group of 10 Broca's aphasics and 12 fluent aphasics. Both groups found the functor in the medial position extremely resistant to deletion. However, the functor in initial unstressed position was again selectively difficult for the agrammatics (mean scores of 5.7 out of 12 versus 7.7 by fluent aphasics). Moreover, the agrammatics omitted the unstressed auxiliary of the simple interrogative significantly more often than the corresponding stressed form of the negative interrogative. For the nonagrammatics, the difference between the two was insignificantly small.

Stress, Saliency, and Agrammatism

The observation of the almost invariant association of agrammatism with a halting output is now supplemented by the finding that the first word of each utterance is perferentially a stressed word—usually a contentive. In fact, the often repeated observation that agrammatism entails the omission of small grammatical words must be modified to say that these words drop out as sentence openers, but survive relatively well in medial positions.

A comprehensive formulation has been proposed by the author (Goodglass, 1962, 1968) which links these observations. It is proposed that a basic feature of Broca's aphasia is the increased difficulty of mobilizing the speech output system, which requires a stressed element to put it into action. Once an utterance is underway, it may carry along some unstressed syllables, but the resistance of the system prevents the production of more than a few words between pauses. Another way of putting it is to say that the response threshold for the speech output system is raised and requires an emphatic or salient element in the message to overcome the elevated threshold and begin the flow of speech. The result is that the speaker cannot get going with an unstressed functor and he soon learns to focus on the first salient element—usually a noun.

By the same mechanism, the functor following the initial stressed word can be carried along in the utterance.

What constitutes "saliency" for the purposes of this model? There is no basis at present for anything but a first-order intuitive definition of saliency as the resultant of informational load, affective tone, and increased amplitude and intonational stress. Does this mean that the agrammatic speaker has a complete model of his intended utterance and accepts or rejects the first word after having determined whether it is an unstressed functor? Such a conception would be out of touch with all clinical and experimental observation. Patients do occasionally (but rarely) indicate their knowledge that they have omitted an initial functor, under special test conditions. In one instance, a patient who omitted the opening *if* of a conditional clause wrote the letters *I–F* and pointed as though to indicate the word belonged in the sequence he had produced. Further, as we have noted, the agrammatic patient can reproduce short strings of disconnected functors as well as the nonagrammatic. His behavior in the sentence repetition task, however, is as though the unstressed word simply were not there. This is true both in repetition tasks, as described above and in free conversation. During repetition, of course, he may have access to a memory trace of the prosodic pattern that he has just heard from the examiner. Our hypothesis is that he embarks on the act of speech with an emphatic, effortful set. The unstressed opening word is simply not activated.

Clinical observation tells us further, that while agrammatism is almost invariably associated with an interrupted, effortful delivery, the reverse association is not necessary. Agrammatism is a common but not universal feature of aphasia due to injury of the anterior speech zone. There are aphasic patients who produce effortful, halting speech, but maintain the grammatical integrity of their sentences. These individuals may have more difficulty in writing than in speech. Their output shows that they are able to conceptualize the grammatical structure of a complex sentence and to realize it, word by word. These patients have virtually a purely articulatory disorder. They can, with deliberate effort, evoke and produce words that have an unstressed position in the normal intonational pattern of the sentence. Thus it appears that effortful and halting delivery is a necessary, but not a sufficient, condition for agrammatism. Nor does it explain all features of the disorder, such as the reduction to elementary grammatical sequences or holophrastic expressions and the loss of inflectional endings. However, a number of studies reveal a variety of devices that serve the common end of providing the agrammatic patient with a salient opening word. These will be reviewed below in the section on compensatory devices in agrammatism.

Relation of Agrammatic to Standard Syntax

If the agrammatic patient "lost" certain rules of syntax in an orderly fashion, one might expect to be able to derive his residual grammar from a corpus of his speech. Depending on the severity of the agrammatism and the method of collecting data, diametrically opposite conclusions can be drawn on this score. Taking the free conversation of a very severe agrammatic, Myerson and Goodglass (1972) found that the totality of his grammar could be summed up in transformational terms by a short list of rules. For this patient a "sentence" might consist of either a noun phrase or a verb phrase, optionally followed by an adverb. In some instances, an adverb of place constitutes an utterance. A noun phrase consists of a noun, optionally preceded by a cardinal number (but never by an article or adjective) with the plural marker *s* added to the noun when necessary. Verb phrases consist of verb stem with *ing* as an optional ending, often followed by an adverbial particle (e.g., *falling down*). While there is no instance of verb plus object, an object noun is, in one instance, followed by the verb: *"wood, uh handling"* for *handling wood*. An alternative type of verb phrase consists of a predicate adjective, without expression of the subject or copula. Adverbs of place and time are sometimes juxtaposed (e.g., *one day, Canada*) or at times precede or follow either a noun phrase or a verb phrase. In no instance is the sequence subject plus verb or verb plus object expressed. However, two elements may be joined by *and*.

Question and negative transformations are handled by primitive mechanisms—the question by intonation only and negation by the juxtaposition of *no* either before or after the term to be negated (e.g., *New York, no*). This level of agrammatism illustrates Jakobson's definition, in that virtually all syntactic rules are abolished.

Quite another concept concerning the regularity of syntactic rules in agrammatism emerges from a study by Goodglass, Gleason, Bernholtz, and Hyde (1972). In this case, the patient was less severely impaired and the method of data collection was different. Instead of relying on free conversation, the authors aimed at eliciting a set of 14 predetermined constructions by means of a structured story sequence to be completed by the patient. For example, to elicit a *yes–no* question one of the sequences was:

Mother sent Johnny upstairs to wash and brush his teeth. When he came down, she wondered if he had brushed his teeth. So she asked . . . what?

By this procedure, virtually every construction was elicited from this patient at least once in a series of attempts. For example, the future auxiliary *will* was produced once in 17 attempts and the final *s* marking the third-person singular appeared twice in 43 attempts. These and other instances made it clear that reliance on an inventory of constructions derived from free conversation did not do justice to the patient's latent ability to use English syntactic rules. Further, the patient's persistent efforts at self-correction almost always were in the direction of standard English grammar. It was obvious that he was not agrammatic through economy of effort, nor was he functioning with a set of simplified grammatical rules. Instead, he was constantly striving to recapture the syntactic rules of the language and capable, to a considerable extent, of judging what sounded right and what did not, even though he might ultimately fail in his expression.

A precisely similar observation was made by Ludlow (1973) in a longitudinal study of recovery of syntax by a group of Broca's and fluent aphasics. She found that the order in which syntactic structures reappeared in the speech of the recovering aphasic (whether Broca's or fluent) correlated highly with the frequency of these structures in a sample of normal speech. There was no evidence of a simplified language system at any point or of changes in the rule system of language during recovery—merely of access to a larger number of more complex forms.

Thus, the persistent difficulty in recovering certain forms, which forces the patient to use grammatically incomplete utterances, may create the illusion that he has developed a simplified grammar. In the case of a severely impaired patient, such as the one described by Myerson and Goodglass on p. 254, it is possible to enumerate his full grammatical repertory, but this need not imply that he judges his utterances to be correct within a system of his own. The opposite extreme is to hold that competence is unimpaired in aphasia and that the patient merely suffers from a performance deficit. This notion is made especially attractive by the observation that, as speech returns, the patient's old knowledge of grammatical rules returns spontaneously to some degree, depending on the extent of the recovery. In any case, his syntactic repertory does not have to be relearned. Moreover, with proper cues, as Weigl and Bierwisch (1970) point out, many performances can be at least temporarily "deblocked"—again testifying to their latent availability.

Unfortunately, this effort to reify the construct of "competence" by recourse to certain features of aphasia is as faulty as the notion that the aphasic develops his own simplified grammatical system. The aphasic suffers from an injury of the organic substrate that mediates his recall and recognition as well as his production of language. True, passive recognition of "what sounds right" is generally more spared than the capacity to produce speech, but even this passive recognition has never been shown to be complete, nor is it accompanied by the ability to indicate how an ungrammatical utterance needs to be corrected. Moreover, as aphasia becomes more severe and eventually total, or "global," even passive recognition of correct grammar is lost, and any semblance of "competence" disappears. We surely cannot accept the notion that competence is intact as long as there is a shred of evidence that certain grammatical forms are recognized or sporadically recovered, only to disappear in total when aphasia becomes global. There remains the mystery of why recovery follows the path of previous linguistic knowledge, but recovery is not likely to be explained as the removal of a block to the access to performances that had always been perfectly stored.

Order of Difficulty of Grammatical Forms

Several studies by this writer (e.g., Goodglass, 1968) as well as by Ludlow (1973) failed to reveal differences in the hierarchy of difficulty of grammatical constructions, in comparisons between agrammatic and fluent aphasics. For both groups of aphasics, the sequence of recovery is best predicted by the frequency of occurrence of these forms in speech (Ludlow, 1973). However, the slope of recovery of these constructions is very different for the two categories of patients. Ludlow's recovering agrammatics, for example, reacquired the auxiliary *do*, the copula, and the simple prepositional phrase only a week or two later, on the average, than her fluent aphasics. Other forms, however, such as the use of a relative clause, the perfect form of the verb, and the passive voice occurred within the first month for most of the fluent aphasics, but in the third month for the recovering agrammatics.

Further details on the order of difficulty of syntactic forms in agrammatism comes from an extension of the Story Completion technique of Goodglass *et al.* (1972) described earlier. The results from testing eight agrammatic subjects indicate clear gradations in difficulty, with the transitive and intransitive imperative most readily available, followed closely by adjective plus noun, number plus noun, WH question, and simple declarative. The most difficult were the future and the combination of two adjectives plus noun (e.g., *a big white house*). The earlier finding on the difficulty of initiating sentences with unstressed functors was confirmed in every instance where either articles or personal pronouns could be compared in initial versus medial position. The combination verb plus object (noun or pronoun) was much more stable than subject plus verb—i.e., subjects were omitted more frequently than objects. This phenomenon is not caused merely by the tendency to omit subject pronouns. Rather, it appears that the agrammatic patient may have difficulty crossing the constituent boundary between noun phrase and verb phrase. This difficulty is illustrated by one of the severe agrammatics who iterated *"baby . . . baby"* a dozen times before being able to conclude the sentence with *"Baby cry"* (for *The baby cries*). The subject plus verb versus verb plus object discrepancy was much greater among four severe agrammatics (25% difference in omission rate) than among four mild agrammatics (4% difference).

Comprehension of Grammar

Does agrammatism imply both an encoding and decoding disorder for the significance of grammatical forms? Clinical impression leads one to say that motor agrammatism is primarily an output deficit and that the patient understands perfectly well the relationships that he does not express. This impression, however, is not based on rigorous evidence. Much of what the agrammatic fails to express can be inferred from the context. For example, in the third speech sample, cited on page 239, a patient wishes to say, *Six months after I became fifteen, my mother died*. He expresses this complex idea by the sequence, *"My mother died; me fifteen; six month; my mother pass away."* It is clear that the patient has the underlying concept of the time-dependent relationship between his mother's death and his fifteenth birthday, and this concept is conveyed to the listener without the expression of the verb tenses or the conjunction *after* linking the two clauses.

Zurif, Caramazza, and Myerson (1972) undertook the comparison of agrammatics and normals with respect to the perceived relationship among the contentive and function words in 50 sentences—5 each of 10 different grammatical types. The approach taken was to present the patient with cards, on which appeared all possible sets of three words from a given sentence. As each card was presented, the patient was asked to select the two words most closely related, based on their use in the original sentence. The reference sentence remained exposed before the patient and was periodically repeated for him, to assure that he remained oriented to the task.

On the basis of the subjects' selections, a matrix was developed on which a procedure termed *hierarchical cluster analysis* was performed. This yielded subjective phrase structure trees for each sentence type, which could be compared for Broca's aphasics and normal controls. The trees derived for normal controls were closely similar to the linguistically derived phrase markers. That is, the elements within the noun phrase were tightly linked with each other, as were those within the verb phrase. Articles and demonstratives were most closely linked with their respective nouns. The copula, when used as an auxiliary verb in the passive, was linked to the past participle; as a main verb, it was linked with the predicate adjective.

In contrast, the remarkable feature of the agrammatic subjects was their tendency to ignore articles, pronouns, copulas, and similar unstressed function words. As a result, their perceived clusters often violated the constituent boundaries. The contrast between the normal and agrammatic sorting is illustrated in Figure 3 of Chapter 8, by Zurif and Caramazza, in this volume, which displays the aphasics' perception of the sentence *The man was hurt* as though it read *man hurt*. Thus, in their response to perceived sentences, Broca's aphasics showed a tendency to ignore unstressed function words, in a fashion very similar to the pattern observed in their speech. The heightened semantic value associated with prepositions, however, made them quite different from unstressed articles. Initial WH (who, where, etc.) words were also included in the aphasics' sortings, while the copulas were ignored.

These results are both similar to and different from the findings for expressive language reported by Goodglass *et al.* (1967). As in the latter authors' work, unstressed functors tend to be omitted by agrammatics. However, such omissions occur regardless of initial versus medial position of function word. The fact remains that the agrammatic does not demonstrate understanding of syntax, and the postulate of normal syntactic competence in Broca's aphasia is brought into serious question.

One of the most frequently cited features of aphasia is the tendency to confuse small grammatical words—specifically to confuse pronouns by person and gender and to confuse prepositions with each other. These errors are frequently seen in paragrammatic speech of fluent aphasics; they were also observed in the Story Completion performance elicited in the the authors' laboratory. It does not appear that these errors are discriminative for motor agrammatism.

Another group of grammatical errors is cited by Luria (1970) under the heading of "logico-grammatical disorder." These errors can be characterized as difficulties with reversible relationships in which the direction of the relationship is marked by a grammatical morpheme—usually a preposition. For example, if two objects—e.g., a comb and a pencil—are on the table, the instruction *Touch the comb with the pencil* depends on the word *with* to determine which object is the instrument. A similar reversible relationship is polarized by the morpheme *s* in the expression *My brother's wife*—is it a man or a woman? Obviously, if the expression were *My brother's hat* the semantic nonreversibility would make the final *s* morpheme redundant.

Even prepositions with more distinctive semantic value, such as *before* and *after* are vulnerable when they designate the direction of a relationship between two actions. This type of confusion can be elicited by yes–no questions of the type *Do you put on your stockings before your shoes?* and *Do you put on your shoes after your stockings?* No difficulty is encountered when the question is put in the form *Do you put on your shoes first, then your stockings?* Thus, it is clear that patients preserve perfectly their knowledge of temporal sequence but have trouble decoding such a relational concept out of the information in a single word.

It can be readily shown that aphasics who fail in these logico-grammatical tasks may have good comprehension of difficult vocabulary items and carry out multiple commands well. Selective comprehension disorders of this type, according to Luria (1970), are associated with parietal-lobe lesions. They are not necessarily part of the syndrome of expressive agrammatism.

Compensatory Features in Agrammatism

The performance of agrammatic patients makes it clear that their difficulty does not lie so much in the conceptualization of relationships between terms, as with the recovery of the grammatical forms for their expression. The devices that they use to express themselves, with their limited grammatical repertory, may take specific idiosyncratic forms in individual patients. Among the compensatory mechanisms that can be categorized are the following:

1. *Agrammatic concatenation.* The substitution of a series of juxtaposed simple sentences or fragments for a complex single sentence. A good example of this device can be seen in the sample of agrammatic speech cited on page 239.

2. *Use of direct for indirect discourse.* Since indirect discourse generally entails the use of a main and subordinate clause, the agrammatic commonly bypasses it in favor of direct quotation. For example, the Story Completion Test (Goodglass *et al.*, 1972, p. 210) attempts to elicit an embedded construction with the following item. *The children were being too noisy and mother was annoyed, so she told* [them to be quiet] . . . . Typical of the agrammatic response was *She told them, "Little kids, be quiet, man!"* In some instances these patients will simply name the speaker and follow with a direct quote, as in the text of a play.

3. *Substitution of a stressed for an unstressed opening word.* Earlier cited data was interpreted as indicating the difficulty that patients experienced in beginning an utterance with an unstressed functor. This interpretation is strengthened by observation of a number of devices used by these patients to place an emphatic word in the first position. One device used commonly in the Story Completion Test is the introduction of a vocative (e.g., *Johnny, you brush teeth?*) as a sentence opener where it was not called for in the target sentence. Not only were vocatives used more frequently by severe than by mild agrammatics, but the few used by normal controls were appended to the sentence, rather than being used as opening words.

A second illustration of the insertion of a stressed sentence initiator is the substitution of nouns where the target sentence normally calls for a subject pronoun. This alternative to the complete omission of the pronoun was also several times more common in the case of severe than of mild agrammatic subjects. As an example of a highly individualized adaptation, one of our patients habitually used the expression *this guy* in place of the initial word *he*. Thus, his repetition of the test sentence *He works here* was, *"This guy work here."*

In agrammatism, as in other problems of aphasia, the careful analysis of substituted utterances reveals the nature of the deficit for which they compensate. When such compensatory devices become stereotyped, they give the impression that the patient has developed his own grammatical system. This impression, however, is illusory.

REFERENCES

Berko, J. 1958. The child's learning of English morphology. *Word, 14,* 150–177.
Brown, R. 1973. *A first language.* Cambridge, Mass.: Harvard University Press.

De Villiers, J. G. 1974. Quantitative aspects of agrammatism in aphasia. *Cortex, 10,* 36–54.

De Villiers, J. G., & De Villiers, P. A. 1973. A cross-sectional study of the development of grammatical morphemes in child speech. *Journal of Psycholinguistic Research, 2,* 267–278.

Goldstein, K. 1948. *Language and language disturbances.* New York: Grune & Stratton.

Goodglass, H. 1962. Redefining the concept of agrammatism in aphasia. *Proceedings of the International Speech and Voice Therapy Conference, 12th, Padua,* pp. 108–116.

Goodglass, H. 1968. Studies on the grammar of aphasics. In S. Rosenberg & J. Koplin (Eds.), *Developments in applied psycholinguistics research.* New York: Macmillan. Pp. 177–208.

Goodglass, H., & Berko, J. 1960. Aphasia and inflectional morphology in English. *Journal of Speech and Hearing Research 10,* 257–262.

Goodglass, H., Fodor, I., & Schulhoff, C. 1967. Prosodic factors in grammar—Evidence from aphasia. *Journal of Speech and Hearing Research, 10,* 5–20.

Goodglass, H., Gleason, J. B., Bernholtz, N. A., & Hyde, M. R. 1972. Some linguistic structures in the speech of a Broca's aphasic. *Cortex, 8,* 191–212.

Goodglass, H., & Hunt, J. 1958. Grammatical complexity and aphasic speech. *Word, 14,* 197–207.

Goodglass, H., & Hyde, M. R. 1969. How aphasics begin their utterances. In H. Goodglass, *New measures of aphasic symptom variables.* Unpublished Progress Report, USPHS Grant NSO7615, Boston.

Goodglass, H., & Mayer, J. 1958. Agrammatism in aphasia. *Journal of Speech and Hearing Disorders, 23,* 99–111.

Goodglass, H., Quadfasel, F. A., & Timberlake, W. H. 1964. Phrase length and the type and severity of aphasia. *Cortex, 1,* 133–158.

Howes, D., & Geschwind, N. 1962. Statistical properties of aphasic speech. Unpublished Progress Report, USPHS Grant M-1802, Boston.

Isserlin, M. 1922. Uber Agrammatismus. *Zeitschrift für die Gesamte Neurologie und Psychiatrie, 75,* 332–416.

Jakobson, R. 1956. Two aspects of language and two types of aphasic disturbances. In R. Jakobson & M. Halle (Eds.), *Fundamentals of language.* The Hague: Mouton. Pp. 55–82.

Jakobson, R. 1964. Towards a linguistic typology of aphasic impairments. In A. V. S. De Reuck & M. O'Connor (Eds.), *Disorders of language.* London: Churchill. Pp. 21–46.

Jones, L. V., & Wepman, J. M. 1965. *Grammatical indicants of speaking styles in normal and aphasic speakers.* Publication No. 46. Chapel Hill: University of North Carolina Psychometric Laboratory.

Kleist, K. 1934. *Gehirnpathologie.* Leipzig: Barth.

Ludlow, C. L. 1973. The recovery of syntax in aphasia. Paper presented at the Academy of Aphasia, Albuquerque, October.

Luria, A. 1970. *Traumatic aphasia.* The Hague: Mouton.

Myerson, R., & Goodglass, H. 1972. Transformational grammars of three agrammatic patients. *Language and Speech, 15,* 40–50.

Pick, A. 1913. *Die agrammatischen Sprachstorungen.* Berlin: Springer-Verlag.

Weigl, E., & Bierwisch, M. 1970. Neuropsychology and linguistics: Topics of common research. *Foundations of Language, 6,* 1–18.

Zurif, E., Caramazza, A., & Myerson, R. 1972. Grammatical judgments of agrammatic patients. *Neuropsychologia, 10,* 405–417.

8

Psycholinguistic Structures in Aphasia: Studies in Syntax and Semantics[1]

Edgar B. Zurif

BOSTON UNIVERSITY SCHOOL OF MEDICINE
AND BOSTON VETERANS
ADMINISTRATION HOSPITAL

Alfonso Caramazza

THE JOHNS HOPKINS UNIVERSITY

The work described in this chapter does not present a strict account of the relation between language and the brain. Neither language use nor brain function is sufficiently understood for that. Instead, all we have attempted is a preliminary taxonomic investigation: a classification of the effects of localized brain damage on some aspects of human cognition exemplified both in language use and in a sensitivity to language structure.

In what follows, it will become apparent that our studies have been influenced by linguistic theory. Superficially, this is shown by our reliance on the structural descriptions of generative grammar to organize our data; more significantly, by our implicit acceptance of the notion that relatively abstract structures are required if we are to capture important generalizations of language behavior. However, along with most cognitive psychologists, we have also attempted to treat language as a conceptual and communicative system in which the extralinguistic world is not excluded. In this respect, given the very evident concern of the aphasic to communicate, and his partial capacity to do so, we focus on the nature of the knowledge and the strategies that this capacity entails. Put differently, our aim in the following studies is to determine what tacit knowledge of verbal communication is spared and what disrupted under conditions of brain damage.

[1] The preparation of this chapter and the studies reported in it were supported by NINDS Research Grants 11408 and 06209 to Boston University School of Medicine.

261

SYNTACTIC FORM AND SEMANTIC FUNCTION

Language Knowledge in Aphasia: Linguistic Intuitions of
Agrammatic Aphasics

There are multiple levels of language knowledge, including the linguist's ability
to articulate the rule system. Understandably, however, the clinician is usually
only concerned with language knowledge at the most practical and intuitively
obvious level—specifically, with the patient's ability to use the language: to
follow verbal commands, as one example, and to answer questions, as another.
And at this level, the patient with anterior brain damage often presents a rather
striking dissociation between what he seems to know about his language and his
capacity for expressive speech. Specifically, many patients with anterior lesions
in the left hemisphere, although not all by any means, often seem to enjoy
virtually intact comprehension for commands and questions and seem to know
what they want to say, yet at the same time produce an output that is distinctly
agrammatic and nonfluent. This agrammatic output, typified by the infrequent
usage of most function words such as articles, auxiliary verbs, and prepositions
and by the relative deletion of inflectional forms, persists even when the patient
begins to recover a considerable speaking vocabulary (Cohen & Hécaen, 1965;
Geschwind, 1970; Goodglass, 1968; Green, 1970).

For some investigators (Weigl & Bierwisch, 1970), the dissociation between
speech and knowledge has been taken as a literal manifestation of the linguistically defined competence—performance dichotomy. They propose that the
speaker/hearer has an abstract mental equivalent of a linguistic grammar, and
that, whereas brain damage disrupts the mechanisms of performance that make
use of this mental grammar, the grammatical knowledge, itself, remains unaffected. In a superficially different version, the distinction between spared knowledge and impaired performance is upheld, but the performance disruption takes
a more neurologically focused form (Lenneberg, 1973). In this view agrammatic
production is attributed to a problem of motor coordination of the speech
muscles; the strain of speaking being so great that the patient confines himself to
the barest minimum of words, and as a consequence, to an agrammatic or
telegraphic style. Still, since even in this second scheme comprehension is seen as
relatively unimpaired, the two versions are thus essentially the same: Speech is
affected by anterior brain damage; language knowledge remains relatively intact.

Given the important practical consequences of this distinction, we sought to
determine more about the anterior aphasic's tacit knowledge of English. Obviously, from his capacity to comprehend speech, it appears he has some knowledge remaining of his language. What we wanted, however, was a more explicit
demonstration of the nature of this knowledge: We wanted the aphasic to
become somewhat of a linguist; not, of course, to attempt an explicit formula-

tion of rules, but simply to provide us with some of his intuitions about grammatical relations.

In order to assess such metalinguistic performance, we chose a task that circumvented the aphasic's problems in dealing with language as it unfolds in real time. The specific task we settled on was one in which patients were asked to judge how the words in a written sentence went best together in that sentence, and to indicate these judgments, not by speaking, but simply by pointing at the written words they wanted to group together. The result for each sentence was a word-relatedness matrix from which a phrase structure tree was induced by the application of an algorithmic scaling procedure. This analysis permitted an estimation of the subjective organization of words in a sentence. Specifically, it revealed the extent to which aphasic patients operate on the basis of an implicit hierarchical organization when performing word-relatedness judgments. Also, it allowed us to determine the degree of correspondence between subjective and linguistic phrase markers. In sum, our search was for a syntactically rich rule system, itself unaffected by brain damage, but served by disrupted performance mechanisms. Put less contentiously, the question was whether or not agrammatic aphasic patients have more information about permissible structures than would be expected from their speech.

The three anterior-brain-damaged patients used in this first study were all of the classical Broca's type (Goodglass & Kaplan, 1972): They all produced dysprosodic, nonfluent speech characterized by a striking agrammatism. Yet, upon clinical examination, all were considered to have relatively intact comprehension and all could read aloud. Obviously, their efforts at reading involved awkward articulation and literal paraphasias, but when their attention was focused on each word of a sentence, they invariably read the sentence correctly, including its grammatical formatives (Zurif, Caramazza, & Myerson, 1972).

Four neurologically intact patients served as control subjects.

The patients were tested individually; they worked with a variety of sentences (Table 1); and the procedure was as follows.

First, since each sentence was presented visually, we had to make sure the patient could read. Second, we had to train the patient for the metalinguistic task of grouping the words of a sentence into clusters. Some structure was

TABLE 1 Sentence Types and Associated Examples

Declarative intransitive: *The baby cries.*
Declarative transitive: *The dog chases a cat.*
Passive (truncated): *The man was hurt.*
Comparative: *The girl was taller.*
WH question: *Where are my shoes?*

provided by adopting the procedure of triadic comparisons. In this procedure, all the possible three-word combinations from a sentence were presented, one at a time, to the patient. For each triad, the patient was required to choose the two words that he felt went best together in relation to the sentence from which they were taken.[2]

This scheme, which has been detailed more fully elsewhere (Zurif *et al.*, 1972), proved quite successful. The aphasic patients as well as the neurologically intact controls mastered the procedure without too much difficulty, willingly carried the task through, and, as it turns out, produced consistent clusters.

For each of the constructions shown in Table 1, the data were organized in the form of a relatedness matrix, the cell entries in the matrix representing the number of times a patient had grouped each word with the other. In order to generate sufficient data there were five semantically distinct sentences exemplifying a given surface structure. But for the purpose of analysis, we ignored possible semantic factors and treated the five examples of each construction as equivalent. Following the computation of inter-word relations on an individual-subject basis, we formed group matrices for each sentence type. This was done simply by adding together the entries in the three aphasic-patient matrices and by adding together those in the control-patient matrices. All subsequent analyses were carried out on the group data.

Our selection of a hierarchical clustering scheme (Johnson, 1967) to analyze these data was motivated by the assumption that the triadic comparisons would be influenced by the hierarchically organized structure of the words in the sentence (Levelt, 1970; Martin, 1970). That is, in accord with Levelt's (1970) suggestion, we expected the degree of subjective relatedness of any two words in a sentence to be a function of the height of the theoretical linguistic node dominating the two words in the sentence.

The procedure, itself, simply consists of working backwards from the similarity matrix to induce the hierarchical organization that may have influenced the

[2] The three words forming each triad were arrayed on one card in a triangular fashion that maintained the left-to-right order of the words in the sentence. For example, if the triad consisted of words two, four, and five (from a five-word sentence), word two appeared in the lower left-hand corner of the card, word four in the center just above the midline of the card, and word five in the lower right-hand corner. This left-to-right array was intended to emphasize the fact that the words were from the sentence, yet, at the same time, it permitted the grouping of nonadjacent words. However, to reinforce the notion that our concern was with how the words were related in the sentence, the examiner often repeated the sentence to the patient between triad presentations. It should also be noted that the patient was forced to consider the three possible combinations within each triad before pointing to the two words he wanted to group together. This precaution was taken in order to minimize the role of subvocal rehearsal in the comparison process. That is, we wanted the groupings to reflect the patients linguistic intuitions and not to reflect his agrammatic production.

sortings. It is an iterative procedure. At each stage the two words that are most closely related are merged and treated as a single entry in a new and smaller matrix. A visual account of this sequence of mergings takes the familiar form of a tree graph.

In an ideal hierarchical ordering the two items merged at each stage should be equally related to the other words of the matrix. But in practice, when two words are clustered together they are not often equidistant to a third. Even if we accept the strong assumption that word-relatedness judgments are mainly determined by syntactic structure, there is still likely to be some nonhierarchical noise. That is, semantic factors, idiosyncratic associations, and left-to-right visuospatial strategies can be expected to influence the judgments of relatedness. The problems arise, then, of first, determining whether in fact we are dealing with a hierarchical structure, and second, assigning a numerical value to express the strength of the relationship between a merged unit and the other words of the sentence.

Following Miller (1969), our solution has been to carry out two parallel cluster analyses: one always based on the stronger relations between the cluster and the other words of the matrix [minimum (distance) method], the other always based on the weaker relations [maximum (distance) method]. To the extent that subjects have been sorting on the basis of an implicit hierarchical structure, there should be no difference between the solutions. In practice, if the minimum and maximum solutions produce only numerical differences of the form of different strengths of the same clusters, the data are accepted as being at least minimally compatible with a hierarchical organization. If they yield striking qualitative (topological) differences, such an assumption is usually not supported, although Miller (1969) claims that it ultimately becomes a matter for individual judgment.

Fortunately, we were not faced with these problems of interpretation. For the most part, both the normal and aphasic subjects sorted on the basis of an implicit hierarchical organization. When the minimum and maximum methods of analysis were applied to the group-relatedness matrices, they typically produced qualitatively identical trees. Furthermore, the group trees did not obscure inter-subject differences; neither the aphasic patients nor the controls varied among themselves.

Figures 1 to 4 show subjective phrase-structure trees for several of the constructions. Since the minimum and maximum solutions were qualitatively the same, only the minimum method outcomes are displayed.[3]

---

[3] It will be noted that the phrase-structure trees for the control group in this study are uniformly more compact than those for the aphasic patients. This represents nothing more than the fact that there were four control patients and only three aphasic patients—thus, the group trees for the normal subjects were based on more data (more relatedness judgments) than those for the aphasic patients.

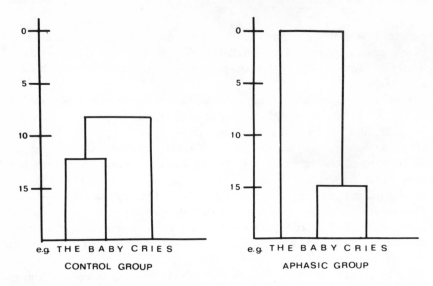

Figure 1 Declarative intransitive frame: induced phrasemarkers for control group and aphasic group. (Vertical axis represents frequency of inter-word groupings.) (From Zurif, Caramazza, & Myerson, 1972. By permission of Pergamon Press.)

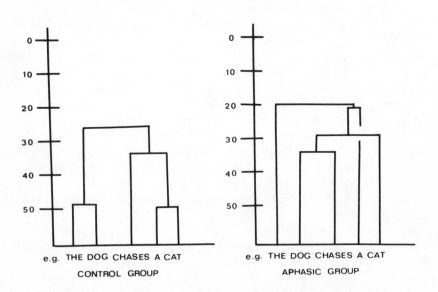

Figure 2 Declarative transitive frame: induced phrase markers for control group and aphasic group. (From Zurif, Caramazza, & Myerson, 1972. By permission of Pergamon Press.)

266

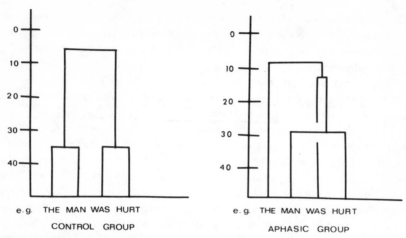

Figure 3 Passive frame: induced phrase markers for control group and aphasic group. (From Zurif, Caramazza, & Myerson, 1972. By permission of Pergamon Press.)

As shown in the figures, the relatedness judgments of the control subjects were constrained by the surface syntactic properties of these four sentences, while those of the aphasic subjects were not. The normal group generated tight linkages between articles and their nouns, which resulted in well-organized subject and object noun phrases. In contrast, the aphasic patients operated on these sentences by coupling the content words together, ignoring the functors to a noticeable degree, and thereby violating the linguistic unity of the noun phrases.

tight link

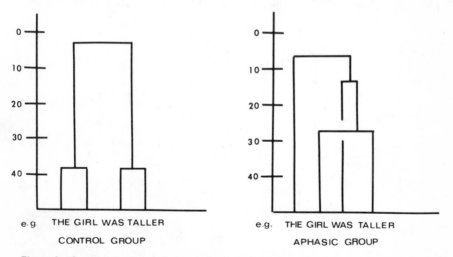

Figure 4 Comparative frame: induced phrase markers for control group and aphasic group. (From Zurif, Caramazza, & Myerson, 1972. By permission of Pergamon Press.)

The aphasic patients did not disregard the functors altogether, however. Note that on each of the trees but one (the declarative intransitive), articles and other functors were clustered at greater than zero. But what is of greater importance is that when the aphasic patients did attend to the functors, they sorted them in a less focused manner than did normals: For example, relative to the control subjects, they more often grouped articles with verbs or with other articles, and correspondingly, less often grouped articles with their appropriate nouns.

For one frame, however, the WH question (Figure 5), the aphasic patients did manage to construct a stable noun phrase marked by a function word. Specifically, they linked the functor preceding the final noun with that noun, the functor in this case being either a demonstrative pronoun as in *Who are these people?*, or a personal pronoun marked for the possessive as in *Where are my shoes?*. The tightly organized noun phrase generated by the aphasic patients on this frame stands in contrast to the weak article–noun relations, and suggests that the patients are at least somewhat sensitive to gradations of lexical meaning within the class of function words.

But aside from this one exception, the aphasic patients appeared to have a firm knowledge only of the bare essentials necessary to communicate an idea. They were unable to compute full structural descriptions for the sentences.

How justified are we in reaching this conclusion? Obviously, the evidence does not provide a direct line to whatever it may be that is termed linguistic competence. At best we are dealing with a type of metalinguistic performance about which little is known (Bever, 1970; Brown, 1973), and the problem is to distinguish between what the patient could not do and would not do. One possibility, therefore, is that the task was insufficiently refined to elicit all that

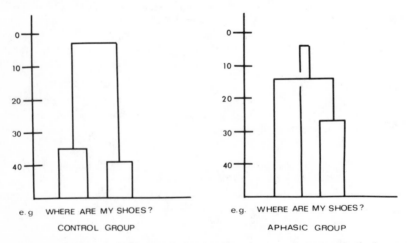

Figure 5   WH question frame: induced phrase markers for control group and aphasic group. (From Zurif, Caramazza, & Myerson, 1972. By permission of Pergamon Press.)

the aphasic patients know about the surface forms of sentences. Not being linguists, these patients may simply have been more concerned with the possibilities of reference than with syntactic niceties. Articles and the like, although heeded, may have been discarded in favor of a search for more basic semantic relations.

But this seems a rather unlikely possibility. First of all, as we have already mentioned, the agrammatic patients did not just ignore articles, they also clustered them inappropriately, or at least inappropriately in terms of the syntax of each sentence. Second, it is probably more than coincidence that the aphasics' unvocalized intuitions captured the regularities of their own speech behavior in such precise fashion. Finally, there is the performance of the normal subjects to consider. However compelling the semantic factor might have been for them on this task, they still did not overlook the structural signals of referential specificity. And they, too, after all, are not linguists.[4]

A more likely possibility, we think, is that anterior brain damage exerts the same pattern of disruption to the underlying knowledge of language as it does to speech. Moreover, for brain damage to exert such similar effects at two different levels, it would seem also that the judgmental processes underlying linguistic intuitions are not independent of the specific psychological operations that produce and interpret utterances. That is, whether the adult aphasic is required to focus on his language as a system independent of any actual use or is simply required to use the language, many of the same mechanisms seem to be called

---

[4] We have recently completed an experiment that firms up the conclusion that agrammatic aphasics do not just ignore articles because they are irrelevant, but rather that such aphasics are relatively incapable of understanding the article's modulating role in a sentence. The paradigm was such that the inclusion of articles in utterances either hindered or aided the specification of an intended referent. As an example, subjects were faced with an array of three figures: a white circle, a black circle, and a black square. In some instances they were given instructions that were entirely appropriate to the situation: "Press *the* white one," or "Press *the* square one." In other instances, the definite article employed in the instruction was inappropriate: "Press *the* black one," or "Press *the* round one," when, as in the example, there were two objects that were black and two objects that were round. Anomic aphasics showed significantly longer response latencies on those trials in which the referent was inappropriately specified by the article than on those trials in which the article was appropriate. This was so even though the anomic aphasics were unable to verbalize the anomaly. Further analysis revealed that the longer reaction times reflected a process whereby the anomic subjects restructured the situation as did neurologically intact subjects so that they chose the object which shared its non-named feature with the ineligible member. Faced with a white circle, black circle, and black square, and asked to press *the* black one, they chose the black circle, that is, the black one of the two circles. In contrast, the Broca's agrammatic aphasics gave no indication of processing the article, whether it was appropriate to the situation or not. Their latencies did not differ between those trials in which the use of the article was anomalous and those trials in which the definite article was appropriate. Nor did they restructure the situation for the inappropriate utterances as did the anomic aphasics (Goodenough, Zurif, Weintraub, & von Stockert, 1975).

upon and similarly constrained. In this view, then, the particular effects of anterior brain damage are not limited to speech; nor are these effects due to an economy of effort. Rather, at no level does the agrammatic patient appear fully capable of processing the small words of language, especially those words that function as syntactic markers for implicit grammatical structure.

Language Knowledge in Aphasia: Gradations of Sensitivity to Functors

As Brown (1973) has pointed out, functors form a class of words that can be characterized only by a partial but imperfect convergence of many features. They occur more frequently in normal adult language than do contentives (e.g., Thorndike & Lorge, 1944). Also, unlike contentives, their numbers are few and additions are not readily admitted. Yet, in terms of their semantic value, functors cannot be lumped together—either formally or in relation to the agrammatism resulting from anterior brain damage.[5] While none of the functors make reference in any very straightforward sense, they do differ among themselves in terms of their informational value. For example, the contrastive use of the definite and indefinite articles somehow seems less referentially important than the distinction between the possessive pronouns, "my" and "your." Compared to the articles, the pronouns seem to carry greater defining qualities; to be less redundant, in other words.

Admittedly, it is an intuitive distinction, but it is one to which aphasic patients may be sensitive, or at least partially so. In the preceding study, recall that the aphasics, although unable to use articles as structural signals, could mark the one noun phrase in which the functor was either a possessive or demonstrative pronoun.

Aside from this one exception, however, the prospect of the aphasic's graded sensitivity to functors remained undetermined. Accordingly, together with others at the Boston Aphasia Research Center (Zurif, Green, Caramazza, & Goodenough, 1975) we decided to use the relatedness judgment paradigm again. But this time we chose sentences that, in contrast to one another, would permit functors to vary somewhat more systematically in terms of their contribution to meaning.

In addition, we wanted to explore a wider range of comprehension deficit in aphasia, and so have greater leeway in which to chart the relation between knowledge of language at the level of metalinguistic judgment and knowledge signaled by comprehension for ongoing speech. It should be emphasized here

---

[5] In this context (as well as from the results to follow) it should be apparent that our use of the term functor is for descriptive convenience only, and that we are not assuming a tidy distinction between grammatical formatives and content words.

that anterior brain damage does not always produce the classical Broca's syn-drome in which nonfluent, agrammatic speech coexists with relatively intact comprehension. In our experience there are many patients with anterior lesions who present not only agrammatic output but also comprehension defects that are sufficiently noticeable to disallow the clinical judgment of "relatively intact" comprehension.

We, therefore, studied three groups of patients. One group consisted of three anterior-brain-damaged patients who showed the classical Broca's-aphasia syn-drome. Specifically, these patients, like those in the previous study, were agrammatic, yet showed good verbal comprehension on the Boston Diagnostic Aphasia Test (Goodglass & Kaplan, 1972).[6] The second group also consisted of three anterior-brain-damaged, agrammatic patients; they, however, showed com-prehension impairments on the Boston Diagnostic Aphasia Test. These patients will be referred to as *mixed anterior aphasics*. Also, we included a group of three neurologically intact control patients matched to the aphasics on age and education.

The procedure, including the use of triadic comparisons, was the same as that of the preceding study. Our initial fear that the agrammatic group with compre-hension problems would not be able to cope with the metalinguistic demands of the task proved groundless. They could and they did. Perhaps, as Bever (1970) puts it, the capacity to reflect upon language is as basic as the capacity to understand that words have reference.

In any event, the characteristics of the sentences we chose are as follows. First, to assess more carefully differential sensitivity to articles and possessive pro-nouns, we placed both types of functors in comparable sentence frames (1 versus 2).

(1)   *The dog chased a cat.*
(2)   *My dog chased his cat.*

Second, we constructed a rather unusual frame in which to place a definite article:

(3)   *He hates the burning rubbish.*

Insensitivity to the article in this frame leads to a sentence that is, at best, ambiguous, but more likely to be interpreted as *He hates to burn rubbish.* Finally, we assessed relatedness judgments for prepositions using sentences such as 4 and 5.

---

[6] The Boston Diagnostic Aphasia Test contains a section devoted to the assessment of auditory verbal comprehension. Patients had to obtain a z-score rating of at least +.5 on this section to be considered as having relatively intact comprehension. Moreover, this assess-ment had to be consistent with the results of an independent clinical work-up.

(4)   *Gifts were given to John.*
(5)   *Gifts were given by John.*

The results appear as tree graphs in Figure 6 to 11. To anticipate what follows, the implications of the data are clear on two counts: (*1*) Once again, aphasic patients are shown to have no better control of functors on the level of metalinguistic judgment than in spontaneous speech; and (*2*) such control as is shown, seems determined more by the semantic force of a functor (if it has such force) than by a fully computed syntactic representation. At least this appears to be the case for patients with relatively preserved comprehension. These patients, although insensitive to the structure-marking role of a functor (e.g., articles), seem to have a somewhat firmer grip on functors that encode semantic relations (e.g., prepositions).

Examining the three tree graphs in each of Figure 6 and 7, one sees that the relatedness judgments of the two agrammatic groups do not differ from each

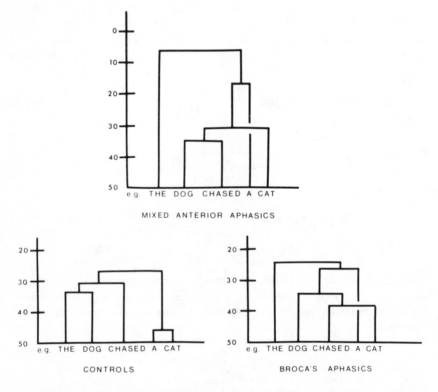

Figure 6   Sensitivity to articles: induced phrase markers for control group, Broca's aphasics, and mixed anterior aphasics.

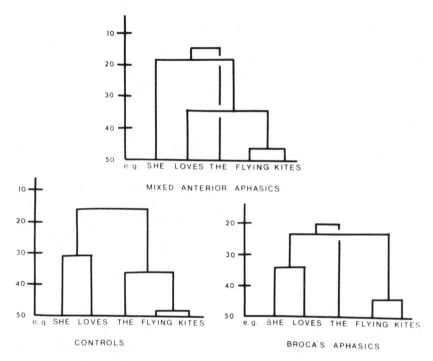

Figure 7 Sensitivity to articles: induced phrase markers for control group, Broca's aphasics, and mixed anterior aphasics.

other, but that they contrast with the normal group's relatedness judgments. Furthermore, the discrepancy between the aphasic and neurologically intact groups is very much in line with that shown in the first study. The agrammatic patients, whether or not presenting clinically intact comprehension, again coupled the content words together and either ignored the articles or sorted them on a relatively unfocused basis.[7] In comparison, the control patients incorporated the articles appropriately, generating compact subject and object noun phrases.

One additional detail of the control group's tree graph on the declarative transitive frame warrants consideration: specifically, the fact that the typology of the tree reveals a ((subject verb) object) organization. Although this finding is not altogether typical (see initial study), it is not an uncommon one (Levelt, 1970; Martin, 1970; Zurif et al., 1972). Perhaps ordinary language users view

[7] Actually, the minimum and maximum solutions did not produce qualitatively identical trees for the Broca's group on either frame. But the main point—that Broca's aphasics are less able than normals to focus on the use of the article as a determiner—was not invalidated.

sentence structure somewhat differently from linguists. Or, as has been suggested (Levelt, 1970), the outcome may be determined in part by the degree of transitivity of the verb, full transitives (e.g., *hit*) being more likely to cluster with the object noun phrase, and middle verbs (e.g., *eat*) with the subject noun phrase. We did not control for these transitivity differences in either triadic comparison study. And while the possibility is an interesting one that deserves further investigation, it is not part of the main concern of this paper.

As shown in Figure 8, the substitution of possessive pronouns for articles on the declarative transitive frame had no effect on the relatedness intuitions gathered from the mixed anterior aphasics. These patients with comprehension problems were no more successful at marking noun phrases with pronouns than they were with articles. The Broca's aphasics offer somewhat of a contrast in this respect in that they generated tighter links between the pronouns and their nouns. Still, their sensitivity to the pronouns on the comparison task was far less than that shown by the neurologically intact subjects, and for that matter, far less than what would have been predicted on the basis of the first study (Figure 5).

In the first study, the Broca's aphasics integrated the possessive pronoun into a compact noun phrase (Figure 5). In the second, this neat hierarchical representation broke down (Figure 8): The possessive pronoun signaling the object noun phrase was no more tightly linked to the noun than was the verb; and the relation between the subject noun and its possessive pronoun marker was even less compact. Also there was evidence of hierarchical instability on the declarative transitive frame in the second study. The maximum solution of the Broca's relatedness judgments on this frame (not shown here) did not fully conform to the minimum solution. Topological inversions occurred for the two weakest relations, one of which involved the initial possessive pronoun.

To our minds there is a good reason for the differences shown on the two studies; that is, for the less focused use of possessive pronouns in the second study and the corresponding hierarchical instability. It derives from the fact that in the triads involving possessive pronouns, the alternatives in the second study were more semantically compelling than those in the first study. Specifically, in the first, the alternative to be sorted was often an informationally useless copula, whereas in the second, it was a referentially important transitive verb. That is, the informative value of the competing triadic elements increased from the first to the second study, and we think it is this change that blurred the Broca's focus on the semantic role of possessive pronouns.

This suggestion, it should be noted, is not intended to imply that agrammatic patients are really sensitive to functors on this task, but ignore them in favor of semantic salience. This argument was considered earlier in relation to the relatedness judgments involving articles, and it was dismissed then because we

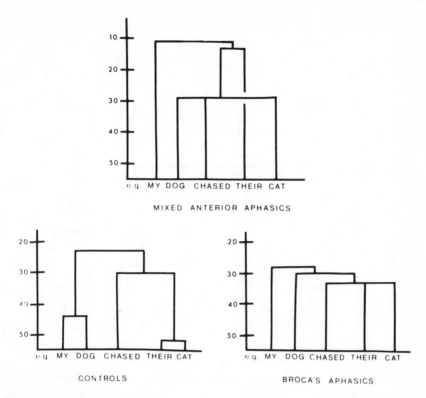

Figure 8 Sensitivity to pronouns: induced phrase markers for control group, Broca's aphasics, and mixed anterior aphasics.

had found that the aphasic patients were not only ignoring articles but also sorting them incorrectly in terms of their syntactic function (see also Footnote 4). The same also holds for their sorting of possessive pronouns. That is, the pronouns, too, were often inappropriately sorted, being clustered with the verbs of the sentences, for example, or with the other pronouns in the sentences. The notion we are left with at this point, then, is that Broca's aphasics are not much more than minimally aware of the difference in semantic value between an article and a pronoun.

The Broca's metalinguistic control of prepositions, however, is shown to be relatively well-preserved in the relatedness judgment task. Furthermore, the Broca's sensitivity to prepositions on this task is not shared by those aphasics who have obvious comprehension problems. As the frames in Figures 9 and 10 indicate, only the aphasic patients with relatively preserved comprehension performed like the neurologically intact controls. Specifically, both the control

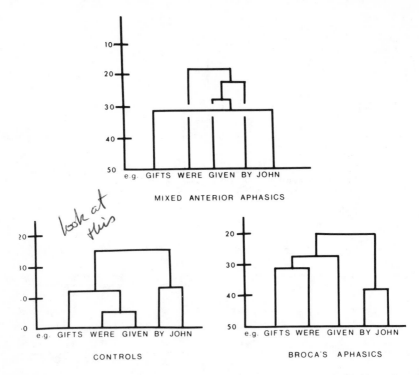

Figure 9 Sensitivity to prepositions: induced phrase markers for control group, Broca's aphasics, and mixed anterior aphasics.

group and the Broca's group formed a strong link between the noun and the preposition that signaled its semantic role. In contrast, the mixed anterior aphasics did not form this link.

It should also be noted that it is solely the informational value of the preposition to which the Broca's aphasics were sensitive. When the functor *to* appeared as an infinitival complementizer, the Broca's responses were no longer appropriately focused (Figure 11).

The distinction between articles and, to some extent, pronouns, on the one hand, and prepositions, on the other, is a semantically important one. For the most part, articles, as Brown (1973) puts it, serve to tune or modulate the meaning associated with a noun in the sense that they signal what the noun refers to as being either specific or nonspecific, a distinction that is often quite apparent on nonlinguistic grounds. Admittedly, pronouns are more likely to have independent semantic content than are articles; yet, in the sentences used here it may be argued that the role of the pronoun was also predominantly a modulating one. The prepositions, in contrast, did more than simply modulate

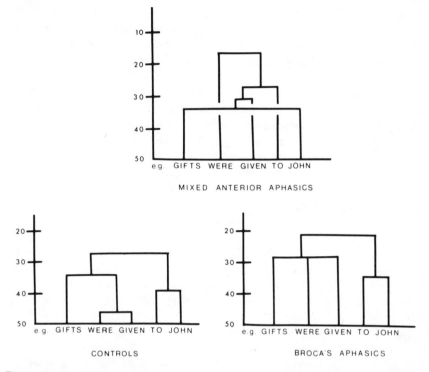

Figure 10 Sensitivity to prepositions: induced phrase markers for control group, Broca's aphasics, and mixed anterior aphasics.

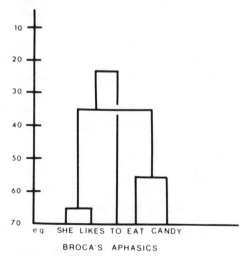

Figure 11 Sensitivity to marking of the infinitive: induced phrase markers for control group, Broca's aphasics, and mixed anterior aphasics.

meaning. Rather, they served to encode semantic relations between a noun phrase and a verb; that is, they served to index the semantic role of the noun phrase (Fillmore, 1968). Thus, in the above examples (Figures 9 and 10), only the prepositions signal that *John* is in one instance the agent of the action, and in the other instance, the recipient of the action.

What the data suggest, therefore, is that a Broca's aphasic, although insensitive to determiners, will be able to process those functors that typically play an important role in encoding semantic relations. This notion implies, of course, that the Broca's aphasic retains a knowledge of the basic semantic roles noun-phrase constituents can assume, even though, as mentioned above, he is no longer fully able to process the determiners that mark such constituents.

Language Knowledge and Triadic Comparisons: A Summary

Obviously not all aspects of performance on the relatedness judgment tasks can be viewed as a reflection of the underlying organization of the aphasic's language, or, for that matter, of the normal adult's language. There were undoubtedly some nonlinguistic intrusions, mostly of a visuospatial nature. But a review of the results will show that, on balance, such factors played a minimal role.

Had the aphasic patients been restricted to a nonlinguistic, visuospatial strategy, the strength of the interword clusters would have been solely a function of their spatial proximity in the surface structure of the sentence. Furthermore, the clusters would have been approximately of the same strength. That this did not occur is obvious.

Consider also that the weak links between functors and contentives did not lessen the semantic cohesion of most of the sentences, at least not of the simple sentences. If anything, the weak links served to frame the essential semantic relations, leading in a sense to unadorned deep structural outputs. In addition, where the functor did play a critical semantic role, it was more fully acknowledged. And what is particularly interesting is that it was acknowledged only by those aphasics one would expect to be capable of doing so—namely, the agrammatic aphasics judged to have relatively preserved comprehension.

The evidence, when taken all together, suggests to us that the aphasic patients viewed the task as a linguistic one, and that they were able to reflect upon and use whatever language knowledge was spared to them in the service of the task.

Metalinguistic evidence on its own, however, can be rather disquieting. In the preceding tasks, for example, the important determinants of the aphasic patients' performance seemed to be semantically based. However, even given reasonable assurance that some knowledge of semantic relations has been spared, there remain the problems of determining how such knowledge fares in the face of increased syntactic complexity and in the face of decreased semantic constraints. There is also the question of how dependent such knowledge is upon the luxury of not working in real time. In what follows we present some data bearing on these questions.

The Aphasic Patient's Ability to Comprehend
Center-Embedded Sentences

In a study not yet fully completed we have been assessing the ability of aphasic patients to comprehend center-embedded sentences. Our primary motivation for choosing such sentences was a practical one: They are complex enough to tap a wide range of perceptual strategies involved in language comprehension (Bever, 1970); yet, in some forms—specifically those we used—simple enough to be comprehended by six-year-old children (Caramazza, 1974). What we were interested in was the aphasic's ability to recruit various perceptual strategies: strategies that draw upon semantic plausibility, for example, or lexical strategies such as attending mostly to verbs (Healy & Miller, 1970); in short, strategies that by their very nature, are neither represented in formal grammar, nor directly observable on a word-relatedness judgmental task.

The center-embedded sentences we used were all picturable and of the type:

(6) $\qquad$ S $\quad$ NP$_1$ (S$_1$) VP$_1$
$\qquad\qquad\qquad$ S$_1$ $\quad$ NP$_2$ VP$_2$

They differed, however, in terms of semantic constraints. One type of sentence was semantically nonreversible. That is, sentences of this type combined lexical items in a unique manner, as in example 7:

(7) $\qquad$ *The apple that the boy is eating is red.*

In this sentence, it is clearly the case that the boy is doing the eating and not the apple. A second type of sentence (8), in contrast, did not have any differential semantic constraints.

(8) $\qquad$ *The boy that the girl is chasing is tall.*

Both boys and girls can chase and both can be tall. Finally, we provided well constructed but situationally improbable center-embedded sentences such as 9.

(9) $\qquad$ *The boy that the dog is patting is fat.*

This sentence is syntactically well-formed; but it clearly deviates from what we know about the real world.

Filler sentences were also used. These were declarative constructions of the type shown in 10.

(10) $\qquad$ *The boy is eating the red apple.*

In the sense that there are two underlying propositions to this type of sentence, it may be claimed that the level of semantic complexity has not been drastically reduced.

The sentences were delivered by the experimenter at a conversational pace with normal intonation. While listening to the sentence the aphasic had before him two pictures: one, a correct depiction of the sentence; the other, an incorrect pictorial representation. His task was to point to the correct picture.

The incorrectly pictured alternative took one of four forms. Consider, in this respect, the following example (11):

(11)   *The cat that the dog is chasing is black.*

One type of incorrect alternative focused on the complement or, more specifically, on the predicate adjective of the matrix sentence: The cat was pictured as brown rather than black. (To avoid confusion the dog was always pictured in a color that was neither brown nor black.) A second type of contrast incorrectly depicted the verb: The dog was pictured as biting rather than chasing the cat. A third, combined the first two contrasts; that is, the dog was shown as biting the cat, and the cat was drawn in brown. And a fourth incorrect alternative showed a subject–object reversal: The black cat, not the dog, was pictured as doing the chasing. To reiterate, however, these four types of alternatives were not all presented at the same time. Rather, for each sentence there was the correct alternative and only one of the above incorrect contrasts.

At this stage we have only tested four patients with anterior brain damage; and while all four present nonfluent, agrammatic speech, only two can be considered to have relatively intact comprehension. In addition we have tested two patients with left posterior damage who present the syndrome of Wernicke's aphasia.

The speech output of Wernicke's aphasics is in striking contrast to that found in patients with anterior lesions. It is a "fluent" output marked by facility in articulation and many long runs of words in a variety of grammatical constructions (Goodglass & Kaplan, 1972). However, unlike agrammatic speech it is strikingly devoid of information; indefinite noun phrases such as *thing* are substituted for the expected noun, and when a noun with specific reference is chosen it is often the wrong one (Goodglass & Kaplan, 1972). Further, and again in contrast with the anterior aphasic, the Wernicke's comprehension is usually impaired.[8]

Despite the very evident differences between the effects of anterior and posterior damage, however, the pattern of results that has emerged thus far on this test is the same for the two groups. Admittedly, more patients have to be assessed before any firm conclusions can be reached, either about the similarity

---

[8] Not surprisingly, their metalinguistic abilities are also limited. They were unable to cope with the demands of the triadic comparison task.

of the anterior and posterior patients' performance, or, indeed, about the performance of each group individually. Yet, since the pattern of results is rather compelling, we present the data as they stand.

First, every patient tested has shown better comprehension for the filler sentences than for the center-embedded sentences. This is what we should expect, given that filler sentences are the only ones in which word order serves as a reliable semantic heuristic.[9]

Second, the aphasics' limitations appear to be clearly defined in terms of the cues they can focus upon. On those trials in which the incorrect alternative presented a double contrast with the correct picture, that is, when both the verb and complement contrasted, the aphasic patients performed at their most accurate. When the verb and complement were tested separately, however, the verb appeared to be the more potent cue. The aphasic patient was less likely to err when the alternative incorrectly depicted the verb than when it incorrectly depicted the complement.

What is especially interesting is that the aphasic patients performed poorest when faced with a subject–object contrast. Given the degree of communicative competence spared by anterior brain damage, one would have expected that at least the agrammatic patients would notice the change in grammatical roles of the noun phrases. They did not perform well, however, and further analysis reveals some of the factors responsible. When performance on the subject–object contrast was analyzed as a function of semantic constraints, it emerged that the inability to notice subject–object reversals was more apparent for semantically reversible sentences (64% correct) and most marked for sentences that violated real-world knowledge (50% correct). When faced with alternatives that offered subject–object reversals for the semantically constrained sentences, the aphasic patients performed at a relatively higher level of accuracy (71% correct).

Actually, the relative importance of semantic factors in determining performance revealed itself differently in the four contrast conditions. For the verb and/or complement contrast conditions, since the contrasts were codified in lexical items (e.g., black versus brown in the complement contrast; bite versus chase in the verb contrast), subjects did not have to rely on whether or not semantic constraints were imposed on the sentence as a whole. As a result, performance across the different sentence types (i.e., constrained versus reversible, versus implausible) differed less markedly in these conditions and was uniformly better than in the subject–object contrast condition.

Thus, at this stage of our study, it would appear that when the aphasic patient cannot rely on the heuristic of word order and cannot rely either on differential semantic constraints or on lexical semantics, his comprehension

---

[9] It should be remembered that the anterior aphasic patients we tested with the center-embedded sentences do not all have relatively preserved comprehension.

ability is dramatically reduced. These experimental facts seem to apply as much to the agrammatic patient, who has some knowledge of semantic roles and relations, as they do to the more dramatically impaired posterior aphasic patient. At this point, neither group appears able to compute syntactic relations independently from semantic content.

Grammatical Knowledge in Aphasia: Some Conclusions

The preceding studies suggest that when syntactic features are absent on the level of spontaneous speech they are unlikely to be preserved at other levels of language. Thus, while articulatory problems are undoubtedly important determinants of nonfluency in anterior aphasia, the concomitant agrammatism, in itself, does not appear to be the result of an economy of effort. Rather, the agrammatism appears to reflect a true language limitation.

Moreover, such sensitivity to structure as is shown in comprehension seems to be heavily reliant on either lexical or general semantic constraints. As we have found with center-embedded sentences, when these factors are unavailable and when the semantic roles of noun phrases are complexly stated in the surface form of an utterance (i.e., when there is departure from an actor–action–object sequence), the anterior aphasic's comprehension becomes dramatically reduced. It would appear, then, that agrammatic patients might be capable of processing contentives and certain functors in terms of the semantic roles they establish in a sentence, but probably only to the extent that these roles and relations can be made out on independent grounds—that is, on the grounds of word meaning and semantic plausibility.

There is, of course, the possibility that aphasic patients rely unduly on semantic and lexical constraints because of an impaired immediate memory span. But while this may serve as a partial explanation, it is certainly not the complete one. For when the aphasic patients' metalinguistic performance is also taken into account, agrammatism appears to be best explained as a limitation upon language capacity (see also Cohen & Hécaen, 1965; Parisi & Pizzamiglio, 1970; Whitaker, 1970).

LEXICAL SEMANTICS

If the evidence discussed in the preceding section can be said to prove any point, it is that when processing an utterance the aphasic patient is much more dependent on the semantic properties of individual lexical items and upon the plausibility of their surface arrangement than is the normal speaker. The structure of lexical meaning in aphasia, therefore, assumes considerable importance; and it is this issue that forms the concern of most of the remainder of this paper.

Subjective Lexical Organization in Aphasia

As with most aspects of language in aphasia, vocabulary disruption is usually never total, except in the most severely striken (e.g., Wyke, 1971). A moderately impaired anterior aphasic typically understands at least the referential part of word meaning. And although his search through memory for a word may be slower than normal, whether in spontaneous speech or in a formal naming test, the outcome is more than infrequently successful. Even when the naming response is not correct, as is often the case with posterior aphasics, it is usually better described as out-of-focus with the target rather than random (e.g., Lhermitte, Derouesne, & Lecours, 1971; Pizzamiglio & Appicciafuoco, 1971). Correspondingly, when the posterior aphasic is tested for word comprehension, his mistakes are usually restricted to the broad semantic category from which the item is taken (e.g., The aphasic might point to his ear, when asked to point to his nose).

Given these well-established clinical forms of word comprehension and production, especially the pervasive fact of word-finding difficulty, it seemed appropriate to determine how the subjective lexicon might be organized under conditions of brain damage.

A number of recent studies have explored some of the possible forms lexical organization might take in the normally intact brain. For the most part, such studies incorporate the notion of an internalized data structure based on semantic features (e.g., Miller, 1967, 1969, 1972; Quillian, 1968). These features, typically mapped as single words (+ *male*) or phrases (+ *who is married*), are taken to represent the lexical information available to the language user. They are meant to capture the concepts in a word as well as to define the range of semantic relations that a word can enter into with other words. Yet, aside from questions concerning the possible organizations of such feature representations in memory and methods for their discovery (e.g., Henley, 1969; Miller, 1969; Perfetti, 1972; Rips, Shoben, & Smith, 1973), there remains the issue of whether or not the act of retrieving words in ongoing speech actually exploits componential information of this kind (Zurif, Caramazza, Myerson, & Galvin, 1974).

This last problem lends a double significance to the task of representing the parameters of lexical storage in aphasia. In the first place, determining whether or not word-finding difficulties can be traced to restrictions in lexical knowledge and organization is of interest in its own right. But more than this, if such underlying restrictions are demonstrated in aphasia, they also can serve as a test of the psychological validity of semantic feature representations in general. That is, to the extent that taxonomic schemes are actually of relevance to the study of word retrieval and production, one would expect the contrast between normal and aphasic word-finding abilities to be mirrored by some sort of meaningful contrast in subjective lexical organization.

The exploration we undertook of how aphasics organize verbal concepts again made use of the triadic comparison procedure. This time, however, rather than having the patients assess the relatedness of words within a sentence, we required them simply to point to two of three common nouns that they felt were most similar in meaning. It was assumed that in order for a patient to settle on two words in any one triad, he had to ignore some of their distinguishing features while attending to others. By analyzing the resultant clusters, we could assess which features had been ignored and therefore indirectly discover which features are central to the subjective lexicon.

As Miller (1972) has pointed out, it is difficult to evaluate semantic features thus obtained without using a comprehensive sample of words. This problem, however, was somewhat mitigated for us. Our intent was not to systematize the subjective lexicon; rather, it was to determine the relation between word-finding difficulties and lexical organization in aphasia. Accordingly, we chose only a small number of words—12—as a case study (Table 2). These words were concrete nouns of relatively high frequency (Thorndike & Lorge, 1944), with the further restriction that the features contained in them could be cast into a hierarchical relation. Thus, not every word in our array has a value for every feature and certain features dominate others. For example, those items that are classified as + *animal* may be further classified as + *fish* or + *reptile*; that is, the

TABLE 2 Stimuli[a]

Noun	Definition given to subject
MOTHER	A woman who has given birth to a child.
WIFE	A woman who is married.
COOK	Someone who prepares food.
PARTNER	Someone who shares something.
KNIGHT	A man who has been honored for his bravery.
HUSBAND	A man who is married.
SHARK	A fish that is scary and vicious.
TROUT	A fish that is harmless and good to eat.
DOG	An animal that is usually kept as a pet.
TIGER	An animal that is ferocious.
TURTLE	An animal called a reptile that has a bony shell.
CROCODILE	An animal called a reptile that is long-tailed and vicious.

[a]Note: The decision to use *animal*, rather than *mammal*, as the superordinate, or general semantic feature in DOG and TIGER was an intuitive one. It should be noted, however, that people generally use these two features synonymously (Rips *et al.*, 1973).

feature, *animal* dominates the latter two. But those items that are classified as ¬*animal* are undefined for either *fish* or *reptile*. It should be noted that the most central or dominating feature of the word array presented in Table 2 can be viewed as being ± *human*. That is, six of the nouns are names of humans and six are not. We felt that unless the patients could capture this feature in their comparisons, there would be little likelihood of any useful data emerging from this procedure.

Of the ten aphasic patients who carried out the triadic comparisons for the 12 nouns, five had anterior damage and five, posterior damage. The patients with anterior lesions were clearly of the classical Broca's type. And of those with posterior lesions, four presented the Wernicke's aphasia syndrome. The fifth posterior patient, although also showing a "fluent" empty output, could comprehend speech at a somewhat better level than is typical in Wernicke's aphasia and this set him apart from the other posterior patients. In addition, five male patients chosen from nonneurological wards served as control subjects. Before testing began, the patients were screened on their ability to read the 12 nouns and to recognize from an array of choices each of the definitions when read aloud.

With respect to formal testing, the words were all individually printed on 3-X-5-inch cards and the three words forming each triad were arrayed in a triangular fashion to permit the grouping of nonadjacent words. There were 220 such triads (i.e., C_3^{12} triads). These were delivered in the same predetermined quasi-random order to all of the subjects; however, the placement of the words within each triangular arrangement was randomized anew for each patient.

A similarity matrix was constructed for each patient's data, the cell entries in the matrix representing the number of times the subject had grouped each of the 12 words with the other. The entries in the five anterior aphasic's matrices were then added together; likewise, those in the five posterior aphasic's matrices, and those in the five control patient's matrices. All subsequent analyses were based on these group data.

Given that the set of items we had chosen could be hierarchically organized, we applied a hierarchical clustering program to these data (Johnson, 1967). However, a second type of analysis was also performed. This consisted of scaling the words by means of a nonmetric multidimensional scaling program (TORSCA, Young & Torgerson, 1967). The combined use of these two analyses permitted us to assess the extent to which there was internal variation within a semantic class. As might be expected, internal variation was not entirely absent, But if the semantic features were not precisely of the "all-or-none" kind, they were sufficiently discrete to permit an analysis in terms of hierarchical class structures. Since the outcome of these analyses are presented in great detail elsewhere, however (Zurif *et al.*, 1974), what follows is simply a verbal summary of the results.

The major patterns in the data can be summarized as follows: The control patients clearly clustered the human items separately from the animal items. The anterior aphasics also recovered the basic semantic feature of *human* versus *nonhuman*, with one intriguing exception—the item DOG was clustered more with names of humans than with the remaining animal items. The posterior aphasic patients, on the other hand, did not convincingly separate the human items from the animal items, despite their having been able to recognize the definitions of the nouns we used. In fact, the only human–nonhuman distinction the posterior aphasics could manage was to cluster the human items more compactly than the animal items. The posterior aphasics also differed from the other two groups in terms of how they based their similarity-of-meaning judgments. The anterior-aphasic and control groups appeared to focus on the meanings of the words independently of their potential use in sentences (paradigmatic classification). Their occasional verbalizations were usually of the form, "Cooks and mothers are both found in homes." The posterior aphasics, however, seemed to sort on the basis of how easily any two words could be used in a copula sentence (syntagmatic classification), as, for example, "My mother is a good cook."

What is of particular interest are the similarities and differences between the group clusters *within* each of the human and animal semantic domains. Both the anterior patients and the control patients appeared to classify the human items on an implicational basis, rather than on the basis of systematic or general semantic features. That is, the referential part of word meaning seemed to emerge as the most significant factor for these groups such that they effected the relation of one item to another from a knowledge of social relationships that is not systematically represented in a dictionary. Thus, the most closely linked items could be viewed as being members of a household unit—MOTHER, WIFE, HUSBAND; the weakest linked, being KNIGHT—a person known to have existed, but with whom no social relations are possible.

Notwithstanding the similarity of their human-item clusters, the control and anterior-aphasic groups were guided by very different considerations when judging the animal items. The control patients combined the items in terms of shared species membership. That is, they judged SHARK to be most similar in meaning to TROUT; TURTLE to CROCODILE; and DOG to TIGER. The anterior aphasics, in contrast, generated two major clusters: one consisting of SHARK, CROCODILE, and TIGER, all ferocious, wild, and remote; and the other consisting of TROUT and TURTLE, both partially edible and both quite harmless. In addition, as already mentioned, the anterior aphasics clustered DOG more often with the human items than with the animal items.

Can one or both of these animal-item clusters be accounted for within a semantic feature framework? We think so, but only if a distinction is made between defining and characteristic semantic features (Smith, Shoben, and Rips, 1974). In this scheme, features such as *+ human, + male, + mammal,* and the like are termed defining features in the sense that they can be applied technically to many entries in the dictionary and are thus relatively systematic in the language (Katz & Fodor, 1963; Bolinger, 1965; Miller, 1972). Yet, the concepts that characterize our judgments of similarity and difference among the meanings of words are not likely to be derived solely from these defining semantic features. Characteristic features are also quite likely to play an important role in subjective lexical organization. These latter features—including size distinctions and other perceptual attributes—only incidently relate members within a given superordinate domain.

Within the framework of this classificatory scheme, it seems reasonable to suggest that, by focusing on the species membership of the items, the control patients applied technical semantic features when judging the similarities and differences among the meanings of the animal items. In contrast, the anterior aphasic patients, by using *± ferocity,* would appear to have carried out the task on the basis of incidental or characteristic features.

The legitimacy of categorizing *± ferocity* as an incidental component essentially becomes a matter for individual judgment. For example, this feature could probably be applied as widely to the dictionary as *± mammal.* On the other hand, compared to *species membership, ferocity* seems more tied to empirical knowledge (first or second hand) and less dependent upon an understanding of systematic interlexical relations. In fact, *ferocity* is not even listed under the dictionary entries for the senses of SHARK and CROCODILE conveyed here; and even TIGER is only "proverbial for its ferocity" (*Oxford Universal Dictionary,* 1955). After all, the extent to which sharks, tigers, and crocodiles are ferocious is in large measure a function of extralinguistic setting. Thus, even though it may be argued that all semantic elements ultimately derive from a knowledge of the world, *+ ferocity* still seems to us to be a much more empirical or perceptual concept than *+ mammal,* for example.

The fact that the anterior aphasics classified the animal items on the basis of ferocity may, of course, have been partly a function of the form of the definitional statements given to them. Recall that contrary to standard dictionary entries, this information was included in our definitions of the animal terms (Table 2) and passed along to the patients during the screening sessions. But even so, the aphasics still had the option of creating a classification based on species membership, that is, on technical semantic features. The point to be emphasized is not that the anterior patients were guided or unduly influenced by the definitional statements, but rather that they seemed constrained by a recognition of the similarities and differences among the attributes of each noun's referent. What this suggests is that, compared to the lexical structure underlying normal language use, the memory code in anterior aphasia is more restricted in its range of conceptual integration. In effect, verbal concepts in anterior aphasia appear to be more tightly tied to affective and situational data.

Consistent with this notion is the finding that DOG was clustered more often with humans than with animals. Insofar as anterior aphasics gain the meaning of a word in terms of the extralinguistic events it signals, this outcome is to be expected. That is, DOG and the human items presumably got grouped together on the basis of something like dog being man's best friend (e.g., Leach, 1964).

Not to overemphasize the limitation, however, the internalized dictionary of the anterior aphasic does reveal an organized set of features. Moreover, the organization seems intuitively valid in terms of everyday language use. It might be more restricted and less efficient than that underlying normal language behavior, but that is what would be expected for a patient who must search his memory so laboriously before finding the word he needs. To this extent there appears to be a relation between the psychological processes underlying verbalization and the present description of the internal lexicon.

In summary, then, the semantic structures that emerged for the three groups seem to differ in the range of their application. Within the context of our limited data base, normal adults could shift from a categorization partially related to the referential conditions of their immediate social environment (as shown by the human-item clusters) to one based on an explicit notion of class membership (as shown by the animal-item clusters). The aphasic patients, on the other hand, did not show this shift, being restricted, for the most part, to a more concrete-emotional form of word categorization. Thus, the interpretation we favor is that, although the normal adult has a number of levels at which he can organize his lexicon—some referentially practical, others linguistically practical—the adult aphasic mostly retains those features of words that relate to perceived or imagined environmental situations, especially the affective components of such situations.

The data also indicate a relation between lexical organization and knowledge of words within aphasia, itself. The structures produced by the anterior aphasics were arranged in a meaningful, even if somewhat restricted, manner; those produced by the posterior aphasics showed much less order: Anterior aphasics very often find the appropriate contentive for an utterance and generally seem to understand words; posterior patients, especially Wernicke's aphasics, very often use indefinite nouns or nouns that are "out-of-focus," and generally have a low level of comprehension.

In this sense, although the analyses presented here say nothing of the processes that might be required to exploit the features of lexical organization, they do suggest that describing what a person knows about his dictionary is of relevance to the exploration of factors affecting actual language performance.

Lexical Knowledge: Extralinguistic Factors

The preceding data suggest an intriguing possibility. If left-sided anterior brain damage disrupts knowledge of the semantic relations of a word to other words in the language, but spares knowledge of a word's referential ties, is it not likely that words learned in a multiplicity of referential contexts will be better retained in aphasia than words learned in a definitional or linguistic context? This notion receives some interesting support from a study reported by Howard Gardner, one of our colleagues at the Aphasia Research Unit (Gardner, 1973).

Gardner assessed the performance of aphasic patients on an extensive naming test. The patients were shown pictures of simple objects and asked only to provide their names. As expected, those items which were easiest for all aphasic patients to name were those whose names occur more frequently in the language. Of particular interest, however, was the contribution of object "manipulability" to naming capacity. Specifically, with word frequency controlled, the aphasic patients found it easier to name elements that lend themselves to manipulation and have appeal to multiple sensory modalities than to name elements that allow little potential for manipulation and thus are encountered and known only in limited ways. A picture of a rock, for example, was more easily named than a picture of a cloud; the former being manipulable, the latter appealing exclusively to the visual sense. The operativity of an element, in fact, was a more potent contributor to ease of naming than was its frequency.

Gardner's results, of course, are not directly comparable to our analysis of lexical organization. We have extracted metalinguistic knowledge, while he has focused on the level of speech and naming; we have studied the distinction between lexical interrelatedness and reference, while he has distinguished only between different aspects of extralinguistic ties. Yet, we think that the implications of the two studies converge on one very essential point: The more a word lends itself to the encoding of reference, the more likely it is to be retained in the face of left-sided brain damage.

Parenthetically, to the extent that aphasia dissociates word meaning into the separate components of lexical sense and reference—disrupting the former, sparing the latter, Goldstein's (1948) long-standing dictum—that aphasia results in a loss of abstract attitude—would appear to be rather apropos. The aphasic patient seems less capable of sampling from the complex matrix of relations (interlexical, especially) that determine a word's meaning (Leontiev & Luria, 1972; Rahmani, 1968).

CONCLUDING REMARKS

The preceding investigations were intended to bear upon the characterization of some aspects of aphasic language. In this respect, we believe that the work has yielded a modest number of general statements. The first is that when syntactic features are absent on the level of spontaneous speech they are unlikely to be preserved at other levels of language. Agrammatism is thus a limitation on language use and language knowledge; it is not primarily the outcome of an economizing effort to circumvent articulatory problems.

The second point is that agrammatism in aphasia is not a deficit that can be described simply as a sparing of content words and a dropping out of functors. Rather, the aphasic's control of a functor—whether on the level of metalinguistic judgment, or in speech, or in comprehension—seems primarily determined by the typical usefulness of the functor in imparting meaning. Thus, as we have shown, the Broca's aphasic is more likely to be sensitive to the lexical contrast between the prepositions *to* and *by* than to the contrast between the definite and the indefinite article. The former contrast entails a considerable difference in lexical meaning and a corresponding difference in structural meaning; the latter, a difference in referential specificity that is usually otherwise quite apparent. In any event, full syntactic processing is disrupted in Broca's aphasia.

Finally, there are our findings that comprehension is sufficiently dependent upon semantic constraints to proceed, and what is more, to appear relatively intact, even though the anterior aphasic is unlikely to process anything more than some of the bare essentials of meaning. Running through all our data, therefore, is the theme that even though the patient with anterior brain damage is incapable of full linguistic participation, he has retained sufficient cognitive structure to exploit the redundancy of language and hence succeed in achieving adequate communication.

ACKNOWLEDGMENTS

We are indebted to Harold Goodglass, Howard Gardner, Gene Green, Sheila Blumstein, Jill de Villiers, and Harry Whitaker for their helpful comments on an earlier draft of this chapter.

REFERENCES

Bever, G. 1970. The cognitive basis for linguistic structures. In R. Hayes (Ed.), *Cognition and the development of language*. New York: Wiley. Pp. 279–362.

Bolinger, D. 1965. The atomization of meaning. *Language, 41,* 555–573.

Brown, R. 1973. *A first language: The early stages*. Cambridge, Mass.: Harvard University Press.

Caramazza, A. 1974. Some cognitive aspects of language acquisition. Unpublished doctoral dissertation, Johns Hopkins University.

Cohen, D., & Hécaen, H. 1965. Remarques neurolinguistiques sur un cas d'agrammatisme. *Journal de Psychologie, 3,* 273–296.

Fillmore, C. J. 1968. The case for case. In E. Bach & T. Harms (Eds.), *Universals in linguistic theory*. New York: Holt. Pp. 1–87.

Gardner, H. 1973. The contribution of operativity to naming capacity in aphasic patients. *Neuropsychologia, 11*, 213–220.

Geschwind, N. 1970. The organization of language and the brain. *Science, 170*, 940–944.

Goldstein, K. 1948. *Language and language disturbances*. New York: Grune & Stratton.

Goodenough, C., Zurif, E. B., Weintraub, S., & von Stockert, T. 1975. Aphasics' attention to grammatical morphemes. *Language and Speech* (in press).

Goodglass, H. 1968. Studies on the grammar of aphasics. In S. Rosenberg & J. Koplin (Eds.), *Developments in applied psycholinguistics research*. New York: Macmillan. Pp. 177–207.

Goodglass, H., & Kaplan, E. 1972. *The assessment of aphasia and related disorders*. Philadelphia: Lea & Febiger.

Green, E. 1970. On the contribution of studies in aphasia to psycholinguistics. *Cortex, 6*, 216–235.

Healy, A. F., & Miller, G. A. 1970. The verb as the main determinant of sentence meaning. *Psychonomic Science, 20*, 372.

Henley, N. M. 1969. A psychological study of the semantics of animal terms. *Journal of Verbal Learning and Verbal Behavior, 8*, 176–184.

Johnson, S. C. 1967. Hierarchical clustering schemes. *Psychometrika, 32*, 241–254.

Katz, J. J., & Fodor, J. A. 1963. The structure of a semantic theory. *Language, 39*, 170–210.

Leach, E. 1964. Anthropological aspects of language: Animal categories and verbal abuse. In E. H. Lenneberg (Ed.), *New directions in the study of language*. Cambridge, Mass.: MIT Press. Pp. 23–63.

Lenneberg, E. H. 1973. The neurology of language. *Daedalus, 102*, 115–133.

Leontiev, A. N., & Luria, A. R. 1972. Some notes concerning Dr. Fodor's reflections on L. S. Vygotsky's *Thought and language. Cognition, 1*, 311–316.

Levelt, W. J. M. 1970. A scaling approach to the study of syntactic relations. G. B. Flores d'Arcais & W. J. M. Levelt (Eds.), *Advances in psycholinguistics*. Amsterdam: North-Holland Pub.

Lhermitte, F., Derouesne, J., & Lecours, A. R. 1971. Contribution a l'etude des troubles semantiques dans l'aphasie. *Revue Neurologique, 125*, 81–101.

Martin, E. 1970. Toward an analysis of subjective phrase structure. *Psychological Bulletin, 74*, 153–166.

Miller, G. A. 1967. Psycholinguistic approaches to the study of communication. In D. L. Arm (Ed.), *Journeys in science: Small steps—Great strides*. Albuquerque: University of New Mexico Press. Pp. 22–73.

Miller, G. A. 1969. A psychological method to investigate verbal concepts. *Journal of Mathematical Psychology, 6*, 169–191.

Miller, G. A. 1972. English verbs of motion: A case study in semantics and lexical memory. In A. W. Melton & E. Martin (Eds.), *Coding processes in human memory*. Washington, D.C.: Winston. Pp. 335–372.

Oxford Universal Dictionary. 1955. New York: Rand McNally.

Parisi, D., & Pizzamiglio, L. 1970. Syntactic comprehension in aphasia. *Cortex, 6*, 204–215.

Perfetti, C. A. 1972. Psychosemantics: Some cognitive aspects of structural meaning. *Psychological Bulletin, 78*, 241–259.

Pizzamiglio, L., & Appicciafuoco, A. 1971. Semantic comprehension in aphasia. *Journal of Communication Disorders, 3*, 280–88.

Quillian, M. R. 1968. Semantic memory. In M. Minsky (Ed.), *Semantic information processing*. Cambridge, Mass.: MIT Press.

Rahmani, L. 1968. Some remarks on the study of abnormal concept formation. *Israel Annals of Psychiatry and Related Disciplines, 6*, 1–12.

Rips, L. J., Shoben, E. J., & Smith, E. E. 1973. Semantic distance and the verification of semantic relations. *Journal of Verbal Learning and Verbal Behavior, 12*, 1–20.

Smith, E. E., Shoben, E. J. & Rips, L. J. Structure and process in semantic memory: A featural model for semantic decisions. *Psychological Review*, 1971, *81*, 214–241.

Thorndike, E. L., & Lorge, I. 1944. *The teachers' workbook of 30,000 words.* New York: Columbia University Press.

Weigl, E., & Bierwisch, M. 1970. Neurospychology and linguistics: Topics of common research. *Foundations of Language, 6*, 1–30.

Whitaker, H. A. 1970. Linguistic competence: Evidence from aphasia. *Glossa, 4*, 46–54.

Wyke, M. 1971. Dysphasia. *British Medical Bulletin, 27*, 211–217.

Young, F. W., & Torgerson, W. S. 1967. TORSCA, FORTRAN IV program for Shepard-Kruskal multidimensional scaling analysis. *Behavioral Science, 12*, 498.

Zurif, E. B., Caramazza, A., & Myerson, R. 1972. Grammatical judgments of agrammatic aphasics. *Neuropsychologia, 10*, 405–417.

Zurif, E. B., Caramazza, A., Myerson, R., & Galvin, J. 1974. Semantic feature representations for normal and aphasic language. *Brain and Language, 1*, 167–187.

Zurif, E. B., Green, E., Caramazza, A., & Goodenough, C. 1975. Metalinguistic judgments of aphasic patients: Sensitivity to functors. *Cortex* (submitted).

9 Transcortical Motor Aphasia

Alan B. Rubens

HENNEPIN COUNTY MEDICAL CENTER
MINNEAPOLIS, MINNESOTA

Damage to the dominant frontal lobe, particularly to those regions marginal to Broca's area, produces a disturbance of verbal output which affects mainly spontaneous speech and tends to spare speech evoked through external stimulation, such as repetition, reading aloud, and naming of visually presented objects. Comprehension remains at a high level. The disturbance of spontaneous speech ranges in severity from near muteness to mild reduction of word fluency and is often unaccompanied by other signs of psychomotor retardation outside the sphere of verbal behavior. This disturbance has been labeled transcortical motor aphasia by Wernicke, and frontal dynamic aphasia by Luria.

The first to mention this symptom complex was Lichtheim (1885), who described a patient with gross impairment of spontaneous speech and writing, but with preservation of repetition, writing to dictation, reading aloud, and comprehension of spoken and written material. The essential feature was the ability in a patient with good comprehension to repeat words and sentences that could not be uttered spontaneously. This peculiar sparing of repetition could not be fitted into Wernicke's model of motor aphasia in which destruction of Broca's area results in loss of speech movement images with more or less equal impairment of spontaneous and imitative speech. Lichtheim, therefore, proposed that since nonlanguage thought processes and motor speech function were intact, this symptom complex resulted from an anatomical separation between the intact motor speech center (Broca's area) and certain nonlanguage cerebral areas (Lichtheim's "concept center") responsible for activation of the speech area during volitional, nonimitative speech. Lichtheim made it clear that the "concept center" did not represent a circumscribed cortical area, but rather the

293

activity of the entire "sensorial sphere" and that the white matter pathways linking this center to the speech area were not distinct entities but rather converged upon the motor speech area from many unidentified regions. For that reason he suggested that a lesion in white matter pathways at the posterior end of the inferior frontal gyrus directly underlying Broca's area would be in the best position to intercept these converging radiations and produce the syndrome. Wernicke (cited by Freud, 1891) accepted this formulation but replaced Lichtheim's label of central commissural aphasia (*zentrale Leitungsaphasia*) with the now generally accepted term *transcortical motor aphasia*.

Although few authors have denied the occurrence of the symptom complex described by Lichtheim and Wernicke, many have rejected the anatomical explanations attached to it and have pointed out the inappropriateness of the use of an anatomical label such as *transcortical* to refer to a disturbance of verbal behavior. The occurrence of gross damage to the motor speech area in some patients with this disturbance has provided many counter examples to the transcortical model (Gloning, Gloning, & Hoff, 1963). Neissl von Mayendorf (1911) firmly believed that even with complete destruction of Broca's area, repetition may be spared by virtue of the function of the minor hemisphere. Bastian (1897) asserted that transcortical motor aphasia represents nothing more than a mild dysfunction of the motor speech area itself. He proposed the widely accepted theory that mild damage produces a heightened threshold of excitability in which reaction is still possible in response to externally derived auditory stimuli, but not to internally generated volitional stimuli. In other words, varying degrees of damage result not only in quantitative changes in behavior but in what appear to be qualitative changes as well. This view is supported by the superiority of repetition occasionally observed during recovery from motor aphasia, particularly of the posttraumatic variety (Goldstein, 1948).

Perhaps no author has dealt with the question of transcortical motor aphasia in greater depth or detail than Goldstein (1915, 1948). Goldstein recognized two forms, one compatible with Bastian's theory of heightened excitability threshold, due solely to mild damage to Broca's area, and the other in which transcortical motor aphasia appears more as an entity in its own right. The first type is usually transitory and is often seen during recovery from motor aphasia (Goldstein's peripheral motor aphasia) particularly after penetrating missile wounds. As might be expected with partial damage to Broca's area, there are mild motor speech defects and a less striking discrepancy between spontaneous speech and repetition. Writing is usually on a par with speech. Reading aloud is also superior to spontaneous speech. As a rule, there are no other abnormalities in thought or language behavior. It is easier for the patient to name objects presented through a particular sensory channel than to evoke names during spontaneous speech. This is in marked contrast to the naming disturbance of patients with damage to the temporal or parietal regions in which confrontation naming is the more difficult task. In Goldstein's second type of transcortical motor aphasia, articulation is normal, but there is a striking lack of speech impulse. The inability to initiate speech may be severe enough at times to approach muteness. Hypokinesia other than that relating to the speech sphere is absent. Here again, as in the other form of transcortical motor aphasia, the patient may be able to name objects placed in front of him even though spontaneous speech is impossible. According to Goldstein, echolalia does not occur without a significant defect of auditory comprehension, and for that reason he excludes cases with echolalia from the category of transcortical motor aphasia. Although he specifically rejected the concept of speech centers and the anatomical implications of the term transcortical, Goldstein attributed the lack of speech impulse to a loss of frontal lobe volitional influence on the speech apparatus produced by a lesion situated midway between the frontal lobe and the motor speech area. This comes very close to Lichtheim's original formulation. In fact, Goldstein chose to cite as a particularly illuminating anatomical example the case of Rothmann (1906) in which the speech disturbance was found to be associated with a small lesion of the white matter directly beneath the motor speech area, the location previously hypothesized by Lichtheim.

Interest in transcortical motor aphasia per se peaked in the early decades of the twentieth century and then gradually declined. Most of the well-studied cases were published in the German literature during this period and have been reviewed by Goldstein. However, a similar if somewhat attenuated form of the disorder was discussed in the German literature, particularly by Kleist (1934) under the term *Adynamie der Sprache*. Kleist studied patients with war injuries involving the dominant frontal lobe but generally sparing Broca's area. Although nonaphasic by conventional testing, these patients manifested reduction of spontaneous speech with normal articulation. They had difficulty evoking appropriate words and sentences, sometimes to the point of agrammatism. Kleist placed the lesion responsible for this type of defect in the posterior end of the second frontal gyrus (area 9 of Brodmann) just superior to Broca's area. Marie (1917) had also related damage to this area with marked slowness of speech and idea formation, normal auditory comprehension, and naming. According to Marie, the major difficulty was in bringing ideas together and condensing them into phrases.

More recently Luria (1970) and Luria and Tsvetkova (1968), acknowledging the work of Kleist and other German neurologists, described in great detail under the term *frontal dynamic aphasia* a disturbance which appears to be identical in almost all respects to transcortical motor aphasia (and some cases that Goldstein would probably have called *mixed transcortical aphasia* because of minimal comprehension deficits). Lesions responsible for dynamic aphasia are located in the frontal lobe, just anterior to Broca's area, but in some cases may be placed more superiorly in the premotor zone. In Luria's dynamic aphasia, the patient has minimal spontaneous speech, seldom uses it for purposes of communication, and yet is able to repeat words and sentences. There is no abnormality in thought processes, auditory comprehension, or motor speech performance. The disturbance affects written as well as spoken performances. As in Goldstein's transcortical motor aphasia, patients do better at naming objects presented to them through the visual sphere or other sensory modality than they do on spontaneous speech. The severity of the disturbance ranges from near speechlessness with inability to generate even simple phrases to milder difficulties in relating stories or describing pictures. In contrast to Goldstein's description, patients with extensive and deep damage to the frontal lobe are likely to respond echolalically to questions that they fully comprehend. According to Luria, the basic defect is an inability to convert initial thought into sentences, to propositionize. Following Vygotski, Luria and his co-workers view inner speech as a transitional step between initial thought and final verbal expression. The discontinuity between thought and verbal output results from an underlying disturbance of inner speech with its predicative function. To support this hypothesis, they note that patients with this syndrome have more difficulty generating a list of verbs than of nouns in a timed interval. This is the reverse of what is seen with most aphasics. Furthermore, even when given specific words such as "horse" and "carriage" they are unable to construct a sentence. This inability to make sentences from individual words which are supplied or to describe a simple picture suggests a deficit in the "linear scheme of the phrase" resulting from an underlying disturbance of the predicative function of inner speech. When presented with a series of nonverbal cues such as blank sheets of paper laid out on a desk before them, these patients are able to describe pictures by pointing to each cue in order and uttering successive elements of the intended sentence. These external cues are viewed by Luria as substitutes for the lost linear scheme of the phrase which is mediated in the normal state by inner speech. Physiological evidence for a deficit of inner speech prior to actual motoric expression comes from electromyographic recordings which show (in contrast to normals) an absence of preparatory lip movements when patients with dynamic aphasia are asked to ready a verbal response. With the aid of the nonverbal cues mentioned previously, normal preparatory muscular activity is recorded. These miniature prevocal lip and tongue muscular contractions are looked upon as representing the transition from inner to external speech, and their facilitation by external nonverbal cues is presented as evidence for the restitution of the lost linear structure of the phrase.

Milner (1964) has reported similar findings in patients with left frontal lobectomy, anterior to and sparing Broca's area. After surgery these patients have a distinct reduction of spontaneous speech and tend to answer questions with as few words as possible. Although no aphasia in the strict sense can be demonstrated, and verbal intelligence is normal, as measured by such tests as the

Wechsler Adult Intelligence Scale, these patients have great difficulty with tests of word fluency (Thurstone & Thurstone, 1949). When asked to write out a list of words beginning with a certain letter of the alphabet, in a given time, they show a great amount of discomfort and can provide few words. Many look around the room for real objects to name. This defect is not found with comparable lesions of the right frontal lobe, nor of the left anterior temporal lobe, although lesions of the latter region result in clear-cut disturbances of verbal memory. The reduction of word fluency is dissociable from abnormalities in abstract thinking as measured by the Wisconsin Card Sorting Test. These findings have been confirmed by Benton (1968). Ramier and Hécaen (1970), on the other hand, have reported minimal but definite reduction of word fluency with right frontal lobe cases as well, and concluded that the overall defect depends on a combination of defective initiation of action owing to frontal lobe damage in general and diminished verbal ability associated with left-hemispheric damage in particular.

Our own experience agrees with the literature that damage to the dominant frontal lobe, which spares Broca's area, results in a defect of spontaneous speech ranging from muteness to mild loss of verbal fluency. In severe forms the distinction between the state of muteness and that in which repetition is "preserved" is often arbitrary and depends on the tenacity and perserverence of the examiner in coaxing a response from the patient. For example, one of our patients could not name objects or repeat sentences unless the examiner bent down, placed his ear directly before the patient's mouth, and assumed the air of an intent and expectant listener. Another could respond only with embarrassed silence when requested to name objects, repeat sentences, and answer questions; yet to the surprise of both patient and examiner, when instructed to remain silent and merely mouth his responses, the patient was able to articulate silently the names of objects and to repeat long complex sentences.

Along another continuum, there is no distinct cutoff between cases with "preserved repetition" and those with classical Broca's aphasia. A significant number of patients with Broca's aphasia are able to repeat a word or two that they are unable to utter spontaneously, and in some cases naming may be slightly superior to spontaneous speech. With the recent availability of objective quantifiable aphasia batteries, such as the Boston Diagnostic Aphasia Test (Goodglass & Kaplan, 1972), which provide measures of repetition graded for increasing levels of phonetic and syntactical complexity, it is now possible to compare, objectively, repetition skills with spontaneous speech in the same patient and to relate these abilities to the performances of others. At present, despite its acknowledged shortcomings, we believe it is useful to apply the term *transcortical motor aphasia* to those cases with good comprehension who are able to repeat consistently full sentences of varying syntactical and phonetic complexity and yet who manifest little or no useful spontaneous speech.

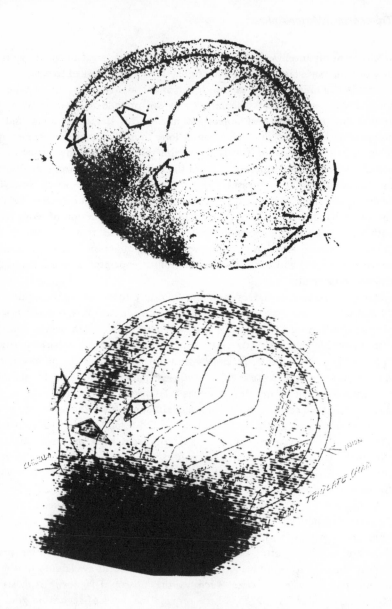

Figures 1A and 1B Superimposition of a template (revised from Marie, 1917) of the lateral surface features of the left hemisphere over a radioisotope brain scan of two stroke patients with transcortical motor aphasia. In addition to the normal accumulation of isotope, seen as darkened areas in the scalp and facial regions, the isotope accumulates in areas of brain damage (infarcts) which appear as the darkened areas indicated by three large arrows. 1A. There is abnormal isotope uptake in a region just anterior to Broca's area in the inferior frontal gyrus. 1B. An area of abnormal isotope uptake indicating cerebral infarction in the territory of the left anterior cerebral artery affecting mainly the superior frontal gyrus in the region including the supplementary motor cortex.

Our experience indicates that from the clinical standpoint the presence of transcortical motor aphasia is highly predictive of lesion location. For example, in 172 consecutive cases of aphasia caused by cerebrovascular disease, in which the area of brain damage was outlined by radioisotope brain scans, eight out of nine cases of transcortical motor aphasia were found to have well-delineated lesions in the left frontal lobe that spared Broca's area (see Figures 1A and 1B).

The single exception was a case in which there was total destruction of Broca's area and the facial sensory motor region directly posterior to it (see Figure 2). The patient was an ambidextrous, 62-year-old man, with excellent confrontation naming, auditory comprehension, and ability to complete long phonetically and syntactically complicated sentences, but who in conversation had only a few short stock phrases at his command. He usually incorporated the examiner's questions echolalically into his replies. For example, to the question, "How did you come here today?" he responded, "How did I come here today? I'll tell you how I did come here today, I came here today by . . . for goodness sakes . . . by taking a . . . by coming here today." He performed at normal levels for his age in tests of reasoning and abstract thinking, as measured by Ravens Progressive Matrices and Weigl Sorting Tests. Dichotic Listening tests with consonant–vowel syllables and with digits revealed a very superior right-ear score suggesting that the auditory region of the left hemisphere was the major area responsible for decoding speech. Since brain scans demonstrated that Broca's area and the left

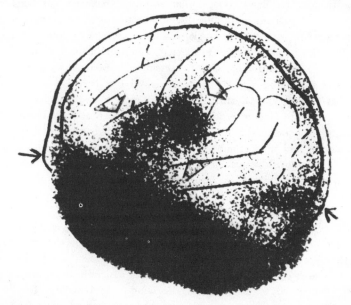

Figure 2 Radioisotope brain scan indicating extensive infarction (indicated by three arrows) of Broca's area and the sensory-motor cortical facial area of the left hemisphere.

motor facial area had been destroyed, repetition must have taken place by a sharing of the functions of both hemispheres. The message was first decoded in the left temporoparietal region, transferred across the corpus callosum, and encoded in the intact right motor speech area for repetition. This case, and a case recently reported by Gott (1973) of a 12-year-old girl, who 2 years after left hemispherectomy could repeat six- and seven-word sentences and who had good auditory comprehension with severely restricted spontaneous speech, support the contention that in certain instances, such tasks as repetition, but not serviceable spontaneous speech, are occasionally mediated via the intact right hemisphere.

Approximately one-third of our transcortical motor aphasia cases had either vascular or traumatic lesions located at a considerable distance from Broca's area, in the vicinity of the supplementary motor cortex of the dominant hemisphere. Included among these cases were three with cerebral infarction in the territory of the left anterior cerebral artery, and two with bullet wounds to the left parasagittal region. These speech findings are consistent with evidence from the literature that the supplementary motor cortex plays a significant role in speech function. For example, electrical stimulation in and around the region of the supplementary motor cortex of either hemisphere in man has been shown to produce either arrest of ongoing speech or initiation of repetitive involuntary vocalizations (Brickner, 1940; Erickson & Woolsey, 1951; Penfield & Roberts, 1959; Penfield & Welch, 1951). Similar abnormal behavior has been noted during seizures of patients with epileptogenic tumors situated in the area of the left supplementary motor cortex (Alajouanine, Castaigne, Sabouraud, & Contamin, 1959; Arseni & Botez, 1961; Carrieri, 1963; Erickson & Woolsey, 1951; Guidetti, 1957; Petit-Dutaillis, Guiot, Messimy, & Bourdillon, 1954; Sweet, 1951). Botez and Barbeau (1971) have reviewed the literature on speech disturbances associated with dysfunction of this region and conclude that the supplementary motor region represents the major cortical structure mediating the "starting mechanisms for speech." They identify the ventral lateral nucleus of the thalamus and the periaqueductal gray matter of the mesencephalon as subcortical elements of this system. We have found that damage to the dominant supplementary cortex frequently results not only in loss of speech initiative, but in dysphonia as well, a feature not usually associated with more inferiorly placed lesions bordering on Broca's area.

As Luria indicated, the fundamental defect in these patients is in generating a full sentence or in milder cases, a string of sentences necessary for conveying sufficiently detailed information in a particular context. We have recently reported two such cases which illustrate this disturbance (Rubens, in press). For example, when asked to look out of the window and make a full detailed statement about the weather, one patient could say after much delay "fine." She could then repeat "It is a beautiful, warm, sunny day outside." When the examiner struck a match and asked what had occurred, the patient replied "fire." When urged to make a full sentence she said "I can't," yet she could then repeat "Doctor, you took out a box of matches from your back pocket and lit one." She was unable to describe how one prepares spaghetti beyond the statement "cook it." Serial speech (days of the week, alphabet, etc.), completion of open sentences, recitation of well-known nursery rhymes and naming all approached normal levels. Another patient when asked to discuss his medical history responded "I don't know" or on another occasion "I can't remember." However, with questions about particular aspects of his illness, such as "Where were you when you became ill?" his one- or two-word replies were correct and indicated a full memory for events which he was unable to discuss in the form of a lengthy discourse.

Although our patients had no trouble naming visually presented objects, even the mildest cases had great difficulty supplying the name plus certain adjectives (attributes such as color, shape, or size) necessary for distinguishing the particular object from a group of similar objects. Thus, four cases who had originally manifested a marked transcortical motor aphasia, but who had improved over a period of several months in all respects, except for a borderline reduction in tests of word fluency, still manifested a disturbance in what might be called the referential function of speech. For example, when they were shown a card with drawings of four chairs and four tables varying in size and color and were asked "Which one am I pointing to?" these patients tended to report only the name of the object, or the name and only one attribute, or even to provide the wrong qualifying words. The same patients were able to reverse the process and point when requested to the "large red chair" or the "small black table" without hesitation. The severity of the disturbance did not depend on the degree of diminution of spontaneous speech or on abnormalities of abstract thinking. Several of the patients had regained what appeared to be normal spontaneous conversational speech and did well for their age level with Ravens Matrices and the Weigl Sorting Test. This performance was quite inferior to that of a group of patients with right frontal lobe disease and to the performance of a group with minimal anomia resulting from temporoparietal damage matched for severity of aphasia by scores on the standard aphasia batteries. According to our preliminary data, this test promises to be a sensitive instrument for detecting mild disturbances of verbal output caused by left frontal lobe disease.

To summarize, transcortical motor aphasia is one of a number of labels which have been applied to a symptom complex characterized by a disproportionate disturbance of spontaneous speech, compared to speech evoked through external stimulation. The defect is generally considered to result from loss of frontal lobe volitional influence on the speech apparatus, most often resulting from damage to the dominant frontal lobe, to connections between frontal lobe and the speech area, or to mild damage to the speech area itself. According to Goldstein the transcortical aphasias represent damage of the relations between speech and nonspeech mental processes. Similarly, Luria describes dynamic aphasia as standing on the borderline between a speech disturbance and a disturbance of thought processes. It would seem that this entity affords an excellent opportunity to investigate a particularly interesting stage in the transition from initial thought to final verbal expression. As such, it provides an opportunity to study in pure form the lack of speech initiative which is a major element of Broca's aphasia.

REFERENCES

Alajouanine, Th., Castaigne, P., Sabouraud, O., & Contamin, F. 1959. Palilalie paroxystique et vocalisations intératives au cours de crises épileptiques par lésion intéressant L 'aire motrice supplémentaire. *Revue Neurologique* 101, 685–697.

Arseni, C., & Botez, M. I. 1961. Speech disturbances caused by tumors of the supplementary motor area. *Acta Psychiatria et Neurologica Scandinavica* 36, 279–299.

Bastian, H. 1897. Some problems in connexion with aphasia and other speech defects. *Lancet* 1, 933–942, 1005–1017, 1131–1137, 1187–1194.

Benton, A. L. 1968. Differential behavioral effects in frontal lobe disease. *Neuropsychologia* 6, 53–60.

Botez, M. I., & Barbeau, A. 1971. Role of subcortical structures, and particularly of the thalamus, in the mechanisms of speech and language. *International Journal of Neurology* 8 (2, 3, 4), 300–320.

Brickner, R. M. 1940. A human cortical area producing repetitive phenomena when stimulated. *Journal Neurophysiology* 3, 128–130.

Carrieri, G. 1963. Sindrome da sofferenze dell 'area supplementare motoria sinistra nel corso di un minengioma parasagittale. *Rivista di Patologia Nervosa e Mental* 84, 29–48.

Erickson, T. C., & Woolsey, C. N. 1951. Observations on the supplementary motor area of man. *Transactions of the American Neurological Association* 76, 50–56.

Freud, S. 1891. *On aphasia*, a critical study. (Trans. E. Stengel) New York: International Universities Press.

Gloning, I., Gloning, K., & Hoff, H. 1963. Aphasia–a clinical syndrome. In L. Halpern (Ed.), *Problems of dynamic neurology*. Jerusalem: Jerusalem Post Press. Pp. 63–70.

Goldstein, K. 1915. Die transkortikalen Aphasien. *Ergebnisse Neurologie und Psychiatrie* Jena: G. Fischer.

Goldstein, K. 1948. *Language and language disturbances.* New York: Grune & Stratton.

Goodglass, H. & Kaplan, E. 1972. *The assessment of aphasia and related disorders.* Philadelphia: Lea & Febiger.

Gott, P. S. 1973. Language after dominant hemispherectomy. *Journal of Neurology, Neurosurgery, and Psychiatry* 36, 1082–1088.

Guidetti, B. 1957. Désordres de la parole associés a des lésions de la surface interhémisphérique frontale postérieure. *Revue Neurologique* 97, 121–131.

Kleist, K. 1934. *Gehirnpathologie* Leipzig: Barth.

Lichtheim, L. 1885. On aphasia. *Brain* 7, 433–484.

Luria, A. R. 1970 *Traumatic aphasia* Mouton: The Hague.

Luria, A. R., & Tsvetkova, L. S. 1968. The mechanism of 'dynamic aphasia'. *Foundations of Language* 4, 296–307.

Marie, P., & Foix, C. 1917. Les aphasies de guerre. *Revue Neurologique* 24, 53–87.

Milner, B. 1964. Some effects of frontal lobectomy in man. In J. M. Warren & K. Ackert (Eds.), *The frontal granular cortex and behavior.* New York: McGraw Hill. Pp. 313–331.

Niessl von Mayendorf, E. 1911. *Die aphasichen Symptome* Leipzig: Engelmann.

Penfield, W., & Welch, K. 1951. The supplementary motor area of the cerebral cortex, A clinical and experimental study. *Archives of Neurology and Psychiatry* (Chicago) 66, 289–317.

Penfield, W., & Roberts, L. 1959. *Speech and brain mechanisms* Princeton, New Jersey: Princeton Univ. Press.

Petit-Dutaillis, D., Guiot, G., Messimy, R., & Bourdillon, Ch. 1954. A propos d 'une aphémie par atteinte de la zone motrice supplémentaire de Penfield, au cours de l 'évolution d 'un anéurisme artério-veineux. Guerison de l 'aphémie par ablation de la lésion. *Revue Neurologique* 90, 95–106.

Ramier, A. M., & Hecaen, H. 1970. Role respectif des atteintes frontales et de la latéralisation lésionnelle dans les déficits de la 'fluence verbale. *Revue Neurologique* 123, 17–22.

Rothmann, M. 1906. Lichtheimshe motorische Aphasie. *Zeitschrift für Klinische Medizin* 60, 87–121.

Rubens, A. B. Aphasia with infarction in the territory of the anterior cerebral artery. *Cortex* (in press).

Sweet, W. 1951. Discussion of Erickson and Woolsey. *Transactions of the American Neurological Association* 76, 55.

Thurstone, I. L., & Thurstone, T. 1949. *Examiner manual for the SRA primary mental abilities.* (rev. ed.) Chicago: Illinois Scientific Research Association.

Subject Index

A 6
B 7
C 8
D 9
E 0
F 1
G 2
H 3
I 4
J 5